NORTH CAROLINA

A Proud State in Our Nation

William S. Powell

Professor Emeritus of History, University of North Carolina at Chapel Hill

D.C. Heath and Company
Lexington, Massachusetts / Toronto, Ontario

Reviewers

Larry S. Krieger, Social Studies Supervisor, Edison, New Jersey
Dr. Percy E. Murray, Chairman of the Department of History
and Social Science, North Carolina Central University
Dr. H. Trawick Ward, Research Archaeologist, Research
Laboratory of Anthropology, University of North Carolina at
Chapel Hill

Executive Editor   **Christopher Johnson**
Supervising Editors   **Susan Belt Cogley, Marian Cain**
Editors   **Nadia Yassa, Jo Pitkin, Deborah Parks**
Design Manager   **Robin Herr**
Designer   **Pamela Daly**
Assistant Designer   **Joan Williams**
Photo Research   **Linda Finigan**
Production Coordinator   **Dorshia Johnson**
Cover Photo Coordinator   **Carmen Johnson**

International Standard Book Number: 0-669-29964-2

5 6 7 8 9 10   VHP   02 01 00 99 98

Contents

NOVA BRITANNIA.
OFFERING MOST
Excellent fruites by Planting in
VIRGINIA.
Exciting all such as be well affected
to further the same.

LONDON
Printed for SAMVEL MACHAM, and are to be sold at
his Shop in Pauls Church-yard, at the
Signe of the Bul-head.
1 6 0 9.

UNIT 7   Growth in the State and Nation   251

UNIT 8   The Twentieth Century   279

Primary Sources

Graphs, Diagrams, Tables and Time Lines

UNIT 1

The Stage for Action

NORTH CAROLINA

Time Line

THE AMERICAS

10,000 B.C. Asian hunters, later to be known as Native Americans, enter the Americas via a land bridge where the Bering Strait is now.

Nomadic hunters wander the land of North Carolina. **8000 B.C.**

8000 B.C. Temperatures warm, and the land bridge disappears.

People in North Carolina begin to settle in villages. **500 B.C.**

100 B.C. The Hohokam and Anasazi people settle in the deserts of the American Southwest.

The mound builders take over land in southern North Carolina. **A.D. 1300**

A.D. 1300s The Iroquois League and other councils of Native Americans are formed.

A.D. 1400s Forest-covered land east of the Mississippi is cleared to make way for fields and villages.

An estimated 35,000 Native Americans live in North Carolina. **A.D. 1492**

A.D. 1492 Columbus leads three ships from Europe to the Americas.

What's Ahead

Chapter 1

A Land of Diversity

Where is North Carolina?

North Carolina belongs to the geographic region in the United States known as the South—the block of states shown on the map entitled Regions of the United States in the atlas section of your text. On the north, it shares a border with Virginia, on the west with Tennessee, and on the south with Georgia and South Carolina. The Atlantic Ocean forms its eastern boundary.

The wonder and variety of North Carolina's land and climate amaze its visitors.

North Carolina ranks 28th among the 50 states in size. It ranks in size about halfway between Alaska (the largest state) and Rhode Island (the smallest state). Its total land area is about 52,712 square miles. Within its borders, North Carolina boasts landforms ranging from sandy seashores in the east to towering mountains in the west. Each year, more than 1,300 kinds of wildflowers bloom throughout the state. The songs of nearly 400 species of birds fill the air. These are but some of the many natural wonders found in North Carolina.

Swamps and cypress trees on the shore of Albemarle Sound

Think Ahead

Read about North Carolina's diversity, including its three different regions, its variety of climates, and its natural resources.

1 North Carolina's Land Regions

In studying North Carolina's **topography,** or physical terrain, geographers have divided it into three distinct regions. A **geographic region** is a large area of land with similar features. In the case of North Carolina, geographers have used elevation to identify regions. Going from east to west, the three main regions are: Coastal Plain, Piedmont, and Mountains. The Coastal Plain has been divided further into an inner coastal plain and an outer coastal plain called the Tidewater. The eastern limit of the Coastal Plain is marked by the Outer Banks. In which region do you live?

To glimpse the North Carolina landscape, imagine taking an east-west journey across the state. The journey begins with a string of islands that seem to form an arc around North Carolina's eastern shore.

People, Places, Terms

topography
geographic region
Outer Banks
primary source
Coastal Plain
Tidewater
Piedmont
fall line

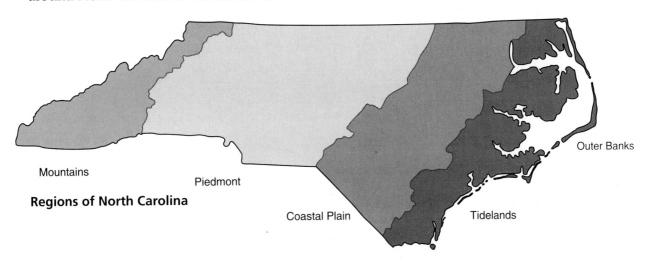

Regions of North Carolina

Mountains

Piedmont

Coastal Plain

Tidelands

Outer Banks

Coming unglued.   "The east coast of North Carolina looks as if it was just coming unglued, with long strips of land floating out to sea." This is how one observer described the fringe of islands off the North Carolina coast. Over the centuries, hundreds of ships have wrecked in the shallow waters that surround some of the islands. Even now, the remains of long-lost wooden vessels sometimes turn up on a beach as the wind, rain, and tides shift the sands.

Today the **Outer Banks,** as the long chain of sandy islands are called, form one of North Carolina's natural wonders. Sandbanks on some islands rise only several feet. Others tower over 100 feet. Jockey's Ridge at Nags Head is the highest sand dune along the Atlantic Coast.

Pinning down the Banks.   In the 1980s, the writer William Least Heat Moon interviewed a North Carolinian

Maps Matter
Maps often summarize a great deal of information in visual form. They give you at a glimpse what may take pages of words to explain.
■ *To Do:* Make a list of the main ideas in Lesson 1 shown in this map.

The Outer Banks are more than 175 miles long. Before bridges and highways were built during the twentieth century, a traveler could only get to them by boat. This tree on the Outer Banks has been shaped by the wind.

who lived along the Outer Banks. Least Heat Moon, who takes his name from one of his Native American ancestors, recorded this interview in *Blue Highways,* which is the story of his journey across the United States. The interview is an example of a **primary source**, or firsthand account. As you read the following quotation from the interview, look for natural forces that have made it impossible to "pin down" the Outer Banks.

Primary Source

> *The sea never forgets where it's been, and it's been over that land [the Outer Banks] many times. . . . New people don't know that. They come in and see open beach and figure they've found open land. But the Banks aren't ordinary islands. . . . They're barrier islands. Some of that land's moving south as much as twenty feet a year. It's a natural process, the way the sea washes sand over the islands from the coast and drops it on the . . . [inland] side. . . . Today we've got bridges over land and roads ending up in the water. Been millions of dollars spent trying to pin down the Banks.*

—WILLIAM LEAST HEAT MOON, Blue Highways

Heading inland to the Coastal Plain.   Several large bodies of water separate the Outer Banks from the mainland. These sounds, or channels of water separating islands from the mainland, include Pamlico, Albemarle, Bogue, Core, Croatan, Currituck, and Roanoke. The Pamlico Sound is the largest sound on the eastern coast of the United States. Because of these sounds, North Carolina has more water surface than all but two other states in the continental United States. Nearly 3,645 square miles of its total area are water-covered.

Running inland from the ocean is a broad, flat region called the **Coastal Plain;** it extends westward some 100 to 150 miles. These flat lands belong to an Atlantic Coastal Plain that stretches from New York to the Gulf of Mexico. Along much of the eastern edge of North Carolina's Coastal Plain, land lies at less than 20 feet above sea level. Here numerous swamps, lakes, and rivers drain the region. Because of low elevations, waters near the mouths of rivers rise and fall with the ocean tides. As a result, this low-lying area has become known as the **Tidewater,** or Tidelands.

The Piedmont.   As you head farther inland from the Coastal Plain, the land rises into gently rolling hills. These hills mark the start of the **Piedmont**—a region with elevations climbing from roughly 500 feet in the east to 1,500 feet in the west. The Piedmont, like the Coastal Plain, belongs to a long belt of land that runs from southern New York to northern Georgia. Rain turns its red clay soil into thick, sticky mud, while dry weather turns it into powdery dust or hard earth.

Rivers and streams in the Piedmont often flow through deep cuts made in the clay soil. In some places, elevations between the Piedmont and Coastal Plain change so sharply that rivers spill off the Piedmont in rocky rapids or low waterfalls. This geographic feature led people to name the dividing line between the Piedmont and Coastal Plain the **fall line.**

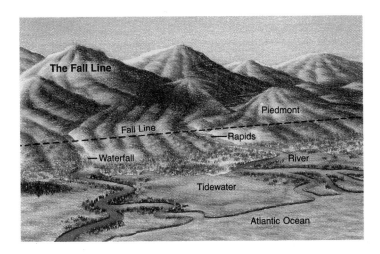

The Mountains.   At the western edge of the Piedmont rises a chain of mountains called the Appalachian Mountains. The chain forms a backbone down much of the eastern coast of North America. It stretches some 2,000 miles from Newfoundland in Canada to central Alabama. The chain received its name from Hernando de Soto, who, in 1540, became the first European to set foot in the region. The Spanish explorer named the mountains after the Apalachee, a group of Native Americans along the Gulf Coast of Florida.

The Appalachians rise to their highest elevations in North Carolina. North Carolina has the highest mountain east of the Mississippi River, Mt. Mitchell. Some geologists, or scientists who study the earth's crust, also think North Carolina may have the oldest mountains in the world.

Think Twice

1. What three land regions make up North Carolina?
2. Why do you get a better overview of North Carolina by traveling east to west rather than north to south?
3. In which of North Carolina's land regions would you prefer to live? Explain.

The Linn Cove Viaduct, Grandfater Mountain, is part of the scenic Blue Ridge Parkway in the Appalachian Mountains.

2 North Carolina's Climate and Weather

Nearly every day, people turn on the television or radio to learn about the weather. They want to find out whether the day will be hot or cold, warm or dry, cloudy or sunny. Weather has been described as "the momentary state of the atmosphere" at a given place or time. **Climate** is the main kind of weather that a region enjoys over an extended period. North Carolina, for example, lies in a region known as the **Sun Belt**—a strip of warm-weather states that runs across the southern United States. What factors help shape a region's climate?

Location. One of the most important factors influencing climate is a region's location on the earth. The closer land lies to the equator, the warmer its climate is. The farther land lies from the equator—traveling either north or south—the cooler its climate is. North Carolina is far warmer than Canada because it is nearer to the equator. However, Florida is warmer still because it is even closer. In general, North Carolina is near enough to the equator to have a moderate year-round temperature. The length of the winter day provides enough sunshine to warm the earth's surface, which warms the surrounding air, so that cold periods are usually short.

Besides location on the earth, a region's climate is also affected by its situation, or relationship to other natural features. North Carolina is situated on the eastern edge of the North American continent. It borders the Atlantic Ocean, so its air has more moisture than does that of inland states. Also, because water tends to hold the sun's heat, the Atlantic warms the air above it, which then passes over nearby land. Therefore, North Carolina generally has warm, humid summers and cool, damp winters.

Altitude. Altitude also influences climate. Air cools as it rises above the surface of the earth, so the higher the elevation, the cooler the air. In North Carolina, elevations range from sea level along the Atlantic shore to nearly 6,700 feet at the top of Mt. Mitchell. On a July day when the average temperature is 67°F in a mountain community, the temperature might reach 80°F along the coast. Because of these wide variations in temperature, one tourism brochure for North Carolina promises, "Whatever climate you want, we have it in North Carolina."

The Appalachian Mountains affect the state's climate in another way. Because weather tends to move across the

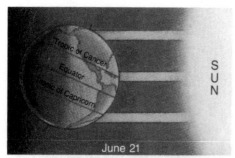

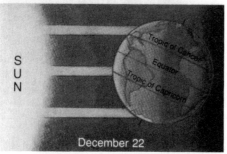

Diagrams Describe

This diagram shows the way the sun's rays reach the earth. Note the different position of the sun on June 21 and December 22. Even when the sun shines on the poles, the rays are slanted. In which hemisphere do the sun's rays shine most directly in June? In December?

6

continent in a west-to-east direction, the mountains act as a barrier. They stop many masses of cold air headed southeast from the interior. However, the mountains do not stop winds that sweep off the Gulf of Mexico or the tropical Atlantic Ocean. As a result, weather patterns in the Caribbean sometimes have a greater impact on North Carolina than do weather patterns on the Great Plains.

Precipitation. Precipitation, or water released from the atmosphere, can fall to the earth in many forms: rain, sleet, hail, snow, fog, or dew. The type of precipitation a region receives goes hand-in-hand with the prevailing temperatures. North Carolina, as you might expect, has far less snow than upstate New York. However, snow still falls in the state, especially at higher elevations in the mountains. Although snow rarely falls on the state's southern coast, four inches a year might fall on the northern coast.

Precipitation in the form of rain or snow is distributed fairly evenly over the state throughout the year. The largest amount of rain usually falls in July and August and the least in October and November. Even so, most areas have no special rainy or dry seasons. Thunderstorms do occur frequently during the hot months, especially in the mountains and along the southern coast. A hail storm may occur in most sections once or twice a year. However, damage to growing crops is generally limited to small areas during any particular storm. Hurricanes from the Atlantic Ocean and the Gulf of Mexico sometimes deliver damaging blows.

RECORD LOW TEMPERATURES

	Wilmington	Asheville
Jan.	5	−16
Feb.	11	−2
Mar.	9	9
April	30	22
May	40	29
June	48	35
July	59	46
Aug.	55	42
Sep.	44	30
Oct.	27	21
Nov.	20	8
Dec.	9	−7

Tables Teach

This table shows record low temperatures for Wilmington and Asheville. One of these cities is located near the coast. The other is located inland. Based on the temperatures in the table, which city is located near the coast? Which city is located inland?

Up from the Caribbean

The Taino, the Native Americans who lived in the Caribbean some 500 years ago, called them *huracans.* The Spanish who first met the Taino placed an accent on the term and added it to their language as *huracáns.* Today English-speaking people call them hurricanes.

Like the word itself, these tropical storms originate in the Caribbean. They usually start in the West Indies as violent, whirling cyclones of wind and rain. From a satellite, hurricanes look like circular patterns of clouds. At the center of a hurricane is an "eye" about 14 miles in diameter, which is relatively calm and free of clouds.

Officially, a storm becomes a hurricane when its winds reach 75 miles an hour. Hurricanes with winds much faster than that have slammed into North Carolina, sending huge walls of ocean waves crashing into the shores. Needless to say, damage can be quite severe. Ask friends and relatives to name and describe some of the most dramatic hurricanes they remember in North Carolina's history.

High winds erode coastal sand dunes and often expose wrecked sailing vessels.

Winds.   For much of the year, winds blow into North Carolina from the southwest. The exception is September and October when they come from the northeast. Wind speeds vary, but they tend to run about 13 miles per hour along the coast, 10 miles per hour along the eastern Coastal Plain, and 8 miles per hour farther inland. Wind speeds decrease at night, pick up at sunrise, and reach their maximum around mid-afternoon.

North Carolina's winds have played a role in the state's history. In the past, sailors found the winds off North Carolina dangerous. The winds could change direction suddenly and blow a ship off course or force it to crash onto a beach. Even today, ship captains pay heed to wind forecasts as they approach the coast of North Carolina. In the past, too, North Carolinians used the winds to power windmills for energy or to pump water from underground wells. Windmills can still be seen in some parts of the state today. For the most part, though, electricity has proven cheaper and more efficient than the windmills.

Throughout time, coastal winds have shaped and reshaped the state's coastline. Wind erosion presents a serious problem in some places. This is especially the case on the Outer Banks, where sand dunes have engulfed cottages. Winds have also mishaped or stunted the growth of trees. Today, picket fences and various kinds of grasses sometimes anchor these shifting dunes.

Think Twice

1. How do weather and climate differ?
2. What factors help shape North Carolina's climate?
3. A generalization is a general statement based on a group of available facts. (a) What generalizations can you form about North Carolina's climate? (b) What facts from the text support your generalization?

3 North Carolina's Natural Resources

People, Places, Terms

environment
natural resource
loam

"The thing I remember most about North Carolina are the flowers. The spring seemed to be filled with color. There were dogwoods, rhododendrons, and wild azaleas. Papa used to drive us to the mountains to see them. It was quite a display." That's how one New York woman, Haroldine Gold, remembers her home state of North Carolina. Her memories describe just one aspect of the North Carolina **environment,** all the living and nonliving things that make up a region. Different environments offer different types of **natural resources,** the parts of nature that people use in some way. A natural resource might even include the flowering trees that are among the features that draw tourists to the mountains each spring. What are some of the region's other natural resources?

Soil. Over time, the forces of nature—heat, cold, rain, and wind—wear down rocks into small particles. The decaying remains of plants and animals mix with these particles to form soil. The soil in North Carolina varies from region to region. In the Tidelands, silt and muck fill the marshes because of poor drainage. In canals that run alongside some roads, the water seems almost black because of the number of decaying plants that have fallen into the water and rotted.

A thick, black **loam** covers the rest of the Coastal Plain. This mixture of clay, sand, and decaying plants can be up to 36 inches deep. Farmers' plows slice easily through the loam because it has few rocks and is well drained. The first European settlers in North Carolina quickly spotted this fact. "The goodliest soile under the cope [canopy] of heaven," announced one settler in 1585.

In the center of the state, in the Piedmont, more rock and less plant life have developed a soil that has a larger percentage of clay. Colors vary from shades of red and yellow to gray. Rocks fill the rolling hills of the Piedmont and make the land difficult to farm. Here and there, big boulders can be seen. Over time, farmers have learned to till the land, but because of the rockier soil, farms tend to be smaller than those in the Coastal Plain.

The thinnest and rockiest soil in the state of North Carolina is found in the Appalachian Mountains. In addition, numerous rocks mark the land. Even so, the plentiful rains and cool air have made the region home to many different types of trees. The state's forests have greatly enriched North Carolina.

Rhododendron blooms in June on Roan Mountain in Pisgah National Forest near Bakersville.

Dogwood and longleaf pine have virtually become natural trademarks of North Carolina.

*T*o show the distribution of natural resources, geographers often display the data on a special purpose map. ■ *To Do*: In the atlas section of your text, locate the map entitled The South: Land Use and Resources. What natural resources are found in the region where you live?

———————

Rocks and minerals. North Carolina possesses at least 300 different kinds of rocks and minerals. They range from the official state gem, the emerald, to gravel, a resource used to build roads. Both the variety and quantity of minerals found in the state provide the basis for a slogan sometimes applied to North Carolina: "Nature's sample case." To glimpse the state's mineral wealth, you might visit the Museum of North Carolina Minerals near Spruce Pine.

Rocks, minerals, and soil vary with the geographic region. In the east, clay, sand, gravel, and phosphate rock can be found. Peat, often used to mulch plants, occurs in much of the swampy land where trees have fallen. In ancient times, the seas covered part of the lands along the coast. Here marine life took refuge in low spots. Their remains formed beds of crumbling shells and sand—the source of lime for generations of farmers who have used it as fertilizer.

The Piedmont provides a wealth of building materials such as slate, granite, and good clay for bricks. It also offers mica and quartz for glass and insulation. Other industrial minerals found here include copper, iron, manganese, chromium, titanium, and tungsten. The Piedmont also supplies nearly 80 percent of the nation's lithium, the lightest of all known minerals.

The mountains offer yet more rocks and minerals. In addition to those found in the Piedmont, the mountainous region provides marble, limestone, and talc. Gemstones such as rubies, garnets, and even a few diamonds have been found. One town, Sapphire, takes its name from the blue gemstone found in its vicinity.

The only mineral fuel found so far in North Carolina has been coal. Some geologists estimate that some 70 to 100 million tons of low-grade coal may be available in the state. They also think that there may be pockets of offshore oil. However, cracks in the earth known as faults have made it dangerous to mine for coal, while environmental threats have made it costly to search for offshore oil.

Plants and wildlife. North Carolina's warm, gentle climate has made it home to an amazing variety of plants and wildlife. Early European settlers saw North Carolina as a kind of paradise. In Europe, people had long since cut down many trees, so the sweeping woodlands that settlers found in the North Carolina region were impressive to them. They also marveled at the great abundance of wildlife, especially a "shaggy cow" now known as the buffalo. The plants and wildlife so impressed Dr. John Brickell that he published, in 1737, some drawings in a book entitled *The Natural History of North Carolina*.

Primary Source

—DR. JOHN BRICKELL, The Natural History of North Carolina

Think as a Historian

A secondary source is information written after an event has taken place. Many history books are secondary sources because they are based on a historian's research into accounts of the past. ■ *To Do*: To practice the skill of writing a secondary account, summarize the information in Dr. Brickell's picture in paragraph form.

From dogwoods to Venus's-flytraps. Today an endless variety of flowers, berries, herbs, and trees still fill the woods and fields of North Carolina. They range from the state flower, the dogwood, to the exotic Venus's-flytrap. Of all the state's plants, perhaps the most important economically are its trees. The wealth of trees found in the state makes North Carolina the nation's leading producer of wooden furniture.

Trees in eastern North Carolina include loblolly and longleaf pines, bay trees, oak, sassafras, and others. Farther west are hickory, poplar, beech, and maple. Spruce, fir, balsam, cedar, and other types of evergreens blanket the mountains. Nearly 145 types of trees have been identified in the Great Smokies alone.

Today forests still cover about 60 percent of all the land in North Carolina. Most of these forests are in the Tidelands and the Coastal Plain. The rest are distributed across the Piedmont and the mountains.

Game, birds, and fish. North Carolina is home to a wide variety of wildlife. Some species seen by Dr. Brickell, such as the buffalo, no longer populate North Carolina. However, a number of other species still roam the mountains or unsettled forest areas. Black bears, opossums, wildcats, deer,

Many natural features in North Carolina bear the names given to them by European settlers. Others still have the names given to them by the Native Americans who first settled the region. ■ *To Do*: Use the map of North Carolina in the atlas section of your text to find two or three names that you think have a Native American origin.

Maps Matter

Look at the map of the principal rivers in North Carolina. ■ *To Do:* Which river is east of Raleigh? West of Raleigh? Use the scale on the map to measure the length of the Tar River.

and rabbits thrive. So, too, do many types of birds. North Carolina has set aside several bird rookeries, or breeding places, to protect endangered species.

Water—offshore and inland. The offshore waters of North Carolina provide another valuable natural resource in the form of fish. Off Cape Hatteras alone, sailors can haul in channel bass, sea mullet, tuna, blue marlin, and more. Fishing boats also bring in large catches of menhaden, a fish used to make oil, fertilizer, and animal feed.

In addition to easy access to the ocean, North Carolina has vast inland water resources. Much of the state possesses high water tables that make it easy for people to drill wells for fresh drinking water. The state also has a number of long navigable rivers, including the Cape Fear, Pee Dee, French Broad, Neuse, and Roanoke rivers. Over the centuries, these rivers have provided important transportation and shipping routes. The state possesses many lakes, too. The largest lake, Mattamuskeet, is a natural lake. However, the state also boasts a number of created lakes. As a result of all these resources, North Carolinians are never far from fresh water—one of the most valuable resources on earth.

Principal Rivers of North Carolina

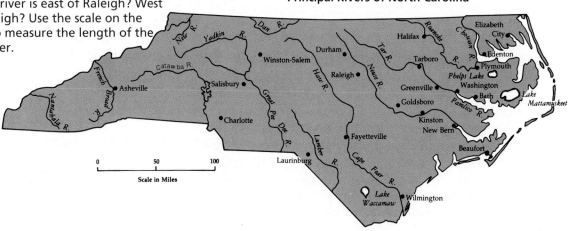

Scale in Miles

Think Twice

1. Why has North Carolina been nicknamed "nature's sample case"?
2. One way of summarizing information is to place it in the form of a chart. What headings would you select to organize information in this section into chart form? What are some of the details that might appear under each heading? Use your headings and details to create a chart.

Chapter 1 Review

Choose from the following menu of activities.

Think Back: Main Ideas

On your paper, answer the following questions.

1. How does elevation, or altitude, divide North Carolina into regions?
2. (a) What climate trait or traits do North Carolina's three geographic areas share with the rest of the United States? (b) How do North Carolina's three geographic regions differ from one another?
3. How does soil differ in the three geographic regions?
4. What are the major natural resources of North Carolina?
5. Do you think the title of this chapter—"A Land of Diversity"—is appropriate? In a paragraph, explain why or why not. Use specific examples from the chapter to defend your opinion.

Maps Matter

Use the map entitled "Regions of the United States" in the atlas section of your text to answer these questions.

1. How does location help identify the South as a region?
2. (a) In terms of situation, how are the Northeast and South alike? (b) What aspect of location helps explain the different climates in the two regions?
3. What are the other two major regions in the United States?
4. The South is sometimes divided into two smaller regions: Southeast and South Central. In which of those two regions would North Carolina be found?

Word Wizard

1. A *suffix* is a word part that can be added to the end of a word. The suffix *er* or *ist* can be added to a noun to describe an occupation or a profession. Use a dictionary to find which ending should be added for a person who works in each of the following fields: geology, geography, topography, and climatology.
2. *Piedmont* comes from two Latin words meaning at the foot (*pied*) of a mountain (*montis*). Using this information, write a definition of the North Carolina Piedmont.

Working Cooperatively

Each year, thousands of people from the United States travel to North Carolina to see its natural wonders. Working in small groups, design a brochure to promote tourism in the state. Use the following steps to guide you.

1. Look at several travel guides in your school or community library for ideas on the type of information most useful to tourists.
2. Select several of the geographic features mentioned in the text to emphasize in more detail in the brochure.
3. Use postcards or pictures from North Carolina magazines to illustrate your brochure.
4. Organize the pictures and descriptions in a way that would interest people in coming to see these sights for themselves.

Curriculum Connection

Using an encyclopedia or a copy of an earth science textbook, find out more about how a hurricane is formed. Present your findings in the form of a diagram.

Learning through Literature

Hatteras Journal, by Jan De Blieu
Ocracokers, by Alton Ballance

The First North Americans

A Native American from Roanoke drawn by Englishman John White in the 1500s ▲

When and how did the first people arrive in the Americas?

The search for answers to these questions has led scientists on a remarkable journey. No written records guide them along the way. Instead, the path is marked by ancient **artifacts**, objects fashioned by human hands. A stone spearpoint, a bone tool—these are the clues that have helped **archaeologists,** scientists who study the remains of early people, to track down the first Americans. The trail of evidence has taken them back to a time some 12,000 years ago. A great Ice Age gripped much of Earth. Ocean levels fell as cold temperatures froze water into icy glacial masses. A land bridge existed where the Bering Strait is now located. Most archaeologists believe that this land bridge formed the pathway from Asia to the Americas.

By the time Europeans arrived, the Americas held millions of people with many diverse ways of life.

For hundreds of years, bands of Asian hunters wandered into North America. Then, around 10,000 years ago, temperatures warmed, glaciers melted, and the land bridge disappeared. However, by this time a band of hunters had reached the most distant tip of South America.

Think Ahead

Early people on all continents lived very close to the land. They molded their lives to take advantage of their surroundings. Read about how the first North Americans—and the first inhabitants of what is now called North Carolina—developed ways of life suited to the land on which they lived.

Bering Strait

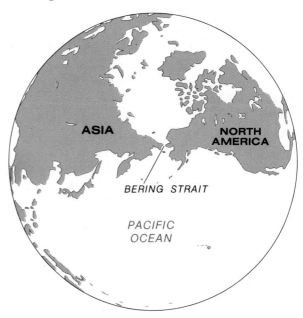

ASIA

NORTH AMERICA

BERING STRAIT

PACIFIC OCEAN

1 The People of North America

In September 1492, three small specks bobbed on the Atlantic Ocean. The sailors aboard Christopher Columbus's three ships scarcely imagined that they would soon change the course of world history. Millions of people lived in both Europe and North America, yet neither knew of the other's existence. That situation changed when Columbus landed on an island off the coast of Florida. Thinking he had reached the Spice Islands of the Indies, Columbus mistakenly called the people there Indians. However, each people had its own name. The names, when translated, often showed a strong connection to the land: "The First People," "The Ancient Ones," "The Original Ones," and so on. Today the Indians are known as Native Americans, or people "native to" the Americas.

By the time Columbus arrived in the Americas, Native Americans had developed very different cultures. A **culture** is a people's way of life. It includes the kinds of tools people make, the food they eat, and the language they speak. Culture also includes how people teach their children and the way they view the world. To study the cultures of early people, scientists have grouped them into

Maps Matter

Mapmakers can only guess at the cultural face of North America around 1500. Many Native Americans moved from place to place. ■ *To Do:* How do you think archaeologists have helped mapmakers in putting together culture region maps such as this one?

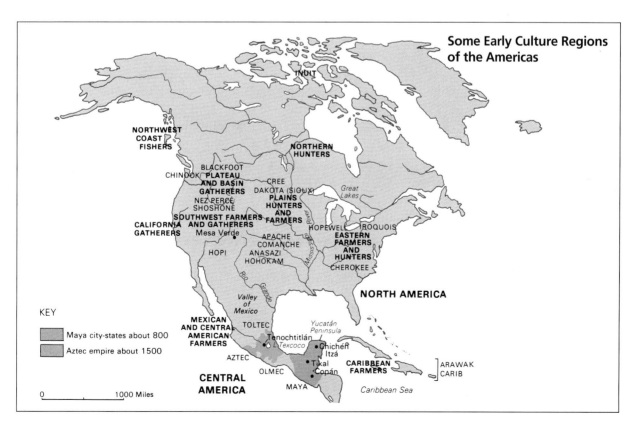

Some Early Culture Regions of the Americas

KEY

Maya city-states about 800
Aztec empire about 1500

0 — 1000 Miles

*I*n speculating about the past, historians develop what is called "historical imagination." That is, they try to look at the period from the viewpoint of the time in which the events took place rather than from the viewpoint of the present. ■ *To Do*: Use your imagination to write a description of one of the culture regions mentioned in the text from the viewpoint of the Native Americans who lived there in 1492.

Native Americans of the Pacific Northwest relied upon the ocean as a source of food.

culture regions, places where methods of living were alike. In which culture region did the first inhabitants of present-day North Carolina live?

The Pacific Northwest. The first fishing-whaling people arrived in the Northwest from 7,000 to 9,000 years ago. Among their descendents were the Makah.

Each spring, cedar canoes 20 to 40 feet long sliced through the Pacific. Up to eight men in each canoe paddled furiously toward pods of gray whales. Each whaler had prepared for battle by swimming gently in a secret pool within the forest. Whalers hoped such rituals would convince a whale's spirit to swim gently, too. In cedar longhouses along the shore, the whalers' wives lay still so the whales would not thrash about. They turned their faces inland so the whales would swim to shore.

In the 1400s, such scenes occurred in Makah villages along the northwestern coast of what is now Washington state. Amid pitching waves, courageous men hurled huge harpoons into whales. Cedar-bark ropes and sealskin floats slowed whales down as they raced away. An injured whale might sink a boat or haul it far out to sea. To capture a whale, however, meant extra food and lots of oil for trade.

The Makah, like other people in the Pacific Northwest, lived in a land of plenty. The ocean and inland rivers yielded a wealth of fish—sweet rock cod, halibut, and all kinds of salmon. The shores harbored shellfish such as clams, mussels, periwinkles, and sea urchins. Inland, the woods contained game, wild cranberries, huckleberries, and more. Tall cedar trees provided straight, sturdy planks for oceangoing canoes and multi-family longhouses. Strips of cedar bark could be woven into rope, blankets, and clothing.

The Desert Southwest. In the deserts of what is now the American Southwest, afternoon temperatures sometimes topped 100°F. Lizards and small rodents burrowed into the sand to escape the hot desert sun. Only cactus, sagebrush, and prickly yucca plants seemed to thrive. Yet some 2,100 years ago, an ancient people known as the Hohokam, or "Perished Ones," settled in the region. Using wooden tools and woven baskets, they dug irrigation ditches to the Salt and Gila rivers. The Hohokam used the water to coax gardens from the deserts.

The Anasazi, or "Ancient Ones," moved into the region around the same time. These master builders constructed huge apartment-like complexes out of sun-dried clay bricks called adobe. To protect themselves from invaders, the Anasazi hauled timber and adobe into the crevices of

The Anasazi built their homes on rock ledges in the cliff walls of the mesas of the Southwest.

canyons and the tops of **mesas,** or plateaus that soared high above the desert floor.

By the time the Spaniards arrived, the Hohokam and Anasazi had deserted their fields and towns. Some archaeologists believe they fled enemies or drought. Others think they simply gave way to people who claimed to be their descendants—the Hopi, Pima, Zuni, Tewa, and others. Like their vanished ancestors, these desert people continued to farm the parched land. They, too, built adobe villages that the Spaniards called **pueblos,** the Spanish word for "town". The Spaniards mistakenly named all the people who lived in such villages the Pueblo. In reality, though, a number of people made up the Pueblo. One of the largest groups was the Hopi, or "Peaceful Ones." Most of the Hopi lived by farming.

The Plains.   Another culture region stretched from the Rocky Mountains to the Mississippi River—the sweeping grasslands of the Great Plains. Here buffalo roamed in herds thousands of animals strong. Sometimes buffalo blackened the land as far as the eye could see and shook the earth with their pounding hooves. To the people of the

Plains, the buffalo meant life itself. Few trees and little water existed on the Plains. As a result, even though the Plains people farmed part of the year, they depended upon the buffalo to supply most of their needs. They used the meat for food, skins for clothes, and bones for tools.

Since buffalo were not afraid of wolves, Native American hunters wearing wolfskins could creep very close to a herd of buffalo without frightening them away.

Plains people, such as the Pawnee, followed the buffalo herds during spring and autumn migrations. During these migrations, people lived as nomads, wandering from place to place. For the rest of the year, however, most Plains people lived in semi-permanent villages. Among the Pawnee, each village was independent and had several leaders and priests. A leader always had a sacred bundle—a group of objects that the Pawnee believed came from a star. Leadership and sacred bundles passed from father to son, but a village might also select an outstanding warrior as a leader. Such a person could then buy a sacred bundle from a priest.

The Eastern Woodlands. While the Great Plains lacked trees, forests covered lands east of the Mississippi during the 1400s. In the Eastern Woodlands, the people hunted and farmed. In doing so, they did not leave the forests unchanged. Time and again, they cleared land for fields and villages by the **slash-and-burn** method. Using a stone axe, they sliced the bark off trees, leaving the trees to die. They then set fire to the dead trees and surrounding brush.

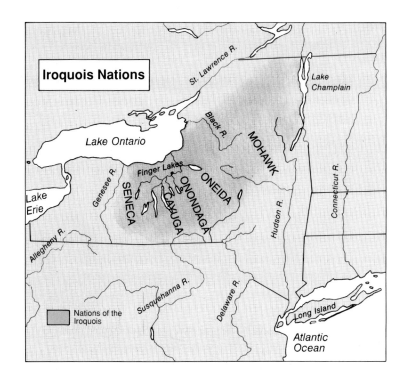

Iroquois Nations

Maps Matter

The league had members from the five different nations that made up the Iroquois people. Chiefs from the nations made laws and agreed upon customs that were to be upheld by all the Iroquois. ■ *To Do:* Which Iroquois nation was located the farthest east? The farthest west?

Amid the ashes, women planted seeds that grew into beans, maize, squash vines, and sunflowers. When the soil wore out, the people moved on. Gradually, new trees and undergrowth reclaimed the land.

If you look at the map on page 15, you will see some of the groups who lived as farmers and hunters in the Eastern Woodlands, including the Iroquois. In the 1300s, the Mohawk, Oneida, Onondaga, Cayuga, and Seneca wanted to end warfare among them, so they formed a council known as the Iroquois League. A league is an alliance for a common purpose. Because property and descent passed down among women, the leading women of each nation chose members of the council. The resulting unity among the Iroquois made these people a powerful force in the north. To the south, however, other people developed equally impressive cultures. Among them were the first inhabitants of what is now North Carolina.

Think Twice

1. In 1492, what Native American culture region included present-day North Carolina?
2. How did the Native Americans in each culture region use their environment for food?
3. How did many Native Americans of the Eastern Woodlands develop unity?

Wigwams—and later, longhouses— had frames of poles lashed together.

2 The First North Carolinians

People have lived in North Carolina for more than 10,000 years. At first, they wandered the land as nomadic hunters. Then, about 2,500 years ago, they began to settle in semi-permanent or permanent villages. Freed from the toil of the hunt, they developed many crafts. Artifacts show that most Native American groups were skilled at craftwork. By 1500 B.C., for example, artists fashioned clay pottery, stone pipes, and soapstone cooking vessels. People prized these treasures so much that they placed them in the graves of loved ones. Archaeologists have also discovered evidence of tightly woven baskets and painted jars and bowls that were both useful and attractive. Native American jewelry made of fine shells or pounded copper has been found as well.

Like other Native Americans, early North Carolinians left no written records. Yet they speak to us through the objects they left behind and through their **oral histories,** stories passed down from generation to generation. Other information comes from the first European explorers to set foot in North Carolina. Together these sources provide a glimpse of the first inhabitants of North Carolina.

Native Americans of North Carolina, 1500

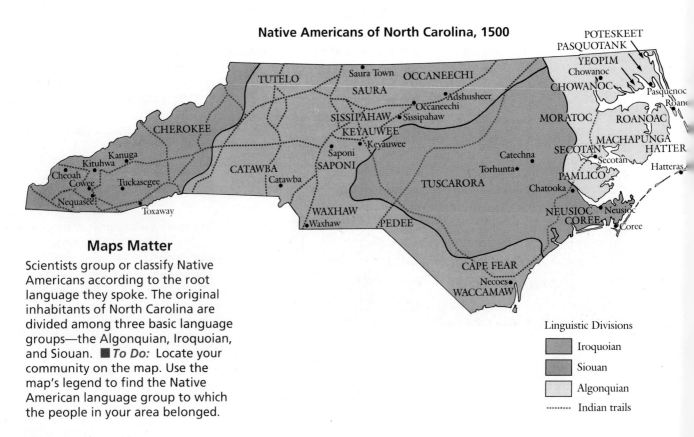

Linguistic Divisions
- Iroquoian
- Siouan
- Algonquian
- .... Indian trails

Maps Matter

Scientists group or classify Native Americans according to the root language they spoke. The original inhabitants of North Carolina are divided among three basic language groups—the Algonquian, Iroquoian, and Siouan. ■*To Do:* Locate your community on the map. Use the map's legend to find the Native American language group to which the people in your area belonged.

"A well shap'd clean-made People." An estimated 35,000 Native Americans lived in North Carolina around 1492. The five largest groups living in North Carolina at that time were the Hatteras, Chowanoc, Tuscarora, Catawba, and Cherokee. Scientists think that some 34 separate Native American groups may have lived in the state at one time or another.

The Europeans who first set eyes on the people of North Carolina marveled at their endurance and strength. "The Indians of North Carolina are a well shap'd clean-made People," wrote John Lawson, who came to the region in 1700. Lawson and other Europeans also observed the darker skin color of North Carolina Native Americans and their straight dark hair. Nearly all Europeans remarked on the lack of clothes worn by the Native Americans and the use of paint or tattoos to decorate their bodies. Europeans, of course, seemed just as oddly clothed and decorated to the people who were already in the region.

In addition to his observations of the physical characteristics of the Native Americans, Lawson lived

The Mound Builders

Around A.D. 1300, warlike invaders pushed into southern North Carolina near present-day Mount Gilead. They sent peaceful farming people scrambling north as they took over lands along the banks of the Pee Dee River. Here they built a permanent town fortified by a great wooden stockade.

At the center of the town lay a huge earthen mound. Workers carried tons of soil, basket by basket, to build the mound. On top of the mound sat a square temple made of thatch. Other smaller mounds dotted the area. Within these mounds, the invaders buried their dead and objects of value—freshwater pearls, copper plates, stone pipes, and turquoise from as far away as Mexico.

After about 100 years, the people that archaeologists call the "mound builders" left the region. Like the Southwestern Anasazi, their fate remains a mystery. Today, however, people in North Carolina can see evidence of the culture of these mound builders at Town Creek Indian Mound in Montgomery County. Shown in the photo above, it is one of the state's many historic sites.

Thare sitting at meate.

The broyling of their fish ouer the flame of fier.

In the 1580s, Englishman John White made many watercolor drawings of birds, plants, and other wildlife and of the people he met in the area that is now called North Carolina. "Indian Man and Woman Eating" and "Cooking Fish" are two examples that can be found in the British Library.

intimately enough with the Native Americans to be able to understand them. He truly was concerned for the well-being of these people.

Leaving a mark on the land.   The native people from the Outer Banks to the Appalachians used whatever the land offered. Many of these people lived in the Coastal Plain. Here, stone hoes easily turned the sandy loam into gardens. People also took advantage of plants for food. Tall cypress trees along the Tidewater rivers provided rot-resistant wood for dugout canoes and posts for wood-and-thatch huts. The long gray moss that hung from trees supplied tinder for fires and material for ropes. In some places, women even wove the moss into skirts.

People in the Piedmont and the mountains used the land, too. Like other Eastern Woodland people, they created fields from the forests by using the slash-and-burn method. Along the fall line, they captured large numbers of fish heading upstream to spawn, or lay eggs, and hunted in the forests for deer, bear, and other game. They prowled in the meadows and brush for wild turkeys and birds. In the mountains, people collected minerals such as mica and quartz. Southeastern people especially valued quartz because they believed its crystals foretold the future. Declared one Cherokee myth: "The future is seen mirrored in the clear crystal as a tree is reflected in the quiet stream."

Patterns of life.   Although ways of living varied, most native people in the North Carolina area shared certain cultural traits. For most groups, the extended family provided the basis of life. Within the family, people traced their descent through women. **Clans,** or groups of related people, tended to live in settlements of ten or twelve houses.

A chief ruled but succession fell not to the chief's son but to his sister's son. In other words, the original people of North Carolina traced their ancestry through the women of the family rather than through the father's line as we do today.

Almost all of the people in North Carolina saw life as a web of relationships, not only among humans but among plants and animals as well. It took non-Native Americans a long time to understand the way Native Americans viewed the connections between themselves and the world around them. One of the first to study this was James Mooney, an **anthropologist,** or scientist who studies human culture. Below is a legend retold to him by Swimmer, an honored Cherokee story teller. As you read it, think about how Native Americans might have viewed nature.

Primary Source

> *When the Plants, who were friendly to Man, heard what had been done by the animals, they determined to defeat the latter's evil designs. Each Tree, Shrub, and Herb, down even to the Grasses and Mosses, agreed to furnish a cure for some one of the diseases named, and each said: "I shall appear to help Man when he calls upon me in his need." Thus came medicine; and the plants, every one of which has its use if we only knew it, furnish the remedy to counteract the evil wrought by the revengeful animals. Even weeds were made for some good purpose, which we must find out for ourselves. When the doctor does not know what medicine to use for a sick man the spirit of the plant tells him.*

> —SWIMMER, *"The Sacred Formulas of the Cherokees"*

Europeans brought new beliefs and attitudes to North Carolina and the rest of the Americas. As you will read in Unit 2, they held views of the land that contrasted sharply with those of the Native Americans. In the years after 1492, Native Americans suddenly found their entire way of life threatened by the arrival of new, non-American cultures.

Think Twice

1. How have historians learned about the first North Carolinians?
2. Name the five largest Native American groups that lived in what is now North Carolina in 1500.
3. How did Native Americans use the land in different regions of what is now North Carolina?
4. What similar ways of life developed among the native people in the area of North Carolina?

Think as a Geographer

Geography, as you might have guessed, includes more than mountains and rivers. It also involves the human beings who interact with the environment where they live.

■ *To Do:* On posterboard, draw a large outline map of North Carolina showing the state's main topographic regions—Coastal Plain, Piedmont, and mountains. Then sketch diagrams on the map depicting how Native Americans used the resources in each area.

Chapter 2 Review

Choose from the following menu of activities.

Think Back: Main Ideas

On your paper, write answers to the following questions.

1. How did the Makah people take advantage of the abundance of natural resources in the Pacific Northwest?
2. How did the Anasazi adapt their lives to the environment of the American Southwest?
3. In what ways did the Plains Indians use the resources of the Great Plains?
4. The ways of life of the Coastal Plain inhabitants of North Carolina were similar to those of the people in the Piedmont and the mountains.
   a. How did each group use the land?
   b. What natural resources were available to each group, and how were the natural resources used?

Maps Matter

Use the culture regions map on page 15 to answer the following questions about Native American ways of life in the 1500s.

1. Which culture region lived primarily by fishing?
2. To which culture region did the Cherokee belong?
3. What groups lived directly to the west of the Southwest farmers and hunters?
4. What group lived farthest north?

Word Wizard

Each of the following word pairs is linked in some way. Using information in the text, write a sentence explaining how each pair of terms is connected.

1. artifact, archaeologist
2. Indian, Native American
3. culture, anthropologist
4. oral history, primary source

Working Cooperatively

Select a Native American group in the North Carolina area from the map on page 20. Working with a team of students, design a museum display of artifacts created by that group. Use these steps to guide you.

1. Photocopy paintings of tools, clothing, artwork, and other interesting articles made by the people.
2. Organize the pictures by categories on separate pieces of construction paper or posterboard. (For example, all pictures of clothing should appear together.)
3. Design a brochure or make a tape recording that will lead other students through the display.
4. Organize the display across the front of the classroom. Make copies of the brochure or the tape recording available so that your classmates can take a guided tour into the past.

Curriculum Connection

Read the following poem written by a Native American. Write a paragraph in which you explain what the poem says to you about nature.

Trail Warning
Beauty is no threat to the wary
   who treat the mountain in its way,
     the copperhead in its way,
      and the deer in its way,
knowing that nature is the human heart
made tangible.
         — Anonymous

Learning through Literature

Ancient Indians: The First Americans, by Roy A. Gallant
Myths of the Cherokee, by James Mooney
North Carolina Indian Legends and Myths, by F. Roy Johnson

Seeking and Settling

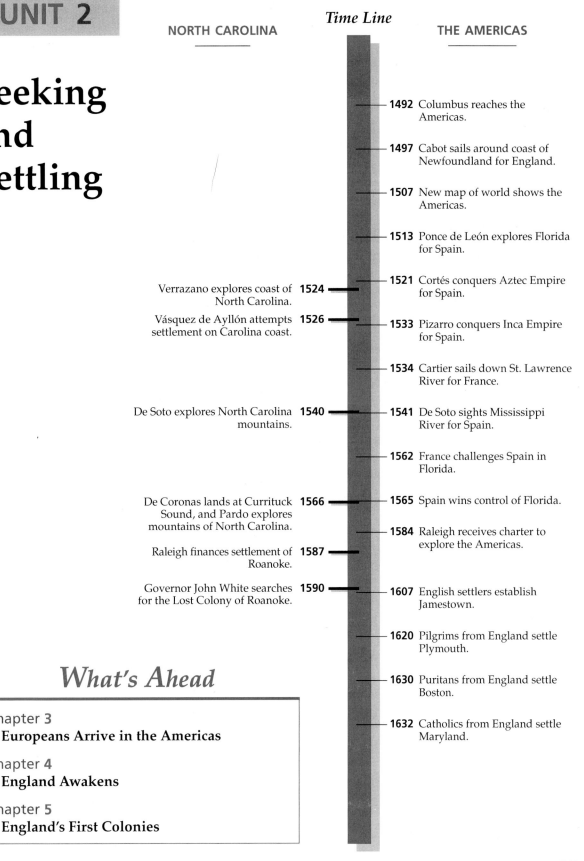

Time Line

NORTH CAROLINA		THE AMERICAS

1492 Columbus reaches the Americas.

1497 Cabot sails around coast of Newfoundland for England.

1507 New map of world shows the Americas.

1513 Ponce de León explores Florida for Spain.

1521 Cortés conquers Aztec Empire for Spain.

Verrazano explores coast of North Carolina. **1524**

Vásquez de Ayllón attempts settlement on Carolina coast. **1526**

1533 Pizarro conquers Inca Empire for Spain.

1534 Cartier sails down St. Lawrence River for France.

De Soto explores North Carolina mountains. **1540**

1541 De Soto sights Mississippi River for Spain.

1562 France challenges Spain in Florida.

De Coronas lands at Currituck Sound, and Pardo explores mountains of North Carolina. **1566**

1565 Spain wins control of Florida.

1584 Raleigh receives charter to explore the Americas.

Raleigh finances settlement of Roanoke. **1587**

Governor John White searches for the Lost Colony of Roanoke. **1590**

1607 English settlers establish Jamestown.

1620 Pilgrims from England settle Plymouth.

1630 Puritans from England settle Boston.

1632 Catholics from England settle Maryland.

What's Ahead

Chapter 3

Europeans Arrive in the Americas

Muslim trader

Muslim merchants made the journey from Southwest Asia to the East.

For hundreds of years, Europeans had bought treasures like silks and spices from China, India, and other countries in Asia. Yet few Europeans ever made the trip themselves. Instead, they bought the goods from Italian merchants who had purchased them from Muslim merchants in the markets of Southwest Asia.

In 1492, Columbus journeyed west across the Atlantic Ocean.

By the 1400s, many European navigators believed that the fastest, safest route to the East was by sea. Most chose to sail south and then east around Africa. Only one navigator, Christopher Columbus, dared to sail west across the Atlantic Ocean. Ten weeks into his journey, Columbus sighted land on October 12, 1492. He believed he had reached the East Indies, near Japan and China. In fact, Columbus was nowhere near Asia. Instead, he had landed on San Salvador, an island in the Caribbean Sea.

A European ship in the late 1400s ▶

Think Ahead

Other European explorers quickly joined the search for a western route to the East. Read about their acts of courage and cruelty in the following pages. Find out who among them was the first to visit the land now called North Carolina.

1 The Search for a Northwest Passage

People, Places, Terms

Christopher Columbus
John Cabot
Giovanni da Verrazano
Amerigo Vespucci
latitude
longitude

When Europeans realized that two large continents blocked the westward route to Asia (see below), they began looking for a route around the Americas. In the early 1500s, explorers sailing for England and France searched for a northwest passage to Asia. Although they never found one, both England and France claimed parts of North America as a result of these early voyages.

The English try first. The first explorer to look for a northwest passage was the Italian navigator John Cabot. Financed by English merchants, Cabot set sail from England and reached the coast of North America in 1497. He then sailed north along the fog-bound shores of Newfoundland, now a part of Canada. Although Cabot never found a northwest passage, he did claim Newfoundland for England.

France enters the race. Like England, France was eager to find a northwest passage to Asia. In 1524, the French king Francis I chose the best navigator he could find—Giovanni da Verrazano—a skilled navigator whose influential Italian family had banking connections with France.

Why America?

Columbus made four trips westward from Spain. Although he never found the treasures he was looking for, he died believing he had found a western route to Asia. However, between 1497 and 1503, a Florentine merchant named Amerigo Vespucci proved Columbus wrong. During those years, Vespucci crossed the Atlantic four times and described in his letters the plants and animals found along the coastline of the land known today as Brazil. Noting that these plants and animals were unknown in Asia, Europe, or Africa, Vespucci concluded that this land must be a new continent unknown to Europeans.

In 1507, a German mapmaker drew a new map of the world based on Vespucci's information. The map showed a great mass of land west of the Atlantic, and the mapmaker labeled this land America in honor of Amerigo Vespucci. When Europeans realized that America was not one continent but two, they simply called the two continents North America and South America.

NORTH AMERICA
EUROPE
SPAIN
AFRICA
ATLANTIC OCEAN
San Salvador
WEST INDIES
Caribbean Sea
SOUTH AMERICA

Giovanni da Verrazano was an experienced Florentine navigator in the service of the king of France. As a young man, Verrazano had traded in the Muslim markets of present-day Saudi Arabia for Asian spices and other treasures. King Francis I hoped Verrazano would find a passage around North America to eliminate the extra cost of trading through Muslim merchants.

Verrazano sails for France.   On January 17, 1524, Verrazano set sail from a "deserted rock" near Madeira, a group of islands off the North African coast. After sailing through a storm as "severe as ever a man who has navigated suffered," he and his crew continued the treacherous trip across the Atlantic. Two months later, in mid-March, they sighted land near the mouth of North Carolina's Cape Fear River. Verrazano became the first European to visit what is now North Carolina and to record his impressions of the North American continent. His report to the king of France, dated July 8, described the wholesome air, "faire fields and plains," and some "mightie great woods."

As Verrazano and his crew explored the ragged coastline, Verrazano was certain he had found the route to Asia at each large bay he saw. Along the Outer Banks of North Carolina, he saw Pamlico Sound and Albemarle Sound, but he did not see the mainland beyond. As a result, he mistook the large body of water behind the narrow sand banks for the Pacific Ocean. For a century and a half after Verrazano's journey, mapmakers and explorers thought the Pacific Ocean, or the South Sea as they called it, was not very far to the west of the North Carolina coast.

Maps Matter

Maps matter because they help us picture information. Sometimes a map shows us information we have learned through our readings. Sometimes a map introduces new information. ■ *To Do:* Study the map to the right. What information from the chapter does the map help the reader picture more clearly? What new information does the map present?

Search for the Northwest Passage
→ Route of Verrazano, 1524
→ Route of Cartier, 1534
⋯⋯► Route of Cartier, 1535-1536
⋯⋯► Route of Cabot, 1497

Gulf of St. Lawrence

Newfoundland

L. Superior

L. Huron   L. Ontario

L. Michigan   L. Erie

St. Lawrence R.

ATLANTIC OCEAN

NORTH AMERICA

Delaware Bay

Ohio R.

Mississippi R.

FLORIDA

Gulf of Mexico

0   300   600 Miles
0   300   600 Kilometers

N E S W

Verrazano describes the land. Much of what is known about Verrazano's trip comes from a letter he wrote to King Francis I. The following passage taken from Verrazano's letter gives his first impression of Cape Fear— "the land first seen at 34 degrees N. Latitude."

Primary Source

> *After going ahead, some rivers and arms of the sea were found which enter through some mouths, coursing the shore on both sides as it follows its windings. Nearby appears the spacious land, so high that it exceeds the sandy shore, with many beautiful fields and plains, full of the largest forests, some thin and dense, clothed with as many colors of trees, with as much beauty and delectable appearance as it would be possible to express.*
>
> *And do not believe, Your Majesty, that these are like the Hyrcanian Forests or the wild solitudes of Scythia and northern countries, full of rugged trees, but [these forests are] adorned and clothed with palms, laurels, and cypresses, and other varieties of trees unknown in our Europe.*

> —VERRAZANO, *"Letter to King Francis I"*

Verrazano describes the people. Culture is the way of life of a group of people. It includes the foods they eat, the languages they speak, how they teach their children, and the way they view the world. It also includes the technology they use and the kinds of tools they make.

What was it like, then, for the Native Americans and the members of Verrazano's crew to meet face-to-face for the first time? What happened when these two totally different cultures collided on the sandy shores of North Carolina's coastline? The following excerpt from Verrazano's letter (page 30) contains one of many descriptions that Verrazano wrote about his crew's encounters with the various Native American groups who lived along the eastern shores of North America.

In this particular encounter, Verrazano attempted to send a boat ashore in Onslow Bay (near present-day Wilmington, North Carolina), but waves breaking on the beach prevented the ship from landing. A few Native Americans appeared and directed the sailors to a landing place. However, one impatient young sailor jumped out of the boat and started to wade ashore. He was tossing some pieces of paper, small mirrors, bells, and other trinkets to the Indians when he was knocked down by a fierce wave. Verrazano described what happened next.

Think as a Geographer

*I*n the primary source to the left, Verrazano gives his impression of Cape Fear—the land first seen at latitude 34 degrees N. ■ *To Do*: Locate a map of present-day North Carolina. Make sure that lines of latitude and longitude are on the map. Find latitude 34 degrees N. Was Verrazano correct? Locate three present-day cities or towns that lie at or near latitude 34 degrees N.

This drawing shows how a Spanish artist of the late 1500s viewed Columbus's arrival in the West Indies.

29

Across Cultures

Since the Native Americans did not have a written language, there are no accounts of their impressions of the Europeans. Yet they must have been struck by the color of the newcomers' skin, their clothing, their sailing vessels, and other parts of European culture.

■ *To Do*: Rewrite or retell Verrazano's account from the point of view of the Native Americans. Compare and contrast the two versions. What do they have in common? How do they differ?

An important navigational tool used by Columbus and other sailors of his time was the astrolabe. The astrolabe was a brass circle with carefully adjusted concentric rings marked off in degrees. Using these rings to sight the stars, a sea captain could measure **latitude**—his distance north or south of the equator. The astrolabe enabled Columbus to measure latitude, but he had no device to measure **longitude**, whose lines run from the North Pole to the South Pole and indicate how far east or west a traveler has gone.

Primary Source

[The young sailor] was tossed by the waves [and] almost half dead was carried [by the waves] to the edge of the shore. The people of the land ran immediately to him. Taking him by the head, legs, and arms, they carried him some distance away. Where, the youth, seeing himself carried in such a way, stricken with terror, uttered very loud cries, which they did similarly in their language, showing him that he should not have fear.

After that, having placed him on the ground in the sun at the foot of a little hill, they performed great acts of admiration, regarding the whiteness of his flesh, examining him from head to foot. Taking off his shirt and hose, leaving him nude, they made a very large fire near him, placing him near the heat. Which having been seen, the sailors, who remained in the small boat, full of fear, as is their custom in every new case, thought they wanted to roast him for food.

His strength recovered, having remained with the [Native Americans] awhile, he showed by signs that he desired to return to the ship; who with the greatest kindness, holding him always close with various embraces, accompanied him as far as the sea, and in order to assure him more, extending themselves on a high hill, stood to watch him until he was in the boat.

—Verrazano, *"The Young Sailor"*

Verrazano continues northward. After this adventure, Verrazano sailed further north. Because his ship was so far out to sea, he failed to notice two giant bays—the Chesapeake and the Delaware. He did, however, make a brief stop at the bay near what is now New York City. Verrazano then landed briefly on the coasts of present-day Rhode Island and Maine and finally reached Newfoundland in Canada. From there, he returned to France.

Think Twice

1. Why were English and French explorers searching for a northwest passage to Asia?
2. What mistake in geography did Verrazano make?
3. What were Verrazano's impressions of North Carolina?
4. What were Verrazano's impressions of the Native Americans he encountered?
5. Based on what you have read about Verrazano's travels, what were qualities of the area of North Carolina that would later be attractive to European settlers?

2 Spain's Search for Treasure to the South

People, Places, Terms

conquistador
Hernán Cortés
Montezuma
Francisco Pizarro
Atahualpa
empire
viceroyalty
missionary
mission

Spain's earliest settlements in the Americas were on Cuba and Hispaniola—islands that Columbus had claimed. Sailing west from these islands, Spanish fortune hunters, called **conquistadors**, set out to find gold and glory. Their early expeditions took them to lands located to the south of present-day United States. Later they searched for cities of gold farther north while destroying ancient civilizations and enslaving millions of native people. They also spread the culture of Spain and brought the Catholic religion to the Americas. Be a judge of history as you read about their deeds.

Cortés conquers the Aztec.   Hernán Cortés was one of the Spaniards who came to the Americas in search of gold and silver. Sailing from Cuba in 1519, Cortés found the treasures he sought in Tenochtitlán (tay NOHCH tee TLAHN), the capital city of the vast Aztec Empire that covered much of present-day Mexico.

It did not matter to Cortés that the treasures belonged to the Aztec. In fact, within two years, Cortés had destroyed Tenochtitlán and taken over its enormous wealth. The quick capture of Tenochtitlán was due to the superior technology of the Spanish as well as an ancient Aztec myth (see below). This event marked the beginning of Spanish rule in Mexico and Central America.

Human or God?

According to an ancient Aztec legend, Quetzalcoatl (KEHT zahl KOH tl), the god of wisdom and civilization, had once ruled Mexico, disguised as a bearded white man. Driven out centuries before, the god had threatened he would return in a "white-winged ship" from across the eastern sea.

In 1519, messengers began bringing reports to Montezuma, emperor of the Aztec, in his capital city of Tenochtitlán in the Valley of Mexico. The reports told of white-skinned, bearded men arriving at the coast in winged towers. Were these strangers merely men from distant lands, or was their leader, as Montezuma feared, the ancient ruler-god of the Aztec returning to claim his kingdom? As fate would have it, the bearded Cortés arrived in the same year that Quetzalcoatl had been expected to return. Believing that Cortés was the god Quetzalcoatl, Montezuma welcomed him into his city as an honored guest. The invitation sealed the fate of the Aztec Empire.

This Inca figurine, made of gold, was found covered with a robe of Peruvian cloth.

Pizarro searches for the Inca. Francisco Pizarro was a conquistador who came to the Americas in search of the fabulous Inca Empire. A gray-bearded man of sixty-two, Pizarro landed on the coast of Peru in 1532 with about 200 soldiers. They then traveled up the western slopes of the Andes in search of the ancient empire.

At that time, the Inca Empire stretched for 2,500 miles, from what is now southern Colombia in the north to central Chile in the south, an area larger than present-day California, Oregon, and Washington combined. Once again the Spaniards used superior technology and force to conquer a Native American civilization. Over 2,000 Inca lost their lives, including the Inca emperor Atahualpa (AH tah WAHL pah). Held captive by the Spaniards, Atahualpa promised to give them a roomful of gold and two smaller roomfuls of silver in return for his freedom. The Spaniards accepted the offer, took the treasure, but then killed the emperor. In the 100 years that followed, the Spanish would conquer all of Peru and seize a fortune in gold, silver, and jewels.

Maps Matter

Today Mexico, Central America, and South America make up a cultural region known as Latin America. The region is called Latin America because the people there speak Spanish or Portuguese. These languages developed from Latin, which was spoken about 2,000 years ago in southern Europe. ■ *To Do:* Study the map. What European country took control of Brazil in the 1500s? What language do the people of Brazil speak today?

Spain's American Empire

KEY
■ Viceroyalty of New Spain
□ Viceroyalty of Peru

0   1000 Miles

Spain rules an empire in the Americas. An **empire** is made up of a nation and the lands and people it governs. The empire built by the Spaniards in the Americas was 20 times larger than Spain. To govern this vast area, the Spanish king Charles V decided to divide it into two large colonies called **viceroyalties.** One was the viceroyalty of New Spain. Its capital was Mexico City, which Cortés had built on the ruins of Tenochtitlán. The other was the viceroyalty of Peru, with its capital in Lima.

Charles V rewarded the conquistadors and other Spanish officials by giving them Native American laborers. The conquistadors also purchased land in the Americas on which they could raise sheep or cattle. Yet the Spaniards did not do the work themselves. Instead, they used the Native American laborers granted to them by the king.

The Spaniards enslave Native Americans. From the beginning, the Native Americans were treated as little more than slaves. Many Spanish landowners cared more about quick profits than the health of their workers. They pushed the Native Americans to exhaustion. Thousands died from overwork. Many more died from diseases the Spanish brought from Europe to the Americas.

The Spanish bring enslaved Africans to the Americas. During the 1500s, the Spanish began buying slaves from the west coast of Africa to replace the Native Americans who had died. These African slaves had been captured by other Africans in wars, and the Spanish brought them in chains to the Americas. By 1540, there were 100,000 enslaved Africans working for Spanish settlers in the Americas.

Think as a Historian

*T*he Aztec emperor Montezuma, the Inca emperor Atahualpa, and King Charles V of Spain were all absolute rulers. Their word was law, and within their empires they did not have to answer to anyone.
■ *To Do*: Can you identify a country leader of the twentieth century who ruled through absolute power? Use a world history book or encyclopedia to help you. Then explain why this person can be considered an absolute ruler.

This artwork, which was drawn by a Native American, shows the brutal treatment received at the hands of Spanish conquistadors.

The San Miguel Mission, built in Santa Fe, New Mexico in 1610, shows what early mission buildings looked like.

This scene, drawn by a Native American after the Spanish conquest of Mexico, shows a Spanish priest baptizing an Aztec. ▶

Spanish priests bring Catholicism to the Americas.
Although the Spanish conquistadors came in search of gold and glory, other Spaniards had a completely different motive for coming to the Americas. For these people, the search for glory meant the spreading of the Catholic religion—a quest that brought not conquistadors but priests. The priests came as **missionaries**—people who teach their religion to people of other faiths. They did their work on **missions,** which usually included a church, homes, and a fort. Within these missions, Spanish priests tried to care for the Native Americans and relieve their suffering. The priests also struggled to learn the Native American languages so that they could more effectively teach Christianity to the native people.

Many religious people questioned Spanish motives for coming to the Americas. As one soldier in Cortés's army wrote, "We came here to serve God and also to get rich." Could one do both at the same time?

Think Twice

The text on pages 31-34 helps explain an important landmark, the Plaza of the Three Cultures, which stands today in the heart of Mexico City. At the center of the plaza are the ruins of an Aztec market. At one side of the ruined market is a 400-year-old Roman Catholic church. On the other side, rising above both the market and the church, is a modern skyscraper with apartments, shops, and a school.

1. (a) Who were the Aztec? (b) In what present-day country did they create their empire?
2. How was the Roman Catholic religion brought to Mexico?
3. What do the modern skyscrapers in the plaza represent?
4. How does the history of Mexico help explain why this plaza is known as the Plaza of the Three Cultures?

3 Europeans Reach North Carolina

People, Places, Terms

Ponce de León
Lucas Vásquez de Ayllón
Hernando de Soto
Jean Ribaut
René de Laudonnière
Pedro Menéndez
Pedro de Coronas
Juan Pardo

As Spain was building a great empire in the south, Spanish adventurers were also scouring lands north of Mexico for treasure. In their quest for gold, they would establish colonies in what is now the United States. Along the eastern coast, their reach would include present-day North Carolina.

Ponce de León explores Florida for Spain.   During his years as governor of Puerto Rico, the gray-haired Juan Ponce de León had listened with increasing interest to a Native American story. It described a nearby land with a wondrous fountain that restored youth to whoever bathed in it. Determined to find the fountain, the aging governor paid for ships and soldiers and set sail with high hopes.

On Easter Sunday in 1513, Ponce de León landed near what is now St. Augustine. Upon landing there, he was so taken by the flowers that he named the region Florida after the Spanish festival at Easter called Pascua Florida, "Feast of Flowers." For the next 200 years, the name Florida would apply to the entire southeast coast of what is now the United States.

Ponce de León's expedition explored the east and west coasts of Florida in search of this magic fountain. However, because of Florida's shape, Ponce de León never realized that his ships were sailing around a peninsula instead of an island. Consequently, he claimed the "Isle of Florida" for Spain before returning home.

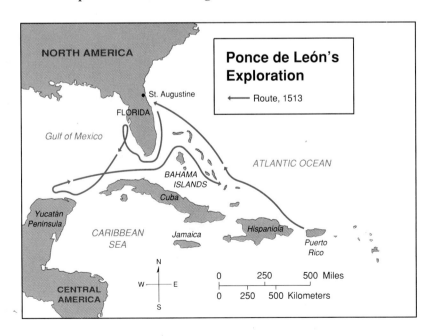

Maps Matter

Trace Ponce de León's route around Florida. ■ *To Do:* Why was he unable to tell that Florida was a peninsula rather than an island?

Ponce de León claims Florida for Spain. Seven years later, an aged Ponce de León tried once again to find the Fountain of Youth. On February 10, 1521, he wrote the following to King Charles V of Spain.

Primary Source

> *Among my services I discovered, at my own expense, the Island of Florida and others in its district . . . I intend to explore the coast of the said island and see whether it connects with [Cuba], or any other; and I shall endeavor to learn all I can. I shall set out to pursue my voyage in five or six days hence.*

—Ponce de León, *"Letter to King Charles V"*

Several days later, Ponce de León set out with two ships and 250 men. This time he tried to establish a settlement in Florida, but Native Americans attacked his party and drove out the intruders. Severely wounded, Ponce de León died a few days after reaching Cuba. Although he never found the Fountain of Youth, his travels gave Spain a claim to much of the southeast coast of North America.

Vásquez de Ayllón lands at Cape Fear. In 1526, five years after Ponce de León's death, the Spanish made the first attempt by Europeans to settle North Carolina. The leader of this expedition was Lucas Vásquez de Ayllón, a man of wealth and education who lived in Hispaniola.

A River in the Ocean

In 1513, Ponce de León and his men were sailing south from St. Augustine along the Florida coast. A brisk tail wind filled their sails, yet the ships were barely moving. An opposing force stronger than the wind was driving them northward, back to St. Augustine.

The force was the Gulf Stream—the mighty "river in the ocean" that carries warm water from the Gulf of Mexico all the way across the Atlantic to the west coast of Europe. Between Florida and Cuba, the Gulf Stream flows with the volume of a thousand Mississippi rivers. Although Ponce de León's ships were fighting the Gulf Stream in 1513, the Spaniards would soon learn to depend upon it to speed their treasure ships homeward toward Spain.

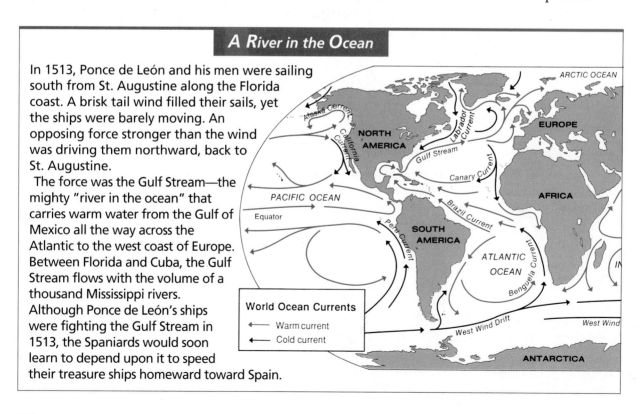

Financing the expedition at his own personal expense, Vásquez de Ayllón set sail in June 1526 with over 500 men, women, and children—including several enslaved Africans—and nearly 90 horses. At about latitude 33°40'N, they entered the mouth of what is now known as the Cape Fear River and began taking their supplies ashore.

Vásquez de Ayllón's expedition moves south.   After several days, Vásquez de Ayllón's group found the site unsuited for settlement because it was swampy and full of insects. As a result, the party moved south into what is now South Carolina. Some of the settlers journeyed south by boat. Others traveled by horseback, following a Native American path, much of which became known as King's Highway, now United States Route 17.

The new Spanish settlement, however, did not prosper. Fever and starvation took many lives, and Vásquez de Ayllón himself died in October, leaving the expedition without a leader. In addition, the enslaved Africans revolted, and Native Americans, fearful of losing their land, attacked some of the settlers. In the winter of 1527, the 150 survivors sailed back to Hispaniola. Vásquez de Ayllón's failed expedition was Spain's first and only attempt to establish a settlement in North Carolina.

De Soto lands in Florida.   Although the Spanish did not attempt another settlement in North Carolina, they did continue their search for gold. The most noted Spanish explorer in the region was Hernando de Soto. De Soto had been a soldier with Pizarro in Peru. Although his conquests there had already made him a rich man, De Soto decided to search for the "gold-bearing mountains" described by the Native Americans.

In May 1539, De Soto and an army of about 600 men set out from Cuba and landed in what is now Tampa, Florida. The men had about 200 horses and several hundred squealing pigs, which De Soto had brought along as food. Large quantities of supplies were unloaded by Native Americans whom the Spanish forced into service along the way. In contrast to the lightly clad Native Americans, the Spaniards were dressed in plumed hats and heavy coats of mail, which caused them great discomfort in the stifling heat of the South.

De Soto reaches the mountains of North Carolina.   By early 1540, De Soto and his men had made their way north through present-day Florida, Georgia, and South Carolina. The expedition entered southwestern North Carolina through present-day Jackson County and then traveled west to the mountains of Macon, Clay, and Cherokee counties.

Many sources of the time portray De Soto as both a cruel and brilliant man. At the Spanish court, he put on a great show of elegance and won from the Spanish king a prized title—"Governor of the Island of Cuba." When De Soto set sail from Cuba in April 1538, he left his wife Doña Ysabel to rule the island. He died after sighting the Mississippi River and never saw his wife again.

The account of Ribaut's voyage entitled *The Whole and True Discoverye of Terra Florida* may have inspired a young English gentleman named Walter Raleigh to learn more about the Americas. In much the same way, a book written by Marco Polo fired the imagination of Christopher Columbus. ■ *To Do*: Think of a book or magazine article on history or current events that inspired you to learn more about a topic. Be prepared to summarize the book or article for the class and to describe how it increased your desire to learn more.

Maps Matter

Look at the political map of the United States in the atlas section of your text. ■ *To Do:* Compare this map of the United States with the map of De Soto's route. List in chronological order the states through which De Soto passed. Through which part of North Carolina did he travel?

The soldiers remained in the mountains for about a month, enjoying the hospitality of the Native Americans. Horses grazed in the valley meadows while the men searched in vain for gold. When the intruders were ready to leave, the Native Americans sent them on their way with baskets of corn.

De Soto sights the Mississippi.   After leaving North Carolina, the group headed southwest. By April of 1541, De Soto and his men had reached the Mississippi River, making them perhaps the first Europeans to see it. The group then traveled north along the Mississippi and Arkansas rivers as far as present-day Oklahoma. Although De Soto and his men never found any treasure, their journey gave Spain a claim to land in the southern and eastern parts of what is now the United States.

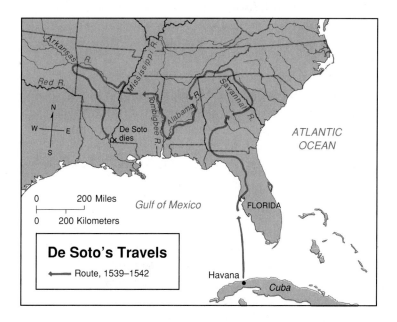

De Soto's Travels
⟵ Route, 1539–1542

France challenges Spain in Florida.   After De Soto's journey, Spain appeared to lose interest in North America, and the French saw their chance to take action. In 1562, an expedition of French Protestants—called Huguenots—sailed under the command of a French navigator named Jean Ribaut. Crossing the Atlantic, they took a middle route to avoid being sighted by the Spanish.

After landing near present-day St. Augustine in Florida, Ribaut and his crew sailed north along the coast until they reached a bay in South Carolina—"one of the greatest and fayrest havens of the world," which Ribaut named Port Royal. Here, high on a bank of Port Royal Island, the French founded a tiny post called Charlesfort, now Parris Island, South Carolina.

However, when Ribaut returned to France for reinforcements, trouble developed among the colonists, who had little to do to keep them busy. They built a small ship and sailed for home, but their craft was not seaworthy. In the Atlantic Ocean, they were rescued by an English ship and eventually reached home.

The French try again in Florida.   In 1564, France chose René de Laudonnière to lead a second expedition to Florida. The group established Fort Caroline near present-day Jacksonville, Florida. Unfortunately none of the settlers knew how to hunt, fish, or farm. As a result, the colony was a dismal failure. The colonists waited in despair for help from France.

The Spanish win control of Florida.   The French colony angered Spain's King Philip II because it was much too close to the territory claimed by Spain. In September 1565, Spanish warships under the command of Admiral Pedro Menéndez approached a French fleet before it could unload supplies. The French fleet quickly fled into the deep waters of the Atlantic Ocean.

Menéndez put his troops safely ashore at an inlet he named St. Augustine. Later, Menéndez's forces massacred the Huguenots. Menéndez eventually established St. Augustine as a Spanish fort. Today St. Augustine is the oldest city in the United States.

De Coronas lands at Currituck Sound.   Even though France had lost its gamble for Florida, the Spanish remained fearful of further French attempts. As a result, the Spanish king introduced a plan that would convert the Native Americans to Catholicism so that they would support Spain against any further challenges from France.

As part of this plan, Menéndez sent Pedro de Coronas, 15 soldiers, their officers, and two friars to the Chesapeake Bay area. However, while traveling north along the Atlantic coast in August 1566, the men encountered a hurricane that beached their ship at what is now Currituck Peninsula in northeastern North Carolina.

While repairs were being made, a party explored the peninsula, crossed Currituck Sound, and visited some of the mainland. Returning to the beach, they erected a cross and claimed the land for Spain. When repairs were completed, the group continued north, but the storm prevented them from sailing very far. Once again the expedition was beached, and Spain claimed land at a second location in the northeastern section of North Carolina.

Laudonnière established Fort Caroline in eastern Florida on the south bank of the St. Johns River about 15 miles from the Atlantic. Built in the shape of a triangle, the fort had a roomy open space in the middle. Fort Caroline was destroyed in 1565 by Spanish troops under Menéndez.

Pardo explores mountains of North Carolina. After De Coronas's failure to reach the Chesapeake Bay, another Spanish expedition made its way to the North Carolina region. The goal of this group was to search for a land route to Spain's gold mines in Mexico.

In 1566, the group landed near what is now St. Helena Sound on the coast of South Carolina. Under the leadership of Captain Juan Pardo, the expedition traveled in a northwesterly direction to the foot of the Blue Ridge Mountains. The expedition marched through Macon, Clay, and Cherokee counties, following the route De Soto had taken 25 years earlier. Leaving the mountains of North Carolina, the group passed through Georgia and Alabama before giving up and going back to South Carolina.

Not much is known about the expedition, since there are no surviving records of it. However, in recent times, archaeologists have found rusty buckets, shovels, and bits of rope in mountain caves near Franklin in Macon County. These artifacts seem to date back to this expedition.

Spain gives up. In 1570, the Spanish established a mission in the Chesapeake Bay region, but a few months after they arrived, the members were killed by Native Americans. After this, Spain gave up its efforts to establish outposts and to spread the Catholic religion north of St. Augustine. Next it would be England's turn to attempt to do what Spain had failed to do. The English would prove more than worthy of the task.

Think Twice

Throughout the 1500s, Spain and other European countries "took formal possession of" or "claimed" lands they explored in the Americas. Make a chart of the European explorers in this chapter. (Use the names in the box at the beginning of each lesson to help you.)

a. In the first column, write the name of the explorer.
b. In the second column, describe the claim.
c. In the third column, write the name of the country for which the claim was made.

Now use your chart to answer the following questions. Be prepared to support or defend your responses.

1. What was required in order for an explorer to claim land?
2. How justified was each claim in the eyes of a competing European nation?
3. How justified were the claims in the eyes of the Native Americans, who had inhabited the land for hundreds of years before the arrival of the Europeans?

Chapter 3 Review

Choose from the following menu of activities.

Think Back: Main Ideas

1. What was the main reason for the European exploration of the Americas?
2. What impact did the expeditions of Cortés and Pizarro have on Native Americans in Mexico and South America?
3. What role did slavery play in the Spanish colonies of the Americas?
4. What were the goals of the Catholic missionaries in the Americas? How did these goals differ from those of the conquistadors?
5. Who made the first attempt by Europeans to settle what is now North Carolina? What was the result of this attempt?

Maps Matter

The map entitled "Countries of the World" in the atlas section of your text helps explain why Columbus was confused about where he had landed. Use the map to answer the following questions.

1. (a) At about what latitude is India located? (b) At about what latitude are the West Indies located? (The West Indies are also known as the Caribbean Islands, which include Cuba, Jamaica, and Puerto Rico.)
2. (a) At what longitude is India? (b) At what longitude are the West Indies?
3. In Columbus's time, sailors had instruments to measure latitude but not longitude. Why did Columbus think the West Indies were islands near India?

Word Wizard

1. What two words from the chapter refer to lines on a map? What do these words mean?
2. A *suffix* is a word part that can be added to the end of a word. Use a dictionary to find out the meaning of the suffix *ary*. How does this suffix explain the connection between *mission* and *missionary*?
3. Use your text to write down the meanings of *empire* and *viceroyalty*. Now use a dictionary to find the meanings of *emperor* and *viceroy*. (a) What does an *emperor* do for an *empire*? (b) What does a *viceroy* do for a *viceroyalty*?

Working Cooperatively

Columbus's voyages to the Americas marked the start of the Columbian exchange—a transfer of people, goods, and ideas between the Americas and Europe. Working in groups of three, investigate the Columbian exchange.

1. Look under *Columbus* or the *Age of Exploration* in an encyclopedia or book.
2. Scan for headings, such as *The results of exploration*.
3. Look for information on plants, food, animals, and diseases that were part of the Columbian exchange.
4. Choose an interesting way to display your information to the class. For example, set up a display or create a marketplace of goods.

Curriculum Connection

After Cortés and his soldiers destroyed Tenochtitlán, an anonymous Native American voiced the grief his people felt for the ruin of the city. Here is the first verse of the poem.

> Broken spears lie in the roads;
> we have torn our hair in grief,
> The houses are roofless now, and their
>   walls
> are red with blood.

The poet tells a whole story in this one verse. What do you learn from these four lines?

Learning through Literature

Secret of the Andes, by Ann Nolan
The Legend of La Llorona: A Short Novel, by Rudolfo A. Anaya

Chapter 4

England Awakens

John Cabot's voyage to North America in 1497 had lasting results for England.

Although Cabot never found treasure in North America, his claim of Newfoundland was England's first land claim in North America. Soon English fishing fleets began making regular trips to Newfoundland. Cabot's voyage paved the way for future English exploration in North America.

In the 1580s, England sought to challenge Spain in the Americas and at sea.

During the reign of Queen Elizabeth I, England was ready to begin exploring the vast lands across the Atlantic. However, Spain had already established an empire in the Americas and had a powerful navy. England wanted bases from which to attack Spanish ships sailing in the North Atlantic. By establishing settlements in North America, England hoped to decrease Spain's power and wealth while increasing its own.

Queen Elizabeth I (1533-1603) ▶

Think Ahead

In the following pages, read about England's first attempts to explore and plant colonies in North America. Find out why the English chose Roanoke Island in North Carolina as the location for the first attempted English colony in North America.

1 The Amadas and Barlowe Expedition

People, Places, Terms

Walter Raleigh
colony
charter
sea dog
Francis Drake
Amadas and Barlowe
Manteo and Wanchese

The discoveries of Spanish and French explorers fired the imagination of an English adventurer named Walter Raleigh. Raleigh knew that England already had interests in the Americas. In 1497, the English king Henry VII had aided the voyage of a merchant named John Cabot. Raleigh also knew that in 1577, a bold captain named Francis Drake had stopped at a bay on the California coast and had claimed that region for England. Raleigh dreamed of planting English settlements in North America and of establishing an English nation there. He would devote much of his life and his fortune to this end.

Raleigh's plans. Raleigh and others were anxious to put their country in a position to protect itself against military threats by Spain. They also wanted England to share in the wealth of the Americas through the establishment of **colonies**—groups of settlements far from home but ruled by the home country.

In March of 1584, Raleigh requested and received from Queen Elizabeth a **charter**—a legal document that gives permission to explore, settle, and govern land. This charter actually was a renewal of an earlier charter from the failed 1578 expedition of Humphrey Gilbert, Raleigh's half-brother. Through the charter, Raleigh was given permission "to discover and inhabit strange places." However, before sending settlers to North America, Raleigh wisely decided to send a small exploratory expedition to study and report on the region.

English Sea Dogs

In the mid-1500s, English rulers secretly urged bold sea captains, called **sea dogs**, to capture Spanish treasure ships. One of the most successful sea dogs was Francis Drake. In the early 1570s, Drake took part in raids off the coast of Panama. The Spanish called him a pirate and nicknamed him *El Draque*, "the Dragon."

In 1577, Drake sailed from England to raid Spanish settlements on the west coast of the Americas. To reach them, he planned to sail through the Strait of Magellan into the Pacific. No other English captain had dared to sail so far into Spanish waters. Drake and his men surprised the Spanish and captured large stores of Spanish treasure. The full value of this treasure may never be known.

Drake knew that Spanish ships would be ready to attack if he returned home by way of the Atlantic Ocean. As a result, he decided to set a course for England by sailing west across the Pacific. Drake succeeded in his journey, making him the second person, after Magellan, to sail all the way around the world.

Amadas and Barlowe. Raleigh selected 19-year-old Philip Amadas and Arthur Barlowe as captains of the two-ship fleet that sailed from Plymouth on April 27, 1584. Passing through the West Indies but avoiding the Spanish outposts there, the ships followed the Gulf Stream up the coast. They arrived near Cape Lookout off the coast of North Carolina on July 4, 1584, making them the first people of English descent to set foot on what is now North Carolina. Continuing up the coast, the expedition arrived on July 13 at an inlet opposite Roanoke Island and claimed land 600 miles north and 600 miles south for Queen Elizabeth.

First impressions. The men were struck immediately by the beauty of the coast and the sweet odors that drifted from the land, which Barlowe described as "some delicate garden." The small band of explorers examined the nearby land, marveling at the tall red cedar trees and the wild grapes that trailed down to the edge of the water. The woods contained deer, rabbits, and many kinds of birds.

A friendly welcome. Two days passed before any of the native people appeared. Although timid at first, they soon demonstrated a willingness to welcome strangers. They traded pearls and furs for English trinkets and offered the settlers food and shelter. In his report to Raleigh, Barlowe described the first meeting between the settlers and one of the Native Americans.

Primary Source

> Then the master and the pilot of the admiral, Simon Ferdinando, and the Captain, Philip Amadas, myself, and others rowed to the land, whose coming this fellow attended, never making any show of fear or doubt. And after he had spoken of many things not understood by us, we brought him with his own good liking aboard the ships and gave him a shirt, a hat, and some other things and made him taste of our wine and our meat, which he liked very well. And after having viewed both barks, he departed and went to his own boat again, which he had left in a little cove or creek adjoining. As soon as he was two bowshots into the water, he fell to fishing, and in less than half an hour, he had laden his boat as deep as it could swim, with which he came again to the point of the land, and there he divided his fish into two parts, pointing one part to the ship and the other to the pinnace [ship's boat], which, after he had (as much as he might) requited the former benefits received, he departed out of our sight. . . .

> — BARLOWE, *"Report to Raleigh"*

Following this friendly reception, Amadas and Barlowe made their headquarters on nearby Roanoke Island and spent the next six weeks exploring the mainland, the Outer Banks, and the islands. Here they gathered information and collected specimens of the country's natural resources. When they left, two Native Americans, Manteo and Wanchese, agreed to return to England with them.

Report to Raleigh.   The expedition returned to England in September with a glowing report for Raleigh. Barlowe's catalog described the wonders of America—fertile soil, tall trees, ample fruits and grains, abundant fish and wildlife, and friendly native people. The presence of Manteo and Wanchese aroused even more interest in the region and in the Native Americans, their language, and their culture. Based on Barlowe's report, a document was drawn up and presented to Queen Elizabeth, urging the planting of English colonies in North America.

Recognition from the queen.   Queen Elizabeth was delighted with the findings, and Walter Raleigh was knighted in recognition of his role in England's earliest efforts to settle in North America. From then on, he would be known as Sir Walter Raleigh.

The new land north of Florida was claimed and named Virginia in honor of Elizabeth, "The Virgin Queen." This was the name not only for the region explored but also for the 1,200-mile-long strip of North America that the expedition had claimed for England. As a result of the Amadas and Barlowe exploratory expedition, England looked enthusiastically to the prospect of establishing colonies in North America.

This engraving of Sir Walter Raleigh (1552?–1618) is the only one published during his lifetime.

Think Twice

1. Why was England interested in establishing settlements in the Americas?
2. Why do you think Walter Raleigh was willing to spend so much of his time and money trying to start a colony for England?
3. What was the purpose of the Amadas and Barlowe expedition?
4. In what ways did the location at Roanoke Island seem suitable for a colony?
5. What was the result of the expedition?

People, Places, Terms

Richard Grenville
Simon Fernández
Thomas Harriot
John White
Ralph Lane
Wingina

2 Ralph Lane Colony

Encouraged by the report of the Amadas and Barlowe expedition, Raleigh decided to send another expedition to North America in 1585. This time the goal was to set up a lasting settlement. Basing his choice on the report, Raleigh picked Roanoke Island, off the coast of present-day North Carolina, for the settlement.

A group of 107 men left England for Roanoke Island to set up homes and prepare for the arrival of their families. In the ten months that followed, the men would encounter many hardships and unexpected challenges.

Voyage of the colonists. On April 19, 1585, a fleet of seven ships under the command of Sir Richard Grenville sailed from Plymouth. The fleet was piloted by Simon Fernández, who had also served as pilot on the Amadas and Barlowe expedition. Also on board were Thomas Harriot, a scientist; John White, an artist; Thomas Cavendish, who would later be the second person of English descent to sail around the world; Philip Amadas, who was now designated admiral of the country; Joachim Gans, a mineral expert; and Ralph Lane, who would be commander of the colony once it landed. Manteo and Wanchese, from whom Harriot and others had learned the Algonquian language, also returned. Grenville's fleet sailed through the West Indies, making stops in Puerto Rico and Florida. On June 26, the colonists arrived at the Outer Banks. From there they sent word to Roanoke Island of their arrival.

Maps Matter

Raleigh picked Roanoke Island based on first-hand reports by explorers. ■ *To Do:* What are the bodies of water that surround Roanoke Island? In which direction does each lie?

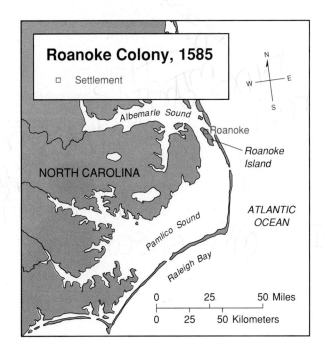

Roanoke Colony, 1585

□ Settlement

Albemarle Sound

Roanoke

Roanoke Island

NORTH CAROLINA

ATLANTIC OCEAN

Pamlico Sound

Raleigh Bay

0   25   50 Miles

0   25   50 Kilometers

Roanoke Island. Landing on the northern end of Roanoke Island, the colonists quickly constructed a fort, which they named Fort Raleigh. On August 17, Ralph Lane took over as governor of the colony. Soon after, Grenville returned to England to seek food and supplies. He left only one small ship for Lane's use in exploring the area. Since food and supplies would not last through the winter, Grenville agreed to return as soon as possible with more.

Exploring the region. The colonists quickly began to explore, map, and paint pictures of the region. Three expeditions set out to explore the area. One of the groups explored the Chesapeake Bay in search of suitable deep-water ports from which to capture Spanish ships. A second group explored the area on and around Roanoke Island. A third expedition, led by Lane himself, traveled to the mainland west of Roanoke Island, which Lane declared "to bee the goodliest soile under the cope of heaven."

Colonists with special skills began to carry out their individual assignments. Thomas Harriot gathered information from the Native Americans and recorded his own observations. John White painted a great many watercolor pictures of plants and wildlife, including birds, fish, and insects. Some of White's pictures showed details of Native American life—different ways of catching fish, cooking, dressing, weaponry, and boats. This information

The Roanoke colonists visited the Algonquian village of Pomeiock in 1585. The woman and her child lived in the village.

would interest people in England. Together, Harriot and White surveyed the land and made maps of the country around Roanoke Island and other parts of the southeastern coast of North America.

Trouble for the colonists. As winter approached, Grenville's ships still had not returned, and food was running out. Because the colonists had not arrived early enough to plant gardens and crops, they were increasingly dependent on Grenville for food and supplies. In addition, the poor growing season that year left the Native Americans with little or nothing to share.

The colonists also experienced problems with their leadership. On the journey from England, Lane and Grenville had disagreed on many things. After Grenville returned to England, many of the colonists were unhappy with Lane's leadership. Lane was a military officer, and most people were not accustomed to being ordered around in military fashion.

It was also clear that after nearly a year of living in the same area together, all was not well between the English and the Native Americans. Lane was known for his harsh treatment of the Native Americans, and they quickly grew tired of the intrusion by the English settlers. Soon conflicts developed. On one occasion, Lane learned of a conspiracy by Native Americans against him, and he secretly led a raid on a native village on the mainland, during which the leader, Wingina, was killed.

Abandoning the colony. While the colonists waited anxiously for Grenville's arrival, fellow Englishman Sir Francis Drake arrived unexpectedly in the area on June 8, 1586. He had been attacking Spanish ships in the Caribbean and stopped by to call on the colony. Discovering the desperate conditions there, he offered to leave food, supplies, and several ships with crews and weapons. Lane was about to accept when suddenly a fierce storm arose. He and the colonists quickly abandoned the

Indian Tree.

Chronicle of a Settler

Based on the notes that he had gathered, Thomas Harriot had a small book printed in London in 1588. It was entitled *A briefe and true report of the new found land of Virginia*. In his book, Harriot wanted to encourage future settlers to travel to North America, so he told about the land and the people. He described the fertility of the soil, the natural resources, the weather, and the medicinal uses of plants. In addition, he explained the lifestyle of the Native Americans, their form of government, their religion, and some of their traditions. He even recorded some of their words. This small but detailed book was published in many languages in 1590, which meant that nearly every literate person in Europe could read about North America.

In 1590, Theodor de Bry published Harriot's book and engraved many of John White's paintings as illustrations. Here is Theodor de Bry's engraving of John White's map of the vicinity of Roanoke Island.

settlement and returned to England with Drake. The settlement at Roanoke Island ended after only ten months.

A few days after Drake's departure, Grenville's long-awaited ships arrived off the coast. After searching for two weeks for the colonists, Grenville learned that they had left with Drake. Leaving fifteen men with supplies to hold the region for England, Grenville returned home.

Achievements of the colony.   Along with 97 survivors, Governor Ralph Lane brought back to England three valuable products. They were tobacco, which the Native Americans called *uppowoc,* corn or maize, called *pagatour,* and the potato, called *openauk.* These potatoes would later be used by Raleigh in 1587 to plant Ireland's first potato crop.

The colony also brought back very important and valuable documents about the region. They were the reports of Thomas Harriot, the watercolor drawings of John White, and several excellent maps. Raleigh was disappointed that Lane had failed in his mission, and he almost lost interest in North America. However, Raleigh would make one final attempt to establish an English colony in North America.

Think Twice

1. What were the main reasons for failure of the Ralph Lane colony?
2. What were some important results of the colony?
3. If you had been responsible for organizing the colony, what would you have done differently? How would you have advised Raleigh to organize the next colony?

3 The Lost Colony

Sir Walter Raleigh was disappointed by the failure of the Ralph Lane colony at Roanoke Island. However, he decided to try once again to plant an English colony in North America. This time the group of 117 colonists included 17 women and 9 boys. The colony had as its governor John White, who had drawn maps and pictures on the previous expedition. What happened to the John White Colony? To this day, the fate of this colony is the source of much mystery and speculation.

The John White Colony. Raleigh's plans for this second colony were different from those for the first attempt. First of all, the new colony would include women and children. In addition, this time the men would be landowners. They would each hold 500 acres of land and would not have to serve the governor. Also, Raleigh planned to establish the colony at Chesapeake Bay because it could be approached more directly by sea.

A change of plans. On April 26, 1587, a fleet of three small vessels sailed from Portsmouth with Simon Fernández again serving as pilot. When the ships landed on the coast near Roanoke Island, Fernández refused to take the colonists to Chesapeake, claiming the summer was too far gone for him to stay any longer. White was helpless. He knew that as long as the colonists were on board the ship, Fernández was in command. As a result, the colonists would have to stay at Roanoke Island.

Findings at Roanoke Island. Arriving at Roanoke Island, the colonists found that the fort from Lane's colony had been totally destroyed, but the other buildings were still standing. The men set to work to repair the damage and to start building new cottages. Except for the bones of one man, there was no trace of the 15 men who had been left behind the previous year.

Events at the colony. Less than a week later, one of the colonists, George Howe, was attacked and killed by a group of Native Americans from the mainland. Manteo, a member of the friendly Croatoan people, assured the colonists that the attackers were members of Wingina's people, enemies to both the settlers and the Croatoans.

Lord of Roanoke. On August 13, Manteo was christened and, following Raleigh's instructions, was made Lord of

Roanoke. The ceremony was in recognition of Manteo's loyalty and service to the colonists. It was the first time the English granted a title of nobility to a Native American.

Virginia Dare. On August 18, 1587, a daughter was born to Eleanor White Dare and Ananias Dare. She was the first child of English parents to be born in North America, as well as the granddaughter of Governor White. As the first child ever born in the region then called Virginia, she was named Virginia Dare. She was the first of two children to be born in the John White Colony.

White's departure in 1587. Like the colony before it, the John White Colony arrived too late to plant seeds to raise food. Once again, the native people had little to share. The colonists convinced Governor John White that he should return to England for food and supplies. Reluctantly he agreed and nine days after Virginia Dare was born, her grandfather set sail for England.

The other leaders were considering moving the colony to a more suitable site. Therefore, they assured White that if the colony relocated while he was away, they would leave him a sign by carving their destination on a post or tree. If they were in danger, they would carve a cross over the destination.

Governor White departed on August 27, 1587. However, when he reached England, his country was at war with Spain. As a result, no ship useful in England's defense was allowed to sail. Only two very small ships were freed, but their attempt to cross the ocean failed. It was not until March of 1590, three years after he had left Roanoke Island, that John White was able to return to his colony.

White's return in 1590. On August 18, the third birthday of his granddaughter, White reached the site from which he had departed in 1587, only to find it deserted. Some of the colonists' heavy gear had been left behind, and several of White's chests had been buried in the sand but uncovered afterwards, and their contents exposed to the elements. His books were torn from their covers and his pictures torn from their frames. Rain had damaged them, and rust had almost eaten through his armor.

White found CRO and CROATOAN carved on a post and a tree. Neither carving had a cross above it to show distress. This told him that his people had probably departed in peace to the portion of the Outer Banks (now known as Hatteras) where Manteo lived. Read John White's description of his findings at the top of page 52.

Read John White's description of his findings at the top of page 52.

Think as a Historian

*I*n 1588, the English surprised the world by defeating the large fleet of Spanish ships known as the Invincible Armada. This defeat marked a major change, or turning point, in European history. It signaled a decline in Spain's strength and an increase in England's power. ■ *To Do*: Think of another event that was a turning point in history. Explain how this event changed history.

Each year, Paul Green's Symphonic Drama, *The Lost Colony*, is performed on Roanoke Island.

Many places in North Carolina were named for both Native Americans and early English settlers to Roanoke Island.

■ *To Do*: Use the North Carolina maps in the atlas section of your text to find the town of Manteo and to find Dare County, named after Virginia Dare.

Primary Source

[CRO] which letters presently we knew to signify the place, where I should find the planters seated, according to a secret token agreed upon between them & me at my last departure from them . . . in Anno 1587 I willed them, that if they should happen to be distressed in any of those places, that then they should carve over the letters or name, a Crosse (✚) in this forme, but we found no such signe of distresse.

— GOVERNOR JOHN WHITE, "Observations"

Searches for the Lost Colony. **Croatoan** was the name of a nearby island on which friendly Native Americans lived. Although White wanted to look for the colonists on Croatoan, a storm broke and the ship was carried out to sea. The captain sailed for England, and White never was able to return to the Americas. Years later, when English sailors finally reached Croatoan, they found no English settlers. No one has ever learned what became of this lost colony.

Raleigh's Lost Colony of Roanoke has been the focus of more speculation than perhaps any other aspect of American history. Some historians believe that the Spanish came north from Florida to destroy the colony. Others believe that the colony was destroyed by Native Americans. Perhaps the colonists did go to Croatoan to join the Native Americans. Perhaps they tried to return to England in a small ship. No one knows for certain what happened to the colonists, and the fate of the Lost Colony remains a mystery to this day.

Results of the Roanoke Colonies. Although Raleigh failed to set up a lasting colony, many people still dreamed of living in North America. It was the experience and knowledge gained with the Roanoke Colonies that prompted England to persist in settling in this area. The experience would ultimately lead to the establishment of the first permanent English colony in North America.

Think Twice

1. How was Raleigh's second colony different from the first? How was it the same?
2. Who was the Lord of Roanoke? Who was Virginia Dare?
3. What did John White find when he returned to Roanoke Island in 1590?
4. What factors contributed most to the failure of the John White Colony?

Chapter 4 Review

Choose from the following menu of activities.

Think Back: Main Ideas

1. What was Walter Raleigh's role in England's first attempts to start colonies in North America?
2. Who led the first voyage to North America that was sponsored by Raleigh?
   a. What was the purpose of their expedition?
   b. What kind of impressions did they have of what is now North Carolina, and what kind of reception did they receive from the native people?
3. Who led the second voyage to North America that was sponsored by Raleigh?
   a. What was the purpose of this voyage?
   b. What were the achievements of these colonists?
4. Who led the second group of colonists that was sent out by Raleigh?
   a. How was the organization of this group different from that of the previous group of colonists?
   b. Who was the governor of the colony and why did he leave and return to England?
   c. Why did it take the governor so long to return to the colony?
   d. Why was this colony called the Lost Colony?
5. How did initial settlements in North Carolina affect future voyages to North America?

Maps Matter

Use the map on page 46 to answer the following questions. Use the map's scale to answer questions 2 and 3.

1. How was the settlement site at Roanoke Island protected from the open sea?
2. Approximately how many miles is Roanoke Island from the mainland?
3. Approximately how long and how wide is Roanoke Island?

Word Wizard

1. Use a dictionary to find two other forms of the word *colony*. Then use each word in a sentence that applies to the colonies at Roanoke Island.
2. The word *charter* derives its meaning from the Latin *charta*. Look up the word *chart* in a dictionary and find the meaning of the Latin word *charta*. How is this related to the meaning of the word *charter*?

Working Cooperatively

Many books, articles, and plays have been written about The Lost Colony at Roanoke Island. What do you think happened to the colonists? Working in a small group, write a skit in which you present your version. Use as characters some of the people mentioned in this chapter. If necessary, create other characters of your own. Present your skit to another group or to the class.

Curriculum Connection

Refer to the engraving by Theodor de Bry on page 49. Then use an encyclopedia or an art book to research the art of engraving. Focus on answering the following questions.

1. What is engraving?
2. How is it done?
3. How accurate is it in reproducing illustrations?
4. Who were some famous engravers? What were some of their works?

Learning through Literature

The Mystery of Roanoke Island, by Jean Bothwell
The Lost Colony, by Paul Green
The Puzzle of Roanoke, by Gwen Kimball

Chapter 5

England's First Colonies

The English find a new way to pay for colonies in North America.

Sir Walter Raleigh lost a fortune trying to build settlements on North Carolina's Roanoke Island. Others did not want to follow in Raleigh's footsteps. In order to start new colonies without taking a huge financial risk, wealthy English nobles, farmers, church leaders, and shopkeepers joined together to form **joint-stock companies.** A joint-stock company is a business that is owned by many people. After English investors bought stock in a company, they became owners of part of the business. As stockowners, they shared both the costs and the rewards of building colonies.

English joint-stock companies support colonists in Virginia and Massachusetts.

During the 1600s, English joint-stock companies sent colonists to live and work in Virginia and Massachusetts. The companies paid for food, supplies, and passage across the Atlantic Ocean. In return, the colonists agreed to work for the company for a number of years and send goods they made back to England. If colonists did not ship goods to the company, their supplies would be cut off and they would have to fend for themselves.

A pamphlet published by the Virginia Company of London ▶

NOVA BRITANNIA.

OFFERING MOST

Excellent fruites by Planting in
VIRGINIA.

Exciting all such as be well affected
to further the same.

LONDON
Printed for SAMVEL MACHAM, and are to be sold at
his Shop in Pauls Church-yard, at the
Signe of the Bul-head.
1 6 0 9.

Think Ahead

Sir Walter Raleigh failed to build settlements on North Carolina's Roanoke Island, but the dream of establishing English colonies in North America did not die. Read about the colonists who settled in Virginia and Massachusetts. Find out why they left England and how they adapted to a new life.

1 Jamestown

People, Places, Terms

joint-stock company
John Smith
Lord De La Warr
John Rolfe
apprentice
indentured servant
House of Burgesses

In 1606, King James I of England granted a charter to the Virginia Company of London, a joint-stock company. This charter gave the company the right to build a colony in Virginia. Seeking gold, a trade route to Asia, and natural resources they could sell or use in factories, the Virginia Company's investors sent colonists to work for them in North America.

The investors also hoped to discover the fate of Roanoke's lost colony. Recent historians claim that the Roanoke colonists gave up hope and moved to the Chesapeake Bay region. There Native Americans may have killed the colonists in an effort to protect their claims to the land.

Jamestown is settled. In December 1606, 144 men sailed from England aboard the *Susan Constant*, the *Godspeed*, and the *Discovery*. During the difficult journey, 39 men died. After 18 weeks at sea, the surviving English colonists reached North America. On April 26, 1607, they entered Chesapeake Bay and sailed up a deep river, which they named the James River.

For a month, the colonists explored and looked for a good place to settle. They found grassy meadows, plenty of wild strawberries, and dense woods filled with deer, beaver, and other game. The colonists finally chose a site 30 miles upriver to build their settlement, which they named Jamestown in honor of King James I.

The Glitter of Gold

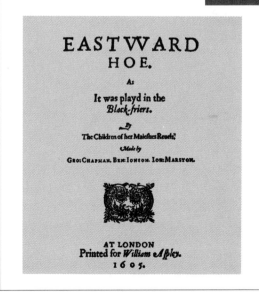

EASTWARD
HOE.

As
It was playd in the
Black-friers.

By
The Children of her Maiesties Reuels.

Made by
Geo: Chapman, Ben: Ionson. Ioh: Marston.

AT LONDON
Printed for *William Aspley.*
1605.

The Virginia Company's investors were anxious to send colonists to North America in search of gold and other treasure. They believed that Virginia had vast mineral deposits. In 1605, a popular play in London called *Eastward Hoe!* made this claim about Virginia: "I tell thee golde is more plentifull there than copper is with us." The play also suggested that people could scoop up rubies and diamonds along Virginia's seashore.

Captain John Smith was a member of the Virginia expedition of 1606. In 1608, Smith set out on his own to explore the land of Virginia and its people. When he returned to Jamestown, he found the colonists with "no talk, no hope, nor worke but dig gold, wash gold, refine gold, and load gold." This "get rich quick" scheme failed; there was no gold in Virginia.

Jamestown, located on the James River, was protected by land on three sides. The Virginia Company's ships could easily bring supplies and more colonists, but the settlement was far enough inland to be hidden from Spanish ships that sailed along the coast of the Atlantic Ocean.

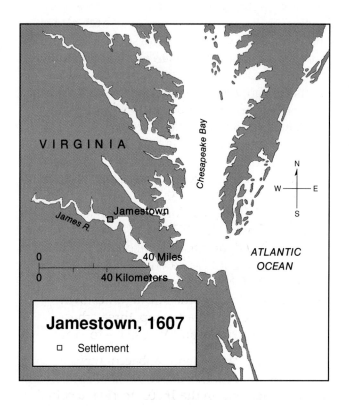

Jamestown, 1607
□ Settlement

The new colony faces trouble.   Despite the bright promise of the future, life in Jamestown was harsh. Colonists ignored the Virginia Company's instructions by choosing to live in a swampy area. Many colonists died from drinking impure water or from diseases spread by mosquitoes during hot months. By January 1608, less than one year after reaching Virginia, only 38 colonists were still alive.

The survivors also faced starvation. They had arrived with enough food to last about 13 weeks. Although colonists planted wheat right away, they were more interested in looking for gold. Many colonists came from cities and had been skilled workers, such as goldsmiths, perfumers, or jewelers. Some had never farmed, hunted, or fished.

Not only were colonists in Jamestown hungry and sick, but they also met Native Americans who resented the arrival of the English. These Native Americans refused to trade corn and other foods. Some colonists were attacked and killed.

Strong leaders emerge.   By 1608, Jamestown was about to fail. Captain John Smith, a 28-year-old adventurer, forced the colonists to plant crops and build. He told them that if they did not work, they would not eat. Smith tried to establish friendly relations with Native Americans and began to trade with them. Conditions at Jamestown slowly improved. Unfortunately, Smith returned to England in 1609 after he was seriously wounded in a gunpowder explosion. The struggling colony again approached the brink of failure.

In the fall of 1608, more settlers, including two women, arrived. The colony now had about 350 people, but the Virginia Company failed to send enough food for them. Colonists, who received daily allowances of a half pint of corn, were forced to eat snails, dogs, cats, rats, boots, and shoes. Following the "starving time," 65 colonists were left in Jamestown.

After the winter of 1610, the remaining colonists boarded a ship enroute to Newfoundland. As they sailed down the James River, they met a Virginia Company ship loaded with supplies and new colonists. Lord De La Warr, the leader who replaced John Smith, ordered the discouraged colonists to return to Jamestown. Lord De La Warr established strict rules. Everyone had to farm, or else they would be imprisoned or killed. Little by little, life at Jamestown improved. Along with strong leadership, three other changes allowed Jamestown—and Virginia—to grow.

The "esteemed weed" flourishes.   Tobacco, which Roanoke Island colonists had discovered Native Americans using, was in high demand in the 1600s. In 1611, a colonist named John Rolfe came to Jamestown. An experienced farmer, Rolfe experimented with growing West Indian tobacco plants. He produced a mild-tasting tobacco, which he sent to England in 1614. Rolfe's tobacco was such a success that nearly everyone in Jamestown began to grow it. Colonists even grew tobacco in the streets. The Virginia Company could now make money by selling tobacco.

Peace brings calm.   Another positive change that helped Jamestown succeed was an agreement with Native Americans. Pocahontas, the daughter of Powhatan, a powerful chief, was kidnapped by colonists. While she lived in Jamestown, she met and married John Rolfe. As a result of their marriage, colonists and Native Americans reached a temporary peace for eight years. Instead of fighting, colonists were able to concentrate on growing crops and improving life in the colony.

New colonists arrive in Jamestown.   By 1618, farms stretched for 20 miles along the James River. Jamestown needed more workers to help farm and to make products for

Captain John Smith was a soldier, an explorer, and a mapmaker. Smith's leadership of Jamestown from 1608 to 1609 helped the colony survive. In *The Generall Historie of Virginia, New England, and the Summer Isles* (1624), Smith described his life in Jamestown.

Tobacco Shipped from Jamestown to England, 1615-1630

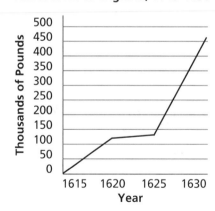

Graphs Teach

Line graphs show how things change over a certain number of years. Look at the graph above. In what year was the least amount of tobacco shipped to England? In what year was the largest amount of tobacco shipped to England?

The Dutch brought the first Africans to the North American colonies to work as indentured servants. After the Africans worked for a certain period of time, they gained their freedom. Later, other European nations brought Africans to North America to work as enslaved people.

the colony. In 1619, the Virginia Company sent 100 boys and girls from London. The new settlers served as **apprentices,** or people who learn a trade from skilled workers.

Indentured servants also came to Jamestown. In return for passage, clothing, and food, they served a colonist for up to seven years. After this time, indentured servants received their own 50 acres of land to farm.

In 1619, about 20 Africans were brought from the West Indies to Jamestown and exchanged for food and supplies. Although colonists may have treated these Africans as indentured servants, Africans were later treated as slaves. These workers contributed to making Jamestown self-sufficient and prosperous. In the same year, 90 women were sent by the Virginia Company. They eventually married colonists and had children. As new families were created in Jamestown, the colony grew stronger.

Colonists find a voice.   Jamestown colonists were at first ruled by a governor and a council who had been appointed in England. As Jamestown grew and new settlements in Virginia developed, colonists demanded a say in how they were governed.

In 1619, the Virginia Company allowed colonists to elect their own leaders. Colonists chose two men for each of the eleven settlements to represent them. These men, called burgesses, met as a legislature, the first ever held in America. In July 1619, the entire group of elected officials, called the **House of Burgesses,** met for the first time. This plan of government modeled on the Parliament in London worked so well in Virginia that it became a model for later English colonies. The eventual success of Jamestown in Virginia encouraged other settlers to come to North America.

The first official Thanksgiving is held.   Near Jamestown on December 4, 1619, the first official Thanksgiving service took place. Captain John Woodliffe, governor of Berkeley plantation, and 38 settlers proclaimed these words: "the day of our ship's arrival at the place assigned for plantation in the land of Virginia shall be yearly and perpetually kept Holy as a Day of Thanksgiving to Almighty God."

Think Twice

1. Where did colonists build the first permanent English colony in North America?
2. How did John Smith help save Jamestown from failure?
3. What changes took place in Jamestown in 1619?
4. Imagine that you lived in England in the early 1600s. Would you buy stock in the Virginia Company?

2 Plymouth

While English colonists who settled in Virginia wanted to become wealthy, the next group of colonists who came to North America had different goals. Jamestown colonists hoped—by finding gold or by farming—to lead comfortable lives. The colonists who settled in Massachusetts sought religious freedom.

Who were the Separatists? In England in the 1600s, there were laws that required all people to follow the rules of one church: the Church of England. Some groups, however, did not want to follow these rules. Because these people wanted to separate from the official Church of England, they were called **Separatists.**

Separatists believed that church services should be simple. They believed that only two ceremonies—baptism and communion—should be performed by the church. Separatists also believed that local churches should make their own rules and choose their own leaders. To worship as they pleased, the Separatists set up their own secret churches but were arrested and imprisoned. They reluctantly decided that they had to leave England.

Separatists seek freedom in the Netherlands. In 1608, a group of Separatists escaped from England. The Separatist leaders paid a Dutch sea captain to take them to the Netherlands, a country where they could worship freely. (See the map to the right to locate the Netherlands and England.)

After settling in the city of Leyden, the Separatists tried to adjust to their new life. The men had a hard time making a living because they had been farmers in England and had to learn new skills. Even when the Separatists did learn to work at skilled trades, the best-paying jobs were given to Dutch men.

The Separatists lived in the Netherlands for 12 years. Their children married into Dutch families and spoke Dutch. The Separatists worried that their children were forgetting English ways and becoming more Dutch, so they decided to look for a new place to live. In order to preserve their customs and their beliefs, the Separatists decided to go to North America.

The plan for a new life. The Separatists had learned about North America in Captain John Smith's book *A Description of New England.* Although some Separatists thought about going to South America, the leaders believed that it would be better to be near other English people in Jamestown.

People, Places, Terms

Separatist
Pilgrim
Mayflower Compact
William Bradford
Massasoit
Squanto

Maps Matter

Maps matter because they help you find out where different countries are located. ■ *To Do:* Find England on the map. What body of water did the Separatists cross to get to the Netherlands? What empire was next to the Netherlands?

Separatists wore simple clothes. The men wore broad-brimmed steeple hats with silver buckles, heavy leather shoes, and cloth breeches. Women wore brown or green long-sleeved dresses that were trimmed with plain linen cuffs and a broad linen collar. In contrast, English fashions of the time included bright colors and fancy lace and braid trimmings.

The Virginia Company granted the Separatists permission to settle just north of Jamestown but lacked money to support them. To raise funds the Separatists needed for building a settlement, a group of 70 English investors formed a joint-stock company, the Merchant Adventurers. The Separatists agreed to send fish, timber, furs, and other goods to the company for seven years.

The Mayflower sails to North America.   The Separatists returned to England to prepare for their voyage. They packed a few personal belongings and crates of vegetables, lemons, limes, dried biscuits, seeds, salted meat, and other supplies. Because the Separatists were taking such a long trip, they became known as **Pilgrims,** or people who make a journey for religious purposes.

In September 1620, a total of 102 passengers, including 41 Pilgrims, crowded onto a small cargo ship, the *Mayflower.* Others who sailed for Virginia were workers, indentured servants, and the ship's crew. After more than 60 days at sea, the colonists spotted land, but they were nowhere near Virginia. The captain's sailing mistakes and raging winds had forced the *Mayflower* off course. On November 9, colonists reached Cape Cod's sandy beaches in Massachusetts. Bad weather prevented them from returning to England or from sailing to Virginia, so the colonists decided to stay.

Leaders sign the Mayflower Compact.   Since the colonists were outside of land controlled by the Virginia Company, they had no government. Before they left the ship, the Pilgrim leaders drew up a compact, or an agreement. The **Mayflower Compact,** signed by 41 adults on board, was an agreement to set up the colony's government. John Carver was chosen as first governor. Once the Mayflower Compact was signed, the colonists looked for a site for their colony. They chose a spot with a harbor and named it Plymouth, after an English town.

Although the colonists chose a good site, they faced cold weather and little food during the first winter. By March, only four months after reaching Cape Cod, over half of the colonists had died, including Governor Carver. Yet they were still determined to build England's second permanent colony in North America.

William Bradford takes charge.   In the spring of 1621, William Bradford was elected the second governor of Plymouth and served for 30 years. The passage on the following page comes from a book he wrote about the Pilgrims that describes their first difficult winter.

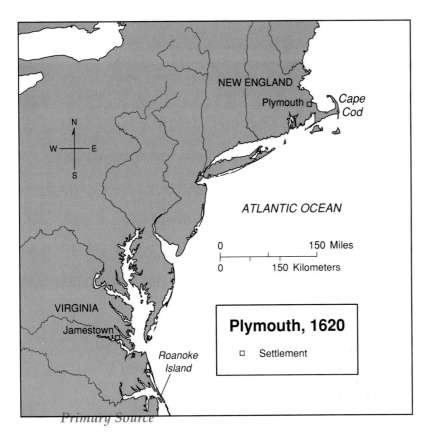

NEW ENGLAND

Plymouth

Cape Cod

ATLANTIC OCEAN

0 — 150 Miles
0 — 150 Kilometers

Plymouth, 1620

□ Settlement

VIRGINIA

Jamestown

Roanoke Island

Primary Source

> [What] was most sad and lamentable was, that in two or three months' time half of [the] company died, especially in January and February, being the depth of winter, and wanting houses and other comforts; being infected with the scurvy and other diseases.

— WILLIAM BRADFORD, Of Plymouth Plantation

Colonists and Native Americans make peace.   One day in March of 1621, Massasoit (MAS uh SOYT), leader of the powerful Wampanoag (wahm puh NOH ag), visited Plymouth. He brought with him as his guide Squanto. Several years before, Squanto had been captured by an English sea captain but had managed to escape. While with the English, Squanto had learned English and was therefore able to serve as an interpreter for the Pilgrims.

Squanto lived at Plymouth and taught colonists how to rake clams at low tide, how to grow corn and pumpkins, and how to make maple syrup. He showed them where to hunt deer and beaver and which wild plants were poisonous. As a result of Squanto's help, colonists learned how to live in their new home.

The first harvest is celebrated.   Little rain fell during the summer of 1621, and young corn plants began to dry out.

Maps Matter

You can find out the distance between two points on a map if you use the scale. To determine direction, you can use a compass rose. ■ *To Do:* Use the scale and the compass rose to answer these questions. About how many miles from Jamestown did the Pilgrims settle? Did they land east, west, north, or south of Jamestown?

Think as a Historian

William Bradford wrote out more than 500 pages by hand to tell the history of the Separatists in *Of Plymouth Plantation.* He described life in the Netherlands, the *Mayflower* voyage, and other important events. ■ *To Do*: Think about your own life. What events would you include in a history that people will read? If you wish, write about one event. Include details that bring the experience to life.

Please Pass the Turkey

Today's Thanksgiving echoes the Plymouth celebration in many ways; however, accounts recorded by Pilgrims make no specific mention of wild turkey. Although turkey may not have been on the menu, the Pilgrims did eat boiled pumpkin, cranberries, eels, oysters, venison brought by the Wampanoags, and other foods.

Since the Pilgrims did not bring cows on the *Mayflower*, they had no milk, butter, or cheese. They had used up all the flour, so their feast did not include bread, pies, or stuffing. Corn was boiled and fried to make corn bread.

To make sauces for meat, they boiled wild berries and sweetened them with wild honey.

Who prepared food to feed more than one hundred people for three days? Of the more than 20 women who sailed on the *Mayflower*, only four women and two girls were left to cook.

If crops failed, colonists would have no food to eat or store for the long winter. The Pilgrims set aside a day of prayer to ask for help; according to Bradford, "sweet and gentle showers" fell that same evening.

During the fall of 1621, colonists harvested their crops. They knew that they would have plenty of food to last the winter. The Pilgrims, other colonists, Massasoit, and 90 other Wampanoags gathered to celebrate the harvest. They feasted for three days on foods such as deer, lobsters, clams, and other local foods.

While Plymouth colonists faced difficulties, they had only one winter of "starving time," made peace with Native Americans, and began to build the kind of community that they wanted.

Think Twice

1. Who were the Separatists?
2. (a) Why did Separatists go to the Netherlands? (b) Why did they come to North America?
3. What was the Mayflower Compact?
4. In what ways did Squanto help the Plymouth colonists?
5. Do you think that English settlers at Jamestown had a first harvest feast similar to the one at Plymouth? Why or why not?

3 Massachusetts Bay Colony

People, Places, Terms

Puritan
Massachusetts Bay Colony
John Winthrop

The Pilgrims were not the only colonists who came to North America seeking religious freedom. Even as the Pilgrims were building Plymouth, more English settlers came to Massachusetts so that they might worship freely.

Who were the Puritans?   Another group of people in England held beliefs similar to those of the Pilgrims. They were called **Puritans** because they wanted to change and "purify" the Church of England. Like the Pilgrims, the Puritans believed that church services should be simpler and that members should have local control of each church.

Unlike the Pilgrims, the Puritans did not want to separate from the official church. Yet they were still treated harshly because of their religious views. As the relationship between the English government and the Puritans grew more tense, one group of Puritans decided to start their own community in North America. They were eager to find a place where they could worship as they pleased.

The Puritans who decided to go to North America differed from the Pilgrims. They were generally better educated, wealthier, and more powerful in English society than were the Pilgrims who settled Plymouth. Some of the Puritans had a great deal of business experience. Others were related to the English nobility.

The creation of the Massachusetts Bay Company.
In 1628, a group of Puritans formed their own joint-stock company, the New England Company, and sent colonists to Massachusetts. A year later, King Charles I granted the New England Company a charter. The company changed its name to the Massachusetts Bay Company. The Massachusetts Bay Company had the right to govern any colony that it established.

In March 1630, the "great migration" began. Four ships sailed from England, carrying supplies, colonists, cattle, and the royal charter. During the course of the year, more than a dozen ships crossed the Atlantic Ocean to bring more than 1,000 Puritans to Massachusetts.

Puritans settle Boston.   In June 1630, Puritans began to build a settlement at Charlestown, but they moved when disease broke out and when fresh water could not be found. The Puritans then established the main center for their settlement near a protected harbor. They named the new settlement Boston, after a town in England.

Across Cultures

*T*he English colonists who settled in New England during the 1600s named their settlements after real places in England. Other New England place names come from Native American words. ■ *To Do*: Make a list of five familiar place names in and around your own community. Use an encyclopedia, *The North Carolina Gazetteer*, or another reference to find the origins of these place names.

John Winthrop, a lawyer and a wealthy landowner, served as governor of the Massachusetts Bay Colony for nine years. Just as William Bradford wrote the history of Plymouth, Winthrop kept a detailed journal in which he recorded the history of the Massachusetts Bay Colony.

Unlike the Pilgrims, the Massachusetts Bay Puritans were well equipped and well prepared for their journey to New England. In addition, the Puritans sailed in March so they could arrive in New England while there was still time to plant a crop for harvesting in the fall. The Puritans also selected a governor before they left England. The governor, John Winthrop, had a clear vision of what the Puritan colony should be.

John Winthrop leads the Puritans.   Governor Winthrop said, "We shall be as a City upon a Hill. The eyes of all people are upon us." He meant that their colony would be an example to others. The Puritans hoped to build a model community to show how much better the world would be if people lived by Puritan beliefs.

Once the Puritans had settled in the Massachusetts Bay Colony, Winthrop ordered colonists to plant crops and to build shelters. He arranged for regular shipments of

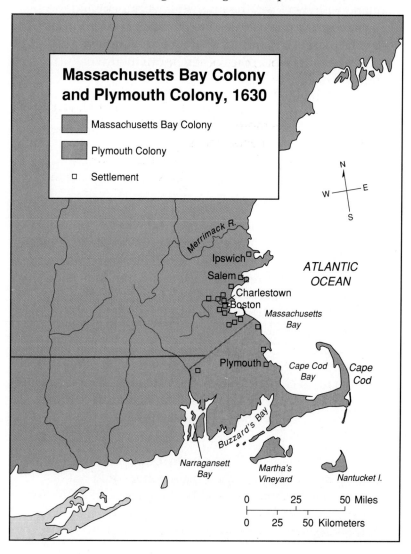

Maps Matter

Maps sometimes use symbols that stand for a place, an object, or an idea. A map legend, or key, helps you understand what the symbols stand for. ■*To Do:* Use the map legend to answer the following questions: How many settlements existed in Plymouth Colony in 1630? How many settlements existed in the Massachusetts Bay Colony in 1630?

This portrait of three New England children—David, Joanna, and Abigail Mason—was painted by an unknown Boston artist around 1670.

supplies from England. With Winthrop's planning and the colonists' hard work, the colony began to grow.

Settlements spread in Massachusetts. In the years between 1630 and 1643, more than 20,000 people went to Massachusetts. As more and more English colonists arrived, new settlements were started. About one third of the colonists settled in Boston, while the rest received permission from Puritan leaders to start settlements nearby.

Plymouth and Massachusetts Bay colonies unite. Seventy years after Plymouth was settled, the colony consisted of 21 towns. In 1691, the Plymouth Colony and the settlements in Massachusetts Bay Colony united to form one large colony, which was called Massachusetts.

England's first permanent colonies — Jamestown, Plymouth, and Massachusetts Bay — each had its own triumphs and disasters. The growth of these colonies encouraged more settlers to come to North America in the 1600s and create settlements up and down the Atlantic coast.

Think as a Geographer

*T*he Puritans established many settlements along New England's coast. They found many natural resources, or things that people find in or near the earth. ■ *To Do*: Use an encyclopedia or another reference to identify two natural resources that Puritans found in this area. What are two natural resources that are found in your own community?

Think Twice

1. Who were the Puritans?
2. Why did Puritans come to New England?
3. In what ways were Puritans prepared to build a colony?
4. About how many English colonists came to Massachusetts during the "great migration"?
5. Why do you think that Plymouth and the Massachusetts Bay colonies united in 1691?

Chapter 5 Review

Choose from the following menu of activities.

Think Back: Main Ideas

This chapter describes the first English colonies—Jamestown, Plymouth, and Massachusetts Bay. Answer the following questions about each of these colonies.

1. Describe the location of each of the following settlements: (a) Jamestown, (b) Plymouth, (c) Massachusetts Bay.
2. (a) Which of the above colonies was the first to be started? (b) What group of people started it?
3. Compare the Puritans and the Pilgrims. (a) How were they alike? (b) How were they different?
4. How did the goals of the English colonists who settled Virginia differ from the goals of the Separatists who settled Plymouth?
5. Write a sentence that describes each of the following people and the role he played in the Americas: (a) John Smith, (b) John Rolfe, (c) William Bradford (d) John Winthrop
6. Describe the significance of Squanto's visit to Plymouth.

Maps Matter

Use the maps in this chapter to answer the following questions.

1. Turn to the map of Jamestown on page 56. Use the map to name the river on which Jamestown is located.
2. The map on page 61 shows Roanoke, Jamestown, and Plymouth.
   (a) Which settlement lay farthest south?
   (b) Where was Roanoke located?
   (c) Which settlement was located near Cape Cod?
3. The map on page 64 shows the Massachusetts Bay Colony and Plymouth. Use the map's scale to tell approximately how far Plymouth was located from Boston.

Word Wizard

1. *Separatist* and *colonist* are formed from the base words *separate* and *colony* by adding the suffix *-ist,* which means "one who does, believes in, or is an expert in." Think of other words that end in *-ist* and define them.
2. Use a dictionary to find the different definitions of the word *compact.*

Working Cooperatively

Work in groups of three to five for this activity. Your teacher will assign one of these colonies to each group—Jamestown, Plymouth, Massachusetts Bay.

Review the information in Chapter 5 about the colony to which your group has been assigned. Look for information in the chapter about the land and resources that might attract people to your colony. Then make a poster or pamphlet similar to the one on page 54. In your poster, include information about the positive features that might attract newcomers to settle in your colony.

Curriculum Connection

Colonists in Jamestown successfully grew and sold tobacco. In the seventeenth century, tobacco smoking was considered harmful. In 1604, England's King James I wrote *A Counterblaste to Tobacco,* a pamphlet that discouraged people from smoking. Use an encyclopedia to find the harmful effects associated with tobacco smoking. Create a pamphlet that explains these health risks.

Learning through Literature

Constance: A Story of Early Plymouth, by Patricia Clapp
The Double Life of Pocahontas, by Jean Fritz

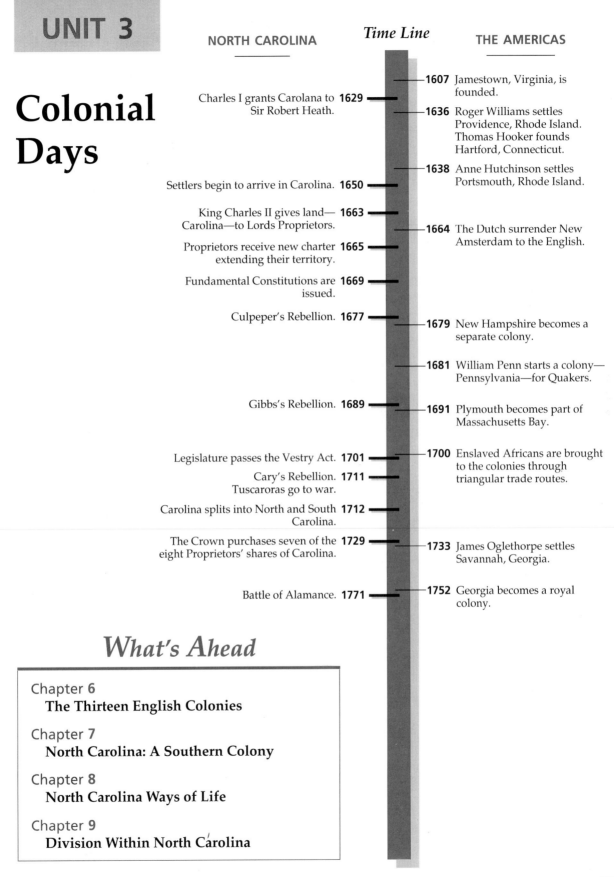

UNIT 3

Colonial Days

NORTH CAROLINA   *Time Line*   **THE AMERICAS**

1607 Jamestown, Virginia, is founded.

Charles I grants Carolana to **1629** Sir Robert Heath.

1636 Roger Williams settles Providence, Rhode Island. Thomas Hooker founds Hartford, Connecticut.

1638 Anne Hutchinson settles Portsmouth, Rhode Island.

Settlers begin to arrive in Carolina. **1650**

King Charles II gives land— **1663** Carolina—to Lords Proprietors.

1664 The Dutch surrender New Amsterdam to the English.

Proprietors receive new charter **1665** extending their territory.

Fundamental Constitutions are **1669** issued.

Culpeper's Rebellion. **1677**

1679 New Hampshire becomes a separate colony.

1681 William Penn starts a colony— Pennsylvania—for Quakers.

Gibbs's Rebellion. **1689**

1691 Plymouth becomes part of Massachusetts Bay.

Legislature passes the Vestry Act. **1701**

1700 Enslaved Africans are brought to the colonies through triangular trade routes.

Cary's Rebellion. **1711** Tuscaroras go to war.

Carolina splits into North and South **1712** Carolina.

The Crown purchases seven of the **1729** eight Proprietors' shares of Carolina.

1733 James Oglethorpe settles Savannah, Georgia.

Battle of Alamance. **1771**

1752 Georgia becomes a royal colony.

What's Ahead

The Thirteen English Colonies

Shipbuilding in New England ▲

A German weaver in the Middle Colonies ▶

Thousands of people come to North America.

During the 1600s and 1700s, people built more and more settlements along the Atlantic coast of North America. Most settlers were from the British Isles—Scots, Irish, Welsh, and English. However, people from other lands, such as the Netherlands, Germany, and Sweden, also built settlements, which the British eventually took over. People came to North America for different reasons—to make their fortune, to escape religious persecution, to escape famine, to get land of their own. Whatever drew them, people found plenty of land and many opportunities for building new lives in North America.

Think Ahead

By 1770, the settlements on the Atlantic coast of North America had been grouped into thirteen colonies. These colonies were divided into the New England Colonies, the Middle Colonies, and the Southern Colonies, of which North Carolina was a part. Find out how these colonies were similar and different.

1 The New England Colonies

People, Places, Terms

New England Colonies
elder
common
Roger Williams
Anne Hutchinson
profit
triangular trade

You have read about the earliest settlements in **New England**—Plymouth and Massachusetts Bay. Plymouth became part of Massachusetts Bay in 1691. The other New England Colonies were Rhode Island, Connecticut, and New Hampshire. Today, New England includes Maine and Vermont, but in colonial times they were part of other colonies. (See map on page 71.)

The land and climate of New England presented the colonists with both problems and opportunities. Much of the land was hilly and rocky. The climate was colder than most colonists were used to. Yet New England had thick forests full of valuable lumber and fur-bearing animals. In addition, the waters off the New England coast teemed with fish.

Puritans in Massachusetts organize their towns.   Since the **elders,** or leaders, of Massachusetts Bay Colony controlled all the land in the colony, they alone could give land to newcomers. The elders chose to give land only to Puritan church groups, not to individuals or families. That way they could be sure that the people in new communities would live according to Puritan beliefs. The elders also made sure that only Puritan men could vote or have a say in government.

Each Puritan town was organized around a **common,** a field where townspeople could graze their cows and sheep. At one end of the common was the meetinghouse where church services and town meetings were held. Town leaders also set aside land for a school. The minister and other important citizens had first choice of the remaining land on which to build their homes. The rest of the citizens drew lots for home sites. Each family also received land outside the village for farming.

During the 1600s, thousands of people went to Massachusetts. As land along the coast was taken up, more and more people moved inland or settled outside of Massachusetts. Some of these people were newcomers, but many were the sons and daughters of early settlers. Others were people who disagreed with some of the Puritan laws.

Williams and Hutchinson found Rhode Island.   One person who objected to certain Puritan laws was Roger Williams, although he was a Puritan minister himself. He did not think that people should be fined for not attending church. He also believed that the church should be separate from the government.

Across Cultures

Not everyone in the colonies had the right to vote. In most colonies, only men who owned land or goods could vote. In some colonies, such as Massachusetts, a voter also had to belong to a certain church. Women were not allowed to vote, no matter what church they joined or how much property they owned. ■ *To Do*: It was over two hundred years before women were allowed to vote. Find out which amendment of the United States Constitution gave women the right to vote.

Although Anne Hutchinson spoke well at her trial, she was banished, or forced to leave Massachusetts.

Diagrams Describe
Notice the orderly plan of a 1700s New England village. What was at its center? ▼

In spite of warnings from the leaders of the colony, Williams continued to voice his ideas. Finally the leaders expelled him from the colony. In the spring of 1636, he and a few followers built a settlement south of Massachusetts that is now the city of Providence, Rhode Island.

The following year, the Puritans forced another outspoken settler to leave Massachusetts. Her name was Anne Hutchinson. In the spring of 1638, Hutchinson and her husband and some of their friends also settled in what is today Rhode Island, starting the town of Portsmouth.

In time a new colony, Rhode Island, was formed around these towns. Unlike Massachusetts colonists, the people of Rhode Island were free to worship as they chose.

Connecticut is founded. Like Rhode Island, Connecticut was founded by people who disagreed with Puritan rule. The leader of these people was Thomas Hooker, a Puritan minister who believed that men of all religions—not just Puritan men who owned land—should be allowed to take part in town government. Hooker and his followers were also unhappy with the land they had been granted in Massachusetts, which had very poor soil and was not large enough for grazing their livestock. In June of 1636, they founded the town of Hartford in the fertile Connecticut river valley.

A New England Village

Meetinghouse

Inn

Smithy

Common

Ox pasture

Carpenter

School

Field

Cow pasture

New Hampshire is the last New England colony. Some colonists were willing to face the harsh winters north of Massachusetts. Like settlers who had moved south to Rhode Island and Connecticut, some who moved north sought more freedom or better farmland. Others hoped for better fishing waters. Still others wanted to work in the fur trade in the forests to the north. All these people headed into lands that are today New Hampshire, Maine, and Vermont.

At first, Maine, New Hampshire, and part of Vermont belonged to Massachusetts. The rest of Vermont was claimed by the colonies of New York and New Hampshire. Then in 1679, New Hampshire became a separate colony. Maine and Vermont never were separate colonies.

Trade booms. By 1700, New England merchant ships were making regular trips to England carrying lumber, furs, and fish. The ships returned loaded with cloth, furniture, iron tools, and other English goods. Soon New England merchants were trading with other countries and other English colonies. Ship captains used different routes, but the idea was always to make a **profit,** or money left over after paying the cost of doing business, at each stop. For example, ships loaded with rum at Newport, Rhode Island, would sail for West Africa. There the captains,

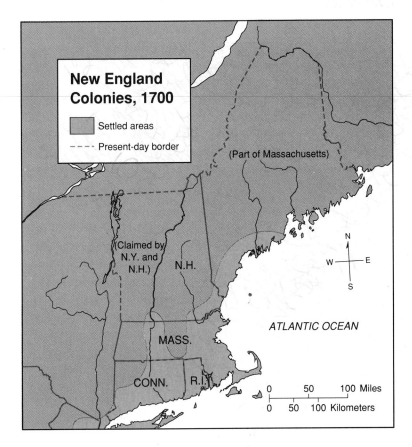

New England Colonies, 1700

- Settled areas
- - - Present-day border

(Part of Massachusetts)

(Claimed by N.Y. and N.H.)

N.H.

N
W — E
S

ATLANTIC OCEAN

MASS.

CONN.   R.I.

0   50   100 Miles
0   50   100 Kilometers

Maps Matter

Notice that the settled area in central Massachusetts was located near a river. ■ *To Do:* In what way might a river be useful to people who live inland?

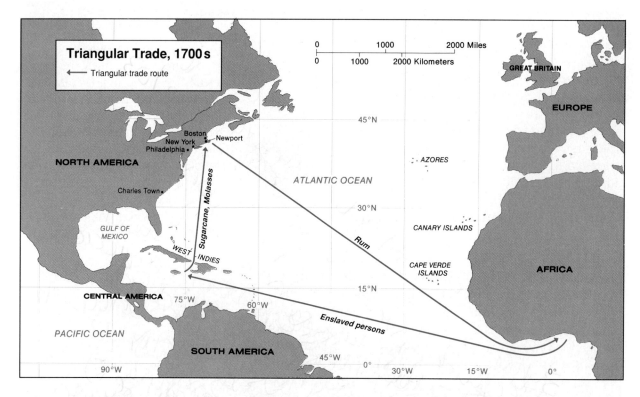

Triangular Trade, 1700s

← Triangular trade route

GREAT BRITAIN

EUROPE

45°N

AZORES

NORTH AMERICA

Boston
New York · Newport
Philadelphia ·

ATLANTIC OCEAN

Sugarcane, Molasses

Charles Town ·

30°N

CANARY ISLANDS

Rum

GULF OF
MEXICO

CAPE VERDE
ISLANDS

AFRICA

WEST INDIES

15°N

CENTRAL AMERICA   75°W

Enslaved persons

60°W

PACIFIC OCEAN

SOUTH AMERICA   45°W   0°

90°W   30°W   15°W   0°

0   1000   2000 Miles
0   1000   2000 Kilometers

Maps Matter

You can easily see how the triangular trade got its name.

■ *To Do:* What was shipped from New England to Africa? From Africa to the West Indies? From the West Indies to New England? Use the map's scale to find the approximate length of the entire route.

working for the merchants, sold the rum to African traders. With some of the money they got for the rum, the captains bought ivory, gold dust, and enslaved African people.

From West Africa, the captains sailed east to the West Indies where they sold some of the enslaved people to wealthy landowners. With money from this sale, the captains bought sugarcane and molasses, which they took to New England to be used in making more rum. Some of the enslaved people were taken to the colonies. Because trading routes, like the example shown above, often looked like triangles, this kind of trade became known as **triangular trade.**

The Puritan way ends.   As trade continued to grow, so did New England's coastal towns. Fishers, whalers, shipbuilders, and merchants settled in the towns to be near their work. Skilled workers, such as shoemakers, leatherworkers, blacksmiths, carpenters, and potters also moved to towns because there was a market for their goods.

Everyone needed or wanted hats, tools, shoes, saddles, tables, and dishes. The merchants could afford certain luxuries, such as fine clothing and jewelry made by skilled tailors and silversmiths. In addition, there were shops where skilled workers made everything from silver bowls to ship's anchors.

With all these people living and working in the towns, the towns grew into cities. As more and more city dwellers became caught up in making money and enjoying what money could buy, Puritan ministers warned against leaving God's path to pursue money. However, the voices of the ministers were drowned out by the bustle of city life.

This engraving shows buildings located near the waterfront in Boston, Massachusetts, during the 1700s.

Think Twice

1. Name the original four New England Colonies.
2. What religious group controlled life in Massachusetts in the 1600s?
3. What did the founders of Rhode Island and Connecticut have in common?
4. Why did triangular trade develop? What did the New England Colonies import? What did they export?
5. The term dissenter refers to a person who refuses to accept the followings of an established church or religion. (a) What role did dissenters have in establishing the New England Colonies? (b) From what established church did they dissent?

People, Places, Terms

Middle Colonies
Peter Stuyvesant
William Penn
Quaker
surplus

2 The Middle Colonies

South of New England were four colonies called the **Middle Colonies**: New York, New Jersey, Pennsylvania, and Delaware. As in New England, large numbers of settlers in these colonies were English. However, the Middle Colonies attracted people from other lands as well. In fact, Dutch and Swedish settlers were already living in several parts of the area when the English first landed in what was to become New York. In time, settlers by the thousands arrived from Germany, Ireland, Scotland, France, and other places. Each group brought its own culture, adding variety to life in the Middle Colonies.

The English develop the Middle Colonies.   In 1664, English ships sailed into the harbor of New Amsterdam, one of the main settlements of the Dutch colony of New Netherland. The English captain told the Dutch governor, Peter Stuyvesant, to turn over the colony to England. Stuyvesant blustered that he would not give up without a fight. The Dutch colonists, however, had tired of their governor's harsh leadership and would not fight. In the end, Stuyvesant surrendered before a shot was fired.

After the capture of this colony, the English controlled an uninterrupted broad swath of land up and down the east coast of North America as far as Spanish Florida. The harbor at New Amsterdam (now called New York) was a splendid one, easily reached by ships from the other English colonies. The English king, Charles II, gave part of the land in the Middle Colonies area to his brother, the Duke of York. The duke divided it into two colonies: New York and New Jersey. The king gave the rest of the land to a man named William Penn. That land became the colony of Pennsylvania. Delaware was later carved out of some of the Duke of York's land and was first added to Pennsylvania, then made a separate colony.

New York is sparsely settled.   Patterns of settlement varied in each of the Middle Colonies. In New York, most people lived in the southeast near the mouth of the Hudson River. Northern and western New York had very few settlers for several reasons. First, land was hard to buy in the north because much of it was in the hands of a few wealthy Dutch landowners who would rent some of their land but not sell any. Second, fur traders and trappers didn't want farmers settling in the area. They knew that the fur-bearing animals would leave when farmers cut down the forests to plant crops. Third, the French claimed much of the land and were

Think as a Geographer

*N*ew York City's location played a large part in its growth. It had a protected harbor for oceangoing ships. People and goods could be transported on the Hudson River. Finally, the city's central location meant that trade could be carried on with both the New England Colonies and the Southern Colonies. ■ *To Do*: Find a map of the United States in an atlas. Name ten cities in the eastern United States. How many are near an ocean or a river?

willing to fight to keep it. Finally, the Iroquois lived in the area and they, too, were willing to fight for their land.

New Jersey grows quickly. The owners of New Jersey hoped to get rich from the colony, so they attracted many new colonists by offering land at low prices. They also promised the colonists religious freedom and the right to govern themselves. Thousands responded to their offer, joining the Dutch, Swedes, and New Englanders who were already there. People came from the West Indies, Scotland, France, and the German states. Soon small villages and towns sprang up, and farms spread throughout the colony. A few people made a living producing lumber and shingles from the forests in the middle of the colony.

All faiths are accepted in Pennsylvania. The founder of Pennsylvania, William Penn, had been imprisoned in England several times as a young man. Penn was a member of a religious sect known as the Society of Friends. Members of this sect, also known as **Quakers,** suffered greatly in England. In those days, people living in England were forced to follow the religion of their ruler. The English ruler, Charles II, belonged to the Church of England, and everyone in England had to follow the practices of his church.

Quaker beliefs clashed with those of the Church of England in many ways. Unlike Anglicans (members of the Church of England), Quakers believed that every person had an inner light and needed only to live by it to be saved. Similarly, the Quakers thought all people were equal—men and women, rulers and ordinary people. As a result, they refused to honor one person over another. They considered titles meaningless.

Penn dreamed of starting a colony where Quakers would be safe from persecution. Finally, in 1681, he received a grant of land from King Charles II, who insisted that the land be called Pennsylvania after Penn's father. Penn planned carefully for his colony. He studied maps, drew up plans for a city, wrote a plan of government, and advertised throughout Europe that the new colony offered religious freedom and rich farmland. True to his Quaker beliefs, he made sure to buy the land the king had given him from the people who lived on it—the Native Americans.

Penn's methods paid off. The city he had planned, Philadelphia, grew quickly, but in the orderly way he had wanted. Sturdy farms spread out in the surrounding countryside. Joining the thousands of English Quaker settlers were Germans, Scots-Irish, and various other groups. Some, like the Quakers, came for religious freedom. Others were looking for land of their own and a

Two Quakers on trial, wearing hats. To show their belief that all people are equal—that only God is superior—Quakers refused to remove their hats in the traditional sign of respect.

Ben Franklin, one of Philadelphia's most famous citizens. He published an almanac and one of the city's newspapers. He helped start the fire company (the first in the United States), a college, and a hospital. He was also a well-known inventor. (*The Granger Collection, New York*)

chance to build a new life. All—Quakers, Catholics, Jewish people, members of the Church of England, and other Protestants—were accepted.

The Middle Colonies prosper.   With New England to the north and Virginia to the south, Middle Colonies settlers had an advantage over early English settlers. When supplies of food or goods were low, they didn't have to wait for ships from England. They could trade easily with neighboring colonies. This trading—plus rich resources—helped the Middle Colonies prosper.

Settlers in the Middle Colonies used the resources well. Farmers raised livestock on the rolling pastureland and tilled the fertile soil. They produced so much food that they sold their **surplus**, or the amount that was over what they needed, at home and abroad. Millers used rushing rivers to power flour mills and sawmills. On other rivers, ships carried beef, pork, flour, furs, and lumber to harbors on the coast. As in New England, the growth of trade led to the growth of the shipbuilding industry. Other industries included a glass-making factory and 73 ironworks in Pennsylvania. Cities grew rapidly.

By 1750, Philadelphia had a public library, a college, a medical school, a hospital, and a theater. Thanks to Benjamin Franklin, many streets were paved and lighted.

Think Twice

1. What four colonies made up the Middle Colonies?
2. Why did William Penn dream of starting a colony in the Americas?
3. How did the location of the Middle Colonies help them grow and prosper?

3 The Southern Colonies

People, Places, Terms

Southern Colonies
Lord Baltimore
James Oglethorpe
plantation
Middle Passage

The settling of the **Southern Colonies** took place over many years. It began with the founding of Jamestown, Virginia, in 1607. Then, in the 1630s, the colony of Maryland was started north and east of Virginia. During the middle and late 1660s, English settlement spread south to the Carolinas, which were started at about the same time that the Middle Colonies were being settled. The southernmost colony, Georgia, was the last English colony begun on the Atlantic coast.

A haven for Catholics is founded.   George Calvert—known by his title, Lord Baltimore—was a Roman Catholic, but as a friend of the king, he escaped being put to death or sent to prison for practicing his religion. Still, Calvert was troubled that Catholics could not worship as they pleased in England. Moreover, they were not welcome in most of the colonies in North America. So Calvert asked the king for land to start his own colony, where Catholics could worship without fear.

In 1632, the king gave his friend land along the Chesapeake Bay north of Virginia. George Calvert died before he could begin his colony there, but his son Cecil took up the dream. In 1634, the new Lord Baltimore began the colony, naming it Maryland to honor an English queen.

Carolina becomes North Carolina and South Carolina. In l663, King Charles II of England gave land south of Virginia to eight Lords Proprietors to whom he was grateful for help in restoring him to his throne after a civil war. They hoped to make money by selling land and collecting rent in Carolina, but in this they failed. Only a few settlers moved into the northern part of the colony, and it was seven years before the first colonists reached the southern part. They settled near the coast where Charleston, South Carolina, is now located. Over the years, the two parts of the colony grew very differently, with the southern part being far more prosperous than the north. Finally, in 1712, the colony was officially split into North Carolina and South Carolina.

The last colony grows slowly.   Georgia was started by a group of Englishmen, called Georgia Trustees, with two goals for their colony. One goal was to provide debtors with a place where they could build new lives. In England, debtors unable to repay what they owed might be thrown into prison. The other goal was to keep the Spaniards in Florida from settling farther north.

The reign of King Charles II lasted from 1660 to 1685. The period of his rule is known as the Restoration because he restored the monarchy to England.

Maps Matter

An inset map helps you see places on a larger map from a different point of view. Here, the larger map is a close-up of the thirteen British colonies. The inset shows these colonies from a distance—in relation to all of North America.

■ *To Do:* Which map helps you see how much of North America was taken up by the colonies?

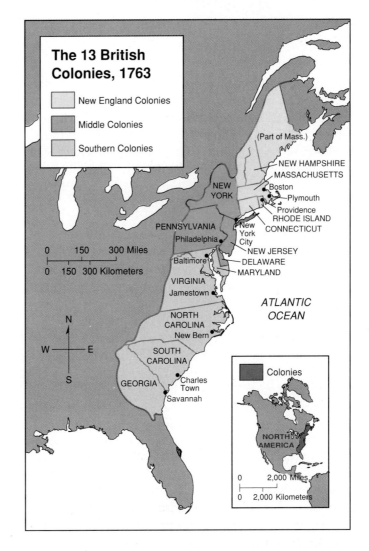

The 13 British Colonies, 1763

- New England Colonies
- Middle Colonies
- Southern Colonies

(Part of Mass.)

NEW HAMPSHIRE
MASSACHUSETTS
Boston
Plymouth
Providence
RHODE ISLAND
NEW YORK
CONNECTICUT
PENNSYLVANIA
New York City
Philadelphia
NEW JERSEY
DELAWARE
Baltimore
MARYLAND
VIRGINIA
Jamestown
ATLANTIC OCEAN
NORTH CAROLINA
New Bern
SOUTH CAROLINA
GEORGIA
Charles Town
Savannah

0 150 300 Miles
0 150 300 Kilometers

N W E S

Colonies

NORTH AMERICA

0 2,000 Miles
0 2,000 Kilometers

The first leader of Georgia was a trustee, James Oglethorpe, who arrived in 1733 with 35 families and began the settlement of Savannah. The colony grew slowly, however. Only a few debtors went to Georgia. Moreover, war broke out with the Spaniards, and Native Americans, fearful of losing their homes and land, kept attacking the colony.

The main reason for the colony's slow growth was that many of the first farms failed. The trustees had made very strict rules for the colony. No one was allowed to own more than 50 acres of land, slavery was prohibited, and settlers were to do certain types of farming. Unfortunately, the climate and soil in Georgia were wrong for those types of farming. In 1752, the trustees' charter expired, and Georgia became a royal colony.

Southerners lived on the land. While in New England and the Middle Colonies many people gradually turned from farming to town and city life, most Southerners continued farming. The size and type of farm depended in part on its location.

For example, large farms called **plantations** were common in Virginia and Maryland. A plantation is a large farm on which crops are grown for sale and on which the people who raise the crops live. Settlers heading for Virginia and Maryland usually sailed up the great Chesapeake Bay. The smaller bays along the Chesapeake created many good harbors where oceangoing ships could dock to load and unload goods. Along the Chesapeake is the Atlantic Coastal Plain, where the land is broad, flat, and rich enough for large farms. Since the rivers of the area were wide and deep enough for oceangoing ships, people could settle far inland on the plain. Most plantations in this part of the colonies were large tobacco plantations.

The widespread use of tobacco in England and in other parts of Europe made it a popular crop on plantations in the Southern Colonies.

Ways of life in North and South Carolina differed.
People in North Carolina were not so fortunate. Few rivers along the coastal plain were deep enough for ships, and the coast had few good harbors. As a result, farms in North Carolina tended to be small ones on the western part of the plain. People raised only enough to feed themselves. (See Chapter 7 for more information on the early settlement of North Carolina.)

In South Carolina, the coastal plain became swampy. This warm and mostly wet area proved ideal for growing rice, and soon settlers built vast rice plantations—much larger than the tobacco plantations of Virginia and Maryland. In the 1700s, people began raising indigo, a plant from which a blue dye can be made. This plant grew well in the higher, drier ground that wasn't good for rice.

After the king took over Georgia in 1752, he dropped some of the strict rules of the trustees. People were allowed to own as much land as they could afford, and they could grow whatever crops they chose. In time, Georgia planters, like their South Carolina neighbors, were growing rich on rice and indigo.

Plantation owners and workers lived very different lives.
Of all the different ways of life in the South, perhaps the biggest difference was between the plantation owners, or planters as they were called, and the enslaved Africans.

Plantation owners lived lives of great comfort. Many decorated their homes with satin curtains, gilded wallpaper, and costly pictures. Planters and their families occasionally visited Charles Town, South Carolina, and other port cities. There, women and men dressed in the finest London fashion to attend dinner parties and other amusing activities.

From Africa to the Americas

The slave trade began in the 1500s. Its growth was closely linked to the growth of Spanish colonies in the Americas. The Spaniards began gold mines and silver mines and planted crops such as sugarcane. At first, they forced Native Americans to do the work. As more and more Native Americans died from disease, the Spaniards bought Africans from Portuguese, Dutch, and English traders. By the 1700s, American colonists were also taking part in the slave trade. In that century, about 6 or 7 million Africans were shipped to the American colonies as slaves. They were packed side by side onto ships for the **Middle Passage,** the ocean journey across the Atlantic. (See below.)

Unlike slaves in earlier times or in other parts of the world, enslaved Africans in the Americas had no rights. Everywhere wealthy European landowners used or punished the enslaved Africans in any way they chose. No laws existed to protect slaves. The slave trade hurt more than just those who were forced into slavery. All of Africa suffered. Families were torn apart. Groups that had lived together for hundreds of years began to raid one another's villages to get slaves.

This engraving shows enslaved Africans making the ocean journey from West Africa to the Americas.

To others, however, Charles Town and other seaports meant misery. It was there that enslaved people were sold to planters. Listen to Jacob Mason, from Raleigh, North Carolina, as he describes his life as a slave.

Primary Source

I belonged to Colonel Bun Eden. His plantation was Warren Country, and he owned about 50 slaves or more. There were so many of them there that he did not know all his own slaves.

Our cabins were built of poles and stick-and-dirt chimneys, one door, and one little window at the back of the cabin. Our clothing was poor and homemade. Many of the slaves went bareheaded and barefooted. Some wore rags around their heads, and some wore bonnets. We had poor food, and the young slaves was fed out of troughs. The food was put in a trough and the little [children] gathered around and [ate]. The children was looked after by the old slave women who were unable to work in the fields, while the mothers . . . worked. The women plowed and done other work as the men did. No book or learning of any kind was allowed.

— BELINDA HURMENCE (ed.), My Folks Don't Want Me To Talk About Slavery

---

Think Twice

1. Name the five Southern Colonies.
2. When did Carolina split into North Carolina and South Carolina?
3. How did the Georgia Trustees hurt the growth of their own colony?

Chapter 6 Review

Choose from the following menu of activities.

Think Back: Main Ideas
On your paper, write answers for the following questions.

1. What was the main way people earned a living in the New England Colonies? In the Middle Colonies? In the Southern Colonies?
2. In which group of colonies was city life slow to grow?
3. In which group of colonies were the first and last English colonies established?
4. How did trade affect the New England and the Middle colonies?
5. Name three people who started colonies to ensure religious freedom and name the colony that each started.

Maps Matter
Refer to the map on page 78 of the 13 British colonies to answer the following questions.

1. If you traveled north from Jamestown 400 miles, would you be in the Southern, Middle, or New England colonies?
2. What were the names of the four New England Colonies? The names of the four Middle Colonies? The names of the five Southern Colonies?
3. Describe the size of the thirteen colonies compared to the size of North America.
4. Which map, the large map or the inset map, would you use to compare the sizes of the three groups of colonies?

Word Wizard
1. Two terms from the chapter, *elder* and *common*, have other meanings than the ones used in the chapter. Use a dictionary to find one other meaning for each term.
2. What is the difference between an *indentured servant* and an *enslaved person*?

3. The names *Massachusetts* and *Connecticut* are both Native American words. Look in an encyclopedia to find their meanings.
4. How did the religious beliefs of a *Quaker* differ from those of a *Puritan?*
5. (a) What are the meanings of *surplus* and *profit*? (b) How does having a surplus affect the profit of a business?

Working Cooperatively
In colonial times, most people made many of the things they needed, such as clothing, tools, and furniture. Working in groups of three or four, choose a topic such as making clothing, getting food, building a home, or making furniture. Prepare a report in which you contrast the colonial way of doing the task with the modern way. Use these steps.

1. Research the topic and take notes for your report.
2. Use diagrams, drawings, and flowcharts to illustrate your report.
3. Present your report orally or in writing.

Curriculum Connection
Sculpture is one of the arts that flourished in Africa during ancient times. Skilled artists used beautifully grained woods from the rain forests and different kinds of metals such as gold and bronze to create their finely crafted objects. Use a book on art history or African history to find examples of sculptures created by the Yoruba people.

Learning through Literature
The Many Lives of Benjamin Franklin, by Mary Pope Osborne
Life in Colonial America, by Elizabeth George Speare
To Be a Slave, by Julius Lester

Chapter 7

North Carolina: A Southern Colony

North Carolina grows slowly.

You learned in Chapter 6 about the founding and settling of the 13 colonies, ending with Georgia in 1732. This chapter takes you back in time for a more detailed look at the settling and growth of the area that would become the colony of North Carolina.

The first settlers in the area were not part of an organized group, the way the Jamestown and Plymouth settlers were. Instead, they were people from Virginia who drifted south, hardly noticing how far they had ventured. No boundary line existed then, and the vast forests of oaks and pines, sluggish creeks, and swamps differed little from one place to another.

Later on, when the area was part of the colony of Carolina, people did come in groups, but the North Carolina area was slow to grow. Part of the problem was geography—the area had few navigable rivers and no deepwater harbors. Another part of the problem was that for much of its history, North Carolina suffered from unstable government.

Settlers from Virginia head to Carolina ▶

Think Ahead

North Carolina was known as the most unruly and rebellious of the English colonies. Read about the stormy times that gave the colony its reputation.

1 A Proprietary Colony

People, Places, Terms

John Pory
naval stores
Robert Heath
quitrent
prerogative party
popular party
Culpeper's Rebellion
duty
John Jenkins
George Durant
Thomas Eastchurch
Thomas Miller
Seth Sothel
Philip Ludwell
John Gibbs
Gibbs's Rebellion

Although the Virginia Company's grant included most of what is today North Carolina, there are no records of any settlers in the area while it was under the control of the company. The first recorded visit to the area was made in 1622 by John Pory, who had just served a term as secretary to the Virginia Colony. While awaiting a ship to take him home to England, he traveled first along the Potomac River and then down the Blackwater and Chowan rivers into northeastern North Carolina.

Along the Chowan, Pory found wide stretches of tall pines that would make good masts for ships, and from which huge supplies of pitch and tar could be produced. Pitch and tar were called **naval stores** because they were used in shipbuilding. At the time, England depended on Scandinavian countries for these stores, so Pory's discovery might be very important. Pory also discovered that the area's Native Americans could grow two crops in the same year on the same land. He found the Native Americans anxious to trade with the English. In a letter to an official in England, Pory described his findings, and soon his report was being widely discussed.

Heath receives a grant of land.   By 1624, King James had grown unhappy with the Virginia Company's management of its colony, so he revoked its charter, thus clearing the way for the making of new grants. James died before he could do so, but in 1629, his son, Charles I, gave a vast grant to his attorney general, Sir Robert Heath. Heath's land extended from the southern shore of Albemarle Sound almost to present-day Florida.

For a while, Heath tried to attract European settlers to his new colony, which the king had insisted be called Carolana, from *Carolus*, the Latin form of *Charles*. Heath was not successful, however, and in 1638, he turned over his interests in America to a friend. The friend succeeded in getting some settlers as far as Virginia, but they couldn't find transportation to Carolana. A few, however, eventually made their way south some years later.

Virginians move into Carolana.   Attempts to colonize from abroad had failed, but people in nearby Virginia grew more interested in the region. By the early 1650s, officials in Virginia were granting land beyond the southern limits of their own territory. Merchants, traders, farmers in search of better land, as well as restless explorers seeking adventure began to appear in Carolana. By the early 1660s,

Sir Robert Heath's charter from Charles I required him to have on hand a 20-ounce gold crown for the king's use if he should visit Carolana.

North Carolina's first known permanent settler was a man named Nathaniel Batts, who in 1655 built a small house along Salmon Creek at the western end of Albemarle Sound. Batts made a living trading with Native Americans in the area.

probably 500 people lived in the area between Virginia and Albemarle Sound.

Charles loses his head.   While Virginians were moving south, a civil war broke out in England between supporters of the king and supporters of Parliament. The crown lost, and Charles I was beheaded in 1649. The monarchy was not restored until Charles II was crowned in 1661. The new king owed a great debt to those who made the restoration possible. The king repaid this debt in many ways—titles, positions, estates in England, and land abroad.

Eight Proprietors receive grants of land.   In 1663, eight men who had helped make Charles's return possible received a grant for a vast tract of American land of which they were to be the Proprietors. This land, which in the Proprietors' charter was called Carolina, was the same land that had been granted earlier to Sir Robert Heath. In 1665, the king extended the grant north far enough to include the settled areas on the Virginia frontier. He also extended it south into Spanish Florida.

Like Heath's charter, the Proprietors' charter gave them great powers, including the right to confer titles of nobility, establish towns and counties, build forts, and collect taxes.

THE LORDS PROPRIETORS OF CAROLINA	
Name	**Position**
Edward Hyde, Earl of Clarendon	Lawyer, member of Parliament, adviser to Charles I and Charles II, Lord High Chancellor of England
George Monck, Duke of Albemarle	Army general
William Craven, Earl of Craven	Army officer, friend of royal family
John Lord Berkeley	Fought for royal cause during civil war, joined royal family in exile
Anthony Ashley Cooper, later Earl of Shaftsbury	Chancellor of the Exchequer
Sir George Carteret	Naval officer, housed some of royal family at his home on the Isle of Jersey while they were in exile
Sir William Berkeley	Governor of Virginia at various times between 1641 and 1677, had knowledge of Carolina
Sir John Colleton	Planter on Barbados in the West Indies, had knowledge of Carolina

Tables Teach

Two of the Lords Proprietors were also the Proprietors of New Jersey. Can you find a clue in the table to tell you who one of them was?

On the other hand, the colonists were to have rights such as those that the people of England enjoyed. Laws for the colony were to be made with the "advice, assent, and approbation of the Freemen" or by their representatives in an assembly. In these ways, the charter reflected a new idea developing in England—that citizens' rights could be protected in a written document.

Counties are created.   The Lords Proprietors included two men who had some knowledge of Carolina. One of the two, Sir William Berkeley, was governor of Virginia at the time. At first, the Proprietors relied on him to take charge. Almost at once, he began authorizing grants for land, and soon the other Proprietors sent instructions for the creation of three counties: Albemarle, Clarendon, and Craven.

Albemarle included the settled area near the Sound; Clarendon was in the area near Cape Fear; and Craven was in what is now South Carolina.

Albemarle County already had settlers, and although more joined them, the county grew slowly. The first settlers in Clarendon County abandoned their settlement but were replaced by a group from Barbados in 1664. The county flourished for a while but was abandoned in 1667. The third county, Craven, was not settled until 1670.

Government is established.   The early government of Albemarle County included an Assembly, a governor, and a Council. The Assembly, made up of delegates elected by the male landowning settlers, decided how the colony's money was to be spent.

The governor was appointed by and represented the Proprietors, not the people. He was expected to carry out the Proprietors' wishes and to keep them informed about affairs in the colony. The governor held office only as long as he pleased the Proprietors. His salary, however, was set by the Assembly.

Charles II (center with hat and long hair) at the time of the restoration. Undoubtedly some of the men around him are the soon-to-be Lords Proprietors.

The Fundamental Constitutions of Carolina

Disappointed by the fate of Clarendon, and by the slow growth of Albemarle, the Proprietors issued a document called the Fundamental Constitutions of Carolina in 1669. This document, intended to protect property rights and to encourage settlement, called for a complex system of land ownership and government. This document never had much effect in the colony, but if it had, there would have been manors with workers similar to medieval serfs, a parliament, ranks of nobility, and restrictions on the rights of the people to govern themselves. The titles of nobility, different from those in England, had the odd names of palatine, cacique (kuh SEEK), and landgrave. A few people actually received these titles. Although the document was revised several times, it was never approved by the colonial Assembly, and was eventually abandoned.

The governor had far-reaching powers. He set the dates for meetings of the Assembly and could send the members home if he didn't like their decisions. Sometimes he called them back when he thought they might have changed their minds. No law could be passed without his approval. The governor had a wide range of additional powers, such as punishing officials who violated their duties.

The Council assisted the governor and, with the governor and Assembly, made laws for the colony. With the governor, the Council also acted as a court. At first, Councilors were usually named by the governor, but later they were named by the Assembly and the Proprietors.

In the 1690s, the name Assembly was used for a lawmaking body made up of an upper house and a lower house. The Council, whose members were now all appointed by the Proprietors, formed the upper house. What was once the Assembly became the lower house, known as the House of Commons.

To help cover the costs of governing the colony, the Proprietors established a land tax called a **quitrent**. The tax got its name because it "quit" the landowner from certain duties to the Proprietors.

Political parties arise. Quite early in the history of Albemarle County, two political parties arose. The governor, Council, and men who owed their positions to the Proprietors or governor made up one party, the **prerogative party.** They believed that a government as independent of the people as possible would serve the best interests of the colony. Against this group was the **popular party,** which believed that the will of the people through their representatives in the Assembly should determine government actions.

Disagreements between the two parties grew in part because many people had already settled in Albemarle before the Proprietors took over. Resenting any interference from the Proprietors, they often rebelled at what they saw as unfair orders. The colony, in fact, earned the reputation as the most unruly of the English colonies. Long and bitter quarrels arose over the governor's salary, quitrents, taxes, paper money, and many other matters.

People are slow to settle Albemarle. Land was the colony's most important form of wealth for the Proprietors, since no gold had been found there. To make money from their land, the Proprietors needed settlers to buy it and pay taxes (quitrent) on it. Unfortunately for them, however, settlers were slow to come to Albemarle. There were several reasons for the slow growth. For one

WEST JERSEY

Cape May

LOWER COUNTIES OF DELAWARE

MARYLAND

Potomac River

Western boundary of the
Fairfax Proprietary

Germanna

Shenandoah River

Route of Spotswood's Expedition

Rappahannock River

PROPRIETARY (Northern Neck)

VIRGINIA

WILLIAMSBURG

James River

Fort Henry

Yorktown

Norfolk

Northern Boundary of 1663
Carolina under Charter of 1663
36° 30'

Currituck

Northern Boundary of
Carolina under
Charter of 1663
36°

ALBE MARLE

Chowan River

Edenton

Roanoke River

35° 34'

GRANVILLE

NORTH GRANT

NORTH CAROLINA

Neuse River

Bath

Fort
Nohoroco

Pamlico Sound

New Berne

TUSCARORA

Beaufort

CHEROKEE INDIANS

CLARENDON

Cape Fear River

Brunswick

Cape Fear

CATAWBA

Broad River

Saluda River

Wateree River

Peedee River

SOUTH CAROLINA

Santee River

Jamestown

River

ST. JOHN'S BERKELEY

Savannah River

Edisto River

YAMASEE

Ashley River

Cooper River

CHARLESTON

CREEK

Ocmulgee River

Oconee River

Ogeechee River

Beaufort

Stuart's Town

Port Royal

Chattahoochee River

Coweta
Town

Savacola
(Spanish)

(Flint River)

Altamaha River

Fort
King George

Southern Boundary of Carolina under Charter of 1663   31°

Santa Cruz
de Savacola (Spanish)

AYUBALE

San Luis (Spanish)

APALACHE

Apalachicola River

Ochlockonee River

St. Mary's River

St. John's River

St. Augustine
(Spanish)

CAROLINAS
AND VIRGINIA
1663-1729

Southern Boundary of
Carolina under Charter of 1663
29°

MILES
25 0   50   100

Drawn under the supervision of E. MERTON COULTER

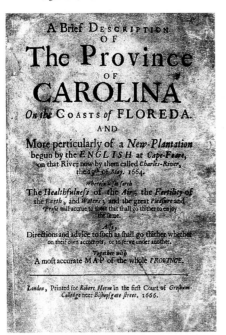

A pamphlet in which the Lords Proprietors advertised Carolina's attractions.

Think as a Geographer

You have read that North Carolina's slow growth was partly the result of its geography—there were few navigable rivers and no deepwater harbors. ■ *To Do*: Write a paragraph explaining the relationship between North Carolina's inadequate waterways and its slow growth.

thing, Albemarle was isolated from the outside world. Forests, swamps, and rivers made inland travel difficult. The inlets, sounds, and rivers of Albemarle were shallow, and only small vessels could use them.

In addition, the Proprietors' land policy kept people away. Although there was plenty of land, the Proprietors allowed only small grants, probably because they did not understand how large their colony really was. To make matters worse, surveys were often inaccurate, and officials kept poor records. Also, quitrents were double those in Virginia.

Although the Proprietors advertised the colony's fertile soil, good weather, and other favorable conditions, the colony continued to grow slowly. Finally the Assembly asked the Proprietors to change their land policy. The Proprietors did so, giving the settlers of Albemarle the same terms as those found in Virginia. The Assembly tried to do its part by passing several new laws. Newcomers did not have to pay taxes for a year; they were free for a year from lawsuits because of debt and from trial for crimes committed outside Albemarle.

The colony suffers from poor government. Neither the Proprietors' actions nor the Assembly's laws helped attract more settlers. In fact, the failure of the Proprietors to set up a strong, stable government was one of the colony's greatest handicaps. Some of its governors were weak and unable to get anything done. Some were dishonest and took advantage of their position for personal gain. The governors failed to preserve order or to protect the people.

The trade laws are unpopular. Under such conditions, it is little wonder that the settlers were unhappy—at times, to the point of open rebellion. The first such rebellion was **Culpeper's Rebellion.** To understand the causes of the rebellion, you need to remember the two political parties in Albemarle. You also need to know that England had passed several trade laws, called the Navigation Acts. These laws stated that colonial trade goods could only be carried on British and colonial ships. Also, certain goods, including tobacco, could only be shipped to England. If the settlers wanted to ship tobacco to other colonies, they had to pay a **duty,** or tax, on it.

These laws were very unpopular with the people of Albemarle since most of their income came from the sale of tobacco to New England traders. So, in 1672, at the request of the Assembly, the governor went to England to try to convince the Proprietors not to enforce the laws. This effort eventually failed.

While the governor was away, the president of the Council, John Jenkins, became acting governor. Jenkins was a member of the popular party. Although he appointed a collector of the duties on tobacco, he had no intention of making sure that the collector did his job. Jenkins had the backing of George Durant, Albemarle's most influential political leader, as well as that of a newcomer, John Culpeper. Culpeper was a man with a reputation as a troublemaker, and had in fact been "invited" to leave Charles Town in southern Carolina. Opposing these three were Thomas Eastchurch, Speaker of the Assembly, and Thomas Miller, both supporters of the Proprietors.

Two factions clash. Jenkins, trying to crush the opposition, had Miller jailed for speaking out against the way the government was being run. Jenkins also tried to keep Eastchurch from getting word to England about what was going on in the colony. Jenkins then tried to disband the Assembly, but it was loyal to Eastchurch. Instead, the Assembly accused Jenkins of wrongdoing and jailed him. Miller, in the meantime, had escaped from jail, and he and Eastchurch went to report to the Proprietors in England.

The Proprietors must have believed their account, because in 1676 they appointed Eastchurch governor and ordered him to halt the illegal trade with New England. At the same time, Miller became secretary and collector of the duties. On the voyage back to Albemarle, their ship called at an island in the West Indies. There Eastchurch met a wealthy widow and delayed his return until he could court and marry her. He sent Miller on ahead with orders to serve as acting governor.

Miller reached the colony and installed himself in most of the various offices. He seized a large quantity of tobacco and goods that had been illegally imported and collected quite a sum in duties. As governor, however, Miller's power apparently went to his head. He meddled in local elections, imposed heavy fines, and jailed several important men.

Matters soon came to a head, and Durant, Culpeper, and their supporters armed themselves, captured Miller, and imprisoned him. After the rebels had arrested other officials, they took over the government. For two years, they governed ably, and the colony enjoyed a period of peace and quiet.

To make their peace with the Proprietors, the colonists sent Culpeper to England with promises to obey the authority of the Proprietors. However, Miller had escaped from jail and gone to England. When Culpeper arrived, he

Culpeper's Rebellion as shown in a museum diorama.

was charged with treason. The Lords Proprietors were afraid that the uprising would make the colony appear to be poorly governed, so one of them, Anthony Ashley Cooper, defended Culpeper at his trial. He was found not guilty of treason. Thus ended Culpeper's Rebellion, one of the first popular uprisings in any of the English colonies.

Sothel is appointed. After the rebellion, the Proprietors were determined to improve conditions in Albemarle. They needed a good leader and someone who would not take sides with either group in the colony. They chose Seth Sothel, who was a Proprietor because he had bought the share of one of the original Proprietors. Sothel seemed to be a sober, moderate man who could "settle things well." On his way to Carolina, however, Turkish pirates captured Sothel and took him to Algiers in North Africa, where they held him prisoner for several years.

Meanwhile, in Albemarle, the Council chose—and the Proprietors approved—John Jenkins as governor. Although Jenkins had the title, George Durant was the one with the real power. Through Jenkins, Durant maintained order, enforced laws, collected duties, and saw to it that the rebels were pardoned.

This happy state of affairs changed drastically when Sothel finally took his post in 1683. If he had been qualified when he was appointed, perhaps his personality had changed while he was a prisoner. At any rate, he soon proved to be one of the most arbitrary and corrupt governors in any of the English colonies. He jailed his opponents without trial, held some on the false charge of piracy, illegally seized estates, "detained" cattle and other property, accepted bribes, and ignored the orders of the other Proprietors.

Finally the people could no longer stand Sothel's behavior, and in 1689, he was tried by the Assembly. Found guilty on 13 charges, Sothel was banned from the colony for a year and from ever again holding government office there.

Ludwell takes over.   Still determined to settle Albemarle's problems, the Proprietors named Philip Ludwell governor. Arriving in 1689, the new governor barely had time to unpack his trunk when he was faced with an unpleasant incident. Captain John Gibbs, a relative of Proprietor George Monck, claimed to be the governor. Probably he based his claim on the fact that he expected to be Monck's heir and also because he was a cacique. **Gibbs's Rebellion,** as it is called, was settled quickly. After a minor incident or two in which no shots were fired, both Gibbs and Ludwell went to London to report to the Proprietors. The Proprietors supported Ludwell and sent him back. This time he went to Charles Town in southern Carolina, with instructions to appoint a deputy governor for the northern part of the colony.

For the next 15 years, the people of northern Carolina enjoyed orderly, able, and peaceful government. This situation was due in part to the deputy governors, who were all old-timers, and like Ludwell, honest and sensible.

The colony expands.   About the time that Ludwell took office, people began to move across Albemarle Sound to settle along the Pamlico River. In 1694, the Proprietors, trying to encourage settlement, ordered the deputy governor to establish as many counties as necessary for the better government of the colony. As a result, Bath County was created in 1696. It took in the entire area from Albemarle to Cape Fear.

Now that peace reigned in the area, settlers began arriving rapidly. A great many were from a French Huguenot settlement in Virginia, which had been started as a haven from religious persecution. The English, however, had taken the best land, so the Huguenots were hemmed in. In North Carolina, they found a pleasant climate and plenty of cheap land. These hard-working people made a good impression on their new neighbors.

This map of Carolina was published in London in 1708. *(North Carolina Collection, University of North Carolina at Chapel Hill)*

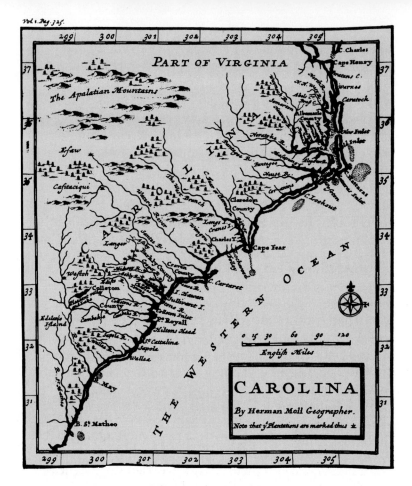

More and more settlers poured into the colony, and in 1706 the town of Bath was established. In 1715, Port Bath was created, and the town became an important trading center for a number of years. Also in 1706, the Council divided Bath County into three parts.

More of the Virginia Huguenots arrived in North Carolina to take up land along the Neuse and Trent rivers. In the same area, a colony of Europeans—Germans and a few Swiss and English—arrived in 1710. The settlement became the town of New Bern, which quickly grew and prospered. In 1675, Albemarle's population had been about 4,000; by 1710, North Carolina's population was around 15,000.

Think Twice

1. Briefly identify each of the following; (a) John Pory, (b) Sir Robert Heath, (c) Seth Sothel, (d) Philip Ludwell, (e) John Gibbs.
2. Name the five major people involved in Culpeper's Rebellion.
3. Why were the Navigation Acts important in Culpeper's Rebellion?

2 War and Peace

People, Places, Terms

Dissenter
John Archdale
Henderson Walker
Vestry Act
Thomas Cary
Edward Hyde
Cary's Rebellion
borough town

Both troubled times and periods of peace marked the years after about 1700. Religious groups in the colony were at odds, Native Americans and settlers warred with one another, and pirates roamed the waters. Despite these problems, the colony managed to survive and even to grow.

Colonists worship as they please.   According to the Proprietors' charter, the official, tax-supported church of Carolina was the Anglican Church, the Church of England. Yet the Proprietors had done nothing about setting up the Anglican Church in the colony. Instead, they had allowed the members of any Protestant group to worship as they pleased.

People who dissented from, or disagreed with, the beliefs and rituals of the Anglican Church were called **Dissenters**. The most numerous of the Dissenters among the colonists were the Quakers.

Anglicans try to take over.   Under the governorship of Proprietor John Archdale (1694–1696), himself a recent convert to the Quaker faith, there were more Quakers than people of any other religion in the government of Albemarle. Such complete control worried the Anglicans, who were anxious to see the Anglican Church take on what they felt to be its rightful role in the colony. These people received some encouragement when an Anglican, Henderson Walker, became governor in 1699.

The new governor convinced the legislature to pass the first church law in North Carolina. Called the **Vestry Act,** it called for laying out parishes, organizing vestries, and building churches, as well as a tax for the support of clergymen. (A parish is the area from which each church draws its members. A vestry is the committee that directs church business.) Delighted Anglicans began at once to carry out the law, creating four parishes in short order.

Quakers, Presbyterians, and even some Anglicans objected to the Vestry Act—some because they didn't believe they should have to support a church to which they didn't belong, others because it increased taxes. These people were relieved when the Proprietors would not approve the law because it gave too much power to the vestries and didn't provide large enough salaries for the clergy.

Quakers protest.   In 1703, another law was passed. This one required that Assemblymen be Anglicans and that all officials take an oath of allegiance to the English queen

93

before taking office. Swearing such an oath was against Quaker belief. To the distress of the Quakers, Robert Daniel, Walker's successor, enforced the law. Because of their complaints about this unfair situation, the governor in Charles Town removed Daniel from office.

The new deputy governor, Thomas Cary, was thought to be friendly to Dissenters, but his actions proved to be even more offensive to them. In response, the Quakers sent John Porter, one of their members, to complain to the Proprietors. With the help of John Archdale, Porter was successful. He was given an order to suspend all oath laws and to remove Cary from office. The Council was to elect a new president who would serve as deputy governor.

When Porter returned, Cary was away on business in Charles Town and Council president William Glover was acting deputy governor. At first the Quakers accepted Glover, but when he too insisted on the oath, they turned

A Quaker meeting. Quakers worshiped in silence, with no minister to give a sermon. Instead, whoever was inspired to speak rose and did so.

to Cary, who had since returned. Apparently he was now willing to change his ways and support the order from the Proprietors.

Since neither Glover nor Cary was willing to give up his claim to office, an election was held for a new Assembly. Whichever man had more of his supporters elected to the Assembly would be the deputy governor. When the representatives arrived, including two sets from some counties, Cary's men won out, and Glover fled to Virginia. Cary held office for the next few years, and during this time the oath law was revoked and a number of Quakers were appointed to office.

Carolina becomes two colonies. Unhappy with the confusion in the colony, the Proprietors decided to appoint a governor of North Carolina to be independent of South Carolina's governor. They chose Edward Hyde, who took the oath of office as the first governor of the colony of North Carolina on May 9, 1712. This date marks the separation of Carolina into two parts—North Carolina and South Carolina.

In the meantime, Hyde had been acting as deputy governor. Under his leadership, the Assembly passed several unpopular laws, including one that revoked all laws made under Thomas Cary. Once again the colony was split into two factions—Hyde supporters and Cary supporters. At first, Cary seemed to be winning. Then while Hyde and his advisers were meeting in a house on the shores of Albemarle Sound, Cary, in a ship bearing six guns, approached and fired on the house. Cannonballs landed on the roof and rolled into the garden. Some of the house servants, dressed in livery, ran outside to investigate the commotion. Cary mistook them for marines sent by Virginia's governor, who had recently offered to help Hyde. In Cary's haste to retreat, he set his sails incorrectly. Instead of sailing away, the ship was driven ashore. Unnerved, Cary and his companions jumped overboard and fled into the woods.

When the governor of Virginia did send marines, other supporters of Cary also fled, making a final end to **Cary's Rebellion.** Cary was captured and sent to England, but was never tried, perhaps because no one was there to testify against him.

Tuscaroras go to war. The early 1700s had their share of troubles between colonists and Native Americans. Tuscaroras and other Native Americans living in North Carolina were upset at being cheated at every opportunity by colonial traders. Further, they resented losing their land.

Edward Hyde, a relative of the Proprietor of the same name, was deputy governor of North Carolina in 1711–1712. He was the first to hold the office of governor after the Proprietors recognized that there were two Carolinas.

They had seen surveyors go into the woods with their instruments and knew that more settlers would soon follow, taking over Tuscarora farmland and hunting grounds. One group of colonists had captured 36 Meherrins, held them for two days without food and water, wrecked their cabins, and threatened to destroy their crops if they did not give up their land. Also, it was not uncommon for colonists to force Native Americans into slavery.

The Tuscaroras knew that the colony had suffered from the conflict between Anglicans and Quakers. They knew that the weather had been bad, crops had failed, and the people were losing hope. Quietly the Tuscaroras decided to take advantage of the situation and put an end to the cause of their troubles. In September 1711, led by their chief, King Hancock, they attacked the settlements along the Neuse and Pamlico rivers, including the town of Bath.

After the attack, which lasted three days, the whole region was described as "totally wasted and ruined," a scene of desolation, blood, and ashes. The settlers had not fortified their homes, supplies were low, and protection was unavailable. Only the Albemarle section was spared

Just before the Tuscaroras attacked the settlements on the Neuse and Pamlico rivers, a founder of New Bern, Baron Christoph von Graffenried, and the surveyor, John Lawson, were exploring the Neuse River north of New Bern. The Tuscaroras captured them and a servant, killing Lawson but letting Graffenried and the servant go. Graffenried was unable to return to New Bern in time to warn the settlers.

because the Tuscarora leader there, Tom Blunt, decided not to join the attack. In appreciation, the colonists set aside a large section of land for his use. The records do not suggest that anyone saw the irony of colonists giving land to Native Americans.

South Carolina sends help. Governor Hyde, facing a very difficult situation, had to ask for help from South Carolina. The colony gave a large sum of money and sent troops consisting of about 30 colonists and 500 of their Native American allies. Under the command of Colonel John Barnwell, this force defeated the Tuscaroras in two battles near New Bern in January 1712. Aided by about 250 North Carolinians, Barnwell then attacked the main force of the Tuscaroras, who were in a fort in what is now Greene County. After a ten-day siege, Barnwell agreed to a peace treaty, thereby saving the lives of a large number of prisoners held within the fort.

Although Barnwell asked the North Carolina Assembly for a grant of land for his men and for money to cover his expenses, the Assembly refused, feeling that he should have broken the power of the Tuscaroras completely. Barnwell became ill and returned directly home, leaving his men to follow. On the way, they discussed the Assembly's ingratitude. Deciding to have *something* for their trouble, they seized some Native Americans and sold them into slavery.

This violation of the peace treaty led to further raids in the summer and fall. At about the same time, many colonists, including Governor Hyde, died in a yellow fever epidemic. Thomas Pollock, the new acting governor, once again called on South Carolina for help. The neighboring colony responded by sending Colonel James Moore with a force of about 30 colonists and 1,000 Native American allies who crushed the Tuscaroras, torturing some and selling others into slavery. The survivors left North Carolina to join relatives in New York.

Good government prevails. The war with the Tuscaroras left the colony in terrible condition. In addition to the loss of life and the destruction of livestock and other property, North Carolina was deeply in debt and very few new colonists were arriving. On the other hand, the threat from the Tuscaroras was gone, and Pollock was an able leader who prepared the way for the equally able governor who followed him, Charles Eden.

Under Eden, the Assembly in 1715 passed laws that went a long way toward solving the colony's long-standing problems: weak government, dishonest or

Across Cultures

*S*ome actions of people of the 1600s, settlers and Native Americans alike, are hideous and inhuman by today's standards. Both groups, for instance, sometimes tortured prisoners.
■ *To Do:* Think about what you hear in the news reports. Then name some things that people do (or don't do) today that will seem as inhuman to the people of the future as the actions of the settlers seem to us.

_____

To add to his fierce appearance when boarding a captured ship, Blackbeard twisted bits of smoldering rope into his hair.

inefficient officials, troubles between Anglicans and Dissenters, and the general confusion about which laws were in effect. In addition, the Assembly passed laws that encouraged business and improved travel on land and water. To promote the development of towns, all towns with 60 or more families were given the right to send a delegate to the Assembly. These towns were called **borough towns.** Bath and New Bern already existed, and in 1722, a town begun a few years earlier became a borough town under the name of Edenton.

Under these laws, the colony began to flourish. Sawmills produced lumber for export, and naval stores also were shipped out. With channels cleared and marked, New England skippers returned to North Carolina, making their way into the sounds and up the rivers to planters' wharves.

Pirates take to Carolina waters.   Unfortunately, the cleared channels and increased trade attracted not only merchants but pirates as well. With their small ships, pirates could slip through the inlets and hide until a richly laden vessel or a passenger ship sailed into view. Then it was simple enough to dash out and capture a valuable cargo. Since the colony still had few merchants from whom goods could be bought, pirates found a ready market for their stolen goods.

The most notorious Carolina pirate was Edward Teach, better known as Blackbeard for his long black beard and hair. Another well-known pirate was Major Stede Bonnet. He was thought to have been a respected army officer at one time who escaped an unhappy marriage by buying a merchant ship on which he would be away for months at a time. Eventually the lure of more and faster wealth turned him to piracy. Although these two were the most famous, there were many other pirates, including some women.

There is some evidence to suggest that some high officials did business with the pirates. Others tried to put an end to the pirates' activities, but it was the governors of the neighboring colonies who struck the blows that finally ended piracy off North Carolina. In September 1718, word reached South Carolina's governor in Charles Town that a pirate ship had been seen off the coast. The governor sent Colonel William Rhett to find it. He found Bonnet's ship lurking behind the sand bars at the mouth of the Cape Fear River, and after a five-hour battle, captured the pirate. Rhett took Bonnet to Charles Town, where he was tried, convicted, and hanged.

Several weeks later, the governor of Virginia secretly manned two sloops with crews from a British warship stationed in the James River. Commanded by Lieutenant

Robert Maynard, they set out in search of Blackbeard. On November 22, they found the pirate's ship and attacked and boarded it. During the fighting that followed, Maynard reportedly cut off Blackbeard's head with a slashing sweep of his sword. Afterwards, Maynard headed for Bath to present several officials there with evidence of their role in some of the pirates' wrongdoing. When Maynard's ship sailed into Bath, the head was hanging high in the rigging. During November and December 1718, 49 other pirates were captured and hanged in Charles Town.

The colony expands.   With the departure of the Tuscaroras, the lessening of piracy, and the leadership of several competent governors, another period of growth began in North Carolina. More and more people arrived, and settlement expanded west and south. Between 1722 and 1730 four new counties were created: Bertie, Carteret, Tyrrell, and New Hanover. Bertie was carved from the part of old Albemarle County on the western side of the Chowan River, Carteret from the eastern part of Bath County, and Tyrrell from the northern end of Bath. New Hanover was in the southeastern corner of the colony on the Cape Fear River.

New Hanover included the area of Clarendon County that had been abandoned earlier. Colonel James Moore had rediscovered the region when he and his troops were returning to South Carolina after helping to defeat the Tuscaroras. Moore and several relatives bought land and moved there. About 1723, other people began to take up land along Cape Fear River, to clear fields and to build houses, against the orders of the Proprietors. Since they had no title to the land, and weren't paying quitrents, the governor took matters into his own hands, giving them deeds and collecting the rents due the Proprietors, as well as opening a land office.

Knowing they could get titles to land, more settlers arrived, many of them by way of a new 100-mile road that had been built from the Neuse River to the Cape Fear River. This road was the result of one of the laws passed by the Assembly of 1715. Other settlers came from South Carolina, the West Indies, New England, Maryland, and Europe. In 1733, Wilmington was established about 30 miles from the mouth of the Cape Fear River. With its excellent harbor, Wilmington was North Carolina's largest city from 1840 to the 1900s.

The Proprietors sell their shares.   Since at least 1689, various advisers to the Crown had been trying to regain the Proprietary colonies as royal colonies. The Carolina Proprietors had already sold South Carolina to the Crown

Production of naval stores in North Carolina

The leader of the surveying crews was William Byrd II of Virginia. The survey, which ran a total of 161 miles, was honestly done and in keeping with the 1665 charter.

in 1719. They knew that they would eventually have to sell North Carolina. In order to sell it, however, they had to know exactly what they owned. There was no boundary between Virginia and North Carolina, partly because Virginia had never accepted the charter of 1665. As a result, the two colonies had been at odds over who owned what land.

By 1727, negotiations between the Crown and the Proprietors had reached the point where a survey was essential. The survey was begun jointly in 1728 by two crews, one from Virginia, and one from North Carolina. After the surveyors had gone 50 miles beyond any known settlement, the North Carolina crew went home, unable to imagine anyone living that far inland. The Virginia crew continued the survey for another 72 miles.

The way was now clear for the Crown to buy North Carolina. On July 25, 1729, papers were signed transferring seven of the eight shares to the Crown. One Proprietor, who was to become Earl Granville, did not sell his share. However, he had to give up any role in the government of the colony. After the American Revolution, the state of North Carolina took over the Granville District.

Think Twice

1. Why were people upset about the Vestry Act?
2. Why did people split into the two factions of Cary's Rebellion?
3. Why did the Tuscaroras attack the settlers?
4. Why was the Assembly of 1715 important?
5. When did North Carolina become a royal colony?

Chapter 7 Review

Choose from the following menu of activities.

Think Back: Main Ideas

1. Where did the first settlers in North Carolina come from?
2. What new idea did the Proprietors' charter reflect?
3. What were the three main parts of the colony's early government?
4. Briefly state the beliefs of the prerogative party and the popular party.
5. Why were the Navigation Acts unpopular?
6. As you have read, the colony's early governors had broad powers. How might North Carolina's history have been different if those powers had been limited?
7. One reason that people resented Quakers was that they refused to go to war, although some Quakers did help equip soldiers when they marched against the Tuscaroras. If you were a settler, would you join Barnwell or Moore in attacking the Tuscaroras? Why or why not?
8. Name two ways the Assembly of 1715 helped North Carolina grow.
9. How did North Carolina's geography help the pirates?
10. Why was it necessary to survey the boundary between Virginia and North Carolina?

Maps Matter

Use the map on page 87 to answer these questions.

1. Find the labels for Albemarle and Clarendon counties. Describe the general location of each.
2. The town of Brunswick (which failed to flourish and was abandoned after the Revolution) was near the future site of Wilmington. On what river would Wilmington be located?

Word Wizard

1. *Store* has many meanings. Use a dictionary to find the one most fitting for the term *naval stores*.
2. One meaning of *prerogative* is a "special right, power, or privilege." Why is *prerogative* a good name for the party so named?
3. *Popular* comes from the Latin word *populus*, meaning "the people." Why is *popular* a good name for that party?
4. In this chapter, the word *duty* is used in the sense of a tax on goods to be shipped. What is another meaning of the word?

Working Cooperatively

Among the Dissenters were Huguenots, Presbyterians, and Baptists, as well as Quakers. Working in small groups, do some research on one of these sects or on Anglicans and prepare a report on the sect's origins and beliefs. Some group members should prepare charts, diagrams, time lines, or other illustrations as needed.

Curriculum Connection

In colonial times, quitrents varied from 1/4 penny to 1/2 penny an acre. If you were a settler, how much would you have to pay on the following amounts of land at 1/4 penny per acre?

1. 100 acres
2. 130 acres
3. 170 acres
4. 190 acres

Learning through Literature

Men of Albemarle, by Inglis Fletcher
Anne Bonney, by Chloe Gartner
Brethren of the Black Flag, by Margaret Hoffman

Chapter 8

North Carolina Ways of Life

In the 1700s, thousands of immigrants poured into North Carolina.

Some people came to North Carolina from American colonies to the north and south. Many of them brought enslaved Africans with them. However, most people who settled in North Carolina in the mid-1700s came from Scotland, Ireland, and Germany. Each set of newcomers followed a different dream—adventure, cheap land, religious or political freedom, economic opportunity, and more. These dreams led people to fill up lands from the Coastal Plain to the foot of the Appalachian Mountains. A few hardy pioneers even pushed across the Appalachians, seeking new frontiers to cross. By 1776, North Carolina ranked fourth among the colonies in number of people.

The large-scale arrival of people sparked a period of progress and expansion among North Carolinians.

The constant immigration of people to North Carolina triggered great economic and social changes. Small farmers used much of the Piedmont for cultivation. Enterprising businesspeople established sawmills to reap profits from the forests. To stimulate trade, North Carolinians carved out rough roads, cleared rivers of debris, and built lighthouses along the coast. Economic diversity led to social diversity as North Carolina became far more than a land of farmers and planters.

A view of Salem in 1787 ▶

Think Ahead

By the mid-1700s, people in North Carolina no longer looked to England as the mother country—except in a political sense. Read about the forces that helped weaken ties between England and a colony of people who called themselves North Carolinians.

1 Newcomers to North Carolina

People, Places, Terms

Highland Scots
Gabriel Johnston
backcountry
Scots-Irish
Pennsylvania Dutch

During the years from 1730 to 1775, North Carolina's non-African population swelled from 30,000 to 260,000. The number of people of African descent grew from 6,000 to more than 40,000. High birth rates accounted for part of this increase. "Most houses [are] full of little ones," declared an Edenton resident, Dr. John Brickell. Women married young, often raising families while still in their teens. However, the rigors of colonial life and frequent childbirth often led to early death. One tombstone in a churchyard in Brunswick Town represents the tragically short lives of some young women.

Primary Source

Rebecca McGwire
Daughter of William Dry and his wife Mary Jane
Born 1749
Married to Thomas McGwire 1763
Died 1766   Age 17

Besides the high birth rate, North Carolina's population boom resulted from another important factor—immigration. During the 1700s, people came from near and far to settle in North Carolina. Some traveled from colonies such as Virginia, South Carolina, Maryland, Pennsylvania, and New Jersey. Others arrived from the crowded cities of England and Northern Ireland. Still others came from the highlands and lowlands of Scotland or the Rhine and Danube rivers in central Europe.

Reasons for immigration.   The settlement of North Carolina took place relatively late among the 13 colonies. As the 1700s unfolded, some colonists viewed North Carolina as an open frontier. In the spring of 1731, for example, Benjamin Franklin carried an article in his newspaper, the *Pennsylvania Gazette*, entitled, "The new Settlement going forward at Cape Fear." Franklin described the many people traveling to Cape Fear "to view the Place and learn the Nature of the Country." Franklin remarked that a large number of people, "especially country people," liked the land so much that they stayed.

Glowing descriptions written by land companies about North Carolina soon reached across the sea, too. The advertisements promised mild climates, fertile soil, and inexpensive land. Royal governors of North Carolina such as George Burrington, Gabriel Johnston, and Arthur Dobbs also did their part in spreading news of the colony overseas.

The advertisements found ready audiences among the people of Europe. German-speaking groups in central Europe saw North Carolina as a place to escape religious persecution and political turmoil at home. People in Ireland and Scotland saw going to the colony as a way to escape crowded conditions or harsh landlords. Together they came by the thousands, creating a culturally diverse region similar to Pennsylvania. The first big wave of immigrants were the **Highland Scots.**

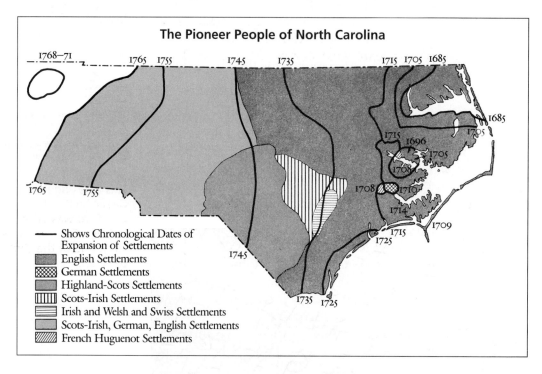

The Pioneer People of North Carolina

— Shows Chronological Dates of Expansion of Settlements
English Settlements
German Settlements
Highland-Scots Settlements
Scots-Irish Settlements
Irish and Welsh and Swiss Settlements
Scots-Irish, German, English Settlements
French Huguenot Settlements

Maps Matter

This map is a special purpose map showing the human side of geography. Based on data on the map, you can form conclusions about colonial culture in North Carolina.
■ *To Do:* Use the map's legend to answer these questions. What was the largest area of non-English settlements? The smallest? Name at least two groups of people that lived in the eastern and central parts of North Carolina. Which people lived in the western part of the colony?

Moving into Cape Fear.   Turmoil in the British Isles drove the Highland Scots from Scotland to North Carolina. England ruled the independent-minded Scots with a tight fist. Gabriel Johnston, a Scot, became royal governor of North Carolina in 1734. He began to promote settlement of the colony and made sure that the call for settlers reached his homeland of Scotland at an early date.

In 1740, the first large group of Highland Scots landed at Brunswick. Numbering about 360, the Highlanders were welcomed by Johnston. He convinced the colonial Assembly to pass a law that excused Protestants from other countries from paying taxes for ten years. The Highland Scots were one of the groups to benefit from this law. Johnston also made it possible for the Highland Scots to obtain large grants of land in what is now Upper Cape Fear.

The Highland Scots found a haven in North Carolina just in time. In 1746, the Highlanders in Scotland rebelled against England. In the defeat that followed, the English government seized huge chunks of farmland in Scotland and gave it to English army officers as grazing land for sheep. Many Highlanders faced near starvation. Inspired by letters from their friends in North Carolina, they moved to Upper Cape Fear by the thousands. The region became so heavily populated that the North Carolina assembly created a separate county in the region called Cumberland.

When revolution swept through the 13 colonies, the once rebellious Highlanders remained loyal to England. Perhaps they feared that losing the Revolution would result in the same harsh treatment they had received from the English at home. Or perhaps the Highlanders did not want to risk losing a profitable trade in naval stores—tar, pitch, and turpentine. Whatever the reason, when rebellion came in 1776, the Highlanders refused to turn their guns against England.

Along the Great Wagon Road.   In the 1700s, a flood of settlers rolled across Pennsylvania and into the so-called "Appalachian barrier." With little desirable land left for the taking in Pennsylvania, these colonists headed south along the foot of the mountains. Their carts and herds of

This title page of a sermon given in Gaelic by the Reverend Le D. Crauford was printed in Fayetteville in 1791. Gaelic was the native language of the Highland Scots and the Irish.

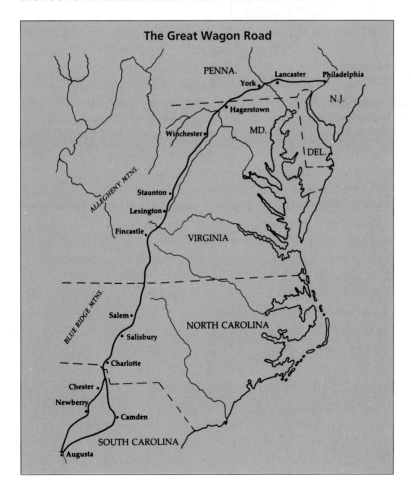

Maps Matter

Many settlers traveled the Great Wagon Road on foot, on horseback, or by wagon from Philadelphia to South Carolina. ■ *To Do:* Trace the route of the Great Wagon Road. Name three towns it passed through in North Carolina.

livestock cut ruts in the land all the way to Georgia. As a result, this 700-mile wilderness trail became known as the Great Wagon Road. By the 1760s, it carried more traffic than any other colonial highway. Along this route, people fanned out into the **backcountry**—thinly populated settlements that stretched from the fall line to the Appalachians.

Two main groups claimed the backcountry as home: the **Scots-Irish** and German-speaking Protestants. Both were largely second- and third-generation colonists whose immigrant parents had arrived in Pennsylvania to farm or to take up a trade. These younger people found land scarce in Pennsylvania just at the time North Carolina opened its backcountry. Soon they began moving into the upper Piedmont section where they farmed, raised livestock, and operated gristmills, tanneries, and forges.

The arrival of the Scots-Irish. The Scots-Irish were descendants of Scots who had been sent by English monarchs to Northern Ireland in the early 1600s to supplant the "unruly Irish" and to industrialize the country. There these people drained swamps, cleared fields, grew flax (from which linen is made) and other crops, and raised cattle and sheep. They were Presbyterians, so in displacing Roman Catholic Irish people they promoted another English objective—to make the country Protestant. This objective was never met, however, and bitter conflict between Protestant and Catholic in Northern Ireland continues to this day. The Scots also developed a thriving linen and woolen industry that began to compete with English mills. As a result, in the 1700s English policy changed, and the Scots-Irish were encouraged to leave Ireland for America.

The Scots-Irish who came to colonial America had no love for England. The frontier experience strengthened the spirit of independence among the Scots-Irish. When the call for revolution came in the 1770s, the Scots-Irish—unlike the Highland Scots—supported it. Because Scots-Irish governor Arthur Dobbs had encouraged a large number of his people to settle in North Carolina, the colony became a hotbed of rebellion.

The arrival of the Pennsylvania Dutch. Joining the Scots-Irish in the backcountry were the **Pennsylvania Dutch.** Their name came from *Deutsch*, meaning *German*. Settlers applied the term Pennsylvania Dutch to all German-speaking people. They were members of several Protestant churches including Lutheran, German Reformed, and Moravian. Most had fled religious persecution by Roman Catholic rulers in German states

Queen Anne, granddaughter of Carolina Proprietor Edward Hyde, helped to provide transportation for the Scots-Irish to Pennsylvania.

along the Rhine River. The largest body of Germans to settle in North Carolina were the Moravians. These people had several close-knit communities where craftsmen provided goods of all kinds for the backcountry. They also had doctors, and they provided medical and dental services for people who came from great distances.

Most German settlers in North Carolina clung to their language until well into the 1840s. Language barriers prevented Germans from taking a large part in the movement toward independence from Britain. However, neither did they hinder the American cause. Instead, most pursued a strict policy of neutrality. When independence from Britain came, the Germans threw their full support behind the new nation.

Settlers against their will. People of African descent played a role in North Carolina history from the very start. Records show that Sir Francis Drake may have left enslaved Africans at Roanoke Island in 1586. If so, their fate is just as mysterious as that of the 1587 Lost Colony. Also, the original Proprietors of Carolina wrote slavery into their first plan of government.

Slavery never took as firm a root in North Carolina as in South Carolina. Of all the southern colonies, North Carolina had the smallest population of enslaved Africans. Hampered by a lack of good ports, North Carolina failed to develop an active slave trade. Moreover, the small farmers of the Piedmont had little need for slaves, and the plantations of the Tidewater never reached the same scale as those of South Carolina, Virginia, and Maryland.

The effects of slavery were further limited by the outspoken Quakers who lived in large settlements in the central part of North Carolina. They urged slaveowners to treat Africans well and to allow them to attend church. In 1770, North Carolina Quakers described the African slave trade as "an iniquitous [sinful] practice" and called for an immediate end to it. Few slaveowners heeded this call. Nonetheless, they tended to treat enslaved Africans less brutally than did owners of slaves who labored on the rice plantations farther south.

Think Twice

1. Why did many immigrants travel to North Carolina in the mid-1700s?
2. Why did the Scots-Irish who settled in the backcountry of North Carolina develop a tradition of independence?
3. How do you think the large-scale arrival of immigrants in the 1700s helped weaken North Carolina's ties with England?

Across Cultures

*T*he arrival of enslaved Africans in North Carolina introduced yet another set of cultural influences into the region. ■ *To Do*: Write to the Afro-American Cultural Center, 401 North Myers Street, Charlotte, North Carolina, to research the contributions of Africans to North Carolina during the colonial period. Ask for examples of art, foods, and music introduced by people of African descent.

NUMBER OF PEOPLE OF AFRICAN DESCENT IN NORTH CAROLINA, 1717–1790	
Year	Number
1717	1,000+
1720	3,000
1730	6,000
1754	15,000
1765	30,000
1767	39,000
1790	100,572 (enslaved)
1790	4,975 (free)

Tables Teach

The first United States census was taken in 1790. Therefore, the population figures in this table prior to 1790 are based on estimates. According to the figures in the table, about how many enslaved Africans lived in North Carolina when the colonists declared their independence from England in 1776?

2 Social Differences

A traveler through the backcountry of North Carolina in the 1700s was shocked by the equality among the people. "Every man in all companies, with almost no exception," wrote the traveler, "calls his wife, brother, neighbor, or acquaintance by their proper name of Sally, John, James, or Michael, without ever prefixing the customary complement of 'My Dear,' 'Sir,' 'Mr.,' etc." The lack of social differences astounded people from the more settled parts of North Carolina. People in colonial times had a keen sense of social class and their place in society. Most people observed that place. The exception, noted the Reverend Charles Woodmason, was "that band of rude fellows" along the frontier.

"Gentlefolk." By the mid-1700s, many people along the Coastal Plain had forgotten the hardships of early settlement. As time passed, they tried to set up a social order similar to the one in England. At the top of society were the so-called "gentlefolk," or **gentry class.** Members of this group enjoyed moderate, or even great, wealth. A few traced their ancestry to the English gentry, adding impressive titles such as "gentleman," "planter," or "esquire" to their names.

The gentry class included professionals such as clergy, lawyers, and doctors. However, the group most closely associated with the gentry were the **planters.** Some planters owned thousands of acres of land and more than a hundred enslaved people. The vast majority, though, owned about 500 acres and fewer than 20 enslaved workers.

The earliest planters built their homes on high bluffs overlooking rivers. These desirable sites allowed them to load or unload goods from boats anchored at their own docks. Most of these plantations were largely self-sufficient. They possessed their own shops, mills, tanneries, looms, and other essential services. Enslaved Africans worked the fields and labored as skilled artisans such as blacksmiths, carpenters, millers, shoemakers, spinners, and weavers.

By the mid-1700s, many planters enjoyed a comfortable life. Luxuries—silver, china, paintings, glassware, and books—marked their homes. Freed of the daily grind of physical labor, planters actively sought public office. Out of respect for their position in society, voters usually elected them. The first serious challenge to the planters' power came when voters in the backcountry decided to challenge the "pen and ink men" of the east.

Think as a Geographer

*I*n the 1700s, the Piedmont Region of North Carolina was a rugged frontier with thinly populated settlements.
■ *To Do*: Use an encyclopedia or other source to find out about the cities, people, and industries of the Piedmont Region today. How has the region changed since colonial days?

"A people very laborious." English observer John Lawson described the mass of North Carolinians as "a people very laborious, and [who] make quick improvements in their way of life." As you read the following glowing description of North Carolinia society, think about how life had changed since the the early years of settlement.

Primary Source

> *Merchants in the town, and considerable planters in the country, are now beginning to have a taste for living. . . . They are generous, well bred, . . . polite, humane, and hospitable. . . . [They] never tire of rendering [giving to] strangers all the service in their power. . . . Their houses are elegant, their tables always plentifully covered and their entertainment sumptous. They are fond of company, living very sociable and neighbourly [lives], visiting one another often. Poverty is almost an entire stranger among them.*

— LAWRENCE LEE, The Lower Cape Fear in Colonial Days

"Folks of a lesser sort." The vast majority of North Carolinians were farmers, servants, and laborers or artisans. Members of the gentry often described them as "folks of a lesser sort." However, the members of this class took pride in the title of "farmer." They also took pride in their achievements, for they formed the backbone of North Carolina society. They pushed the frontier west. They also formed the bulk of the **militia,** or volunteer soldiers.

This artist's drawing of a backcountry house suggests the kind of home that left an impression on visitors to the colony. Large families—five children are shown here—and pigs loose in the yard were also commented on by outsiders.

Following the independent farmers came the indentured servants, people who signed indentures, or contracts, to work for others for a certain number of years. These people constituted an important source of labor. In fact, they seem to have been more important than enslaved laborers during the early years of the colony.

Another category of bonded workers was that of apprentice. Under the apprentice system, parents or guardians placed children in the care of a skilled worker. In exchange for their labor, the children received food, shelter, and instruction in a craft or trade. Apprenticeship records in North Carolina list more than 30 trades, including weaver, blacksmith, mechanic, carpenter, and cooper (barrel maker). Perhaps the best known apprentice in the history of North Carolina was Andrew Johnson, who was apprenticed to a tailor in 1822 and became president of the United States 43 years later.

"Bonded for life." At the bottom of colonial society were people "bonded for life." This phrase was used most often to describe the status of enslaved Africans. The existence of slavery ensured that even free Africans enjoyed little status. **Racism,** or the belief by some that people of one race are superior to those of another, had crept into colonial America along with the first Africans forcibly carried to its shores.

A small number of enslaved Africans won their freedom. Some slaveowners released faithful servants by special provisions in their wills. Occasionally the Assembly granted freedom to an enslaved African as a reward for a brave deed. Newly freed Africans might then purchase family members.

Like the governments of other colonies, the North Carolina Assembly considered enslaved Africans to be property. Laws restricted the rights of enslaved Africans to travel, to meet in groups, or to bear arms. Enslaved Africans still clung to their dignity by keeping alive family and cultural traditions. They held weddings and church services sometimes in secret. They retold stories of their African ancestry. When freedom finally came in the mid-1800s, some newly freed slaves still recalled the name of their "farthest back" ancestor—the first African relative to arrive in the Americas.

Think Twice

1. What social divisions emerged in colonial North Carolina?
2. How did indentured servants differ from apprentices?
3. Why do you think North Carolinians of European descent sharply restricted the activities of enslaved Africans?

3 The Products of Farm, Field, and Forest

People, Places, Terms

cash crop
corduroy road

The mild climate of North Carolina led early settlers to experiment with exotic warm-weather crops such as olives, French grapes, and lemons. When these crops failed, settlers turned to staple crops such as wheat, oats, barley, and rye. These crops flourished, as did a number of Native American crops—including corn, tobacco, potatoes, squash, sunflowers, sweet potatoes, and several varieties of beans and peas.

Struggling settlers also learned to farm like Native Americans. They planted seeds in rows and hills, chopped out weeds with wooden hoes, and set up scarecrows to frighten away birds and animals. Slowly, an agricultural society began to take shape. By the 1700s, perhaps 95 percent of all North Carolinians earned their living through agriculture or some industry related to agriculture, such as milling wheat into flour or corn into meal.

Nature's bounty. North Carolina farmers soon found a ready market for their goods in England and the West Indies. They also sold farm products to New England, where the rocky soil made it difficult for settlers to produce surpluses. The most successful **cash crops** in North Carolina, or crops sold for a profit, were corn, wheat, and tobacco. A taste for corn spread throughout the colonies. People roasted it, fermented it into whiskey, and milled the dried kernels into grits or meal for bread, or with lye water to make hominy. They fed the stalks, cobs, and leftover ears to livestock. Wheat, which required large fields to grow, also sold well in areas with limited land—especially England.

One of the most successful nonfood crops produced in North Carolina was tobacco. The industry developed from sharing among the colonies. North Carolina farmers learned to grow tobacco from farmers in Virginia. In 1666, the governors of the tobacco-growing colonies of Virginia, Maryland, and North Carolina met to discuss ways to keep demand high. They agreed to inspect tobacco and to destroy inferior plants, selling only those of high quality.

By the mid-1700s, North Carolina possessed a thriving tobacco industry. Some tobacco warehouses grew into thriving centers of trade. Here and there, towns sprang up. Historians believe Kinston and Williamston may have had such origins. The demand for Carolina tobacco was so high in Scotland that Scottish merchants sent buyers to the

For many years, there was plenty of land available to settlers. They built fences around their fields and planted crops among the tree stumps. Livestock were permitted to roam at large.

111

Southern Colonies. They even lent money to planters so they could expand production. They accepted tobacco in payment at the end of the growing season.

Besides these cash crops, North Carolina also produced a variety of garden vegetables and fruits for sale. The author of a book entitled *American Husbandry* wrote, "Fruit in none of the colonies is in greater plenty [than in North Carolina], or finer in flavour; . . . peaches . . . are so plentiful that the major part of the crop goes to the hogs."

Hogs proved to be another valuable commodity in the state. Each fall, farmers herded thousands of hogs to markets in towns in Pennsylvania and Virginia. In addition, about one-eighth of all the salt pork in the West Indies came from North Carolina.

Most of the ships that carried products abroad used North Carolina naval stores or wood. By 1768, the colony sold England more than 60 percent of all its naval stores. A number of Highland Scots in the Cape Fear region also pooled their money to open sawmills. The colony's forests supplied wood products in such quantity that in 1772, North Carolina alone exported 7.5 million wood shingles. In addition, the colony supplied England with nearly 10 percent of that country's lumber.

Bumping along the roads. Producing goods for market was one thing. Getting them there was another. Like other colonies, North Carolina suffered from a lack of good transportation routes. Although rivers provided efficient transportation, most highways consisted of little more than stump-filled paths. In some places, settlers put down small tree trunks across muddy roads to form what became known as **corduroy roads.**

The horse was invaluable for travel. Wealthier people had horse-drawn coaches or chariots, while other people owned two-wheel carts. As the backcountry became more populated, so did the number of roads connecting east and west. The process of improving transportation was slow, however, and for much of the 1700s, rivers remained the main arteries of trade.

Think Twice

1. What were the main cash crops of North Carolina?
2. What was the main obstacle facing the colony's farmers?
3. How do you think the colony's poor system of roads helped increase the independence among settlers in the backcountry?

Chapter 8 Review

Choose from the following menu of activities.

Think Back: Main Ideas

In the 1700s, a number of forces worked to weaken colonial ties with the home country. At the same time, bonds continued to link the colonies with England. To understand this relationship, answer the following questions.

1. How did the arrival of immigrants in North Carolina help foster a culture that differed from that of England?
2. How did the existence of a large frontier along the backcountry promote a spirit of independence?
3. Why might many members of the gentry class and the Highland Scots have remained loyal to England?
4. What economic factors linked North Carolina with England?
5. How did trade among the colonies foster unity and independence in the colonies?

Maps Matter

Refer to the North Carolina regions map on page 3 and the map of pioneer people on page 104 to answer the questions below.

1. Which national group or groups lived in each of the following regions: Outer Banks, Coastal Plain, Piedmont, mountains?
2. (a) What region was settled last? (b) Why do you think this region took the longest to settle?
3. Coastal lands remained the most heavily settled region throughout the 1700s. Based on the description of the Coastal Region found in Chapter 1, explain why this part of North Carolina was settled first.

Word Wizard

Sometimes people put together two words to create a new expression. Use a dictionary to look up the meaning of each of the following terms. How do these definitions give you an insight into the reason people may have coined each term?

a. cash crop
b. corduroy road

Working Cooperatively

With several classmates, design a large illustrated map showing the Great Wagon Road and some of the products carried over it. Use these steps to guide you.

1. Using a historical atlas of the United States, locate a map tracing the full extent of the Great Wagon Road.
2. On newsprint or posterboard, draw an outline map that shows the following items: (a) colonial boundaries, (b) the Appalachian Mountains, (c) the path followed by the Great Wagon Road. (You might arrange to borrow an opaque projector from the audio-visual department in your school to project the map onto your drawing material.)
3. Next, look up information on the Great Wagon Road in the encyclopedia or a book on colonial history. Draw sketches on the map that show some of the people and goods that traveled along this highway. (As a tip, many settlers traveled in covered wagons, while others traveled by horseback. Products of the Piedmont traveled most readily along the route.)

Curriculum Connection

Use the table on page 355 of your text to trace the growth of North Carolina's population between 1675 and 1790. When did the sharpest increase in population take place? About how many people came during those years? What information in this chapter supports these findings?

Learning through Literature

Little Benders, by Joe Knox
Purslane, by Bernice Kelly Harris
Wild Cherry Tree Road, by Bernice Kelly Harris

Chapter 9

Division Within North Carolina

Sectional rivalries divide North Carolina.

One of the most important factors in the development of North Carolina has always been **sectionalism**—a strong loyalty to the region or section where a person lives. Many key events in North Carolina's history came about because of sectional rivalries. Conflicts first arose between northern and southern parts of the colony. Other divisions later emerged between the west and the east. Sectional differences continue today in the form of competition between urban and rural areas.

How did sectional rivalries first develop?

Sectional rivalries grew out of North Carolina's great diversity. Not only did land regions differ, but so did the people who settled in each region. Contributing to sectional rivalries were differences in national origins, wide social distinctions, and varied economic interests. Older counties tried to tighten their grip in government as new counties with new interests looked for greater influence in government. The resulting political struggle forms a continuing theme throughout much of North Carolina's early history.

Two examples of provincial paper money ▶

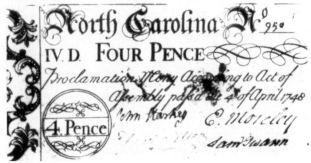

Think Ahead

In the 1700s, settlers in North Carolina battled to win rights or liberties denied to them by local governments. The political struggles had nothing to do with the home country. In fact, the quarreling colonists sometimes perplexed England. As you read, identify the interests that each region sought to protect or win.

1 North Against South

People, Places, Terms

sectionalism
Granville District
Gabriel Johnston
quorum
anarchy
Arthur Dobbs

For nearly 40 years after North Carolina became a royal colony, it did not have a permanent capital. Instead, the capital followed the governor. Lawmakers met wherever the governor lived, and the governor lived wherever he chose. Official records seemed to be stored on wheels as they rolled from place to place. Some documents never survived the trip. One time, when an attendant was hauling a cartload of records across a river, some of the papers blew into the water. The attendant debated whether to jump in to rescue them, but the chilly waters decided the issue. The papers floated away—lost to government and to history.

Settlers in the Albemarle counties complained loudly whenever a governor moved the capital to Cape Fear. Similar grumbling rippled across Cape Fear whenever a governor moved the capital to New Bern. With roads in such rough shape, each section—north and south—saw the move as a plot to control the government. Because of this antagonism, the two sections could not compromise on a permanent site for a capital. Each wanted the capital nearby.

The Granville District. As you have read, in 1729, one of the Proprietors, John Carteret, refused to sell his share of the colony to the crown. Although he had to relinquish all voice in colonial government, he was still entitled to one eighth of

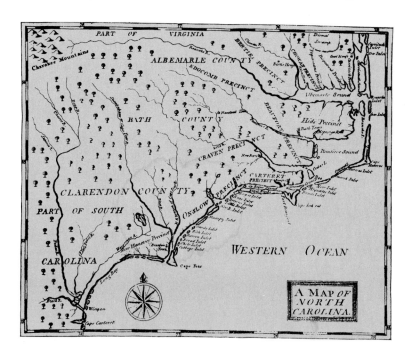

Maps Matter

This map was published in 1737 in Dr. John Brickell's *The Natural History of North Carolina.* It shows North Carolina at the end of the Proprietary period. ■ *To Do:* Use the map to find the names of the following: an ocean, one cape, three counties, and four precincts.

John Carteret, Earl Granville, inherited his great-grandfather's share of Carolina. His family held onto lands in northern North Carolina until the American Revolution. After the war, his heirs tried to regain his property, but their suit was rejected in the United States District Court in Raleigh and never made it to the Supreme Court.

the quitrents collected in North Carolina, South Carolina, and Georgia, the three colonies developed from the original grant. Rather than splitting Carteret's claim among the three colonies, King George II—probably for simplicity's sake—decided to take it all from North Carolina. In 1742, the king ordered that Carteret's share be surveyed and identified, using the Virginia – North Carolina border as the northern border of Carteret's land.

The **Granville District,** as the land became known, included a 60-mile-wide strip across the northern part of North Carolina. It contained nearly two thirds of the colony's population and an even larger share of the wealth. The Virginia-North Carolina line formed the northern boundary of the district. The southern boundary was formed by a survey line that eventually ran from Cape Hatteras to the Blue Ridge Mountains.

The Granville District was the site of trouble from the start. Settlement of the district took place in a haphazard way. For example, most settlers took over unoccupied lands in the district without paying for the land. These squatters, as they were called, often resisted paying quitrents. A quitrent in the form of money exempted, or "quit," people from an obligation to render service to the Proprietors. Although the quitrents in the district were generally lower than in counties to the south, squatters balked at them anyway.

To collect quitrents and taxes, North Carolina had to hire two treasurers—one for the Granville District and one for the rest of the colony. Whenever settlers within the Granville District stopped paying taxes or quitrents, thunders of protest broke out among people living in other sections of the colony. They loudly demanded that the settlers in the Granville District carry their fair share of the burden in the colony. As a result, a struggle emerged between the settlers in the Granville District and settlers in the other districts, particularly in the south of the colony.

A challenge from Cape Fear. Another source of conflict was unequal representation. The five old Albemarle counties had five representatives apiece in the colonial Assembly. However, each time a new county from the Cape Fear region in the south applied for representation, the Assembly allotted the new county only two representatives apiece. As more people settled in Cape Fear, the region demanded an equal voice in government. The people there demanded that the number of representatives in Albemarle be reduced to two per county.

This issue of unequal representation fueled sectionalism within the colony. As Moravian bishop August Gottlieb

Spangenberg explained, "North Carolina is a rather large province, and the condition of the inhabitants varies so greatly that often what is good for the southern part is bad for the northern, and vice versa, which leads to continual strife between the two sections."

A spokesperson for Cape Fear. Cape Fear had an able spokesperson in Governor Gabriel Johnston. Johnston played the game of politics well. In 1734, he moved his home—and therefore the capital—to Cape Fear. As ill feelings grew over the number of representatives from Albemarle, Johnston decided to use location to remedy what he felt was an injustice.

Johnston patiently waited for a time when bad weather made it impossible for Albemarle's representatives to reach the colonial Assembly in Cape Fear. He tried this tactic in 1741 by calling a session in Wilmington, a town in the Cape Fear region. However, enough Albemarle delegates arrived to control the Assembly. Johnston called the next three sessions in New Bern, a town between Albemarle and Cape Fear. Again, the Albemarle delegates turned out. Finally, in November 1746, bad weather struck, and Albemarle's delegates could not reach the Assembly in the south.

Although the Albemarle delegates could not attend the meeting in Cape Fear, they felt sure that the Assembly at Cape Fear would not meet without a **quorum**, or a majority of the members, present. However, they underestimated the anger of the people in the southern counties. With only 15 members out of 54 present, Samuel Swann, the Speaker of the House, called the session to order. Speaker Swann then notified Governor Johnston that the House was ready for business.

Once assembled, the southern counties proceeded to pass laws favorable to themselves. The Assembly raised quitrents in the north to match those in the south. It approved the permanent location of the capital in New Bern. Finally, it cut Albemarle's representation from five members from each county to two members apiece. Johnston dissolved the Assembly and sent the new laws to London for approval.

Albemarle in revolt. Needless to say, people in Albemarle called the Assembly a fraud. Northern delegates angrily protested to King George II. They then withdrew from the Assembly and even considered withdrawing from the colony as a whole. The issue hung in the balance for more than seven years. During this time, chaos reigned in the north. August Spangenberg described the situation as **anarchy,** or a complete absence of government. As you

Think as a Geographer

*T*oday the capital of North Carolina is Raleigh. ■ *To Do:* Find Raleigh on the map of North Carolina in the atlas section of the text. How do you think people in the Albemarle region and the Cape Fear region might have responded to having a capital in this site in the mid-1700s?

read his account, look for reasons that may have led him to this conclusion.

Arthur Dobbs was governor of North Carolina from 1754 to 1765. He was in office during the French and Indian War. During that period, settlement expanded in North Carolina and relations with other colonies were established.

Primary Source

> There is . . . in the older counties [Albemarle] a perfect anarchy. As a result, crimes are of frequent occurrence, such as murder, robbery, etc. But the criminals cannot be brought to justice. The citizens do not appear as jurors, and if court is held to decide such criminal matters no one is present. If anyone is imprisoned, the prison is broken open and no justice administered. In short most matters are decided by blows.

> — Records of the Moravians in North Carolina, vol. 1

Governor Johnston continued to run the colonial government. However, from 1747 to 1754, Albemarle ignored laws passed by the Assembly. Northern counties also refused to pay taxes or to use currency issued by the Assembly. The southern counties had no intention of carrying the burden of government alone. As a result, they refused to pay taxes, too.

Reunion. Governor Johnston died in 1752, and the crown appointed Arthur Dobbs to replace him. Dobbs, from Northern Ireland, settled at Brunswick in Cape Fear, where he looked out for southern interests. However, King George II ordered him to set aside the laws passed in 1746 by the southern counties. In 1754, Albemarle counties were once again entitled to send five representatives apiece to the Assembly. When the Assembly met the next time in New Bern, however, new troubles were brewing—this time in the western part of North Carolina. There, outspoken pioneers were criticizing eastern control of the colonial government.

Think Twice

1. Why was the Granville District created?
2. How did tax collections cause disputes among sections of the colonies?
3. How was unequal representation a cause of conflict among sections of the colony?
4. Why did anarchy develop in Albemarle County?
5. Governor Johnston used trickery to protect the interests of the south. (a) To what did this trickery lead? (b) Suggest a different approach that he might have chosen.

2 West Against East

People, Places, Terms

William Tryon
poll tax
Edmund Fanning
Regulator
War on Sugar Creek
amnesty
extortion
Battle of Alamance

After the death of Governor Dobbs in 1765, William Tryon became governor of the colony. In 1767, the new governor hired English architect John Hawks to begin work on a residence at New Bern. News of the grand project angered people in the backcountry of North Carolina. It would serve both as a capitol and a residence for the governor but in fact it was more like a palace. Fumed one westerner, "Not one man in twenty . . . will ever see this famous house when built."

When the people of Albemarle and Cape Fear heard about protests against the palace in the western regions, they united for once. They worried that westerners might try to move the seat of government to Hillsborough, the unofficial capital of the backcountry. As a result, they hastily approved construction of the governor's palace in New Bern.

Hawks designed an elegant two-story brick building trimmed with marble. In 1770, it stood completed, and the Assembly called the palace "truly elegant and noble." However, when tax officials showed up in the backcountry to collect duties to pay for the palace, westerners described it in far less flattering terms. Debate over the palace revealed the growing split between east and west in North Carolina.

Tryon Palace, New Bern. The wing on the right is original, but the remainder is a restoration.

An inscription on the back of this painting says it is a picture of William Tryon painted in New York in 1767 by John Wollaston. However, the uniform is not that of Tryon's British regiment. As a result, some people question whether the portrait is indeed of Tryon. Whether or not Tryon visited New York in 1767 is still unknown. Nonetheless, in 1771, the crown saw fit to appoint Tryon as New York's royal governor.

Government by the east. If Cape Fear felt it had little voice in the Assembly, the backcountry felt it had virtually none at all. Representation in the Assembly was by county rather than by population. As population in the backcountry increased, the Assembly created more counties in the west. At the same time, however, it created additional counties in the east. This tactic made sure that eastern counties would stay in control of colonial government.

As time passed, political inequalities became more glaring. Between 1740 and 1755, the Assembly carved out seven counties in the west and six in the east. Yet most of the population increase was in the west. By 1754, the six westernmost counties—Anson, Granville, Johnston, Orange, Cumberland, and Rowan—had 22,000 people and only 10 representatives. The remaining counties in the colony had 43,000 people and 45 representatives.

In the years ahead, the differences became even wider. In 1770, nearly one third of the colony's population of European descent lived in the west. However, only 15 representatives out of a total of 81 came from western counties.

The cost of the governor's palace. Construction of the governor's palace brought to a head the issue of unequal representation. The pioneers in the west objected not so much to the palace itself as to its cost. They also squawked loudly at the method of collecting taxes to pay for it. They did not protest the small duty placed on liquor, wine, and other alcoholic beverages. Because the pioneers made their own corn liquor and malt beer, they could escape this tax. However, they could not escape the **poll tax** enacted by the Assembly. This tax charged each person—rich and poor alike—at the same rate.

"Lighted from the Sky"

Tryon Palace in New Bern is named after William Tryon, the governor who oversaw its construction. The palace housed the colony's last two royal governors and the state's first independent Assembly. The inauguration of the first constitutional governor, Richard Caswell, also took place there. Looking at Tryon Palace in 1787, William Attmore wondered whether its elegance was fitting for a democratic people. However, he also saw its beauty, including "the grand Staircase lighted from the Sky by a low Dome. . . ."

In 1791, North Carolina used the palace to host a "magnificent ball" for President George Washington. In 1798, however, a fire destroyed all but the west wing of the building. Over the next decades, the surviving wing served a variety of functions from school building to warehouse to stable to chapel.

Then, in the 1950s, a New Bern native gave the state money, furniture, and art so that Tryon Palace could be authentically restored to all its original splendor. Today, people can visit the palace at New Bern and once again climb a staircase "lighted from the Sky."

Not only was money scarce in the backcountry, but the land in the backcountry was less productive. As a result, the poll tax seemed particularly unfair to these settlers. On August 2, 1768, citizens of Orange County put the matter clearly to a local sheriff. Said a poor farmer, "We are determined not to pay the Tax for the next three years, for the . . . Governor's House. We want no such House. . ."

Thirty citizens in Orange and Rowan counties also sent a petition to the Assembly. They addressed it to the wealthy planters and merchants who controlled the east. Its words drove home the hardships of pioneer life.

Primary Source

> Your Poor Petitioners have been continually Squez'd and oppressed by our Publick Officers. . . . Money is very scarce . . . and we exceeding Poor . . . On your Breath [word] depends the Ruin or Prosperity of poor Families, and so to Gentlemen Rowling in affluence [gentlemen rolling in wealth], a few shillings per man, may seem triffling yet to Poor People who must have their Bed and Bed clothes yea [even] their Wives Petticoats taken and sold to Defray [these charges, think] how Tremendous . . . the consequences [must be]. . . . To be concluded, it now depends on you whether we shall be made happy or miserable.

> — The Regulators in North Carolina, A Documentary History

Edmund Fanning, a native of Long Island, resettled in Hillsborough around 1760. Why might his style of dress have offended settlers in the backcountry?

Government by "foreigners." These political quarrels between the east and the west were exaggerated by other differences between the two regions. For example, the east was populated mostly by people of English descent and by Highland Scots. These groups built economies based in part on enslaved African labor and indentured servitude. The eastern gentry relished all the trappings of the upper class—from ruffled shirts to fancy titles. The west, on the other hand, belonged mostly to the Scots-Irish and Germans. These settlers built small farms based on free labor. They cherished social equality and looked down on the fashionable dress of men and women of the east.

Citizens in the west took special issue with the "foreigners" who gained influence in North Carolina government. Foreigners included all English officials sent to the colony, as well as royal officials who traveled to North Carolina from other American colonies. Many of these officials mixed with the colonial gentry, and the officials took a dim view of the "ruffians" to the west.

Governor William Tryon was a soldier by profession. As a soldier, he realized the value of the sword. However, he

*P*ictures, like written words, can present a point of view. An artist can emphasize certain details or ignore others. The picture at the bottom of this page was made many years after Tryon met the Regulators. ■ *To Do*: Analyze the artist's interpretation of events in the backcountry. How is Tryon depicted? How are the Regulators portrayed?

also recognized the power of compromise and tried to work with Assembly members from all of the regions.

More typical of royal officials of the time, however, was Edmund Fanning, one of Tryon's close friends. Fanning represented everything that westerners detested. A graduate of Yale, he loved the finer things in life—lace and gold buttons on his clothes, good books, a comfortable house, educated friends, and high position. To his equals or "social betters," Fanning proved a picture of charm and grace. To "common people," he revealed nothing but contempt. They willingly returned the same feeling.

Corruption in government. Unlike today, many public officials at the time received their offices as gifts from the crown or the royal governor. Instead of salaries, public officials in North Carolina received fees fixed by law and paid by the people. Collection of these fees earned public officials widespread scorn. In some cases, this scorn was well deserved, as corruption and bribery started creeping into the colonial government. In the backcountry, most officials worsened this situation by living and dressing like the eastern gentry. Wrote one pioneer, "To. . . [the country] come the merchant, the lawyer, the tavernkeeper, the artisans, and court officials, adventurers in the perenial [constant] pursuit of gain."

Most pioneers neither understood the royal system of government nor knew how to change it. At first they complained to the Assembly and governor. However, when these complaints fell on deaf ears, some western settlers began to take matters into their own hands. In the mid-1760s, a group of leaders in Orange County formed

This sketch shows Governor Tryon as he addresses a group of backcountry farmers at the time of the Regulator movement.

what became known as "an association for regulating public grievances and abuses of power." The name soon given to them was the **Regulators.**

The Regulators and the growth of conflict.   Protests and riots had taken place in the backcountry before. In 1765, for example, two landlords—Henry McCulloh and George Selwyn—owned land in Mecklenburg County. These two landlords sent surveyors to Mecklenburg County to map out their land for sale. However, squatters on this land soundly whipped the surveyors in what became known as the **War on Sugar Creek.** Governor Tryon offered **amnesty,** or pardon, to anyone who revealed the names of the riot leaders. Yet no names surfaced.

Another incident later that year further deepened the anger of western settlers against colonial government. Officials of the colonial government arrested George Sims, a schoolmaster and laborer, for not repaying a small debt. Sims, however, refused to suffer his arrest quietly. He issued a statement citing the names of officials who had abused their right to collect fees. The Assembly, however, completely ignored Sims's appeal for justice, continuing what westerners felt was the Assembly's abuse of power.

The conflict in 1766.   In response to abuses like these, the Regulators took action for the first time in 1766. Their leaders included Herman Husband, Rednap Howell, and James Hunter. Howell proved a gifted writer. He composed "ambling epics and jingling ballads" that poked fun at royal officials. One of Howell's targets was Tryon. Most pioneers knew that Tryon had not personally created their problems, but he was the leader of the government and the one responsible for enforcing laws. Therefore, he received regular blasts from Howell's pen. However, the most popular target by far was Edmund Fanning, who lived and collected fees in Orange County.

The conflict in 1768.   Conflict between the pioneers and provincial officials reached a peak in 1768. That year, officials set out to collect new taxes to pay for the governor's palace. Not only did many pioneers refuse to pay, but they also demanded an end to **extortion,** or the illegal fees demanded by some officials. Events quickened when a sheriff in Hillsborough seized a Regulator's horse, saddle, and bridle for nonpayment of taxes. In a burst of fury, the Regulators rode into Hillsborough and recovered the property. What's more, as they fled town, they fired shots into Fanning's home.

The Regulators then invited colonial officials to a meeting to discuss the situation. Edmund Fanning

*T*he differences between the north and the south in North Carolina were caused by political conflicts. The differences between east and west had to do with cultures, or ways of life. ■ *To Do*: Describe the cultural differences that separated the eastern and western sections of North Carolina in the 1700s. Then describe the culture, or way of life, that makes your community distinct. Identify some of the different cultures that are represented by people living in your own community.

declined, saying he would not explain his conduct to "the shallow understanding of the mob." Instead, he arrested two leaders of the Regulators, William Butler and Herman Husband, and sent them to jail. About 700 citizens, including many non-Regulators, threatened to storm the jail. This explosive turn of events prompted Governor Tryon to set out for Orange County with some 1,500 militia. When he arrived in Hillsborough, nearly 3,500 Regulators and their sympathizers were waiting for him.

Tension filled the air as the Orange County court convened in late 1768 to consider two sets of charges. Royal officials charged Husband, Butler, and two other Regulators with rioting. In turn, the pioneers charged Edmund Fanning with extortion. The court acquitted Husband and convicted the other three, but on Tryon's advice, the king pardoned the pioneers. The court also convicted Fanning. However, it ruled that Fanning had not knowingly violated the law and excused him from punishment. Tryon upheld this decision—leading the Regulators to believe that both the court and the governor had failed them.

The conflict of 1770.   If the Regulators had been willing to wait for the long slow process of law to take effect, legal solutions would have eventually solved their problems. In many quarters from the governor on down, officials recognized that changes were needed. However, the Regulators were short on patience.

In September 1770, a mob of 150 Regulators broke into the Hillsborough courthouse in Orange County. Armed with sticks and switches, they drove the judge from the bench. Next, they marched through the streets toward Fanning's home. According to one report, the Regulators dragged Fanning down the courthouse stairs by his heels, banging his head on every step. Before leaving town, the Regulators whipped Fanning, looted his home, and smashed windows throughout Hillsborough.

Neither Tryon nor the Assembly could ignore such lawlessness. The Assembly proclaimed the rioters to be outlaws. The Regulators used the same label to describe all royal officials. In May 1771, Tryon set out to restore order. Along the Great Alamance Creek, a force of 1,450 militia of the colony faced 2,000 Regulators. Tryon demanded that the Regulators lay down their arms or his troops would fire on them. Replied the Regulators, "Fire and be damned!" Tryon obliged them.

For nearly two hours, a battle raged until Tryon's military force carried the day for the colonial government. In the aftermath, the governor showed great restraint. The government executed a total of six rebels for treason.

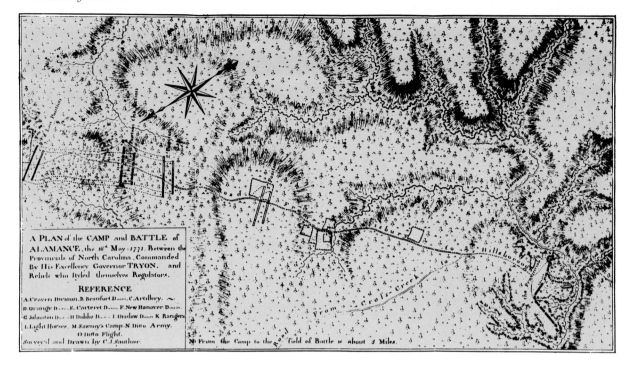

A PLAN of the CAMP and BATTLE of ALAMANCE, the 16ᵗʰ May 1771. Between the Provincials of North Carolina, Commanded By His Excellency Governor TRYON, and Rebels who styled themselves Regulators.

REFERENCE

A. Craven Division. B. Beaufort D..... C. Artillery.
D. Orange D..... E. Carteret D..... F. New Hanover D.....
G. Johnston D..... H. Dobbs D..... I. Onslow D..... K. Rangers.
L. Light Horses. M. Enemy's Camp. N. Ditto Army.
O. Ditto Flight.
Surveyd and Drawn by C.J. Sauthier.

N. From the Camp to the field of Battle is about 5 Miles.

However, Tryon pardoned thousands of others in exchange for their oaths of allegiance to the colonial government.

Although the **Battle of Alamance** ended the Regulator movement, the division between east and west remained. Western protests, however, were soon drowned out by even louder protests in the American colonies against the royal British government. Many eastern North Carolinians had already thrown in their lot with these colonial rebels—called Patriots. The Patriots called for nothing less than complete independence from Great Britain. Western North Carolinians now had to decide whether they would join the movement for independence from Britain.

Maps Matter

The map on this page is a primary source. It was drawn by a Swiss military surveyor named Claude Joseph Sauthier. Sauthier accompanied Tryon to the Great Alamance Creek. ■ *To Do:* How does Sauthier use a north pointer to indicate the site of battle?

Think Twice

1. In what specific ways did eastern and western North Carolina differ?
2. Describe at least two issues that divided the two sections.
3. (a) Who were the Regulators? (b) What prompted them to take action?
4. Describe the conflict that arose in 1768 between the pioneers and the provincial officers.
5. How did the Hillsborough riot in 1770 lead to the Battle of Alamance?
6. Imagine you are a Regulator. Would you side with Great Britain or the Patriots in the struggle for independence?

Chapter 9 Review

Choose from the following menu of activities.

Think Back: Main Ideas

To understand the sectionalism that developed within North Carolina, answer the following questions.

1. How did northern counties gain control of government?
2. How did this tactic lead to friction with the southern counties of Cape Fear?
3. How did the creation of western counties force an uneasy alliance between Albemarle and Cape Fear?
4. (a) What issues led to the rise of the Regulator movement? (b) Why did the assembly and governor take up arms against the Regulators?
5. How did the outbreak of the American Revolution interrupt the quarrel between the eastern and western sections of North Carolina?

Maps Matter

To link past with present, use the County Map of North Carolina in the atlas section of your text and the Regions of North Carolina map on page 3 of your text to answer the following questions.

1. How many counties exist in North Carolina today?

2. The Piedmont is a geographic divider between the eastern and western sections of North Carolina. (a) Roughly how many counties exist today east of the Piedmont? (b) How many counties exist west of the Piedmont?

3. Compare the two answers that you came up with for question 2. Which part of North Carolina today has more counties—the East or the West?

Word Wizard

Below are several terms from this chapter and the Greek or Latin roots from which they are derived. For each term, write a sentence explaining the connection between the root and the English term derived from it. (The translation of each root appears in parentheses.)

1. anarchy/*anarchos* (Greek for "without a leader")
2. amnesty/*amnestia* (Greek for "a forgetting")
3. extortion/*extortus* (Latin for "to twist or to wring")

Working Cooperatively

Working in small groups, review Tryon's treatment of the western counties. Prepare to support or condemn his actions in a classroom trial.

Curriculum Connection

Below are lyrics taken from a poem written by Rednap Howell, "poet of the Regulation."

When Fanning First to Orange Came.
When Fanning first to Orange came,
He look'd both pale and wan:
An old patch'd coat upon his back,
An old mare he rode on,
Both man and mare wa'nt worth five pounds,
As I've been often told;
But by his civil robberies,
He's laced his coat with gold.

1. How does Howell describe Fanning upon his arrival in Orange Country?
2. How did Fanning enrich himself?
3. Based on information in the text, evaluate the inaccuracies and/or accuracies of Howell's description of Fanning.
4. Why might Howell have exaggerated certain details?

Learning through Literature

The Wind in the Forest, by Inglis Fletcher
The Devil's Brigadier, by Don Ryan

UNIT 4

Towards a New Nation

NORTH CAROLINA

Time Line

THE AMERICAS

1754 French and Indian War begins.

1763 Pontiac's Rebellion leads to the Proclamation of 1763.
Treaty of Paris signed.

1764 Britain passes Sugar Act.

War on Sugar Creek 1765
Resistance to Stamp Act in North Carolina.
Tryon becomes governor.

1765 Parliament enacts Stamp Act and Quartering Act.

1766 Stamp Act is repealed.

Non-Importation 1769
Association's plan adopted by North Carolina.

1770 Boston Massacre

Battle of Alamance 1771

1773 Boston Tea Party

Edenton Tea Party 1774

1774 "Intolerable Acts" are passed by Parliament.
First Continental Congress

Mecklenburg Resolves 1775
Governor Martin flees from New Bern.

1775 War for Independence begins.
Second Continental Congress

Battle of Moores Creek Bridge 1776
The Halifax Resolves

1776 Declaration of Independence

Battle of Ramsour's Mill 1780

1781 Articles of Confederation

1787 Shays' Rebellion

Convention in Hillsborough 1788
declines to ratify Constitution.

1788 U.S. Constitution becomes law.

Convention in Fayetteville 1789
ratifies Constitution.

1789 George Washington becomes first President.

James Iredell is appointed to 1790
first U.S. Supreme Court.

1791 Bill of Rights

Raleigh becomes first state 1792
capital of North Carolina.

University of North Carolina 1795
opens.

1803 Louisiana Purchase

1812 War of 1812 begins.

1814 Peace treaty ends War of 1812.

What's Ahead

Chapter **10**
Quarrels with England

Chapter **11**
The War for Independence

Chapter **12**
A New Nation Grows

Quarrels with England

England proclaims a "New Colonial Policy."

Early in colonial history, England paid scant attention to its struggling colonies on the other side of the Atlantic, and the colonists were free to run their own affairs. England regarded the American colonies as a business investment, and North Carolina was simply a small part of the British commercial system. By the mid-1700s, though, the colonies had turned into profitable enterprises. In 1752, for example, North Carolina exported 61,528 barrels of tar, 12,055 barrels of pitch, 10,429 barrels of turpentine, 762,000 wooden shingles, 61,580 bushels of corn, 100,000 hogsheads of tobacco, and huge quantities of other goods. Needless to say, England began to believe the time had come for colonists to share in the costs of the empire. In 1763, after an expensive war with France, England enacted a series of laws to establish what came to be called "the New Colonial Policy." The colonists responded with ringing protests.

Colonists struggle to unite.

Some English officials snickered at the thought of 13 separate colonies uniting to resist England. They had only to recall the divisions between eastern and western North Carolina. If the colonies ever sought independence, remarked one traveler, "there would be a civil war from one end of the continent to the other." As events unfolded, however, colonists astounded the world by rallying behind a common cry: Liberty and Freedom!

A cartoon urging colonists to unite for revolution ▶

Think Ahead

As you can see by the cartoon on this page, some colonists in the mid-1700s began to think of unity among the colonies. As you read through this chapter, trace events that led colonists to draw together. Pay particular attention to instances in which North Carolinians took action with other colonists.

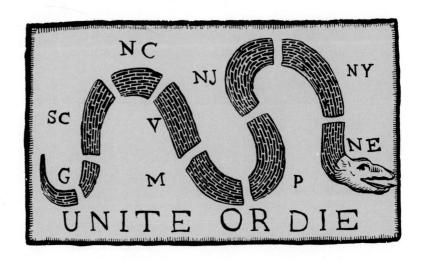

1 Orders from Abroad

People, Places, Terms

George Burrington
veto

In the early 1700s, no direct mail service linked the colonies with the home country. It took from two months to two and a half years for a letter to cross the Atlantic. Pirates or enemies of England boarded ships and stole cargo—including mailbags. Sometimes ships sank in storms. Other times, ships headed first to ports in Africa or the West Indies. Officials in England once waited three years to hear from the governor of North Carolina.

People with pressing business in England often made the wave-tossed journey themselves rather than risk losing their letters. In 1729, George Burrington hastened across the Atlantic to convince the crown to appoint him the first royal governor of North Carolina. Burrington received his commission in January 1730. However, he had to wait nearly a year for his instructions. In the meantime, business went on as usual in North Carolina. Sir Richard Everard, the colony's last Proprietary governor, continued to serve. However, the people of North Carolinia knew a change was in the air. The new governor, George Burrington, would no longer report to a group of private Proprietors. His orders would come instead from a higher authority—King George II of England.

Defending the interests of empire.   When North Carolina became a royal colony, it fell under the jurisdiction, or power, of the English Board of Trade. Members of this board advised the king on colonial policy. In the 1730s, the board wanted to bind the colonies and England together in one large empire. To achieve this goal, the crown appointed all royal governors and judges in the colonies. Royal officials held their positions only so long as they enjoyed the favor of the crown. In addition, the colonial assemblies paid the salaries of most royal officials, but the board fixed the amount of those salaries. These tactics made royal colonial officials more dependent upon England—one of the board's primary goals.

As a royal governor, Burrington came to North Carolina armed with new powers. The king and Parliament gave him the authority to decide how many assembly representatives had to be present for a quorum. They also allowed Burrington to **veto**, or overrule, colonial laws. Acting on the king's authority, Burrington could adjourn or dismiss colonial assemblies as he chose. The board ordered Burrington to use his royal powers to enforce the Navigation Acts.

The Navigation Acts had been passed by the English Parliament in 1660 and 1663. The purpose of these acts was to force the colonists to help the growing English shipping industry. The acts said that all goods shipped to and from the colonies had to be carried by ships that had been built in England or in English colonies and whose officers and crews were English. For the most part, the American colonists freely ignored the Navigation Acts.

Lumber, produced at sawmills such as the one shown here, was a major colonial export. The English believed that the colonies existed mainly to buy their home country's manufactured goods and to supply it with raw materials.

Defending the interests of the people.   England assumed that it had absolute authority over the colonies. The people of North Carolina, however, had other ideas. For years, the Proprietors had allowed the colonies to handle their own affairs. As a result, members of the Assembly saw themselves as a "little Parliament," or an extension of the English governing bodies. When Burrington tried to exert his power over the North Carolina Assembly, it angrily charged that England was trying to restrict North Carolina's charter. In February 1731, Burrington sent a report to England. It shows how the people of North Carolina had come to view royal authority.

Think as a Geographer

*D*istance between England and the 13 colonies helped weaken ties with the home country and pave the way for a distinctly American identity. Today geographic distances no longer separate people as they did in the 1700s. ■ *To Do*: List five technological advances that have broken down geographic distances and barriers between and among people. How have these advances helped create a "global world"?

Primary Source

   The people of North Carolina are neither to be cajoled [flattered] or outwitted. Whenever a governor attempts to effect anything by this means, he will lose his labor and show his ignorance [of the people].

   The inhabitants of North Carolina . . . [have] always behaved insolently [defiantly] to their governors; some they have imprisoned, others they have drove out of the country, and at other times set up a governor of their own choice, supported by men under arms.

— GEORGE BURRINGTON *"Letter to the Board of Trade"*

Controversies between the Assembly and the royal governor marked the entire period from 1731 when Burrington became governor until the American Revolution. Some governors during this time proved more able than others in dealing with the Assembly. Conflict always existed, however, and the source of the conflict was disagreement about the role of the colonial assemblies. Were assemblies the elected representatives of the colonists? Or did they exist simply to carry out the orders of the king? The people of North Carolina and other colonists chose the first view. That is, they believed that colonial assemblies existed to make laws for and carry out the wishes of the colonists. Most officials in England believed differently. To them, the colonial assemblies existed only to carry out the orders from England. As you will read, the 13 colonies eventually united over this very question.

Maps Matter

This map shows the number of North Carolina counties by 1775.
■ *To Do:* How many counties existed at that time? How do you think the organization of colonies by counties strengthened the idea of representative government?

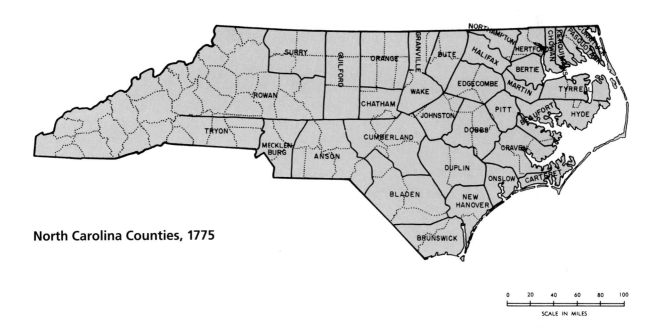

North Carolina Counties, 1775

SCALE IN MILES
0 20 40 60 80 100

Think Twice

1. How did government in North Carolina change after 1731?
2. As a royal governor, what powers did George Burrington have?
3. How did the views of the people of North Carolina and the views of the English differ on colonial government?
4. What role do you think geographic distance played in the growing differences between American colonists and the British government?

People, Places, Terms

George Washington
French and Indian War
Benjamin Franklin
Albany Congress
Treaty of Paris

2   A Contest for Empire

On October 31, 1753, George Washington set out on a dangerous mission. He carried a letter from Governor Robert Dinwiddie of Virginia demanding that the French depart from the rich Ohio River valley, an area that lay in part on the Virginia frontier and was claimed by both England and France. For two months, Washington trudged through deep snows, pathless forests, and frozen swamps. Finally, in late December, he reached a French fort south of Lake Erie in what is today Pennsylvania. The French commander scoffed at the letter handed over by Washington. He insisted that the Ohio River valley belonged to France. Any British colonist crossing into French territory, warned the commander, would be taken prisoner. The English now had a decision to make—lose the Ohio River valley or fight.

Beginnings of the French and Indian War. In May 1754, about four months after Washington's meeting with the French commander, Governor Dinwiddie ordered Washington to build a fort where the Allegheny and Monongahela rivers join to form the Ohio River. Washington soon learned, however, that the French had already built Fort Duquesne (du KANE) on this very site. Washington knew he could not capture a well-armed fort. Therefore, he chose an easier target—a band of French troops camped just outside the fort. Before attacking, Washington ordered the hasty construction of a rough fort named Fort Necessity.

On the evening of May 27, 1754, Washington crept up on the French camp. As the first rays of dawn crossed the sky, he attacked. In a 15-minute volley, his militia killed 10 French soldiers and captured 22 others. Washington later wrote to his brother, "I heard the bullets whistle, and, believe me, there is something charming in the sound."

Washington's victory was short-lived, however. On July 3, the French surrounded Washington at Fort Necessity. After a day of intense fighting, Washington surrendered. The French sent him back to Virginia with a message: Stay out of French territory!

News of the fighting spread like wildfire. Governor Dinwiddie requested help from North Carolina and other neighboring colonies. The British ordered troops to set sail for America. Remarked British author Horace Walpole, "The volley fired by this young Virginian [George Washington] in the forests of America has set the world in flames." It was the beginning of the war that American colonists called the **French and Indian War.** It lasted from 1754 to 1763.

This painting shows George Washington as colonel in the Virginia militia.

An alliance with the Iroquois. Even before Washington's encounter with the French at Fort Necessity in 1754, Great Britain had anticipated a war with the French over the Ohio Valley. To help in the war against the French, Great Britain asked its northern colonies to form an alliance with the powerful Iroquois.

In June 1754, while Washington was defending Fort Necessity against the French, a meeting opened in Albany, New York, to discuss the proposed alliance. Attending were delegates from seven colonies—New Hampshire, Massachusetts, Connecticut, Rhode Island, Pennsylvania, Maryland, and New York. The Iroquois attended the meeting. Rather than offering support to the English, they challenged English strength. "Look at the French," said one chief. "They are fortifying everywhere—but, we are ashamed to say it, you are . . . without fortifications." The Iroquois accepted wagonloads of gifts. However, they made few promises in return.

Unity rejected. Benjamin Franklin, a delegate from Pennsylvania, saw the meeting as an opportunity for another kind of alliance. At the so-called **Albany Congress**, he presented a plan for a union among the colonies. The plan proposed a Grand Council made up of representatives from the colonies and a "president general" appointed by King George II. Franklin believed that trouble brewing along the western frontier had made the time right for union among the colonies. To illustrate his views, Franklin published a cartoon of a divided snake in his paper, the *Pennsylvania Gazette.* The cartoon carried the grim warning, "Join, or Die."

By the time the Albany Plan of Union reached the other colonies, they were buzzing with talk of Washington's defeat at Fort Necessity. In North Carolina, the Assembly ordered Franklin's plan printed for discussion at a later time. However, there is no evidence that copies were ever printed or that the matter was taken up again. In the end, only Massachusetts seriously debated the plan. An angry Franklin complained, "Everyone cries, a union is necessary, but when they come to the manner and form of the union, their weak noodles [heads] are perfectly distracted."

North Carolina to the rescue. What the North Carolina Assembly did review in 1754 was Virginia Governor Dinwiddie's request for help following Washington's defeat at Fort Necessity. Before adjourning, members agreed to send troops to Virginia and to levy a special tax for defense of the frontier. North Carolina chose Colonel James Innes who led some 450 militia from North Carolina

JOIN, or DIE.

This original cartoon expressed Franklin's views that colonists should work together to form an alliance, or union, among the colonies. The slogan on the cartoon was changed to "Unite or Die" during the American Revolution. (See page 128)

This crude stone marker in Thyatira churchyard in Rowan County, identifies the grave of 19-year-old Richard King, killed during the French and Indian War.

to meet with Washington. The two leaders agreed to build a fort at the headwaters of the Potomac River. The new fort was called Fort Cumberland.

Innes took command of the fort. He then waited for the arrival of British General Edward Braddock, who would lead the North Carolina militiamen on an attack on the French fort, Fort Duquesne. Events conspired so that Innes and Braddock never met.

Braddock in charge. In June 1755, General Braddock set out once again to defeat the French. Seasoned on the battlefields of Europe, the 60-year-old Braddock expected to fight against the French on open battlefields. Therefore, Braddock ordered troops to cut a rough wilderness road for cartloads of artillery and supplies. His soldiers were easy targets as they marched over the road in bright scarlet uniforms, stepping to the sound of fife and drum.

Several colonial militia units marched with them. Washington rode at the head of the Virginians. General Edward Brice Dobbs, son of Governor Arthur Dobbs, led some 84 North Carolinians, including a band of North Carolina Rangers headed by Major Hugh Waddell. The Rangers were groups of men who rode up and down the frontier to keep roaming bands of Native Americans from disturbing either local Native Americans or settlers. Both Washington and Dobbs warned Braddock that his troops made an easy target for French bullets. Braddock, however, refused to give up the march. One North Carolinian described him as "a bird ready for the snare."

On July 9, the nightmare feared by colonists struck. Nearly 250 French and some 600 Native Americans allied with the French launched a surprise attack. They darted out from behind rocks and trees, picking off red-coated soldiers. Braddock kept his soldiers in tight formation. Washington and Innes, on the other hand, ordered their soldiers to fight "frontier style." The battle proved a miserable defeat for the British. Out of almost 2,000 troops, nearly 900 fell dead or wounded. Washington had two horses shot out from under him. Four bullets seared through his uniform. Another bullet fatally hit Braddock. In the retreat that followed, recalled Washington, the British "broke and ran as sheep pursued by dogs."

A North Carolina victory. At the start of the war, some Native Americans allied with the British. However, most sided with their French fur-trading partners. The French, unlike the English, had taken little Native American land. Many Native Americans, therefore, used the war as an opportunity to strike at English frontier settlements from

New York to Georgia. In North Carolina, Moravians in Bethabara built a stockade to protect themselves. Other settlers also barricaded themselves behind wooden walls. Despite their efforts, there was a terrible loss of life.

In 1755, the North Carolina Assembly approved money to build a fort where settlers could take refuge from Native Americans. Major Hugh Waddell from the Lower Cape Fear took charge of the project. In 1757, he oversaw construction of Fort Dobbs, a few miles north of present-day Statesville. In the winter of 1758, Waddell and about 300 North Carolinians left the fort to support the British fighting the French once again at Fort Duquesne. Disguised as Native Americans, Waddell and another North Carolinian, John Rogers, captured a Native American who knew the layout of the fort. Waddell thus won information that allowed the British to drive the French from Fort Duquesne. Once in control of Fort Duquesne, the British renamed it Fort Pitt, after British Prime Minister William Pitt.

A world conflict. The skirmishes in the Ohio River valley between the French and Native Americans on one side and the British and American colonists on the other side is known as the French and Indian War. This war, which broke out in 1754, was part of a large war for empires being fought among England, France, and Spain.

The Great Wars for Empire started in 1689 and continued on and off into the mid-1700s. For much of the time, the Great Wars for Empire had a direct effect on North Carolina. The people of North Carolina needed protection from two European nations involved in the Great Wars for Empire— the Spanish in Florida and the French along the western frontier. They also faced constant threats from Native Americans. Fearful of losing their lands, the Native Americans made alliances from time to time with either the Spanish or the French—whatever group seemed most able to protect them from England's hold in the Americas.

The British victory at Quebec. British Prime Minister Pitt himself took over the war in the Americas in 1757. Through brilliant planning, he turned the tide of war in Britain's favor. In 1759, under Pitt's leadership, British General James Wolfe captured Quebec at the cost of his own life. This victory gave Britain control of New France.

However, a war still raged along the western frontier. As the 1760s opened, colonists from Virginia to Georgia found themselves in battles with the Cherokee, Creek, Choctaw, Chickasaw, and Catawba. In February 1760, the Cherokee attacked Fort Dobbs, but the North Carolinians beat back the attack. Then, in June 1760, the Cherokee ambushed a

This drawing shows the bookplate used by Hugh Waddell. The Latin inscription means, "A mind that knows the difference between right and wrong." What does the saying tell you about Waddell?

British force of 1,600 Scottish Highlanders at Echoe in the southwestern corner of modern North Carolina. This time, the Cherokee won.

In 1761, militia from Virginia, North Carolina, and South Carolina joined with the British to drive the Cherokee into the mountains. As the troops pushed the Cherokee westward, the colonial militia burned the Cherokee fields and villages.

Peace treaties of 1763. Although local skirmishes continued along the frontier between 1760 and 1763, the British victory at Quebec in 1759 had decided the war's outcome in Britain's favor. In November 1763, Governor Dobbs of North Carolina attended a peace conference in Augusta, Georgia. Along with 25 Native American chiefs,

Maps Matter

The map to the right is a historical map. It shows at a glance how the Treaty of Paris changed the political geography of North America.

■ *To Do:* What lands did Britain hold prior to 1763? What lands did it acquire as a result of its war with France?

British North America, 1763

ARCTIC OCEAN

RUSSIAN TERRITORY

HUDSON'S BAY COMPANY

Hudson Bay

NEWFOUND-LAND

Quebec
Montreal

NOVA SCOTIA

Boston
New York
Philadelphia

LOUISIANA

THE THIRTEEN COLONIES

MISSISSIPPI R.

SPANISH

TERRITORY

Charleston

New Orleans   FLORIDA

ATLANTIC OCEAN

Gulf of Mexico

PACIFIC OCEAN

WEST INDIES

CUBA

PUERTO RICO

BELIZE   JAMAICA   HISPANIOLA

SOUTH AMERICA

KEY

British territory before 1763

Acquired from France

Acquired from Spain

0   800 Miles

General Wolfe's forces on the St. Lawrence River near Quebec. Wolfe's capture of Quebec gave Britain control of New France

four colonial governors, and a British official, Dobbs helped to negotiate the terms of a peace treaty. That same year, the British signed the **Treaty of Paris,** officially ending their war with France. Under this treaty, Great Britain won what is now Canada and most of the French holdings east of the Mississippi. English colonists suddenly found themselves part of one of the world's greatest empires.

For a short time, good spirits prevailed. Colonists up and down the Atlantic coast celebrated their ties with Great Britain. They looked west and saw land for the taking. However, the bonds of affection proved to be short-lived. Officials in London had new plans for their empire—plans that conflicted sharply with those of the colonists.

Think Twice

1. (a) What nation had control of the Ohio River valley in 1753? (b) What nation wanted to gain control of it?
2. Describe General Washington's first encounter with the French in 1754 at Fort Necessity.
3. (a) What Native American group did the British try to entice to help in the British war with France? (b) Did the plan work?
4. Describe the Albany Congress. (a) What plans did Franklin propose at the Congress? (b) How did the colonists respond to the plan?
5. (a) Why did Washington and Governor Dobbs describe the British general as a "bird ready for the snare" in the battle in 1755 between the British and the French? (b) Were Washington and Dobbs correct? Explain your answer.
6. The Treaty of Paris brought an end to the French and Indian War. Do you think the British could have won this war without colonial support? Why or why not?

3 The Road to Revolution

In January 1763, Native Americans in the Ohio River valley learned about the terms of the Treaty of Paris. Some groups, such as the Delaware, had already lost their homelands along the Atlantic coast. They had no intention of giving up yet more territory to the land-hungry British. In May, Native Americans in the Ohio Valley found a leader in Ottawa Chief Pontiac. George Croghan, an Irish trader in the region, described Pontiac as "shrewd, sensible, [and] of few words." He also warned,"Pontiac commands more respect amongst these [Native American] nations than any [person] I have ever seen."

A new proclamation. Throughout the summer of 1763, a total of 40 different Native American groups banded together under Pontiac. Together they attacked one British settlement after another. When word of what became known as Pontiac's Rebellion reached London, King George III decided to act. That October, he signed the **Proclamation of 1763.** This act drew an imaginary line down the spine of the Appalachian Mountains. It temporarily closed all lands west of the line to colonial settlement by English colonists. The king hoped to avoid another costly war with the Native Americans. The tactic worked. Pontiac agreed to end the fighting. Only a handful of the many colonists living in the Ohio River valley protested the proclamation. In the end the colonists were no match for the British army who forced out the settlers by burning the settlers' cabins.

Britain's new colonial policy. With so much unrest in the colonies, the British government decided to keep an army in North America. The British soldiers would also protect colonists from the Spaniards to the south. Around 10,000 red-coated British soldiers arrived in 1764. England claimed the soldiers had come to protect English claims in the Americas. However, colonists feared that England intended to use the army to enforce unpopular British laws.

It was at this time that Britain unveiled its new colonial policy. English citizens in the British Isles already felt the weight of taxes incurred by the French and Indian War. Therefore, Britain decided to shift some of the tax burden to its American colonies. After all, reasoned the British, had Britain not fought that war for the benefit of the colonies?

King George III came to power in 1760 at age 25. The willful young king promised to be more than a symbol. "I will be a king," promised George.

The Sugar Act and the Quartering Act.   The first laws of the New Colonial Policy arrived on the heels of the British army. In 1764, Britain passed the **Sugar Act.** This law raised the duties on luxury items such as wine and silk that Britain sold to the colonies. This meant that colonists would have to pay more money for these items.

The Sugar Act also affected the tax on molasses, which was produced in two different places. One was the British West Indies, which did not make enough molasses to satisfy the sweet tooths of colonists. The other was the non-British West Indies which had a plentiful supply.

In the past, the British had placed a high duty on molasses that the colonies purchased from the non-British West Indies. However, the colonists defied the duty by smuggling molasses from France or by bribing officers. Although the Sugar Act lowered the duty on molasses from the non-British West Indies, the Sugar Act was to be strictly enforced. As a result, King George III armed royal tax collectors with the right to search warehouses for smuggled items.

In early 1765, Parliament enacted the **Quartering Act**. This law required colonies to feed and shelter British troops stationed in the Americas. As it turned out, most troops set up home in port cities—the centers of colonial trade.

The effect on North Carolina.   The Sugar Act and the Quartering Act affected colonies to the north far more than North Carolina. New England merchants complained loudly over the new duties. They resented royal tax collectors who flourished **writs of assistance,** or search warrants. Northern colonies also protested loudly over the thousands of troops stationed in port cities. Agricultural North Carolina, one of the few colonies without a major port, escaped the full weight of these laws. However, North Carolina did feel the full impact of another law.

The Stamp Act.   Within weeks of learning of the Quartering Act, colonists heard of a new law—the **Stamp Act.** According to this law, the colonists had to pay for stamps printed on taxable paper items, such as playing cards, deeds, licenses, newspapers, contracts, pamphlets, and other printed materials. The stamp was proof that the tax had been paid.

Britain expected little reaction to the law because such a tax had been in effect in England for nearly 75 years. The British people had representatives in Parliament who voted for or against taxes. Since the American colonists were not represented in Parliament, they argued that Parliament had no right to tax them. Only colonial

These are examples of stamps the colonists were expected to use on paper items. Stamps in 1765 were imprints rather than the gum-backed stamps used today.

Think as a Historian

*P*rimary sources about the past include more than written material. Primary sources may also include objects made in the past, such as stamps. ■ *To Do*: Study the stamps on this page. What do the crowns on these stamps symbolize?

Women also organized into Patriot groups called the Daughters of Liberty. Notice that the woman is wearing a man's hat and holding a gun and powder horn.

assemblies or legislatures had that right. As an act of courtesy, Parliament asked colonial assemblies to suggest alternative taxes. When no suggestions appeared, Parliament allowed the Stamp Act to go into effect on November 1, 1765.

The effect of the Stamp Act.   British officials had misjudged the mood of the American colonists. Opponents to the Stamp Act soon swung into action. Virginia reacted first. A group of firebrands in the Virginia Assembly delivered heated speeches attacking Britain's right to tax the colonies. Patrick Henry, known as "the very devil in politics," charged that the Stamp Act threatened colonial liberty. He came within a breath of calling King George III a tyrant. The speaker, or the one in charge, of the Virginia Assembly warned Patrick Henry of committing **treason,** or betrayal of one's country. According to legend, Henry reportedly muttered,"If this be treason, make the most if it."

Massachusetts acted next. In June 1765, it invited the colonies to send delegates to a Stamp Act Congress. The congress would meet in New York City in October of 1765. Before the congress assembled, however, mobs took to the streets of Boston. In August, they looted the homes of the royal governor and the colonial stamp agent. The mobs called themselves "Sons of Liberty" because anyone who told the colonists to obey the Stamp Act was an enemy of liberty. British officials, on the other hand, labeled the protestors "lawless rabble-rousers."

Protest in North Carolina.   The Stamp Act Congress met in October 1765. However, it did not include delegates from North Carolina. Governor Tryon of North Carolina, who had replaced Governor Dobbs in late 1764, refused to allow the North Carolina Assembly to meet to elect a delegate to the congress. Nonetheless, the people of North Carolina applauded actions taken by the Stamp Act Congress. In firm, polite words, the members of the Stamp Act Congress accepted Britain's right to make laws for the empire. At the same time, delegates rejected the right of Parliament to tax the colonies. Only colonial assemblies made up of elected representatives had that right, said the congress.

Despite the resolves of the Stamp Act Congress, the Stamp Act went into effect on schedule. Although North Carolina had sent no delegates, the people of North Carolina did not accept the Stamp Act quietly. Even before the meeting of the Stamp Act Congress, the citizens of Wilmington had organized its own group of Sons of Liberty. The Wilmington Sons of Liberty raised their voices in a popular toast, "Liberty, Property, and no Stamp Duty!" Soon Cape Fear became a hotbed of protest. Governor Tryon tried to convince a group of leading merchants in the area to obey the law. But they vowed to resist it to the utmost of their power.

North Carolina protests continued in November 1765. That month a ship named the *Diligence* arrived off the coast of Brunswick, North Carolina, with the first stamped paper. Local Sons of Liberty prevented the paper from being landed. Later, in January 1766, a British ship named the *Viper* prevented two colonial ships without stamped clearance papers from sailing down the Cape Fear River. The people of North Carolinia responded by refusing to sell supplies to British ships. They also arrested a group of British sailors who set foot in Wilmington. Despite all efforts by Governor Tryon, the people of North Carolinia kept the hated stamped papers off their shores.

The North Carolina Sons of Liberty included some of the colony's most distinguished citizens: Hugh Waddell, hero of the French and Indian War; John Ashe, speaker of the Assembly; and Cornelius Harnett and James Moore, members of the Assembly. Although they neither destroyed property nor hid their identities, they steadfastly disobeyed what they considered to be an unjust law. Governor Tryon refused to speak with the Sons of Liberty unless they put down their arms. At the same time, he upheld their right to petition peacefully. Needless to say, both sides breathed easier when Parliament **repealed,** or withdrew, the unpopular law in March 1766.

New taxes.   The colonists' joy over the end of the Stamp Act did not last long. The British Parliament still believed it had the right to tax the colonies. In 1767, it levied a new set of duties on English tea, glass, paint, and lead sold in the colonies. Parliament intended to use the fees to pay the salaries of all royal officials.

News of this action prompted a burst of outrage among colonists. This time, the Massachusetts Assembly devised a new method of protest. It sent what was known as a circular letter to the assemblies in all of the colonies. The letter invited colonists to join a **boycott,** or refusal to buy certain items.

The North Carolina reaction.   John Harvey, the speaker or head of the North Carolina Assembly, introduced the circular letter to the North Carolina Assembly in 1768. Much to his disgust, the Assembly as a whole refused to take any formal action. Instead, members asked Harvey to reply to Massachusetts himself. The Assembly then wrote

King George III "an humble, dutiful, and loyal address" seeking repeal of the latest set of tax laws. The letter contained a phrase famous to colonists: "No taxation without representation."

The king expressed satisfaction at the obedience of the people of North Carolina. He had reacted too soon, though. Speaker Harvey sent a letter to the Massachusetts Assembly pledging that North Carolina stood ready to support other colonies in protesting unjust laws.

North Carolina and the Non-Importation Association. In 1768, Parliament ordered the royal governor of Massachusetts to dissolve that colony's Assembly unless it retracted the circular letter. When the Assembly ignored the order, the governor ended the meeting. Virginia quickly rose to the defense of Massachusetts. It drew up plans for a Non-Importation Association in which the colonists would refuse to buy any British goods. On November 2, 1769, Speaker Harvey presented the plan for the Non-Importation Association to North Carolina. The North Carolina Assembly adopted the plan without a single dissenting vote.

When Governor Tryon learned of the action, he dissolved the Assembly. Because the Assembly still had unfinished business, though, Speaker Harvey called upon members to "take measures for preserving the true and essential interests of the province." Of the 74 members who had attended the Assembly, 64 gathered in the New Bern courthouse. Two days later, they approved the Non-Importation Association. This was the first action taken by a colonial legislature independent of a governor. For this reason, when North Carolina celebrated the Bicentennial of the Revolution in 1976, license plates throughout the state carried the words: "First in Freedom."

The Boston Massacre. The Non-Importation Association was a stunning success. Reeling with the loss of business, British merchants demanded that Parliament repeal the unpopular laws. In 1770, Parliament bowed to pressure and eliminated all the taxes except the one on tea.

Celebration over the repeal lasted only a short time. On the night of March 5, 1770, trouble stirred anew in Boston. That evening, a group of colonists crowded around a British guard posted at the local tax office. First they hurled insults at the red-coated soldier: "You lobsterback!" "You bloodyback!" Soldiers and townspeople rushed to the scene. In the confusion that followed, shots rang out. Five colonists fell mortally wounded, including a formerly enslaved African named Crispus Attucks.

This engraving of the Boston Massacre was made by Paul Revere, a Boston silversmith.

Patriots, as the supporters of colonial liberty were known, used the event to enflame passions. Led by Samuel Adams, the Patriots circulated letters describing what they called the Boston Massacre. The letters vividly told how defenseless citizens had been cut down by British bullets. In the end, Britain brought the soldiers to trial. The trial resulted in the mild punishment of only one British soldier.

Tea parties, north and south.   For the next few years, people traded with England for most goods except tea. For a while, England accepted this situation. Then, in 1773, British tea merchants asked their government for help. Parliament responded with the Tea Act, which cut the price of tea sharply. However, the act had a flaw—it carried a tax.

Again, the Patriots of Boston took the lead in protesting a British action. On the night of December 16, 1773, a small band disguised themselves as Native Americans and boarded several tea ships anchored in Boston Harbor. In less than an hour, they dumped more than 300 chests of tea into the water.

A year later, a group of North Carolina women held a different sort of tea party. Led by Mrs. Penelope Barker, 51 "patriotic ladies" gathered in Edenton to support the Patriot cause. They signed an agreement vowing to do "every thing as far as lies in our power . . . [to promote] the publick good." Because this was one of the first organized protests by women, it attracted widespread attention. The London press mockingly called the event the Edenton Tea Party. When one London resident, Arthur Iredell, heard that his sister-in-law had a hand in the party, he wrote the following sarcastic letter to his brother.

Primary Source

I see by the newspapers the Edenton ladies have signalized themselves by their protest against tea-drinking. . . . Is there a female Congress at Edenton too? I hope not for we Englishmen are afraid of the male Congress, but if the ladies . . . should attack us, the most fatal consequence is to be dreaded. . . . The Edenton ladies . . . are willing, I imagine, to crush us into atoms. . . . The only security on our side . . . is the probability that there are but few places in America which possess such female artillery as Edenton.

— *Arthur Iredell, "Letter to his brother"*

The letter greatly underestimated the support of women to the cause of liberty. It was largely because of women that colonial boycotts succeeded.

This cartoon of the Edenton Tea Party was published in London in 1775. Penelope Barker and the other women at the Edenton Tea Party declared that they could not remain indifferent to whatever affected the peace and happiness of their country.

Across Cultures

Read the primary source letter written by Arthur Iredell about the Edenton Tea Party. ■ *To Do*: What can you infer from this letter about the way in which American women in the late 1700s were viewed? Compose a letter that might be written today. In your letter, reflect the roles of women in present-day society.

Richard Caswell was born in Joppa, Maryland, but at age 16, he moved to North Carolina. Trained as a surveyor, Caswell held a variety of offices that led him into politics. His experiences in the western section of North Carolina helped Caswell to understand the demands of the Regulators. He also sat in the North Carolina colonial Assembly, so he knew from firsthand experience the abuses of executive power.

He also knew how to fight. During the French and Indian War, Caswell marched off to battle with the North Carolina militia. Then, in 1775, Richard Caswell was among those who helped push Royal Governor Josiah Martin from power. When war finally broke out between the colonies and Great Britain, Caswell served loyally and well as wartime governor of North Carolina. He also guided North Carolina through the first trying years of colonial independence from Great Britain.

The Intolerable Acts. In 1774, furious at the destruction of the tea in Boston Harbor, Parliament sealed off the harbor until colonists paid for the damage. King George III appointed a new royal governor and placed the colony under military control. Colonists, finding their life unbearable, called these new actions the Intolerable Acts.

In 1774, the colonies once again organized a meeting known as the Continental Congress. It was to meet on September 5, 1774, in Philadelphia. Josiah Martin, who had replaced William Tryon as governor of North Carolina, made every effort to prevent North Carolina representatives from attending the First Continental Congress. He went so far as to disband the North Carolina Assembly so it could not send delegates. On July 21, 1774, Assembly members agreed to hold a Provincial Congress without Martin's approval. The decision placed North Carolina squarely on the road to revolution. It also set the stage for the removal of the colony's last royal governor. In May 1775, Josiah Martin fled for his life from the governor's palace.

Think Twice

1. Why did colonists challenge British taxes?
2. How did the people of North Carolina resist (a) the Stamp Act, and (b) the tax on tea?
3. How did the people of North Carolina support (a) the colonial Non-Importation Association, and (b) the First Continental Congress?
4. How did the organization of the North Carolina Provincial Congress reflect a long-standing tradition of legislative independence in North Carolina?

Chapter 10 Review

Choose from the following menu of activities.

Think Back: Main Ideas

Many British officials doubted 13 separate colonies could ever find cause to join together. Yet in little more than a decade colonists edged closer and closer toward forming a new nation. To understand the chain of events leading to unity, answer the following questions.

1. How did the French and Indian War help give colonists experience in working together?
2. How did Great Britain provide reasons for colonies to correspond with one another?
3. What experiences in North Carolina's past helped make North Carolina colonists willing to challenge royal authority?
4. How did formation of the Provincial Congress help commit North Carolina to a course of revolution?

Maps Matter

Use the map on page 136 for these questions.

1. Which lands east of the Mississippi did Spain hold prior to 1763?
2. Which country took control of that claim in 1763?
3. Which country controlled the lands directly west of the Mississippi River?
4. Where were Britain's largest holdings in North America before 1763?
5. What were the names of four cities in Britain's thirteen colonies?

Word Wizard

The definitions of some words appeal to the emotions. These so-called "loaded words" can influence opinion by their very use. Below is a list of loaded words used in the text narrative. Imagine you are a Son or Daughter of Liberty. Write a short paragraph in which you use each of these terms to influence public opinion against the British.

1. lobsterback
2. tyrant
3. massacre
4. Patriot
5. liberty

Working Cooperatively

A political cartoon expresses an opinion. Working in groups, draw a political cartoon about one of the events that you learned about in this chapter. Share your cartoons with your classmates.

Curriculum Connection

Below are lyrics taken from a poem written by a Daughter of Liberty. Read the lines carefully, and then answer the questions that follow.

*Let the Daughters of Liberty, nobly
  arise,
And tho' we've no Voice, but a negative
  here,
The use of the Taxables, let us forebear.
Stand firmly resolved and bid
[Prime Minister] Grenville to see
That rather than Freedom, we'll part with
  our Tea.*

1. What action does the poem call upon women to take?
2. What do you think the poet means by the words "tho' we've no Voice"?
3. What power does the poet imply women are fighting for?
4. How do these words compare with the description painted of women by Arthur Iredell on page 143?

Learning through Literature

Settlement on Shocco, by Manly Wade Wellman

145

The War for Independence

The news of events in colonial Massachusetts spreads.

Following the Boston Tea Party in 1773 and Parliament's harsh actions against the people of Boston, many colonists wondered if their colony would be next to suffer from Britain's **tyranny**, or unjust use of power. George Washington believed that all of the colonies must stand together; otherwise, he feared that each colony would fall alone. Many other colonists shared his fear.

The First Continental Congress meets in Philadelphia.

Colonial leaders organized a meeting to protest how the people in Massachusetts had been treated and to discuss how to avoid war with Britain. On September 5, 1774, representatives from every colony except Georgia gathered at Carpenters' Hall in Philadelphia. Among those who attended the First Continental Congress were Benjamin Franklin from Pennsylvania, Patrick Henry and George Washington from Virginia, cousins John and Samuel Adams from Massachusetts, and Richard Caswell, William Hooper, and Joseph Hewes from North Carolina. The representatives sent complaints to King George III and agreed to meet again in May.

Boston Tea Party ▶

Think Ahead

As quarrels between the colonists and the British continued, tension grew. Read about the outbreak of war in Massachusetts and how the American Revolution affected the other colonies. Find out about the role played by North Carolina in the war for independence from Britain.

The Fighting Begins

Few colonists wanted a war with Britain, yet many followed the advice of the First Continental Congress to prepare for battle. Ordinary citizens armed themselves and trained to fight. They called themselves **minutemen** because they could be ready to fight the British at a minute's notice.

The battles of Lexington and Concord. Tension between colonists and the British continued to grow. Patrick Henry called for war in a dramatic speech that he delivered at a meeting in Virginia. Here is part of the speech that he gave in March 1775.

Primary Source

> *The gentlemen may cry, Peace, peace! but there is no peace. The war has actually begun! The next gale that sweeps from the north will bring to our ears the clash of resounding arms! Our brethren are already in the field! Why stand we here idle? What is it that the gentlemen wish? What would they have? Is life so dear or peace so sweet as to be purchased at the price of chains and slavery? Forbid it, Almighty God. I know not what course others may take, but as for me, give me liberty or give me death!*
>
> — *PATRICK HENRY, "Speech to the Virginia Convention"*

People, Places, Terms

tyranny
minuteman
revolution
Loyalist
Patriot
Mecklenburg Resolves
Continental Congress
Declaration of Independence

On March 23, 1775, Patrick Henry gave his most famous speech, urging resistance to the acts of Parliament.

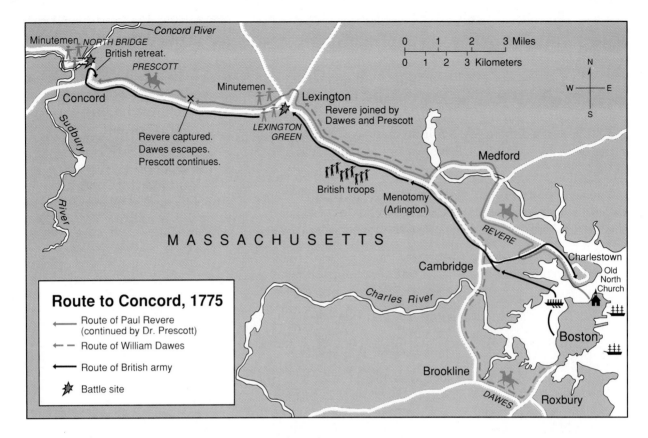

Route to Concord, 1775

← Route of Paul Revere (continued by Dr. Prescott)
←- - Route of William Dawes
← Route of British army
✦ Battle site

Maps Matter

A map can help you plan what route to take to a certain place.

■ *To Do*: Use the map that shows the route to Concord in 1775. Trace the routes that Paul Revere, William Dawes, and Dr. Samuel Prescott each followed to Lexington and Concord. Where did each man begin to ride? What towns did each man go through? Where did each man finally end his ride?

In Massachusetts, General Thomas Gage, the new governor, was ordered to arrest two leaders of the Sons of Liberty and to destroy any guns and gunpowder that minutemen had hidden. John Hancock and Samuel Adams were in Lexington, a village about 20 miles northwest of Boston, and weapons were thought to be stored in nearby Concord. On the night of April 18, 1775, about 700 British soldiers, known as redcoats because of their scarlet uniforms, marched in the moonlight toward Lexington.

The Sons of Liberty learned about the British plan and arranged to warn colonists in Lexington and Concord. Three messengers — Paul Revere, William Dawes, and Dr. Samuel Prescott — rode on horseback by different routes. Revere was captured by a British scouting party just after he left Lexington. On his way to Concord, Dawes was thrown from his horse, and he was also captured. Prescott managed to reach Concord and warn colonists that the British were coming.

By the time British soldiers reached Lexington, about 70 minutemen were waiting on the village green. Both minutemen and redcoats were under orders not to shoot, but a shot was suddenly fired. To this day, no one knows which side fired the first shot that sparked the Battle of Lexington.

After the 15-minute battle, which took place early on the morning of April 19, eight minutemen were dead. Another ten were wounded. At the Battle of Lexington, the tension between colonists and the British had finally exploded.

The British marched on to Concord but found few guns. At the North Bridge, three British soldiers were killed in the Battle of Concord. When the British headed back to Boston, hundreds of minutemen hidden behind farmhouses, stone fences, and barns fired at them, killing 73 men and injuring an additional 174 soldiers.

The shot "heard round the world" had started a **revolution**, or great change. The American Revolution would bring great changes to North America.

The Second Continental Congress. By the time news of the battles of Lexington and Concord reached the other colonies in May, the Second Continental Congress was already in session in Philadelphia. Representatives hoped to deal with the growing threat of war, but even as they discussed the problem, fighting spread to New York and continued in Massachusetts.

Representatives at the Second Continental Congress voted on June 14, 1775, to create an American army, called the Continental Army. George Washington was chosen to lead it.

The Battle of Bunker Hill. On June 17, 1775, one of the fiercest battles of the American Revolution took place north of Boston. To gain control of Charlestown Peninsula, Americans had secretly built a fort on Breed's Hill. The British were ordered to attack the fort and drive the Americans away.

Think as a Geographer

*T*he Americans built a fort on Breed's Hill, which was located on Charlestown Peninsula. A peninsula is land that is almost totally surrounded by water.

■ *To Do:* Study the painting on page 150 or look at an old map of Boston. What landforms and bodies of water do you see? Why do you think Americans chose to build a fort on Breed's Hill?

This painting, "The Battle of Lexington" by Doolittle and Barber, shows minutemen and British soldiers engaged in battle. Compare the two groups shown in the painting. Notice as many differences as you can. How do the two sides differ in position, dress, and number of men?

Although it is called the Battle of Bunker Hill, the battle actually took place on nearby Breed's Hill. This painting of the battle is believed to have been done by an eyewitness to the fight, Winthrop Chandler.

In the Battle of Bunker Hill, British ships shot cannons, and redcoats charged up Breed's Hill. The Americans fought bravely but ran out of gunpowder and had to retreat. More than 200 British soldiers and about 140 Americans were killed. Despite their loss, Americans proved they could fight a trained army.

The Battle of Moores Creek Bridge. In the year following the Battle of Bunker Hill, the war slowly spread north and south. **Loyalists**, or people loyal to Britain, and **Patriots**, or people who wanted independence, clashed from Maine to Georgia.

On February 27, 1776, the first battle of the American Revolution in North Carolina took place at Moores Creek Bridge. Governor Josiah Martin had drawn up a plan to unite North Carolina's Loyalists with British soldiers. After meeting in Wilmington, the combined forces would fight the Patriots to restore British control of the Southern Colonies.

To prevent Loyalists and the British from meeting, Patriots hid along the road to Wilmington near the banks of Moores Creek. They took planks off a bridge and greased its supporting logs with soap and animal fat. Patriots, led by Richard Caswell and Alexander Lillington, surprised the Loyalists trying to cross the slippery bridge.

In a three-minute battle, about 50 Loyalists were killed or wounded. The Patriots lost only one man.

Called the "Lexington and Concord of the South," the Battle of Moores Creek Bridge helped prevent the British from gaining control over the South. This important Patriot victory also encouraged North Carolina to seek independence.

British departure.   Less than a month after the Battle of Moores Creek Bridge, George Washington found a way to drive the British out of Boston. Washington sent for cannons from Fort Ticonderoga in New York, then controlled by Patriots. Soldiers hauled about 50 heavy cannons by sled for hundreds of miles, floated them on rafts down the icy Hudson River, and dragged them up the hills surrounding Boston.

When the British saw the Americans' cannons pointed at them, they knew they had been defeated. On March 17, 1776, more than 150 ships sailed out of Boston Harbor toward Canada.

The Halifax Resolves.   About six weeks after the victory at Moores Creek Bridge, a committee of Patriots met at Halifax. On April 12, 1776, they adopted the Halifax Resolves. These resolves, or formal statements of purpose, made the very first call for independence from Britain.

The Halifax Resolves not only recommended that North Carolina declare independence but also urged all of the colonies to do so together. The resolves were printed in

Think as a Historian

*H*istorians sometimes compare different events to help you understand them. ■ *To Do*: Think about why the Battle of Moores Creek Bridge is often called the "Lexington and Concord of the South." If you wish, make a chart to show how these battles were alike and different. Try to name two other past or present events that you might compare to help people better understand them.

The Mecklenburg Resolves

Colonists in North Carolina's Mecklenburg County were concerned when they heard about the Lexington and Concord battles and Parliament's declaration that the colonies were in rebellion. They met to discuss the situation and adopted the **Mecklenburg Resolves** on May 31, 1775.

The resolves stated that British laws were no longer in effect. To solve this crisis, the resolves provided for the creation of an independent local government to manage Mecklenburg County. This government would act until Britain's unjust actions stopped or until North Carolina's Provincial Congress took control.

The Mecklenburg Resolves, which temporarily severed ties between Mecklenburg County and Britain, were drawn up more than a year before the Declaration of Independence.

William Hooper was one of the delegates from North Carolina who signed the Declaration of Independence.

newspapers in other colonies and read by colonists. More importantly, the resolves were read and discussed by the representatives at the **Continental Congress** in Philadelphia. Not long after the Halifax Resolves had been adopted in North Carolina, the Declaration of Independence was drafted.

The Declaration of Independence. The members of the Continental Congress voted to declare independence. They set up a five-man committee to draft a formal declaration. Thomas Jefferson wrote the **Declaration of Independence** to explain why the colonies decided to separate from Britain and what rights the newly independent states now held. (See Declaration of Independence in the Citizenship Handbook.) The declaration also listed the many wrongs that colonists suffered under King George III.

The Declaration of Independence was approved on July 4, 1776. It was signed on August 2 by 55 representatives, including North Carolina's Joseph Hewes, William Hooper, and John Penn. Although the Declaration of Independence created free and independent states, Britain would not give up the colonies easily. Colonists would have to fight more battles to win their freedom.

North Carolina's first governor. Once the Declaration of Independence was adopted, British laws and royal governors appointed by the king no longer governed the colonies. Each of the 13 new states had to create new laws and governments.

Richard Caswell, a hero at Moores Creek Bridge, became the first governor of the new state of North Carolina. He took the oath of office on January 16, 1777, in Tryon Palace, which served as the state capitol.

Think Twice

1. Which two battles started the American Revolution?
2. What was one result of the Battle of Moores Creek Bridge?
3. (a) What were the Halifax Resolves? (b) Why were they important?
4. What was the purpose of the Declaration of Independence?
5. Do you think that the American Revolution could have been avoided? Why or why not?

2 The Fighting Spreads

The British had been driven out of Boston on March 17, 1776. However, Britain would not give up the colonies without a fight. For the next five years, the American Revolution spread from Massachusetts to other states in the North, West, and South.

War in the North. General William Howe, leader of the British army, did not leave North America. Howe got more ships, arms, and soldiers from Britain while he stayed in Canada. Howe decided that New York could be easily attacked, and he and his army sailed there in the summer of 1776.

Although Washington and his men rushed to defend New York City, the Americans were forced from Manhattan. The British won three battles at Long Island, Brooklyn Heights, and Harlem Heights. By November 1776, Long Island, New York City, Fort Washington, much of Westchester County, and Fort Lee in New Jersey were under British control.

Washington led his army through New Jersey and across the Delaware River into Pennsylvania. At this point, Washington and many other Patriots thought the war was nearly over. Americans had reached a low point in their struggle for independence.

Badly beaten, the American soldiers were discouraged. To encourage them to continue fighting, Thomas Paine, a

People, Places, Terms

Hessian
George Rogers Clark
privateer
John Paul Jones
Lord Charles Cornwallis
partisan
Nathanael Greene

The Will to Win

How could a ragtag army fight against highly trained troops and a superior navy? The British had more men, more money, and more weapons than the Americans. By 1778, their forces included about 50,000 professional British soldiers (see far left) and 30,000 **Hessians**, or German soldiers hired by King George III. Also, approximately 52,000 Loyalists fought for Britain.

On the other hand, the inexperienced Continental Army (see immediate left) at times numbered less than 5,000 men. American soldiers — from young boys to elderly men — had been farmers, shopkeepers, or artisans. They lacked adequate supplies, such as clothing and food, and were poorly paid, earning about 60 dollars a year.

Despite the odds, the Americans kept up the fight during the American Revolution. They used a secret weapon that the British did not have: the will to win.

Some women took an active role in the war. In 1776, Margaret Corbin fought in the Battle of Fort Washington. In 1778, Molly Hays fought in the Battle of Monmouth. Deborah Sampson, shown delivering a message to George Washington, served in the army for 20 months.

This famous painting shows George Washington and his troops crossing the Delaware River in 1776.

former soldier himself, wrote a pamphlet. Washington had the pamphlet read to his troops, including the following passage:

Primary Source

> *These are the times that try men's souls. The summer soldier and the sunshine patriot will, in this crisis, shrink from the service of their country; but he that stands it now, deserves the love and thanks of man and woman.*

> — THOMAS PAINE, "The American Crisis"

On Christmas night 1776, Americans did win a victory. Washington attacked a group of Hessians who were stationed in Trenton, New Jersey. After crossing the icy Delaware River, the Americans surprised the Hessians and won the Battle of Trenton.

While Americans won more victories in New Jersey in 1777, the British planned to defeat them. Their plan called for three armies to meet in Albany and cut New England off from the other colonies. One army, led by General John Burgoyne, would come south from Canada along the Hudson River. The second army would march east from Oswego through the Mohawk Valley. A third army would press north from New York City.

The British plan failed because the three armies never met. At the Battle of Saratoga, General Burgoyne's soldiers were beaten by Patriots. On October 17, 1777, Burgoyne

was forced to surrender. This important American victory was the turning point of the American Revolution.

War in the West. While fighting went on in the North, settlers had begun to move west of the Appalachians. American soldiers, led by a young Virginian named George Rogers Clark, were sent to protect the settlers.

To force the British out of the West, Colonel Clark set out to capture their forts. In the summer of 1778, Clark and his men took the fort at Kaskaskia, located on the Mississippi River in southern Illinois. Clark walked into a British party and said, "Go on with your dance. But remember that henceforth you dance under the American flag."

Clark and his troops also captured forts at Cahokia in Illinois and Vincennes on the Wabash River in Indiana. His victories gave Americans control over much of the land east of the Mississippi River and west of the Appalachians.

War at sea. Not all of the fighting during the American Revolution took place on land. More than 400 British ships sailed along the coast from Massachusetts to Georgia. Many small battles took place at sea.

At the beginning of the war, Americans used **privateers**, or trading ships that were armed for battle, to hunt down British supply ships. After a Continental Navy was created on October 30, 1775, money was raised to pay for about a dozen warships. Some states, including North Carolina, also had their own navy.

The painting below shows the battle between the American ship *Bonhomme Richard* on the left and the British ship *Serapis* on the right.

African Americans who lived in the North and the South during the war supported Loyalists as well as Patriots. Quamino Dolly guided the British through the swamps to capture the city of Savannah. Peter Salem, shown in this picture, and Salem Poor both fought against the British in the Battle of Bunker Hill.

Lord Charles Cornwallis often delayed taking action during his military campaign in the South. These delays allowed Patriots to take advantage of the British and contributed to the British defeat.

An important sea battle took place on September 23, 1779. The *Bonhomme Richard,* commanded by John Paul Jones, and a British warship called the *Serapis* (suh RAY pis) clashed off the northwest coast of England. The Patriots won after three hours of fighting, and Jones became the first American naval hero.

War in the South.   By 1778, the war had already lasted three years. Although the Americans had lost more battles than they had won, they refused to give up. Hoping to end the war, the British tried another plan. They began to fight in the South.

In 1778, the British captured the city of Savannah in Georgia. Two years later, the British captured Charles Town, an important port in South Carolina. Soon after the fall of South Carolina's capital, the Americans suffered a terrible defeat at the Battle of Camden in South Carolina, which took place on August 16, 1780.

Having gained confidence as a result of their victories, the British planned to take North Carolina and then Virginia. Lord Charles Cornwallis was in charge of taking these states, which would give the British control over the South. Yet Cornwallis decided to wait to make his move. The summer of 1780 was very hot and humid, and the British were not used to such weather.

While the British waited for fall, people in North Carolina busily prepared for war. They raised money and gathered supplies. Since the regular Continental Army had left the Carolinas, local groups of **partisans**, or Patriot followers, formed to resist the British as they marched through the area.

These partisan bands also fought their Loyalist neighbors. One such battle took place at Ramsour's Mill on June 20, 1780. After a group of Loyalists gathered to discuss the plans of Lord Cornwallis, about 400 partisans attacked them. Because neither side had uniforms, partisans stuck pieces of white paper in their hats, and Loyalists wore green twigs to identify themselves. The Loyalists, many of whom were not armed, retreated after less than an hour.

Once Cornwallis and his men finally set out for Charlotte on September 8, 1780, bands of North Carolina's partisans slowed them down. While Cornwallis headed north, he sent one of his officers, Patrick Ferguson, to western North Carolina toward the Blue Ridge Mountains. He ordered Ferguson to drum up Loyalist support and to provide protection for the British army.

Ferguson was chased to the top of Kings Mountain, on the border between North Carolina and South Carolina, by

Daniel Morgan was a partisan fighter who had settled in the Shenandoah Valley of Virginia. He was related to the famous frontiersman Daniel Boone. Morgan was about 45 years old when he fought in the Battle of Cowpens.

frontiersmen from Virginia and the Carolinas. The American victory at the Battle of Kings Mountain on October 7 forced the British to give up their plan of taking over North Carolina. Cornwallis returned to South Carolina, having found the countryside around Charlotte to be "the hornet's nest" of the Revolution.

Another important battle took place at Cowpens near South Carolina's Broad River. On January 17, 1781, a group of Patriots commanded by Daniel Morgan defeated British troops led by Banastre Tarleton. After the Battle of Cowpens, Morgan and his men quickly retreated to North Carolina, and an angry Cornwallis left South Carolina in pursuit of Morgan. Cornwallis soon had an unfortunate encounter with other Americans in North Carolina.

The last significant battle that took place in North Carolina during the American Revolution occurred on March 15, 1781. The Patriots, led by Nathanael Greene, caught up with British troops at Guilford Court House near Greensboro. Although the British held the field of battle, they lost one quarter of their men and many of their best officers. Cornwallis took his weakened army to Wilmington.

George Washington selected Nathanael Greene, a Rhode Island native, to command the Continental Army in the South. A skilled leader, Greene often was able to defeat the British with a small number of inexperienced men and few basic supplies.

Maps Matter

A map might show you where important events in history have taken place. This map shows you where Cornwallis went during his military campaign in the South.

■ *To Do:* Trace the route that Cornwallis took. Where did he begin his campaign? Where did his campaign end? What places did he pass through in North Carolina?

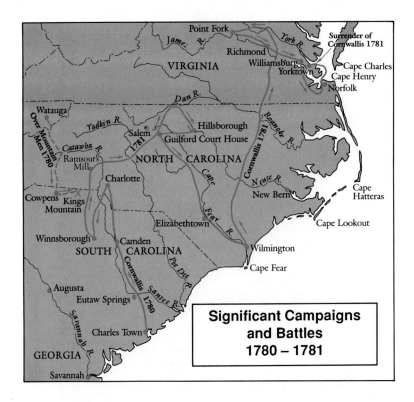

Significant Campaigns and Battles 1780 – 1781

As the British chased after the Americans, they moved farther and farther from their supply bases in the South. When the British leaders realized what was happening, they moved back to the coast. In so doing, however, they left most of Georgia and the Carolinas in American hands.

During the war in the North, West, and South, thousands of lives were lost. Fields were stripped of crops, livestock was killed, and homes and buildings were destroyed. But Americans were fighting for their homes, their families, and the right to rule themselves. The Patriots were determined to win the American Revolution.

Think Twice

1. (a) What are two battles that Patriots won in the North?
   (b) What are three battles that the British won in the North?
2. Who captured British forts in the West?
3. Who was the first American naval hero?
4. (a) What major battles took place in the South?
   (b) Which of these battles took place in North Carolina?
5. The British plans to control the North and the South failed. Think about what you have already learned about the struggle between the British and the Americans. Draw conclusions about the strengths and weaknesses of each side.

3 The End of the War

Following the Battle of Guilford Court House, Cornwallis first went to Wilmington and then headed north to Virginia. He led his army to Yorktown, a port located between the York and the James rivers on a narrow peninsula in Chesapeake Bay. There he set up camp and waited for British ships to bring fresh soldiers and supplies.

The Battle of Yorktown. British soldiers dug ditches and built sandbanks to protect their camp from an inland attack. Cornwallis counted on British warships anchored in the Chesapeake Bay to prevent an attack by sea. Without knowing it, however, Cornwallis had fallen into a trap set by the Americans.

While Cornwallis prepared for battle at Yorktown, an army of more than 7,000 French troops joined the American army stationed in New York. Together, the two armies marched to Virginia before Cornwallis ever learned that they had left New York. American and French soldiers closed the land route off the Yorktown peninsula, trapping Cornwallis by land.

At the same time, a fleet of more than 20 French warships had arrived from the West Indies. The French fleet sailed to Chesapeake Bay and blocked the entrance. This **blockade** prevented Cornwallis from leaving Yorktown by sea.

Maps Matter

To help you picture how the British were surrounded at Yorktown, the map below uses different symbols.
■ *To Do:* Look at the map legend. Use the symbols to help you answer these questions. Where did Washington and his army land in Virginia? What town did Lafayette and his troops pass through? Between what two capes did the French fleet form a blockade?

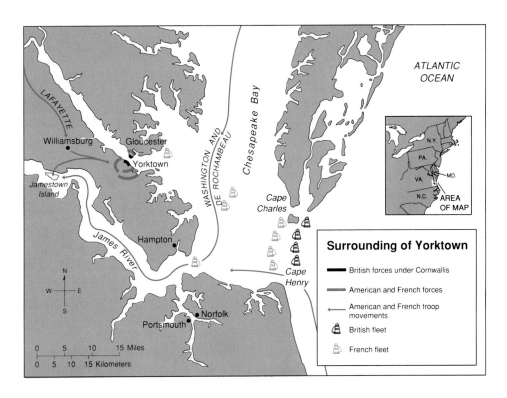

Surrounding of Yorktown

— British forces under Cornwallis

— American and French forces

← American and French troop movements

⚓ British fleet

⚓ French fleet

159

This painting by John Trumbull shows General Benjamin Lincoln accepting the surrender of the British at Yorktown. Washington asked the British to surrender to Lincoln because Lincoln himself had been forced to surrender to the British at Charles Town.

Think as a Historian

*B*ritain was a very strong nation in 1775, yet it lost the American Revolution. ■ *To Do*: Can you think of a war in the twentieth century that was fought between a powerful nation and a much less powerful one? Where did this conflict take place? What was the reason for the war? Which side won? Use a world history textbook, a newspaper, or an encyclopedia to help you.

After the combined French and American forces attacked the British, Cornwallis surrendered to the Americans. On October 19, 1781, thousands of British soldiers put down their guns. During a formal ceremony, British troops filed between two long lines of American and French soldiers while a British band played a popular tune called "The World Turned Upside Down." The Patriots had turned the world upside down: they had won the American Revolution.

Against the odds.   With the surrender of Cornwallis at Yorktown in 1781, one of the greatest armies in the world had been defeated. How had the Americans won? The Americans had advantages that the British did not have.

First, Americans were fighting to defend their homeland. They were more familiar with the climate, the land, and the bodies of water. Many local Patriots served as guides or scouts and furnished boats to help them cross rivers.

Although the Americans were not well trained soldiers, they learned to shoot from behind trees and make surprise attacks. George Washington, a great leader from the beginning of the war, inspired these inexperienced men to keep fighting.

On the other hand, the British were fighting in a strange country that was 3,000 miles from their homeland. The British soldiers — and even more, the hired Hessians — had no personal reasons to fight. Soldiers wanted to return to their families.

The British troops were skilled; however, they were used to orderly fights on battlefields, and their leaders made mistakes. British leaders did not count on strong support for the Patriots, and they were too confident that they could stop the rebellion. After five years of war, however, the British learned that they could not stop the Americans in the North, West, or South.

After the Battle of Yorktown. Although the British surrendered after the Battle of Yorktown in the fall of 1781, fighting did not yet end in the South. Nathanael Greene had to force the British out of Georgia and South Carolina. Civil war took place between citizens living in North Carolina.

In North Carolina, small bands of armed men pretending to be either Loyalists or Patriots robbed and killed people and burned down their homes. Since both British and American forces had left the state, these violent attacks on citizens could not be stopped.

One of the leaders of these armed gangs was a Loyalist named David Fanning. Just one month before the Battle of Yorktown, his band captured more than 200 prisoners in Hillsborough, including Governor Thomas Burke. Even when the news of the British surrender reached him, Fanning refused to give up. He continued his cruel raids in the country and towns until the spring of 1782.

In the summer of 1782, the British finally gave up their posts at Charles Town in South Carolina and Savannah in Georgia. The last of the British forces did not leave New York to sail for England until November 1783, two years after the Battle of Yorktown.

The Treaty of Paris. In June 1781, the Continental Congress set up a committee to work out a peace agreement with Britain. John Adams, John Jay of New York, Thomas Jefferson, Henry Laurens of South Carolina, and Benjamin Franklin were members of this committee.

Formal peace talks began in Paris in the fall of 1782. The Americans were represented by Franklin, Adams, and Jay. The **Treaty of Paris** was signed on September 3, 1783, by Britain and the United States.

The terms of the Treaty of Paris were very favorable to the United States. Britain formally recognized the independence of the 13 colonies, and the borders of this new country were set. The United States would reach from the Atlantic Ocean in the east to the Mississippi River in the west and from the Great Lakes in the north to the northern part of Florida in the south.

The Americans agreed that Loyalists would not be punished for their actions during the war. They also agreed that Loyalists would have the same rights as other citizens and would get back any property that they had lost during the American Revolution.

Important Battles of the
Revolutionary War, 1775-1783

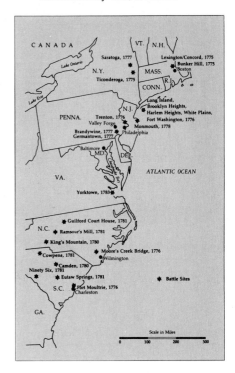

Maps Matter

The American Revolution ended at the Battle of Yorktown. You can use this map to review where other important battles occurred. ■ *To Do*: Look at battle sites in the North. In which state did most of the fighting occur? Look at battle sites in the South. In which state did most of the fighting occur?

The borders of the United States in 1783 were the Atlantic Ocean in the east, the Mississippi River in the west, the Great Lakes in the north, and the northern part of Florida in the south. ■ *To Do*: Look at the map titled The United States: Political in the atlas section of your text. Where are the borders of the United States today?

_____

Both the British and the Americans promised that they would pay back any money that they owed to one another. At last, the British agreed to end the fighting and leave the United States as soon as possible.

A few months after the Treaty of Paris was signed, Benjamin Franklin wrote a letter to his friend Mary Hewson. In part of the letter, he expressed his relief that the peace talks had been successfully concluded and described his desire to settle conflicts by discussion, not by war.

Primary Source

At length we are in peace, God be praised, and long, very long, may it continue! All wars are follies, very expensive, and very mischievous ones. When will mankind be convinced of this, and agree to settle their differences by arbitration? Were they to do it, even by the cast of a die, it would be better than by fighting and destroying each other.

— BENJAMIN FRANKLIN, "Letter to Mrs. Mary Stevenson Hewson"

Once the Treaty of Paris was signed, the 13 colonies were truly independent states. Britain had agreed to give them up. With independence, these states formed a new nation, the United States of America.

The leaders of the American Revolution now faced a huge task. The United States needed a strong government to unite the 13 states and to protect the freedom of Americans. This new government would have to guarantee the people's right to rule themselves — a right that had been dearly won.

_____

Think Twice

1. Who won the American Revolution — the British or the Americans?
2. (a) What major battle ended the American Revolution? (b) When did it take place? (c) Describe the location where this battle occurred.
3. (a) How were Cornwallis and his army trapped by land? (b) How was the British army trapped by sea? (c) Which country sent soldiers and ships to help the Americans trap the British?
4. (a) What was the Treaty of Paris? (b) When was the treaty signed? (c) Why were the terms of the treaty favorable to the United States?
5. The American Revolution brought great changes to North America. Consider the changes that took place after the war. Predict what your life would be like today if the war had ended differently.

Chapter 11 Review

Choose from the following menu of activities.

Think Back: Main Ideas

1. Why was there so much tension between Britain and the colonists in the 1770s?
2. (a) Following the Boston Tea Party in 1773, why did George Washington and many other colonists support Massachusetts? (b) How did they show their support?
3. What were Loyalists, and how were they different from Patriots?
4. (a) When did the first battle of the American Revolution take place in North Carolina? (b) Where was this battle, and to what important northern battle is it often compared? (c) What were two important results of this battle?
5. After the signing of the Declaration of Independence, were the British successful in battles in the South? What was the decisive battle in the South, and what critical tactical error was committed by Cornwallis?

Maps Matter

The Battle of Yorktown led to the British defeat. The map on page 159 shows how French and American forces surrounded Yorktown. Use the map to answer these questions.

1. Where were British forces located?
2. Where did Washington's and Lafayette's forces meet?
3. What might have happened if French ships and troops had not come to help?

Word Wizard

1. *Minutemen* and *warship* are compound nouns made of the words *minute* + *men* and *war* + *ship*. Think of other compound nouns, look them up in a dictionary, and define them.

2. Look up *patriot* in a dictionary. Why were the Patriots well named?

Working Cooperatively

The Catawba were Native Americans who lived in the western Piedmont section of the two Carolinas. During the Revolutionary War, they served the Patriots as scouts to report on British strengths and movements. They played an important role in the defeat of the Cherokee — who sided with the British — at the Battle of Franklin in 1776.

With three to five classmates, find out more about the role of the Catawba and Cherokee during the Revolutionary War. Then create a bulletin board display showing the results of your research.

Curriculum Connection

Ralph Waldo Emerson, a resident of Concord, Massachusetts, wrote a poem for the dedication of a war monument at North Bridge. Here is the first stanza of "Concord Hymn."

By the rude bridge that arched the flood,
Their flag to April's breeze unfurled,
Here once the embattled farmers stood
And fired the shot heard round the world.

Who are the "embattled farmers"? Why does Emerson say they "fired the shot heard round the world"? Write your own poem stanza about the same event. You might try to take the British point of view.

Learning through Literature

Drums, by James Boyd
Johnny Tremain, by Esther Forbes
Betsy Dowdy's Ride, by Nell Wise Wechter
The South Fork Rangers, by Manly Wade Wellman

Chapter 12

A New Nation Grows

The states organize their own governments.

In 1777, one year after the Declaration of Independence, the Continental Congress had asked the states to set up their own governments. By 1780, all of the 13 states had working governments. Each state had its own **constitution**, or a written plan of government, to explain what the government could and could not do and what rights of citizens would be protected. The state constitutions gave the power of government to the people.

The United States creates a national government.

At the same time that state governments were being set up, members of the Second Continental Congress were working on a plan for a government that would protect the rights of Americans and link the states together—a national government. After the war, the 13 states joined together to form a new nation, the United States of America. The United States was a **republic.** A republic is any government that is not ruled by a king or queen and in which power rests with the people. Because most countries in 1783 were headed by either a king or queen, many Americans wondered whether their new republic would succeed and whether the states would remain united.

The Great Seal of the United States ▶

Think Ahead

After the American Revolution, the United States needed a strong government to unite the original 13 states as well as new states in the West. Discover how America's leaders hammered out the framework of government that is still in use. Learn about North Carolina's contributions to the growth of the new nation.

1 Forming a New Government

People, Places, Terms

constitution
republic
confederation
Articles of Confederation
Congress
compromise
elector

The task of creating a national government was difficult. Many Americans felt that the British government had had too much power over them. As a result, Americans wanted to limit the power of the national government. Yet they wanted a government strong enough to hold the states together.

The Articles of Confederation are drawn up. In 1777, while each state worked out its own constitution, the Second Continental Congress finished a plan for a national government. By March 1781, all 13 states had approved the first national constitution, called the Articles of Confederation. A **confederation** is a joining together—in this case, the joining together of states.

The **Articles of Confederation** set up a system of government in which power was divided between the national government and the state governments. However, the articles granted most of the power to the states. The **Congress,** the one body of national government established by the articles, had little power.

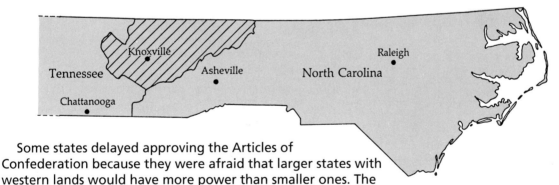

The Lost State of Franklin

Some states delayed approving the Articles of Confederation because they were afraid that larger states with western lands would have more power than smaller ones. The Congress asked Virginia, Georgia, and North Carolina to give up their western lands to the national government. North Carolina's leaders agreed to this plan in April 1784.

People who lived in North Carolina's western lands, which stretched from the Appalachian Mountains to the Mississippi River, were pleased. In December 1784, they created a new state, which they called Franklin in honor of Benjamin Franklin. Leaders held a convention to draw up a state constitution, and John Sevier was elected governor in March 1785. However, many people in Franklin were still loyal to North Carolina, and the new state's government eventually began to crumble. The state of Franklin did exist for four years, until March 1788. This dispute started people thinking about how new states might join the United States.

Under the Articles of Confederation, each state, regardless of its size or its population, had one vote in Congress. Congress could declare war, provide mail service, enter into treaties, and coin money. It did not have the power, however, to collect taxes or to regulate trade. The states alone could tax Americans and control trade. A host of problems developed as a result of these weaknesses of the national government.

Without the power to tax citizens, Congress had trouble raising money to pay the high costs of fighting the American Revolution. Congress could ask the states for money but had no power to force them to pay. Without the power to control trade, Congress could not settle trade disputes between states. Quarrels took place because some states unfairly charged high taxes on goods that passed through them.

As a result of these weaknesses, some Americans worried that a foreign power could take over their new nation. Others were afraid that some states would set themselves up as separate countries. George Washington wrote, "We cannot exist long as a nation without having somewhere a power which will govern the whole union."

Money troubles spark rebellion. Taxes often led to bitter arguments. In the state of Massachusetts, landowners had to pay high taxes. Some people were forced to sell their land in order to pay the government the taxes they owed. Hundreds of farmers in western Massachusetts demanded that the state lower their taxes, but their complaints were ignored.

In January 1787, desperate farmers, led by a veteran of the American Revolution named Daniel Shays, tried to seize guns stored in Springfield. The governor in Massachusetts sent troops to crush Shays' Rebellion.

Although Shays' Rebellion did not last long, the uprising sent shock waves throughout the nation. Massachusetts had requested help from Congress, but Congress did not have the power to help. Was the new national government so weak that a small group of angry farmers could take it over?

The Constitutional Convention is held. Although the Articles of Confederation created the first national government, this government was too weak. Noah Webster of Massachusetts wrote, "Our . . . Union is but a name and our Confederation, a cobweb." To revise the articles and make a stronger national government, the Continental Congress called for a convention to take place in Philadelphia in 1787.

This woodcut shows Daniel Shays, the leader of a Massachusetts rebellion.

The Constitutional Convention had its first meeting in the Pennsylvania statehouse on May 25, 1787. Every state except Rhode Island sent delegates. During the hot summer, the 55 delegates, including North Carolina's Hugh Williamson, William Blount, Alexander Martin, Richard Dobbs Spaight, and William R. Davie, met to discuss how to make the national government stronger. So that delegates could debate their ideas freely, the discussions were kept secret. Guards made sure that no one except the delegates came into the room. In spite of the heat, the windows were often closed.

For three hot, steamy months, the delegates tried to answer important questions. They agreed that the national government should remain a republic. They also decided that the national government should collect taxes as well as control trade among states and with other countries.

In addition, the delegates decided that the government should have three parts — a congress to make laws, a president to ensure that laws were followed, and courts to try cases of national law. The powers and duties of government would be divided among these three parts so that no one person or group could become too powerful.

There were questions, however, on which the delegates did not agree. How many votes should a state have in Congress? How would a President be chosen? How should power be divided between state governments and the national government? These disagreements had to be settled.

Delegates reach compromises. After weeks of heated debate, the delegates found answers to their questions. They reached **compromises**, or agreements in which each side gives up something it wants in order to gain something else.

The delegates agreed that Congress should be divided into two parts, the Senate and the House of Representatives. In the Senate, each state would have two members called senators. The number of members in the House of Representatives would be based on the population of each state. Larger states would have more representatives, and smaller states would have fewer. This plan, known as the Great Compromise, guaranteed that every state would be fairly represented in the national government.

The delegates also decided how the President would be chosen. They agreed that voters in each state would elect representatives called **electors**. The number of electors for each state would equal the number of its senators and representatives. These electors would vote for the President.

James Madison, a Virginia delegate, was nicknamed the "Father of the Constitution." He prepared for the Constitutional Convention by studying the history of governments from ancient Greece to Britain. *(The Granger Collection, New York)*

At the Constitutional Convention in Philadelphia, members elected George Washington to lead the debates. To honor his position of authority, his chair was placed on a platform.

In addition, the delegates determined that the national government would have certain powers over the states. The delegates hoped that these compromises would create a strong national government that would unite the 13 states.

After four months of serious debate, the delegates approved and signed the Constitution. (See the section entitled Constitution of the United States of America in the Citizenship Handbook at the back of your text.) Yet before it could become law, nine states had to approve the Constitution. The states had to hold conventions at which they would decide whether to accept this new plan of government.

The Reverend Absalom Jones, shown in the picture, attempted to win African Americans the right to vote in Pennsylvania. Delegates at the Constitutional Convention compromised to let states count three fifths of enslaved Africans for purposes of representation, but they did not deal adequately with the larger issue of slavery. *(The Granger Collection, New York)*

Think Twice

1. Why didn't the Articles of Confederation work?
2. (a) Why did Shays' Rebellion occur? (b) Why did it alarm people throughout the country?
3. What was the purpose of the Constitutional Convention of 1787?
4. (a) On what issues did the delegates at the Constitutional Convention agree? (b) On what issues did the delegates disagree? (c) How did they resolve their differences?
5. Imagine that you are a delegate at the Constitutional Convention. Do you agree with the ideas proposed for a stronger national government? Why or why not?

2 The Republic Grows Stronger

People, Places, Terms

Federalist
Antifederalist
amendment
Bill of Rights
federal system
checks and balances

In September 1787, delegates to the Constitutional Convention sent their new Constitution to the 13 states. Voters in each state elected people to represent them in state conventions. These representatives hotly debated the merits and drawbacks of the new plan of government.

The debate continues.   The state conventions were marked by sharp debate. **Federalists**, or people who supported the new Constitution, argued that the new government would provide a better balance between the national government and state governments. Their opponents, known as **Antifederalists**, feared that the new Constitution created a central government with too much power. They also pointed out that the Constitution did not have a bill of rights to protect the liberty of individual citizens.

Some states—Pennsylvania, Delaware, Connecticut, New Jersey, and Georgia—quickly voted to adopt the Constitution. On the other hand, debates over the Constitution raged between Federalists and Antifederalists in Virginia, New York, Rhode Island, and North Carolina.

North Carolina's state convention met in Hillsborough on July 21, 1788. In the debate over the new plan for a national government, James Iredell represented the Federalist side, and Willie Jones led the Antifederalists. When the convention ended on August 4, North Carolina's Antifederalists had won. The state decided not to ratify the Constitution because it created too powerful a central government.

The Constitution is approved.   By the end of July 1788, 11 states had voted to approve the Constitution, and it became the law of the land. Two states—North Carolina and Rhode Island—had rejected the Constitution. Both North Carolina and Rhode Island decided to remain totally independent of the United States.

As a result of pressure to join the other states, North Carolina held a second state convention in Fayetteville in 1789. The Antifederalists, pleased that Congress was strongly considering adding a bill of rights, agreed to approve the Constitution on November 21, 1789. North Carolina became the twelfth state to approve it. Rhode Island, the thirteenth state, did not approve the Constitution until May 1790.

At last, the plan for a new government had been accepted by all of the states. The republic could now pursue its ambitious goals, which are best summed up by the introduction to the Constitution.

Washington's inauguration, or the ceremony that made him the President, included fireworks, gun salutes, a parade, and a religious service. ■ *To Do*: Compare Washington's inauguration with that of another President. If you wish, create a chart to show how the two ceremonies were alike and different.

The *Massachusetts Centinel* published this cartoon on August 2, 1788, in an effort to convince North Carolina and Rhode Island to approve the Constitution. Why is North Carolina represented by a tilting column? Why is Rhode Island represented by a broken column?

Primary Source

We the People of the United States, in order to form a more perfect Union, establish justice, insure domestic tranquility, provide for the common defense, promote the general welfare, and secure the blessings of liberty to ourselves and our posterity, do ordain and establish this Constitution for the United States of America.

— *"Preamble to the Constitution"*

The first President takes office.   Once the Constitution had been accepted, the Continental Congress asked the states to hold elections for senators, representatives, and electors. The electors would vote for the President.

George Washington was elected the first President of the United States. In April 1789, Washington left his home in Virginia to travel to New York City, which was the new nation's first capital. There he would take the oath of office. When Washington reached the Hudson River, a barge rowed by 13 oarsmen—one for each state—carried him across the river to New York City.

Thousands of people crowded the shoreline to greet the new President. Although Washington was pleased at the honor of serving as the first President, he said, "I greatly apprehend that my countrymen expect too much from me." On April 30, 1789, he was sworn into office, promising to fulfill his duties to the best of his ability and to protect and defend the Constitution of the United States.

The Bill of Rights is added.   The lack of a bill of rights was one of the reasons that the Constitution was not

REDEUNT SATURNIA REGNA.
On the erection of the Eleventh PILLAR of the great National DOME, we beg leave most sincerely to felicitate " OUR DEAR COUNTRY."

Rise it will.

The foundation good—it may yet be SAVED.

The FEDERAL EDIFICE.

This painting shows the huge, colorful parade of ships in New York Harbor that escorted the future President's barge to New York City.

immediately approved. To gain the support of Antifederalists, Federalists had promised to add a bill of rights. In 1791, Congress formally added ten **amendments**, or changes, to protect the basic rights of citizens. (See the section entitled The First Ten Amendments: The Bill of Rights in the Citizenship Handbook at the back of your text.)

The **Bill of Rights** guarantees such rights as freedom of speech, freedom of press, and freedom of religion. It gives people the right to speak out about their beliefs, to worship in their own way, and to have a trial by a jury. Also, it gives to the states or to the people all powers not already given to the federal government or denied to the states by the Constitution.

With the Bill of Rights, the people of the United States had truly won rights that they had fought for during the American Revolution. The Constitution and the Bill of Rights brought into being a government chosen by the people and based on law rather than on royal power.

The new government begins its work.   The Constitution of 1787, still the basis for government, set up a **federal system** in which power was divided between the national and state governments. The seven parts of the Constitution, called articles, explain the way government should be set up and how the powers should be divided.

Across Cultures

*T*he Bill of Rights protects Americans' freedoms of speech, press, and religion. Many people around the world do not have these same freedoms. ■ *To Do*: Work with a partner to read and discuss the Bill of Rights in the Citizenship Handbook in the back of your text. Then find a news story in a current newspaper that illustrates how the people in another country do not enjoy the same freedoms.

James Iredell, a Federalist from North Carolina, helped secure the approval of the Constitution in his state. He was later named to the first Supreme Court.

The Constitution created a strong national government with three parts—the legislative branch, the executive branch, and the judicial branch. The legislative branch is Congress. Article I of the Constitution lists rules and powers of Congress and tells how its members are chosen. Congress has the power to make laws and treaties, coin money, and regulate trade.

In 1790, North Carolina chose its first members of Congress. Timothy Bloodworth, John B. Ashe, Hugh Williamson, John Steele, and John Sevier served in the House of Representatives. The first senators were Samuel Johnston and Benjamin Hawkins.

The executive branch, which includes the President and Vice President, makes sure that laws are carried out. Article II lists the President's powers and duties and explains how the President is elected. With the approval of the Senate, the President can appoint government officials and make treaties. As you learned, George Washington was the first President. John Adams was the first Vice President.

The judicial branch is the national system of courts. The highest court is the Supreme Court. One responsibility of Supreme Court justices is to decide cases that involve the Constitution. If a case is brought to the Supreme Court, justices decide whether the law in question agrees with the Constitution or whether it is unconstitutional.

In 1790, North Carolina's James Iredell was appointed by George Washington and confirmed by the Senate to the first Supreme Court. In one case, he gave a dissenting statement that later resulted in the Eleventh Amendment to the Constitution. He said that citizens of other states cannot sue a state in national courts.

Diagrams Describe

A diagram shows how something works or how its parts relate to one another. This diagram shows you the relationship among the three branches of the national government. Which branch of government makes laws? Which branch contains the Supreme Court? To which branch does the President belong?

The Three Branches of Government

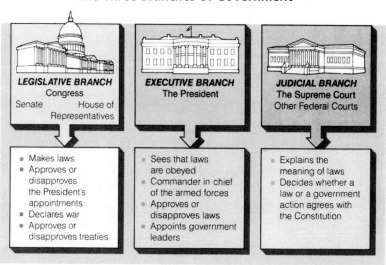

LEGISLATIVE BRANCH
Congress
Senate House of Representatives

- Makes laws
- Approves or disapproves the President's appointments
- Declares war
- Approves or disapproves treaties

EXECUTIVE BRANCH
The President

- Sees that laws are obeyed
- Commander in chief of the armed forces
- Approves or disapproves laws
- Appoints government leaders

JUDICIAL BRANCH
The Supreme Court
Other Federal Courts

- Explains the meaning of laws
- Decides whether a law or a government action agrees with the Constitution

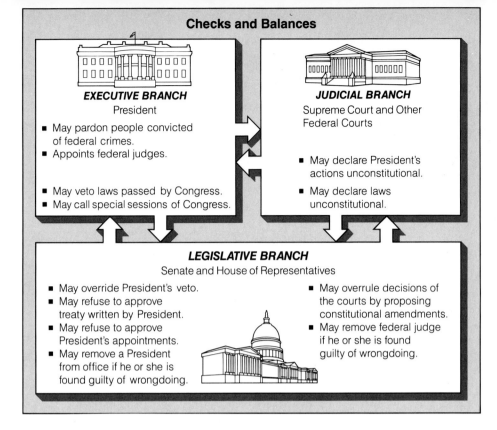

Checks and Balances

EXECUTIVE BRANCH
President

- May pardon people convicted of federal crimes.
- Appoints federal judges.

- May veto laws passed by Congress.
- May call special sessions of Congress.

JUDICIAL BRANCH
Supreme Court and Other Federal Courts

- May declare President's actions unconstitutional.
- May declare laws unconstitutional.

LEGISLATIVE BRANCH
Senate and House of Representatives

- May override President's veto.
- May refuse to approve treaty written by President.
- May refuse to approve President's appointments.
- May remove a President from office if he or she is found guilty of wrongdoing.

- May overrule decisions of the courts by proposing constitutional amendments.
- May remove federal judge if he or she is found guilty of wrongdoing.

By setting up three branches of government, each with its own duties and limits, the Constitution divided the powers given to the national government. This division not only keeps one branch of government from becoming too powerful but also allows each branch to check on another's actions and decisions. The balancing of power and the checking of one branch by another is known as the system of **checks and balances.**

The nation's first leaders encountered many challenges and problems. Although a stronger government was in place, the young republic faced huge debts, threats of war, and a need for new laws as the country began to grow and expand westward.

Charts Teach

A flowchart is a step-by-step chart that shows how something is done. This flowchart shows how one branch of government checks the power of the other two branches. How does the executive branch check Congress and the Supreme Court? How does Congress check the President and the judicial branch? How does the judicial branch check the President and the legislative branch?

Think Twice

1. Analyze the strengths and weaknesses of the Constitution from the viewpoint of the late 1700s.
   (a) How did Federalists feel about the Constitution?
   (b) How did Antifederalists feel about it?
2. Which two states didn't accept the Constitution?
3. (a) Who was the first President of the United States? (b) When and where did he take the oath of office?
4. What are three rights protected by the Bill of Rights?
5. Describe some specific ways that the freedoms protected in the Constitution are important in your life.

People, Places, Terms

Thomas Jefferson
Louisiana Purchase
Meriwether Lewis
William Clark
Zebulon Pike
impressment
War of 1812

3 Heading West

In colonial days, some American settlers had moved west despite the efforts of the British government to stop them. Once the American Revolution was over and a strong national government was in place, thousands of settlers again began to cross the Appalachian Mountains in search of land and new opportunities.

Pioneers settle in the West.   During the 1770s, Daniel Boone left North Carolina and led pioneers across the Appalachians to Kentucky. Later pioneers followed Boone's lead and drove their wagons along trails to Tennessee, Kentucky, Indiana, and Ohio. There they found miles and miles of rolling hills covered with grassland and forests.

Some pioneers floated farther west down the Ohio River on large rafts called flatboats, stopping where they found a good spot. One pioneer who settled in Ohio wrote the following:

Primary Source

> *This is the best country I have ever seen. . . We have seen many buffalo. Deer are as plentiful as are the sheep in New England. Beaver and otter are so numerous that a man may catch a dozen in one night. Wild turkeys are everywhere, and are so tame that they come close to us in the fields.*
>
> — *"Letter of an Ohio pioneer"*

Pioneers in the rich farmlands west of the Appalachians raised enough cattle, hogs, tobacco, and corn to sell. Since overland routes were long and difficult, farmers shipped their goods on flatboats downriver on the Ohio and Mississippi. The goods, bound for overseas markets, were loaded onto ships in the port city of New Orleans.

These farmers were concerned, however, because New Orleans belonged to Spain. Spanish officials who controlled trade through the port made it difficult for Americans to unload and store goods at New Orleans.

The Louisiana Purchase brings new lands.   In 1800, Spain ruled New Orleans and a vast tract of land in the middle of the country. In a secret treaty with France, Spain gave the city and this land to the French. In 1803, President Thomas Jefferson learned the contents of the treaty. To protect the United States and to help western farmers,

While pioneers were moving west, many citizens in North Carolina were busy putting down deep roots. In 1789, the state government approved the creation of the first state university in America. Land in the middle of the state was donated for this purpose, and a university was built in Chapel Hill. The University of North Carolina opened in 1795.

At the same time, North Carolina's leaders realized the need for a permanent state capital. At various times, the legislature had met in Hillsborough, New Bern, Edenton, Bath, Fayetteville, Smithfield, Halifax, Wilmington, Brunswick, and Tarboro. In 1792, the state bought a thousand acres of land in Wake County. State leaders planned a state capital there and named it Raleigh, after Sir Walter Raleigh. (See left.)

Jefferson devised a plan. He asked two officials, Robert R. Livingston and James Monroe, to buy New Orleans and, if necessary, some of the nearby land.

Congress approved $2 million for the purchase, but Jefferson told Monroe and Livingston to pay as much as $10 million for New Orleans. At first, the French leader Napoleon Bonaparte refused the American offer. Suddenly, however, he changed his mind, offering to sell not only New Orleans but all French lands west of the Mississippi.

The American officials acted quickly. They offered Napoleon $15 million for the land. Although they did not have the authority to make this purchase, the sale was made. Federalists criticized the cost, but Congress approved it. As a result of the **Louisiana Purchase**, the United States, which now included New Orleans and land from the Mississippi River to the Rocky Mountains, doubled in size.

Explorers travel west. President Jefferson sent explorers to study the landforms, plants, animals, and natural resources of the newly purchased land. Jefferson also wanted to know about Native Americans who lived there.

Between 1804 and 1806, a party of more than 50 explorers, including a North Carolinian, traveled through the northern part of the Louisiana Purchase. Led by Meriwether Lewis and William Clark, brother of the Revolutionary War hero George Rogers Clark, the explorers traveled by keelboat, canoe, and packhorse from St. Louis to the coast of Oregon. As the party traveled west, they kept detailed journals and made maps.

Think as a Geographer

The 1803 Louisiana Purchase doubled the size of the United States. ■ *To Do:* On the map on page 176, find the borders of the purchase. Now look at the map entitled The United States: Political in the atlas section of your book. Which states were once part of the Louisiana Purchase? What natural resources do you think the United States gained as a result of this purchase?

Americans were very interested in drawings of plants collected by members of the Lewis and Clark expedition to the West. Can you identify these plants?

Two months before Lewis and Clark returned, another explorer named Zebulon Pike set out across the southern part of the Louisiana Purchase. He led his group west across the Great Plains into Colorado and as far south as the Rio Grande. Both expeditions helped Americans learn more about life in the West.

The Walton War erupts. As North Carolina's pioneers pushed westward, they became involved in a dispute known as the Walton War. The 1804 "war" took place on a 12-mile strip of land between North Carolina and Georgia.

Both states had granted settlers land here, yet no one knew the exact location of the state line. After Georgia created Walton County for these settlers, angry North Carolina officials reacted. Soldiers from both states clashed at the border. When the state line was surveyed in 1810, Walton County's settlers discovered that they lived in North Carolina rather than in Georgia.

The War of 1812 begins. Once France no longer held New Orleans after the Louisiana Purchase, Americans focused on problems with Britain. The countries disagreed over the location of the Canada-United States border. In addition, settlers in the West resented the presence of British forts.

Maps Matter

Zebulon Pike and Meriwether Lewis and William Clark led explorers to the West. This map shows you their routes. ■ *To Do*: Trace the explorers' two routes on the map. Where did Lewis and Clark's route begin and end? Which rivers did they use? Where did Pike's route begin and end?

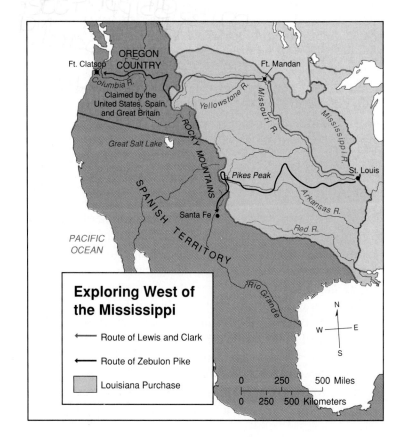

Exploring West of the Mississippi

← Route of Lewis and Clark

← Route of Zebulon Pike

Louisiana Purchase

The British also seized American sailors against their will and forced them to serve in the British navy. Such seizure is called **impressment.** These problems forced President James Madison to call for war in June 1812.

In the **War of 1812,** Americans won key battles on Lake Erie and Lake Champlain. They stopped the British from invading the United States from Canada. However, British forces along the Atlantic coast captured the nation's new capital, Washington, D.C., in August 1814. The British moved north to Baltimore but lost a fierce battle there at Fort McHenry in September 1814.

On Christmas Eve 1814, Britain and the United States signed a peace treaty in Belgium. Because it took two weeks for news to reach the United States, the war's last battle was fought after the treaty signing. The Americans, led by North Carolina native Andrew Jackson, won the Battle of New Orleans on January 8, 1815.

Neither Britain nor the United States won the War of 1812, yet Americans showed the world that their young republic could succeed. After the war, the growing nation faced new challenges.

Two naval heroes from North Carolina fought in the War of 1812. Captain Johnston Blakeley, commander of the *Wasp,* captured two British ships. Captain Otway Burns, shown in this picture, sailed on a privateer called the *Snap Dragon.*

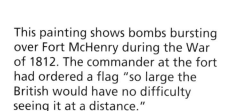

This painting shows bombs bursting over Fort McHenry during the War of 1812. The commander at the fort had ordered a flag "so large the British would have no difficulty seeing it at a distance."

Think Twice

1. Where did pioneers settle in the late 1700s?
2. What was one result of the Louisiana Purchase?
3. Who explored the Louisiana Purchase?
4. What were three causes of the War of 1812?
5. Imagine you are an American in the 1700s. Would you move west or stay and help make your state stronger? Why?

Chapter 12 Review

Choose from the following menu of activities.

Think Back: Main Ideas

1. On a separate sheet of paper, enlarge the diagram below. List similarities and differences to compare the first two plans for a new government of the United States.

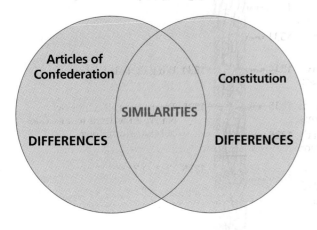

Articles of Confederation

Constitution

SIMILARITIES

DIFFERENCES

DIFFERENCES

2. Name two functions of each branch of government: (a) legislative, (b) judicial, (c) executive.
3. Explain the importance of (a) the Bill of Rights, (b) checks and balances, (c) the Louisiana Purchase, (d) the War of 1812.

Maps Matter

By 1783, the United States stretched from the Atlantic Ocean in the East to the Mississippi River in the West. Use the map entitled Growth of the United States, 1783–1853 in the atlas section of your text to answer these questions.

1. What natural feature marked the western boundary of the Louisiana Purchase of 1803?
2. What natural feature marked the eastern boundary of the Louisiana Purchase?
3. What state was formed in 1845 southwest of the Louisiana Purchase?

Word Wizard

1. *Congress* comes from a Latin word that means "to come together." Is this is a good term for our national legislative body? Why or why not?
2. Read the different meanings of *bill* in a dictionary. Write the definition that relates to the Bill of Rights.

Working Cooperatively

Work with a group of three to five of your classmates. Find out who currently represents North Carolina in Congress. Who are the senators? Who are the representatives? Have your group write a letter to one of these senators or representatives to inquire about his or her job. If you wish, mail the letter to this person's Washington office.

Curriculum Connection

During the War of 1812, Francis Scott Key was a prisoner on a British ship and witnessed the battle at Fort McHenry. He scribbled a poem on the back of a letter. His poem, "The Star-Spangled Banner," was later set to the music of an old song. In 1931, it became the nation's national anthem. Listen to a recording of the song. Then answer these questions.

1. What images do the song lyrics convey?
2. How does the music make you feel?
3. Do you think this song should be the national anthem? Why or why not?

Learning through Literature

The Toad on Capitol Hill, by Esther Wood Brady
Jump Ship to Freedom, by James L. Collier and Christopher Collier
If Pigs Could Fly, by John Lawson

North Carolina: A State On Its Own

NORTH CAROLINA

Time Line

THE UNITED STATES

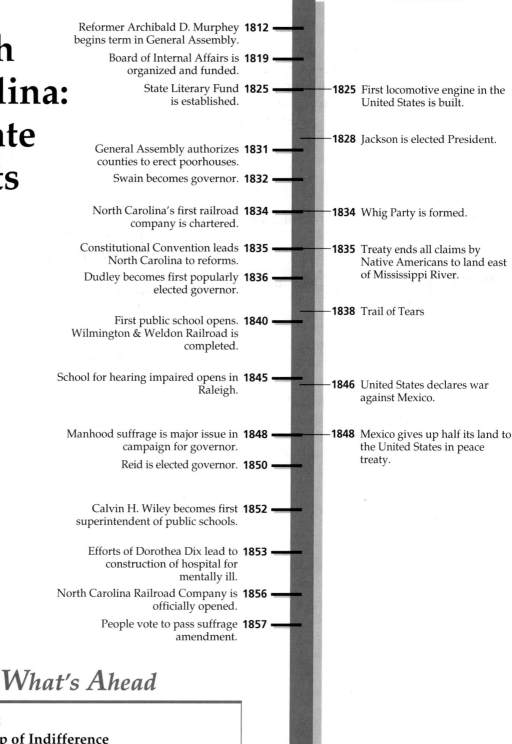

North Carolina	Year	The United States
Reformer Archibald D. Murphey begins term in General Assembly.	**1812**	
Board of Internal Affairs is organized and funded.	**1819**	
State Literary Fund is established.	**1825**	**1825** First locomotive engine in the United States is built.
		1828 Jackson is elected President.
General Assembly authorizes counties to erect poorhouses.	**1831**	
Swain becomes governor.	**1832**	
North Carolina's first railroad company is chartered.	**1834**	**1834** Whig Party is formed.
Constitutional Convention leads North Carolina to reforms.	**1835**	**1835** Treaty ends all claims by Native Americans to land east of Mississippi River.
Dudley becomes first popularly elected governor.	**1836**	
First public school opens. Wilmington & Weldon Railroad is completed.	**1840**	**1838** Trail of Tears
School for hearing impaired opens in Raleigh.	**1845**	**1846** United States declares war against Mexico.
Manhood suffrage is major issue in campaign for governor.	**1848**	**1848** Mexico gives up half its land to the United States in peace treaty.
Reid is elected governor.	**1850**	
Calvin H. Wiley becomes first superintendent of public schools.	**1852**	
Efforts of Dorothea Dix lead to construction of hospital for mentally ill.	**1853**	
North Carolina Railroad Company is officially opened.	**1856**	
People vote to pass suffrage amendment.	**1857**	

What's Ahead

Chapter 13

The Sleep of Indifference

In the early 1800s, apathy and poor conditions earn North Carolina a reputation as the "Rip Van Winkle State."

In most parts of the United States, the War of 1812 spurred business and brought new ideas. This was not the case in North Carolina. In fact, few states had done as little as North Carolina to promote education, science, and the arts. When people in other states became aware of conditions in North Carolina, they began to refer to it as the "Rip Van Winkle State," because it seemed that the state was asleep.

Archibald DeBow Murphey leads the way to reform in North Carolina.

North Carolina lawyer and legislator Archibald DeBow Murphey wanted to improve conditions in his native state. For years he pushed for a program of internal improvements, public education, and constitutional reform. It was not until the Constitutional Convention of 1835 that efforts by Murphey and others would bear results.

Archibald D. Murphey (1777–1832) ▶

Think Ahead

Many factors contributed to North Carolina's slow progress, including isolation of the people, poor farm conditions, migration to other states, and an undemocratic government. Read about the state's struggle to regain its strength and prosperity. Find out how the Constitutional Convention of 1835 aroused North Carolina from its long Rip Van Winkle sleep.

1 A Dismal Outlook

People, Places, Terms

individualism
legislature
academy
economy

Following the War of 1812, citizens of North Carolina seemed unaware of public events and trends, even within their own state. Most people in the eastern section of the state were satisfied with their conditions. Their voice prevailed in the government, and they were content to do little or nothing to improve conditions in the whole state.

In 1810, Thomas Henderson, editor of a Raleigh newspaper, *The Star,* sent a questionnaire to leading citizens in each county to learn about conditions in North Carolina. His results showed that a third of the people in Edgecombe County could not read, and only about half of the men and a third of the women could write. From Caswell County, it was reported that fewer than half the people could "read, write and cypher." Other reports showed that similar conditions existed in the state as a whole. By 1832, North Carolina was many years behind other states in the education of its children. Several factors caused this decline in the state in the early 1800s.

The impact of isolation. The isolation of people within North Carolina played a role in the state's backwardness. People lived far apart on scattered farms. There were few towns and little trade. People in the interior of the state were even more isolated because of the lack of roads and other means of communication. They produced only those goods that were absolutely necessary—and did not miss the luxuries they had never known.

The geographical isolation of the people contributed to a feeling of **individualism**. This meant that people were concerned only with their own individual needs and freedoms. They did not want state officials interfering in their lives or telling them to pay taxes or to send their children to school.

The attitude toward education. Many parents in North Carolina did not feel that education was important. They preferred to have their children stay at home to work on the farm. If their children attended school, farm families would lose a valuable resource—the help of their children at home. Many of these parents were themselves uneducated. They felt that if they could get by without education, so could their children.

The landowners who were in power supported this attitude since it saved them and the state money. They saw no reason why the state should tax their property to pay for the education of the children of poorer families.

Think as a Historian

*T*he first public schools in North Carolina were not started until after 1835. This date lagged far behind other states in the country.
■ *To Do*: Look under the heading of Public Education in an encyclopedia or other reference source. Find out which state had the first public system of education in the country. Based on what you have read so far in this lesson, explain how public education in that state might have benefited its economy and growth.

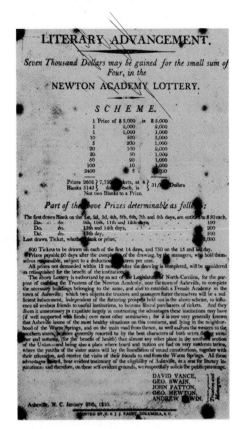

Lotteries often were held to raise money for the academies in North Carolina.

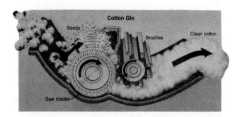

In Whitney's cotton gin, cotton was fed through a row of saw blades. The saw's teeth pulled the cotton—but not the seeds—through a metal grill. Brushes removed clean cotton fiber caught on the saw's teeth.

The state **legislature**, the lawmaking branch of state government, did little to improve attitudes toward education. Although the state constitution of 1776 had stated that schools should "be established by the Legislature for the convenient Instruction of Youth, with such Salaries to the Masters paid by the Public," the legislature made no attempt to enforce these rules. As a matter of fact, in the early 1800s when many other states had passed laws establishing public education, North Carolina had no public schools. Instead it had **academies**—schools that depended on local interest and financing.

By 1825, North Carolina had chartered 177 academies. Only thirteen of these permitted girls to attend. Although some of the schools provided free tuition for a limited number of poor students, many poor families were too proud to take advantage of this opportunity. As a result, schools were attended primarily by those who could afford to pay.

The state's economy.   A state's **economy** is the way people produce goods and services. In North Carolina, the economy seemed to prosper for a while, but then it faltered. This was due in part to the introduction of the cotton gin, invented by Eli Whitney in 1793.

Whitney's cotton gin was a machine that removed the seeds from cotton quickly and thoroughly. Using the cotton gin, a worker could clean 50 times more cotton each day than by using his or her hands. As a result of the cotton gin, planters in North Carolina and other southern states began planting more and more cotton.

The cotton gin gave agriculture an advantage in the state. Before long, manufacturing ceased to interest many people. North Carolina became largely an agricultural state, and in many respects, a one-crop state. The focus on cotton also meant that food crops were neglected and had to be brought in at great cost from other states. With most of its attention and money focused on agriculture, North Carolina had little industry, limited commerce, and inadequate banking.

The system of enslaved labor that existed in North Carolina also contributed to the state's economic woes. First, and most importantly, the system was cruel and repressive to enslaved laborers. Secondly, wealthy landowners invested their money in this unjust system instead of developing industry or improving agriculture.

Farm conditions and migration.   Another reason for decline in North Carolina was poor farm conditions. Farmers rarely made any attempt to improve their land or to preserve its fertility. Therefore, they found it very difficult to carve out an existence on this constantly eroding land. Between 1815 and 1833, the assessed value of land dropped dramatically. In the words of one farmer, the choices were to "move, improve, or starve."

Contributing to this bleak situation was the lack of adequate transportation and communication. Few rivers were suitable for boats or rafts, and roads were poorly maintained. Bridges were rare, and floods were common. This lack of transportation meant that it would cost farmers one half of their crop to get the other half to market. As a result, few farmers bothered to grow more than was needed for their own use.

Poor farming conditions led many families to leave North Carolina. Between 1815 and 1850, one-third of the population of North Carolina migrated to other states. In 1815, it was estimated that 200,000 people had moved to Tennessee, Alabama, and Ohio. In addition, thousands of wealthy people moved to the West where richer land and good river navigation offered better opportunities. By 1850, the census showed that 31 percent of all native North Carolinians living in the United States were residents of other states.

Trail of Tears

People of European descent were not the only group that suffered in the early 1800s. The Cherokee—a Native American group that claimed North Carolina lands long before the arrival of the Europeans—also endured hardship. Their hardship had to do not with poor farming conditions or lack of industry but with the loss of the land on which they lived.

In 1819, the Cherokee were forced by the federal government to give up their claims to land in present-day Henderson, Transylvania, and Jackson counties. However, individuals among the Cherokee were permitted to own land under specific grants. Then in 1835, a treaty ended all claims by Native Americans to land east of the Mississippi River. In 1838, General Winfield Scott and about 7,000 troops were sent into the mountains by President Andrew Jackson to force 3,500 Cherokee to leave their homes and travel to what is now Oklahoma. Most of the Cherokee left the region, suffering greatly on their trek, which has come to be called the Trail of Tears.

Under the leadership of an elderly man named Tsali, about one thousand Cherokee revolted against the inhumanity of the soldiers. An agreement was reached that if Tsali surrendered, a plan would be worked out to permit his followers to remain in North Carolina. Whether Tsali surrendered or was betrayed is debatable. He and some of his relatives were executed. The remaining people were permitted to stay in North Carolina. They were granted United States citizenship, and each family received land. This was the origin of the Qualla Boundary, or Cherokee Indian reservation, still maintained in southwestern North Carolina today.

*T*he richest and most fertile land in the state is in the broad middle eastern section called the Coastal Plain. ■ *To Do*: Study the map of North Carolina in the atlas section of your text. What physical features can you find to explain why this section is the most fertile part of the state?

_____

A government undemocratic in form.   Representation in the legislature was by county. Since most of the counties were in the east, it was the east that governed North Carolina. The voting population of the eastern counties was a very small percentage of the total voting population of the state. However, this population elected a majority of the legislators and dominated elections for governor and other state officials. From 1777 to 1836, twenty-four men served as governor of the state, but only six of them were from western counties. Consequently, the east controlled all the branches of state government.

Frequently, the west tried to get new counties established by naming them after prominent, living eastern politicians. When eastern politicians realized what was happening, they tried to offset the effect of each new western county by dividing an old eastern county. This is why there are so many small eastern counties in the state today.

A government undemocratic in spirit.   The state government was not only undemocratic in form, it was also undemocratic in spirit. Since all state officials were elected by the legislature, and since that branch of government was controlled by wealthy landowners from the east, *property*—not people—controlled the government. Living on their plantations supported largely by enslaved laborers, these landowners were satisfied with their easy existence and often looked down on the majority of citizens, whom they called "the common people." They were opposed to granting the majority of people more political power or spending state money to improve conditions in the state.

_____

Think Twice

1. Explain how each of the following factors contributed to decline in North Carolina in the early 1800s.
   (a) isolation
   (b) attitude toward education
   (c) the state's economy
   (d) farm conditions and migration
2. In what ways was the constitution of 1776 undemocratic?
3. In Chapter 9, "Division Within North Carolina," you learned about sectional rivalries that existed in the state in the 1700s. Which of the rivalries that you read about in Chapter 9 appeared again in the early 1800s? Were the effects of the rivalries in the early 1800s similar to or different from the effects of the rivalries in the 1700s?

2 The Vision of Archibald Murphey

People, Places, Terms

Archibald D. Murphey
Literary Fund
internal improvement
constitutional reform

From 1815 to 1840, a small group of reformers tried to solve North Carolina's problems and set the state on a new course. The leaders of this movement included Bartlett Yancey, Joseph Caldwell, Charles Fisher, David L. Swain, William Gaston, John Motley Morehead, and William A. Graham.

The clear leader in the group, however, was Archibald DeBow Murphey. Murphey fought for a system of public education, internal improvements, and constitutional reform.

Preparation for leadership.   Archibald DeBow Murphey was born in Caswell County in 1777 and attended David Caldwell's school in Guilford County. After he was graduated from the University of North Carolina in 1799, he remained in Chapel Hill for two years as a tutor and professor of ancient languages. During this time, he also studied law and in 1802 began working as a lawyer in Hillsborough. From 1818 to 1820, Murphey was a superior court judge and sometimes served as a special justice on the state supreme court. In addition, he served as a legislator, representing Orange County in the General Assembly from 1812 through 1818. As he traveled throughout the state, Murphey became deeply disturbed by the conditions he observed. Writing to his friend Thomas Ruffin in 1819, Murphey described what he saw.

Primary Source

I know ten times as much of the Topography of this Circuit, as the Men who have lived here fifty Years. I had no Idea that we had such a poor, ignorant, squalid Population, as I have seen. Who that sees these People, and those of the Centre and the West, can wonder that we wish to have a Convention [to amend the constitution]? In the Towns are found decent and well informed Men in Matters of Business, Men who look well and live well. But the Mass of the Common People in the Country are lazy, sickly, poor, dirty and ignorant. Yet this is a Section of the State upon which the Hand of Industry would soon impress a fine Character.

— ARCHIBALD D. MURPHEY, *"Letter to Thomas Ruffin"*

Murphey was aware of modern progress in other states and abroad, and he often cited changes taking place elsewhere. As a legislator and a private citizen, Murphey

Public school reforms generally applied only to children of European descent. These reforms did not include Africans, either free or enslaved. In fact, laws existed prohibiting the education of enslaved laborers throughout the South. ■ *To Do*: Why do you think the education of enslaved people was seen as a threat to those who enslaved them?

A North Carolina canal built in the mid-1830s.

took the lead in support of three important programs that he thought would rouse the state from its long period of relaxation.

The state's Literary Fund. Murphey devoted much of his energy to the cause of public education. He advocated state-supported public schools. Murphey published his findings and proposals in a pamphlet called *Report on Education* so that people could learn about his ideas.

About seven years after Murphey left the General Assembly, more people began to realize the value of his plans for public education in North Carolina. As a result, in 1825, the General Assembly agreed to set aside state money for a **Literary Fund**—a fund that the legislature said would be used to establish a public school system. A Literary Board was appointed to manage the fund.

Unfortunately, the Literary Fund grew very slowly, and its history reflects the legislature's attitude toward education. The legislature rejected all bills introduced to increase money in the fund. As a result, the Literary Fund never grew large enough to pay for public schools throughout the state. Although many people continued to urge the legislature to establish a public school system in North Carolina, legislators refused, saying that they had done all that they could.

Suggestions for internal improvements. Murphey knew that one of the chief factors that slowed North Carolina's progress was the lack of adequate transportion. In 1815, he drew up a plan calling for **internal improvements,** in which the state would pay to improve harbors, construct canals, and build turnpikes. He also wanted the state to drain the swamplands of the east, reclaiming them for agricultural purposes while improving the health of the people who lived near them. Funding was to come from the sale of land taken from the Cherokee and from stock owned by the state.

In 1819, the legislature created a fund for internal improvements and established a Board of Internal Improvements to manage the fund. The board hired a Scottish engineer, Hamilton Fulton, who developed Murphey's ideas and drew up plans to clear the waterways and connect them with canals.

The fund spurred great interest from counties throughout the state. Soon nearly every community in the state came forward with a project to be funded. Unfortunately, the state spent large amounts of money on projects that never should have been funded. The internal improvements program eventually failed, due in large part to bad financing.

In the late 1820s and early 1830s, a new form of transportation, the locomotive engine, captured the imagination of the people of North Carolina. Although this new form of transportation caused work on canals to decline, it offered an improved form of transportation. The locomotive engine had been invented in England in 1804 by Richard Trevithick. In 1825, Colonel John Stevens built the first locomotive engine in the United States. There was great enthusiasm throughout North Carolina for rail transportation. As a result, in 1834, the legislature chartered the first railroad company in the state.

The need for constitutional reform.   The west wanted public schools and transportation, but the east opposed both, and the east controlled the state. Murphey and other reformers realized the state would not be able to improve education or transportion until the undemocratic constitution of North Carolina was changed. They wanted a convention to change the constitution of 1776 so that the west would be more fairly represented.

In 1816, Murphey argued in favor of a convention, explaining that the current constitution violated the principles of democratic government. Murphey recommended that the legislature hold an election and allow the people to decide if they wanted to change their constitution. Murphey hoped that such an election would attract public attention to the issue of changing the constitution, or **constitutional reform.** Unfortunately, Murphey's proposal was rejected by the legislature. During the next few years, other efforts to persuade legislators on this point also failed.

Murphey's legacy.   Archibald D. Murphey devoted his life to the task of arousing the people of North Carolina from their indifference and poor conditions. He pointed out their failings and showed them their opportunities.

Before his death in 1832, Murphey must have thought that his life had been a failure. However, soon a new political party would emerge that would have Murphey's program as its base. In time, this new party would bring about an era of progress that Murphey had so clearly foreseen.

Think Twice

1. Name the three main programs for improving conditions in North Carolina that Murphey sponsored in the early 1800s. Describe the specific plan for each program. Describe the results of each program.
2. Why do you think Murphey felt that public education and internal improvements were important to the state?
3. Before his death in 1832, Murphey believed that his life had been a failure. Do you agree or disagree? Explain your answer.

People, Places, Terms

Andrew Jackson
Whig party
David L. Swain
Nathaniel Macon
William Gaston

3 The Constitutional Convention of 1835

In 1816, Archibald Murphey had supported the idea of a convention to amend the state's constitution of 1776. In 1835, only three years after his death, Murphey's dream for a constitutional convention became a reality.

The Constitutional Convention of 1835 marked a turning point for the state. Although many of the reforms it passed were initially seen as a victory for the west, in time these reforms benefited the entire state. In fact, the reforms would usher in a new age of progress and prosperity for North Carolina.

Rise of a two-party system. For 20 years following the War of 1812, the Republican party, founded by Thomas Jefferson, was the only political party in North Carolina. As a result, there was little political discussion or debate of political issues. The 1828 election of Andrew Jackson as the nation's President was to change this one-party rule in North Carolina.

Andrew Jackson (1767–1845)

In 1828, Andrew Jackson's election to the presidency was applauded by a united North Carolina. However, once President Jackson was in office, he disappointed many North Carolinians, especially those from the west, when he opposed internal improvements, such as building canals and turnpikes.

Rise of the Whig party.   By 1834, the dissatisfied voters in North Carolina were ready to switch their loyalty to a new American political party. The **Whig party** was formed in the United States by those who were sympathetic to banks and internal improvements. Jackson's supporters soon changed the name of their party from Republican to Democrat to show that it represented the will of the people. Thus, two parties, Whigs and Democrats, began a 20-year rivalry that contributed greatly to progress in North Carolina.

Demands of the west.   Most North Carolina Whigs lived in the west. They adopted Archibald D. Murphey's program calling for constitutional reform, public schools, and internal improvements in North Carolina. Newspaper support, mass meetings, and unofficial polls all showed public sentiment in the west in favor of these reforms. When eastern landowners still refused to support any change in the constitution, a great wave of anger swept over the west. Revolution was actually threatened if the demands of the region were not met.

The west needed a leader who could urge the legislature to call a convention. He was David L. Swain, a popular lawyer, legislator, and judge, who became governor of the state in 1832. As governor, Swain spoke often in the cause of the west, and constitutional reform became the chief goal of his administration. In his address to the legislature in 1834, Swain urged the legislature to call a convention to amend the 1776 constitution. His message helped to make it possible for the west finally to win the first victory for consititutional reform in North Carolina since 1776.

The convention.   The convention met in Raleigh on June 4, 1835, with 128 delegates present. Members of the convention included governors, judges, and members of Congress. Nathaniel Macon, an eastern Democrat and long-time legislator, was chosen president of the convention. After working for more than a month, the delegates to the convention proposed several important changes to the state constitution.

An important result of the convention was a change in the old system of representation. Under the new system. the Senate was to have fifty members chosen by districts formed on the basis of taxes paid into the state treasury.

David L. Swain (1801–1868) was governor of North Carolina when he participated in the Constitutional Convention of 1835. A skillful negotiator, Swain helped to bring about important changes in the state constitution.

William Gaston (1778–1844) was one of the most respected men in the state of North Carolina.

Because the east was wealthier and paid more taxes, the majority of Senate members would be from the east. However, the House of Commons was to have 120 members representing counties based on their population. Therefore, the west would have a majority of House members.

Other changes were also made to the constitution of 1776. The question of religious restrictions for office-holding was seriously discussed. William Gaston, a lawyer, legislator, and judge was one of the most highly respected men in the state. As a Roman Catholic, he was uncomfortable with the 1776 constitution that allowed only Protestants to hold certain offices. It was finally agreed that the word *Protestant* would be replaced by *Christian*, thereby allowing Catholics to hold public office. In addition, the delegates approved an amendment to provide for the election of the governor by all male taxpayers of European descent who were 21 years of age or older. The convention also changed the term of governor from one year to two years and set the terms for other state officials.

While these changes were considered improvements, not all of the reforms of the Convention of 1835 were positive. In fact, one reform actually took away rights that had been granted in 1776. These rights had to do with free African men. The constitution of 1776 did not deny these men the right to vote. The 1835 constitution did.

The Convention of 1835 was an important event in North Carolina history. It allowed people from both eastern and western parts of the state to play a role in government and state policies. The east no longer had control of both houses, and the west was able to approve laws for improved conditions. Within a few years, important changes began to take place in North Carolina. It was the Convention of 1835 that finally aroused the state from its long Rip Van Winkle sleep.

Think Twice

1. How did the Constitutional Convention of 1835 finally come about?
2. Name the men who played important roles in the convention.
3. (a) Describe three positive results of the convention.
   (b) Describe one negative result of the convention.
4. In your opinion, what was the most important constitutional reform of the Convention of 1835? Support your answer with facts from the chapter.

Chapter 13 Review

Choose from the following menu of activities.

Think Back: Main Ideas

1. What nickname had North Carolina earned in the early 1800s? Why was this nickname appropriate?
2. Describe three factors that led to the decline of the state of North Carolina in the early 1800s.
3. (a) Why was political power originally held by the eastern part of the state?
   (b) How were the needs in the western part of the state different from those in the eastern part of the state?
4. Describe the contributions of Archibald D. Murphey.
5. What new political party emerged in the state in 1834? Whose ideas formed the base of this party? What were the goals of this party in North Carolina?
6. (a) What were the goals of the Constitutional Convention of 1835?
   (b) Who benefited from changes brought about in the new constitution? What group suffered as a result of the new constitution?

Maps Matter

As a result of the politics of the early 1800s, many western counties today bear the names of eastern politicians. These include the following counties.

Western County	Named for
Ashe	Samuel Ashe of New Hanover
Buncombe	Colonel Edward Buncombe of Tyrrell
Iredell	James Iredell of Chowan
Macon	Nathaniel Macon of Warren

1. Use the North Carolina Counties map in the atlas section of your text to find each of these four western counties.
2. Describe the relative location of each county—that is, describe in what part of the state each county lies and what other counties surround it.
3. For additional research, you may choose to find out more about the eastern politicians for whom these counties were named.

Word Wizard

1. The word *legislature* gets its meaning from the Latin root *legis*, meaning "law." Use a dictionary to find other related words that contain the same root. Write each word and its specific meaning.
2. The word *economy* comes from the Greek word *oikonomia*, meaning "household manager." How has the meaning changed from the original use to today's use of the word *economy*? Use a dictionary to find related words that contain the same root. Write these words and their meanings.

Working Cooperatively

Work in a small group to write the script for a debate between easterners and westerners about one aspect of Murphey's plan—either education, internal improvements, or constitutional reform. Then stage the debate for the class.

Curriculum Connection

Read Washington Irving's tale "Rip Van Winkle." Compare the events of the story to conditions in North Carolina in the early 1800s.

Learning through Literature

Sequoyah, by Grant Foreman

Chapter 14

Alert and Active

Changes in North Carolina politics benefit the state.

The revised constitution, along with the two-party system, generated a new political atmosphere. Under the constitution of 1835, the western part of the state gained a strong voice in state government. The two-party system created healthy competition between the Whigs and the Democrats. This encouraged both parties to support ideas and plans for the public good in order to win votes.

The years before the Civil War are the most progressive in North Carolina's history.

North Carolina thrived in the years between 1835 and 1860. The Whig party was in power for much of this period. The Whigs drew support from throughout the state. As a result, the sharp division between eastern and western North Carolina declined. The benefits that Archibald Murphey predicted came to be true, including public schools, railroads, and other internal improvements. When the Democrats gained the upper hand in 1850, they proved to be capable custodians of the state's growing reputation.

State capitol building in Raleigh, 1840 ▶

Think Ahead

Changes in North Carolina's government woke the state up from its long Rip Van Winkle sleep. The years between 1835 and 1860 were dynamic ones. Read about the improvements and social reforms that made North Carolina one of the most progressive states in the country during this period.

1 Improvements Under the Whigs

In 1836, Edward Bishop Dudley, a Whig from Wilmington, became the first governor elected directly by the population when he defeated Richard Dobbs Spaight, Jr., the Democratic incumbent. Dudley's victory marked the beginning of a long period of Whig-controlled government. During this time, North Carolina made great progress. Railroads were built, public education was established, and services for the needy were established. Some of the money for this development came from a surplus in the federal treasury, which the United States government distributed to the states. North Carolina's share was nearly a million and a half dollars.

The "Iron Horse" in North Carolina.   Interest in railroad development began almost a decade before the Whigs gained control of state government. In 1827, University of North Carolina president Joseph Caldwell published a series of articles in newspapers. In these articles, Caldwell pointed out the advantages of railroads over canals and turnpikes. North Carolinians were quick to see the benefits.

In 1828, about 200 farmers gathered at the farm of William Albright in Chatham County to talk about the possibility of a railroad through central North Carolina. A railroad would be a great help in getting their crops to market. Unfortunately, the farmers lacked both the money and political influence to pursue their dream. That same year, a short experimental railroad was constructed in Fayetteville. It ran from the waterfront docks on the Cape Fear River up the steep bank to a warehouse on higher ground. This was a simple affair, with wooden rails and cars pulled by horses or mules.

In 1833, another experimental railroad was laid in Raleigh. It ran from a quarry to the site of the new capitol building. During the work week, it was used to haul stone for the building of the capitol. However, on Sundays, passengers were taken for pleasure rides. When members of the General Assembly were in town, they also had a chance to try this wonderful new device.

The Wilmington & Weldon Railroad.   The citizens of Wilmington decided the future of their city depended upon the railroad. By 1833, they had raised $400,000 toward the construction of a line from Wilmington through Raleigh. However, the people of Raleigh refused to cooperate and the plans were changed. The new route, chartered in 1836, extended north from Wilmington to the

Edward B. Dudley was born in Onslow County in the eastern part of North Carolina. He was a leader in the Whig party and a strong advocate of state support for railroads and public education. In 1836, Dudley became the first popularly elected governor.

Woodburning locomotives, like this one belonging to the Raleigh & Gaston Railroad, were symbols of North Carolina's progress in the mid-1800s.

Think as a Geographer

*I*t was along the route of the North Carolina Railroad that a string of thriving industrial cities developed in the nineteenth century. ■ *To Do*: Compare the map of North Carolina railroads in 1860 to the map entitled North Carolina: Physical/Political in the atlas section of your text. Name at least three large cities that are located along this line. What role do you think the railroad played in helping them grow?

Roanoke River at Weldon. The **Wilmington & Weldon Railroad** was completed on March 7, 1840.

The new railroad was 161 1/2 miles long—the longest railroad in the world at the time. Although the railroad was a great improvement, it still lacked many of the comforts of today's railroads. A traveler in 1849 reported that it took 11 hours to go from Weldon to Wilmington and that the fare was five dollars. He also noted that "travellers who grumble at the bad condition of the road would not do so if they knew what difficulties the company have had to encounter, and how poorly as yet they have been paid." Another passenger was not so understanding, as the following passage shows.

Primary Source

The cars were constantly filled with dust so that we could not see each other with any distinctness, and what rendered the ride more intolerable, I had no one to fret and fidget with me. . . . I had to wet a towel we had provided ourselves with, having had a foretaste of this when we went to Raleigh. I had to wet this towel whenever we stopped, and clear the dust from my eyes, in order to preserve any kind of vision.

— ANONYMOUS TRAVELLER

The building of the first interstate railroad. At the same time the Wilmington & Weldon Railroad was being built, another railroad was also under construction. Raleigh's citizens worked with officials of the Petersburg, Virginia, railroad to construct the first interstate line. To do this, the state granted Raleigh two charters. One was for a short line from Greensville County, Virginia, to the Roanoke River in Northampton County, which would be known as the Greensville & Roanoke Railroad. This line was soon completed and its southern terminal took the name of Gaston. The other was for a line from Raleigh to the Roanoke River at Gaston. This one was called the **Raleigh & Gaston Railroad**. Except for a break at the river, which had to be crossed by ferry, this line connected the state capitals of North Carolina and Virginia.

Connections by rail.   In 1840, farmers in the eastern part of the state began to ship their cotton, corn, tobacco, and other produce to market by rail. Suppliers started using the railroads to transport fertilizer and equipment to the farmers. People in western North Carolina realized the advantages to be gained from such services. As a result, they wanted railroads in their part of the state.

In response to the demand for more railroad lines, the General Assembly passed a bill in 1849 that chartered the North Carolina Railroad Company. This line was to run from Goldsboro to Charlotte, passing through Raleigh. The state agreed to pay two million dollars of the three million dollars necessary for construction.

The entire state was enthusiastic about the railroad and watched the progress with great interest. The first rails were laid in a ceremony on July 11, 1851, and nearly five years later, on January 29, 1856, the railroad was officially opened. It ran in a great arc across North Carolina, covering a distance of 223 miles.

The Raleigh & Gaston Railroad had a roundhouse and machine shop in Raleigh. A roundhouse is a circular building used for repairing and storing locomotives.

Maps Matter

Maps help us picture information so that we have a clear understanding of it. ■*To Do:* Using the descriptions of the routes of the railroad lines in the text, trace the routes of the Wilmington & Weldon, North Carolina, and Raleigh & Gaston railroads on the map.

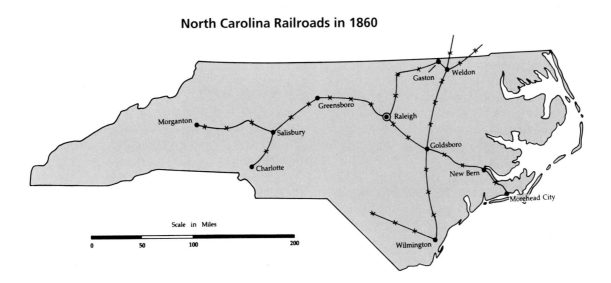

North Carolina Railroads in 1860

Morganton · Salisbury · Greensboro · Raleigh · Gaston · Weldon · Goldsboro · Charlotte · New Bern · Morehead City · Wilmington

Scale in Miles
0   50   100   200

Dorothea Dix was a social reformer in Boston and New York. After touring North Carolina in 1848, she convinced the state to fund a hospital for the mentally ill.

In less than 25 years, rail transportation connected almost all of the regions of North Carolina. Trade grew and the economy improved. Communication increased. The railroads united the people of the state, created a new pride and patriotism, and helped to stop the flow of people out of North Carolina to other states.

Establishment of public schools. Not all of the Whig government's attention was focused on the railroads. Some of the money from the federal government's surplus went into North Carolina's Literary Fund, and late in 1838, the Literary Board presented the General Assembly with a plan for establishing public schools. This plan followed very closely on Archibald Murphey's plan of 1817.

In January 1839, the General Assembly passed the state's first public school law. The bill provided for the division of the state into school districts. It also called for the establishment of a primary school in each district that would be supported through county taxes and money from the Literary Fund. On January 20, 1840, the first "common" or public school opened in Rockingham County.

Defects in the new educational system. Some counties were less supportive of public schools than other counties. As a result, schools varied in quality. Also, the school districts were too large to make the location of the schoolhouses convenient for everyone. Some families lived so far away that their children were unable to make the trip every day. Nevertheless, the establishment of common schools in North Carolina was a significant achievement. Before 1840, a majority of citizens had been either indifferent to public education or actually opposed to it.

To War!

While the attention of most North Carolinians was focused on local affairs, some citizens of the state were on their way to battle. On May 13, 1846, the United States declared war against Mexico over the annexation of Texas. North Carolina was asked to supply a regiment of 1,000 soldiers to help fight the war.

Citizens of North Carolina responded enthusiastically. Many believed it was the "manifest destiny" of the United States to expand westward. They were inspired by a certain amount of state pride as well. James Knox Polk, the President of the United States at the time, was a native of North Carolina and a graduate of the University of North Carolina. Also, quite a few North Carolinians had recently moved to Texas. Their friends and relatives felt it was their duty to defend them.

The war was a success for the United States. In 1848, Mexico and the United States signed a treaty in which Mexico gave up half its land. (See the map entitled Growth of the United States, 1783–1853 in the atlas section of your text.) The land later became the states of California, Utah, Arizona, and Nevada. It also included a large part of what is now New Mexico, Colorado, and Wyoming. In return, the United States paid Mexico $15 million.

Help for the unfortunate. Under the Whigs, the state began to provide more services to the poor. Legally the poor were defined as persons incapable of earning a living because of mental disabilities or physical challenges. Also included were physically challenged children, the aged, and invalids.

In 1831, the General Assembly authorized counties to erect poorhouses, or institutions to house the poor. In the coming years, almost every county had a poorhouse. Institutions were also created to fulfill the needs of other people who required special services, including the mentally ill.

In 1848, the great social reformer Dorothea Dix visited North Carolina. She spent three months gathering information about jails and poorhouses. Dix also studied the treatment of the mentally ill, whose welfare particularly concerned her. She lobbied the legislature to pass a bill to fund special hospitals where the mentally ill could be taken care of properly. A skillful politician, she eventually succeeded. Construction began on the building in Raleigh in 1853.

State plans also included support for the hearing impaired. With the support of Governor John Motley Morehead and the help of William D. Cooke, principal of the Virginia Institute for the Deaf and Dumb, the General Assembly approved funds for a school for the deaf. The school opened in 1845. In 1852, the legislature incorporated the school as the North Carolina Institute for the Education of the Deaf, Dumb, and Blind. (Terms such as "deaf" and "blind" were commonly used in the mid-1800s. Today, these terms have been replaced by the terms "hearing impaired" and "sight impaired.")

Across Cultures

*T*he United States has come a long way since the time of Dorothea Dix in its treatment of people with special needs, such as the poor, the physically challenged, or the mentally ill. ■ *To Do*: Choose one of these groups to research and find out how North Carolina helps to meet their needs. You may wish to write or call your state legislator to find out how to get information from the state about the group you have chosen.

Think Twice

1. How did the changes of the 1835 constitution affect politics in North Carolina?
2. Why is the period between 1835 and 1860 considered to be a progressive time for North Carolina?
3. In what ways did the railroad help North Carolina to prosper?
4. How did state government help the needy?
5. Compare the role of government before and after the changes of the 1835 constitution.

People, Places, Terms

William A. Graham
Charles Manly
William W. Holden
David S. Reid
manhood suffrage
Calvin H. Wiley

2 The End of the Whig Party

The first three Whig governors, Edward B. Dudley (from the east), John M. Morehead (from the west), and William A. Graham (from the center), were young and active. They had the ability and enthusiasm to push their party's program. Under their leadership, North Carolina changed from a backward state to one of the most progressive in the nation. The fourth Whig governor, 54-year-old Charles Manly, was unimpressive by comparison. Manly played a large role in bringing about the end of the Whig party in North Carolina. In 1850, the Democrats took over the leadership of the state.

Changes in the Democratic party.   Young men joined the Democratic party and began to change its program. They favored support for the railroads and public education. Many of them also realized that the requirements for voting had been only slightly changed since 1776 and that the state constitution restricted too many people from voting.

One of the most active and effective of these new Democrats was William W. Holden. At the age of 25 in 1843, he became editor of the *North Carolina Standard*, a Raleigh newspaper. He soon developed it into the leading paper in the state. It also was one of the most attractive, since Holden acquired new type and decorative devices.

Holden, who had come from humble origins in Orange County, stood up for the common people. He urged the Democratic party to adopt a program that would benefit a great many people in North Carolina.

Democratic support for suffrage.   The Democrats had difficulty convincing good men to run for governor. The Whig party was so strong that Democrats just assumed the other party would win and were discouraged from running. Nevertheless, David S. Reid was finally persuaded to run for governor in 1848.

Although the party platform said nothing about broadening suffrage, or the right to vote, Reid chose this issue as his major campaign topic. He was in favor of a constitutional amendment that "all voters for a member of the House of Commons shall be allowed to vote for Senators." This change meant that a person would no longer have to own 50 acres of land in order to vote.

The Whigs chose Charles Manly to run against Reid. At a political meeting in Beaufort, both Manly and Reid were speaking from the same platform when Reid came out

Think as a Historian

*T*he cornerstone of democracy is the belief that citizens have a right to make free political choices. However, this is impossible if, as in the former Soviet Union, there is only one political party. ■ *To Do*: Think about the role of political parties in North Carolina. How did the two-party system benefit the ordinary citizen? How did it help democracy to progress?

strongly in support of **manhood suffrage,** or the right of white males to vote even if they owned no property. Reid's position took Manly by surprise. He refused to commit himself immediately and instead asked for a day or two to think it over. The next day, at another political gathering, Manly decided that he was against manhood suffrage.

Failure of the Whig party.   Manly's stand marked the beginning of the end of the Whig party. Although Manly managed to win the election by a mere 854 votes, his party had a much smaller majority than it had in the previous election when it had won.

(Left) David S. Reid was an attorney, a military officer, and a politician. In 1848, he ran against Charles Manly as the Democratic candidate for governor. Reid raised the issue of free manhood suffrage during the campaign. He served as governor of North Carolina from 1851 to 1854.

(Right) Charles Manly, the Whig candidate for governor in 1848, took a stand against free manhood suffrage. His position against the popular issue contributed to the downfall of the Whig party.

Manhood suffrage became a popular issue. In the legislature that met late in 1848, the Democrats introduced an amendment to broaden the suffrage, but it was defeated in the Senate by the Whigs. Meanwhile, extending the suffrage was gaining more and more popularity with the people of North Carolina. As the Whigs clung to their anti-suffrage position, the party continued to decline.

Victory for the Democrats.   Finally, in 1850, David Reid beat Manly by nearly 3,000 votes. Addressing the legislature for the last time, Manly admitted that many people of North Carolina wished to have the constitution revised.

In 1850, the legislature passed Reid's suffrage amendment. To become effective, however, it also had to pass in 1852. Opposition quickly developed to the amendment, and it was narrowly defeated.

The Democrats had to start all over again to revise the constitution for manhood suffrage. Renewing their efforts, they were finally able to get the bill through two successive sessions of the legislature by 1857. When the amendment was submitted to a vote of the people, it won 50,000 to 19,000. Upon passage, 50,000 more men in North Carolina became eligible to vote for members of the state Senate. As a result, the Senate was more responsive to the needs of the

In 1851, Calvin H. Wiley published *The North-Carolina Reader* for use in the public schools. He thought that information about the state should be available to young people learning to read. This interesting collection of historical and descriptive writings on North Carolina helped to instill state pride in many generations of Tar Heels.

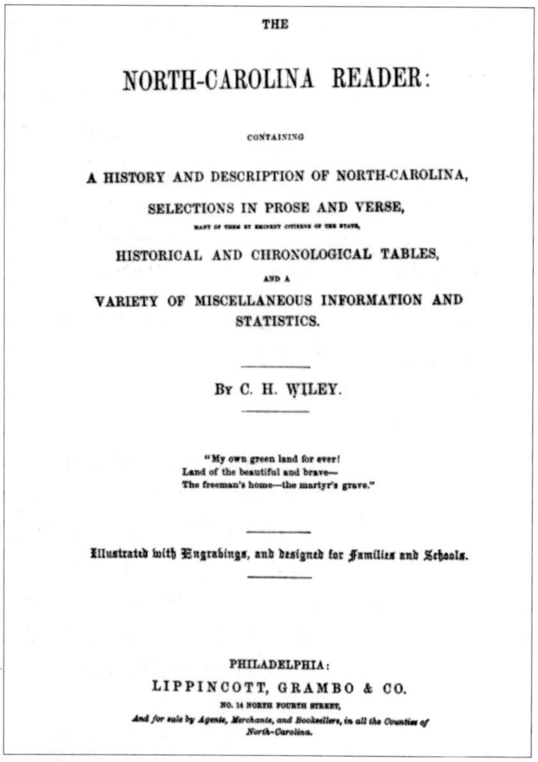

THE

NORTH-CAROLINA READER:

CONTAINING

A HISTORY AND DESCRIPTION OF NORTH-CAROLINA,

SELECTIONS IN PROSE AND VERSE,

MANY OF THEM BY EMINENT CITIZENS OF THE STATE,

HISTORICAL AND CHRONOLOGICAL TABLES,

AND A

VARIETY OF MISCELLANEOUS INFORMATION AND STATISTICS.

BY C. H. WILEY.

"My own green land for ever!
Land of the beautiful and brave—
The freeman's home—the martyr's grave."

Illustrated with Engravings, and designed for Families and Schools.

PHILADELPHIA:
LIPPINCOTT, GRAMBO & CO.
NO. 14 NORTH FOURTH STREET,
And for sale by Agents, Merchants, and Booksellers, in all the Counties of North-Carolina.

people than ever before. The Democratic party's support of suffrage gave it a new image. The party's platform became even more liberal as it began to support programs that it had previously opposed.

Improvement of public education. Public education in North Carolina made great progress under the Democrats. In 1852, a bill passed that reorganized the public school system and created the office of Superintendent of Common Schools. Calvin H. Wiley was appointed the first superintendent. When Wiley took office, he commented that the school system was "obscured in darkness." After spending most of his first year traveling around the state visiting schools, inquiring into conditions, and sounding out public opinion, he noted the following in his annual report.

Primary Source

I feel bound to say that money is not our greatest want. . . . We want more efficient management—a constant embodiment and expression of public opinion—a watchful supervision—a liberal course of legislature, good officers, and patience and energy in all having an official position in the system.

— CALVIN H. WILEY, *"First Annual Report"*

Wiley was a good administrator. During the years that he served as the superintendent, he helped to get more money for the schools and saw that the money was wisely spent. He also established institutes to train teachers, drew up a uniform course of study, and required progress reports. In 1860, he was able to report that "North Carolina has the start of all her Southern sisters in educational matters." In only seven years, he had revolutionized the public school system.

Schools of higher learning. During this period of development for public schools there also was an increasing interest in higher education. Schools sponsored by religious denominations opened with various programs. Some were merely ambitious academies, many were manual labor institutions where students worked to pay their expenses, and others made serious efforts to offer advanced work and to grant degrees. Over the years, as they became more soundly established, their goals changed and while all made important contributions to the youth of the state, many survived to make notable records in their fields.

There was a growing interest in higher education beginning in the 1830s. Schools supported by religious groups opened with various programs. Over the years many of these became well-known private colleges and universities such as Wake Forest College pictured in this drawing in 1834.

Think Twice

1. How did the Democratic party change?
2. What was the Democrats' position on manhood suffrage?
3. How did the issue of suffrage contribute to the fall of the Whig party?
4. What did Calvin Wiley do to help public education?
5. Explain in what ways the Democratic party appealed to the common person.

Chapter 14 Review

Choose from the following menu of activities.

Think Back: Main Ideas

Below is a list of some of the changes that took place from 1835 to 1860. On a separate sheet of paper, copy the list. Beside each change, name one important effect or result of the change.

1. Railroads are built.
2. Dorothea Dix studies conditions in the jails and poorhouses.
3. The Democrats strongly support manhood suffrage.
4. Manly and the Whig party oppose manhood suffrage.
5. Calvin H. Wiley is appointed Superintendent of Common Schools.
6. Edward Bishop Dudley is elected governor.
7. The General Assembly passes the first public school law.

Maps Matter

Use the map on page 195 of your text to answer these questions.

1. What city is located between Charlotte and Greensboro?
2. What is the approximate distance in miles from Goldsboro to Raleigh?
3. What cities would you pass through to get from Raleigh to Morehead City on the railroad?
4. Which city on the map is closest to the place where you live?
5. Which is closer, Morganton to Salisbury or Charlotte to Salisbury?
6. Which is a greater distance, Raleigh to New Bern or Raleigh to Wilmington?

Word Wizard

1. What does the word *suffrage* mean? What is meant by the term "universal suffrage"?
2. Look up *poorhouse* in the dictionary. In what year did it come into use?

Working Cooperatively

Get together in groups of three to five students to do the following activities.

1. Prepare a debate that might have taken place between David Reid and Charles Manly over the issue of manhood suffrage. Choose groups of two students to present the debate to your classmates.
2. In North Carolina, as in the nation, women had few rights. Their husbands, fathers, or other male relatives controlled their lives in many ways. Nevertheless, a number of women, like Dorothea Dix, made notable contributions to life in the state and nation. With the help of your school or local librarian, find out who some of these women were and what they did. Look for women active from about 1800 to the 1850s. Your local historical society may be of help as well.
3. Do research on the following reformers: (a) Horace Mann, (b) Thomas Hopkins Gallaudet, (c) Samuel Gridley Howe. Then write a paragraph about each man.

Curriculum Connection

In 1831, the state capitol burned. It was rebuilt in the Grecian Doric style. Today it is considered one of the most perfect examples of its kind in the United States.

Use an encyclopedia to find out about the Grecian Doric style of architecture. Then find out more about the design and construction of the beautiful capitol building in Raleigh. You may want to ask your librarian or teacher what is the best way to do this research.

Learning through Literature

A Treasure of Carolina Tales, by Webb Garrison
The Black Poet (George Moses Horton), by Richard Walser

UNIT 6

War and Reunion

NORTH CAROLINA | *Time Line* | **THE UNITED STATES**

	1845 Polk becomes President.
	1850 Compromise of 1850.
	1857 *Dred Scott* v. *Sanford*
	1859 Raid on Harpers Ferry
	1860 Lincoln is elected President. Confederate States of America is formed.
North Carolina joins Confederacy. **1861**	**1861** Civil War begins.
Union takes Roanoke Island. **1862**	**1862** Battle of Antietam
Warship *Albemarle* defends coast of **1864** North Carolina.	**1863** Emancipation Proclamation Battle of Gettysburg
Battle of Bentonville. North Carolina **1865** ratifies Thirteenth Amendment.	**1865** Confederates surrender. Johnson becomes President.
	1866 Congress passes new Freedmen's Bureau Bill. Ku Klux Klan is formed.
Republican party is organized. **1867**	**1867** Congress passes Reconstruction Act.
North Carolina ratifies Fourteenth **1868** Amendment. North Carolina is readmitted to Union.	**1868** Congressional vote fails to convict President Johnson in an impeachment trial. Republican Ulysses S. Grant becomes President.
North Carolina ratifies Fifteenth **1869** Amendment.	
Kirk-Holden War **1870**	
Constitutional Convention meets. **1875**	

What's Ahead

Rumblings of Civil War

The issue of slavery provokes a sectional crisis.

By the mid-1800s, three distinct sections had emerged in the nation: the North, the South, and the West. Physical geography and location set the sections apart. So, too, did the views of the people who lived in each section. In Congress, representatives defended the sectional interests of the voters who had elected them. Often these interests clashed, and the halls of Congress erupted in bitter sectional debate. No issue proved more explosive than slavery. Since the founding of the nation, compromise had settled debates over slavery. However, the process of compromise broke down in the 1850s. When it did, the fate of the Union was uncertain.

The South leaves the Union.

In 1860, Abraham Lincoln won election as President. He was swept into office by the Northern and Western states that opposed the spread of slavery outside of the South. Not a single Southern state voted for him. The election convinced Southerners they had lost their voice in government. The states that had elected Lincoln could outvote the South in Congress, too. One by one, the slave-owning states of the South left the Union. On May 20, 1861, North Carolina became the eleventh—and last—state to join the Confederate States of America, or the Confederacy.

The inauguration of Jefferson Davis as president of the Confederacy, February 18, 1861 ▶

Think Ahead

Could the Civil War have been avoided? Historians have long debated this question. As you read this chapter, identify the chain of events that caused the slave-owning states, including North Carolina, to leave the Union. Think about alternate actions that might have prevented war.

1 The Widening Split

People, Places, Terms

James Knox Polk
annexation
Missouri Compromise
David Walker
Nat Turner
slave codes
abolition

In the spring of 1845, a native of Mecklenburg County and an honors graduate of the University of North Carolina stepped forward to take the presidential oath of office. James Knox Polk, the son of a Scots-Irish farmer, knew the restless spirit of the backcountry. Polk's family, like many backcountry families, had crossed the Appalachians into Tennessee, lured by the fertile lands of the West. Here Polk put down roots. As a young lawyer and politician, he both befriended and at times fought with such famous western figures as Andrew Jackson and Davy Crockett. When Polk took office, he spoke for Westerners who dreamed of new frontiers to cross. As a slave owner, he also sympathized with Southerners who wanted to bring the institution of slavery with them as they moved into new lands.

In his inaugural speech, Polk praised the westward march of settlers. "Our people have filled the eastern valley of the Mississippi," boasted Polk. He then pledged to lead Americans across the Mississippi into new western lands. True to his promise, Polk added more territory to the nation than any other President. A stone pyramid at Polk's birthplace near Pineville shows the pride that the people of North Carolina took in his accomplishments.

Spanning a continent.   By 1845, Americans by the thousands had poured into two areas—the Republic of Texas and the Oregon Country. Polk vowed to add both areas to the United States. However, the acquisitions came at the risk of war. To obtain Oregon, the United States faced Great Britain, which also claimed the region. In the case of Texas, the United States squared off against Mexico. Texans had shaken off Mexican rule in 1836. Nonetheless, Mexico refused to recognize Texas independence.

Polk took a firm stand on both issues. In 1846, the United States and Britain avoided war by dividing the Oregon Country between them. They set the dividing line at the 49th parallel, or what is now the northwestern border between the United States and Canada. The matter of Texas proved trickier, though. In 1845, Congress approved a treaty with Texas that opened the way for statehood. News of **annexation,** or addition, of Texas to the Union enraged Mexico. Polk further infuriated Mexican officials by boldly asking to buy California and the New Mexico territory. Mexico refused to even listen to such an offer.

Polk kept up the pressure on Mexico. In 1846, he sent troops into lands along the Rio Grande claimed by both Mexico and Texas. The move provoked the first shots of

James Polk was an alumnus of the University of North Carolina. While he was President, the United States acquired a vast new territory which included California and New Mexico. In total, the United States added half a million square miles of land.

205

*E*conomic ties foster interdependence among geographic regions. ■ *To Do*: Describe the connection between the mills of the North and the plantations of the South. What crop helped link the North and the South?

the Mexican War. (See Chapter 14.) Some historians call the gunfire "the first shots of the Civil War" because the Mexican War helped to sow the seeds of the Civil War.

Seeds of division.　By the time Polk left office in 1849, a bitter quarrel raged over the extension of slavery into newly won western lands. The South wanted to extend slavery into the territories. The North did not.

The quarrels between the North and the South had been brewing for a long time. By the mid-1800s, the North depended for its livelihood upon manufacturing and trade far more than did the agricultural South. As you have read, from colonial times trade was important in both New England and the Middle Atlantic area. It was in New England that machines first replaced hand labor in the textile, or cloth-making, industry. Women and children ran the machines in some of the earliest textile mills there, since they could be paid lower wages than men. The arrival of large numbers of German and Irish immigrants in the 1840s provided an even cheaper source of labor. Consequently, mill owners did not use enslaved workers.

The mills of the North were linked to the plantations of the South by cotton. Invention of the cotton gin by Eli Whitney in 1793 made slavery profitable. (See Chapter 13.) Each year, enslaved Africans turned out thousands of bales of cotton. The raw cotton was then shipped to textile mills in both England and the North. In 1855, South Carolina agricultural writer James H. Hammond proclaimed, "Cotton is king!"

However, the South was not all cotton. The region produced other cash crops, including tobacco, indigo, and rice. The South also had its share of shrewd merchants and mill owners. One of the more economically diverse states was North Carolina. It possessed turpentine stills and gristmills, fishing ports, mines, plantations, and

(Left below) In the early 1800s, factories and mills were busy in the North. (Right below) At the same time, cotton plantations were thriving in the South.

backcountry farms. The table on this page shows the variety of economic activities within the state.

When compared to the North, however, agriculture still formed the backbone of the Southern economy. As a result, political power rested in the hands of Tidewater planters—the people who used enslaved workers. In North Carolina, the number of planters was smaller than in states farther south. However, as in colonial times, they still exercised a great deal of power. Therefore, North Carolina tended to vote with its slave-owning neighbors when sectional issues arose in Congress.

A delicate balance. Debates in Congress in the 1800s often broke along sectional lines. Northerners wanted laws to promote trade and the growth of factories. Southerners wanted laws to protect slavery and the growth of agriculture. As a result, Northerners and Southerners jealously watched the entry of new states into the Union. Both wanted any new western votes to benefit their section.

During the nation's first years, the states managed to keep a balance between free states and slave states. In 1787, the Continental Congress passed the Northwest Ordinance. This law banned slavery north and west of the Ohio River. However, few Southerners protested the law because they were more interested in the Old Southwest, or lands south of the Ohio River and north of Florida. Families such as the Polks moved into the lands and helped organize them into territories. Some brought enslaved Africans with them. Because slavery already existed in the Old Southwest, Congress did not prohibit it in states carved from the region. These states included Kentucky, Tennessee, Alabama, and Mississippi.

As the 1800s began, a spirit of goodwill generally prevailed between the North and the South. However, this spirit began to fade in the early 1800s when the North surged ahead of the South in terms of population. In the House of Representatives, each state was represented on the basis of population. As the North gained in population, it also gained representatives in the House. In the Senate, where each state had two senators apiece, the balance stayed the same. As a result, Southerners waited cautiously to see what new states would enter the Union from lands acquired in the Louisiana Purchase of 1803.

In 1818, a call for admission came from Missouri. Many people in Missouri owned slaves, so it would enter the Union as a slave state. This would have given the South control of the Senate. However, Northerners resisted the entry of Missouri as a slave state. They did not want slavery—or Southern power—to spread west.

OCCUPATIONS IN NORTH CAROLINA, 1860	
Occupation	Number
Farmer	87,000
Laborer	63,500
Artisan	27,000
Professional worker	7,500
Planter (20 or more slaves)	4,000
Merchant	3,500
Teacher	2,000
Clerk	1,500
Manufacturer	1,300

Tables Teach

Based on this table, what generalizations can you form about the main economic activities in North Carolina? How important was manufacturing to the overall economy? How did the number of planters compare with the number of farmers?

Think as a Historian

To understand events, historians need to look at the political framework in which the events developed. For example, some sectional debates had to do with the system of representation set up by the Constitution.
■ *To Do*: Read the portions of the Constitution in the Citizenship Handbook at the back of your book that focus on representation in the House and the Senate. Summarize House and Senate representation in your own words.

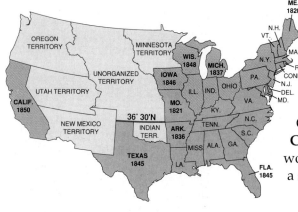

New States and the Missouri Compromise

- ▨ Free States
- ▨ Slave States
- ── Missouri Compromise Line, 1820
- New states between 1820 and 1850 are labelled with a date and bold face type.

Maps Matter

In 1820, lawmakers agreed on the Missouri Compromise. As a result, the number of free and slave states was equal until 1850. ■ *To Do*: Which state joined the Union that year and upset the balance?

For months, the two sides battled. Then, in 1820, Maine, which was still part of Massachusetts, asked to become a separate state. It would enter the Union as a free state. Senator Henry Clay of Kentucky seized on Maine's request as a way to end the debate in Congress. He proposed the so-called **Missouri Compromise**. According to Clay's plan, Maine would enter the Union as a free state and Missouri as a slave state. To prevent future arguments over the Louisiana Territory, Congress drew an imaginary east-west line at latitude 36°30′ north. The line followed the southern boundary of Missouri. Any new state north of the line was to be a free state. Any state south of the line was to be open to slavery.

The compromise quieted sectional divisions. However, many observers saw trouble ahead. In a letter to a friend, Thomas Jefferson shared his reaction to the debate over the Missouri Compromise. Wrote Jefferson, "This momentous question [slavery], like a fire-bell in the night, awakened me and filled me with terror. I considered it at once the knell [death bell] of the Union. It is hushed, indeed, only for the moment."

The South's "peculiar institution."   Southerners loved the Union. Many had given their lives in the Revolution, the War of 1812, and the Mexican War. Yet as the 1800s unfolded, they felt apart from the rest of the nation. Even many non-slave owners blistered under the stinging attacks on slavery. It seemed as if Northerners intended to undermine the entire Southern way of life. Some Southerners, such as John C. Calhoun of South Carolina, rose to defend the South's "peculiar institution." Calhoun argued that enslaved Africans in the South lived better lives than poverty-stricken factory workers of African descent in the North. He called slavery "a good," not an evil.

Reform-minded Americans who visited the South knew otherwise. Treatment of enslaved Africans varied greatly from plantation to plantation. Even so, slavery denied enslaved Africans their basic rights as human beings. At a moment's notice, a husband, wife, or child could be taken to the auction block and sold.

Enslaved Africans resisted slavery in several ways. First, they kept their culture alive. In slave quarters, they told stories of lost family members or recalled their African heritage. These oral histories helped enslaved Africans preserve the past. Second, they denied owners both labor and profit. Enslaved Africans slowed down work, faked sickness, broke tools, or stole food from their owners. Third, some defied owners even though it resulted in brutal whippings.

To survive slavery, enslaved Africans clung to a sense of family by calling each other by names such as "auntie," "uncle," "sister," or "brother." Enslaved Africans also took comfort in holding their own religious services. Under the cover of darkness, they crept off to secret "hush shelters," or wooded areas where tree branches could be bent down to quiet their voices. Here enslaved Africans sang spirituals, or religious hymns, that poured out the sorrows of bondage and dreams of liberty.

A few slave houses still survive in North Carolina such as those at Stagville, the Cameron family plantation north of Durham. Other examples of slave quarters can be seen at Somerset Place in Washington County.

Primary Source

I reckon something inside just told us about God and that there was a better place hereafter. We would sneak off and have prayer meeting[s]. Sometimes the pattyrollers [slave patrols] catch us and beat us good, but that didn't keep us from trying. I remember one old song we use to sing when we meet down in the woods back of the barn. My mother, she sing and pray to the Lord to deliver us out of slavery. . . . [I]t went something like this: . . .

We camp awhile in the wilderness,
In the wilderness, in the wilderness;
We camp awhile in the wilderness,
Where the Lord makes me happy,
And then I'm a-going home!

— *W.L. Bost in* My Folks Don't Want Me To Talk About Slavery

A few of people of African descent turned to the press to protest slavery. One such person was David Walker, a

The Voice of Slavery

"[M]y mammy was a queen in Africa. They kidnaps her and steals her away from her throne and fetches her here to Wake County in slavery." When Ann Parker recalled this story she "reckoned" that she was 103 or 104 years old. She was but one of more than 2,000 formerly enslaved Africans asked in the 1930s to recall their lives in bondage. In the midst of the Great Depression, the federal government created the Federal Writers Project for unemployed writers. The government assigned one group to interview the last generation of people who had experienced slavery firsthand. In North Carolina, 176 African Americans such as Ann Parker took part in the project. Suddenly, the voice of slavery came alive. Stories that might have disappeared were stored at the Library of Congress under the heading *Slave Narratives.* In the 1980s, North Carolina author Belinda Hurmence pored through this collection and edited 21 oral histories. You can read these stories in her book, *My Folks Don't Want Me To Talk About Slavery.*

native of Wilmington, North Carolina. The son of a free mother and enslaved father, Walker fled to Boston in 1829 to demand an immediate end to slavery, by violence, if necessary. The harsh tone in what was known as Walker's Appeal shocked white Southerners. When an enslaved African named Nat Turner led a violent slave revolt in Virginia in 1831, many Southerners blamed Walker.

Southern states banned Walker's book and enacted strict **slave codes,** which forbade educating enslaved Africans and kept them from leaving plantation land without the owner's permission.

The growing crisis. Despite Southern fears, most Northerners in the 1820s and 1830s did not strongly support **abolition,** or an end to slavery. Instead, they wanted to confine slavery to the South. Yet, by the 1850s, the cause of abolition swept through the North.

In part, this change of opinion was the result of events of the 1840s. The lands acquired at the end of the Mexican War fell outside of the Missouri Compromise. As a result, Jefferson's worst fears soon proved true. Once again, the halls of Congress rang with debate over an old question, Who would benefit from western lands—North or South?

Enslaved Population in North Carolina, 1860

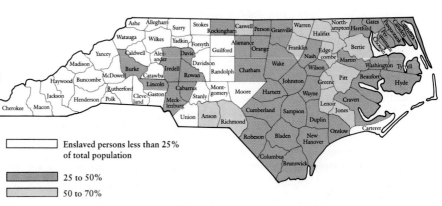

Maps Matter

Most of the enslaved people in North Carolina lived in the eastern part of the state.
■ *To Do*: Based on your reading of Chapter 9, why do you think most of North Carolina's enslaved Africans lived there? Name five counties with the lowest number of enslaved people. Name five counties with the highest percent of enslaved people.

Enslaved persons less than 25% of total population

25 to 50%

50 to 70%

Think Twice

1. What lands did President Polk add to the Union?
2. How did the North and South differ economically?
3. What were the terms of the Missouri Compromise?
4. How did enslaved Africans resist slavery?
5. Suppose you were a senator from North Carolina in the late 1840s. What solution would you propose to the problem of the newly acquired western lands?

2 The Failure of Compromise

People, Places, Terms

Henry Clay
Daniel Webster
John C. Calhoun
secede
fugitive slave law
Frederick Douglass
Sojourner Truth
Henry Highland Garnett
Underground Railroad
Stephen A. Douglas

In blazing headlines around the world, a single word seemed to leap off the page, "Gold!" In 1849, news of a gold strike in California spread like wildfire. Prospectors poured into the territory, and in 1850, Californians requested entry into the Union as a free state. The acceptance of California as a free state would upset the delicate balance between 15 free states and 15 slave states.

The stage was thus set for a grand battle between North, South, and West. To wage the war of words, three famous senators met for the last time. Henry Clay vowed to present one last set of compromises to save his nation. Clay faced two rivals from the past, Daniel Webster, from the North, and John C. Calhoun, from the South. The fate of the nation hinged upon which of the three Congress chose to follow.

The Compromise of 1850.   Clay said that if Congress failed to reach a compromise, some Southern states might **secede,** or leave the Union. To satisfy the North, Clay proposed the Compromise of 1850. The compromise stated that California be admitted as a free state. It also called upon Congress to ban the buying and selling of enslaved Africans in Washington, D.C., the nation's capital. To satisfy the South, Clay suggested that two other territories won from Mexico—Utah and New Mexico—decide the slavery issue for themselves. He further asked Congress for a stronger **fugitive slave law**—a law forcing people to return runaway enslaved Africans.

The proposals satisfied no one completely. Calhoun rejected them outright. He clung to his angry call for special protection of the South. Amid the debate, the ailing Calhoun died, his last words the cry, "The South! The South! God knows what will become of her!"

Meanwhile, Webster struggled with his own conscience. He hated slavery, but he valued the Union more than abolition. In the end, he accepted Clay's compromises and urged other Northerners to do the same. Some Northerners furiously asked Webster how he could speak for a plan that included a fugitive slave law. Webster replied: "I speak not as a Massachusetts man, not as a Northern man, but as an American. . . . I speak today because I do not want the Union broken up." Finally, the Compromise of 1850 passed by a narrow margin. The Union was saved—but for how long?

Secession.   While Congress argued over the compromise, nine slave states, excluding North Carolina, sent delegates to a convention in Nashville, Tennessee, to discuss

Ravaged by a cruel cough, the 73-year-old Henry Clay leaned on the arm of a friend as he walked into the Senate. In his speech to his fellow senators, he tried to win their support for the Compromise of 1850.

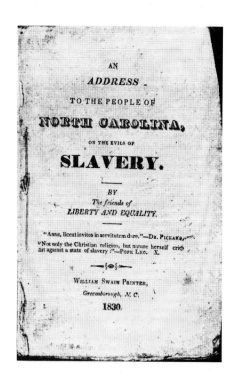

There was considerable antislavery sentiment in North Carolina in the early 1800s. Organizations opposed to slavery faced few or no restrictions in their activities. This pamphlet was issued by a society in North Carolina opposed to the evils of slavery.

The most famous conductor of the Underground Railroad was Harriet Tubman. Slave owners offered a $40,000 reward for her capture—dead or alive. However, no one ever caught up with either Tubman or the more than 300 people she guided to freedom.

secession from the Union. They drew upon historic precedents. New England, for example, had threatened to secede when the nation elected Thomas Jefferson in 1800. New Englanders also talked of secession during the War of 1812. When Congress passed a tariff that hurt Southern agriculture in 1832, South Carolina debated secession, too. The 1850 convention decided to put off the matter on two conditions. First, they expected Congress to honor provisions in the Constitution protecting slavery. Second, they expected the North to honor the Fugitive Slave Act.

The voice of abolition. Some Northerners, however, had no intention of obeying the law. An abolitionist movement had organized during the reform era of the 1820s and 1830s. Even North Carolina had several antislavery societies. While the South, including North Carolina, generally ended these societies after Nat Turner's Rebellion, the North did not. The Fugitive Slave Act stirred them into action. To drive home the evils of slavery, abolitionists invited African Americans who had escaped from slavery, such as Frederick Douglass, Sojourner Truth, and Henry Highland Garnett, to join them on the lecture platform. Truth drove home the pain of lost children and the backbreaking work endured by women. In fiery words, Garnett called for radical action, even rebellion. Douglass, a runaway from Maryland, defied the Fugitive Slave Act.

Abolitionists feared for their safety. William Lloyd Garrison, one of the founders of the abolition movement, fled for his life many times. Yet as the 1850s progressed, the voices of abolitionists grew louder, setting off alarms throughout the South. Southerners especially objected to the efforts of abolitionists to speed escaped Africans out of the South. They viewed this as a direct attack on slavery.

The route to freedom was called the **Underground Railroad.** Quakers such as Levi Coffin, a native of Guilford County, helped set up the railroad, which stretched from the rim of the South to the edge of Canada. When completed, the system was like no other railroad in the United States. Its "tracks" consisted of paths through the forests and fields. Its "stations" included barns, attics, cellars, and any other place where runaways could hide. Its "conductors" were the courageous people, including formerly enslaved Africans, who led the runaways north.

Bloodshed. The daring escapes of fugitives led Harriet Beecher Stowe to publish *Uncle Tom's Cabin* in 1852. Stowe, a Northern abolitionist, wanted to inspire people to resist the Fugitive Slave Act, so she filled the book with tales of cruelty, suffering, and desperate escape. The story was so moving that it sold 400,000 copies within months. Southern states branded the book a pack of lies and banned its sale.

The more some Americans spoke out against slavery, the louder others argued for it. Many government officials did not realize how strongly Americans felt until 1854. That year, Congress agreed to a plan by Stephen A. Douglas, senator from Illinois. The plan opened the Kansas and Nebraska territories for settlement. It stated that settlers in Kansas and Nebraska should decide the issue of slavery themselves.

The decision enflamed Northerners. They quickly pointed out that the two territories lay above the line drawn by the Missouri Compromise and should, therefore, be free states. Douglas disagreed. He felt the Compromise of 1850 had replaced the Missouri Compromise. Northern abolitionists responded by sending a flood of settlers into the territories. Soon proslavery forces from the South rushed in as well.

Nebraska joined the Union as a free state. This left Kansas as the focus of the issues. Here people on both sides committed crimes. Some slave owners from Missouri crossed into Kansas and set up a proslavery government. Antislavery forces set up a second government. Proslavery forces then destroyed the antislavery town of Lawrence. John Brown, a raging abolitionist, vowed revenge. Along with seven followers, he brutally murdered five people. Newspapers across the country labeled the territory Bleeding Kansas. In all, 200 people died in the fighting.

Bloodshed made compromise difficult, if not impossible. On the floor of the Congress, some people packed pistols. On May 22, 1856, Congressman Preston Brooks of South Carolina walked into the Senate and attacked his arch rival Charles Sumner of Massachusetts. Sumner beat Brooks with a cane until he dropped to the floor. Because of his injuries, Sumner was absent from Congress until December 5, 1859. Some people wondered how long the Union could endure such hatred. What, if anything, would save the nation?

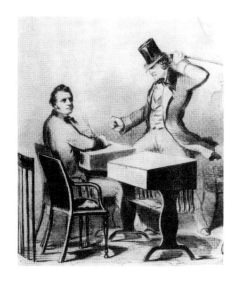

American artist Winslow Homer made this lithograph showing Preston Brooks attacking Charles Sumner as he sat at his desk in the Senate chamber.

Think Twice

1. What were the provisions of the Compromise of 1850?
2. What were some movements for secession in the past?
3. (a) Name at least three leading abolitionists in the 1850s. (b) Describe what each did.
4. How did the Underground Railroad operate?
5. What events led to Bleeding Kansas?

213

People, Places, Terms

Dred Scott v. *Sanford*
Daniel Worth
Harpers Ferry
arsenal
Confederate States of America
Fort Sumter

3 Breaking the Bonds of Union

North Carolina did not escape the passionate debates of 1856. In the fall of that year, the people of North Carolina found themselves caught up in a heated presidential race between two candidates, Democrat James Buchanan and Republican John C. Fremont. Fremont was a famed western explorer and hero of the Mexican War. However, he belonged to the Republican Party, a new political party that opposed the extension of slavery. The new party was not well organized in the South. In fact, many Southern states, including North Carolina, did not have a Republican ticket. As a result, people in North Carolina who supported Fremont could not vote for him. One of these people was Benjamin S. Hedrick, a professor at the University of North Carolina.

Hedrick publicized his views in a series of letters to the *North Carolina Standard.* An uproar went up throughout the state, and people demanded his resignation. When Hedrick refused to bow to pressure, the university declared his professorship vacant. Proslavery forces had scored a minor victory, but they would soon win an even bigger victory.

Thunderbolt from the Supreme Court.   On March 6, 1857, reporters from North and South filed into the Supreme Court to hear the decision in ***Dred Scott* v. *Sanford.*** The case involved two enslaved Africans—Dred and Harriet Scott. The couple sued for their freedom because they had lived with their owners for several years in free territories. The couple had already received freedom upon their owners' deaths. However, abolitionists decided to use the Scotts as a test case for the Supreme Court.

Chief Justice Roger B. Taney, a slaveowner from Maryland, read the majority opinion. The Court ruled that people of African descent—both free and enslaved—were not citizens under the Constitution. Therefore, they could not sue in federal courts. The Court went on to declare enslaved Africans "property." Because people could take their property anywhere, the Court said Congress had no right to ban slavery in the territories. It then ruled the Missouri Compromise unconstitutional. A cry of joy went up throughout the South, but Northerners fumed. To radical abolitionists, such as John Brown, it seemed abolition might only now come at the point of a gun.

Adding fuel to the fire.   At this critical time, a native of Davie County, North Carolina, Hinton Rowan Helper, added fuel to the fire. Helper had left the state to take part in the California gold rush. He then settled in New York. In

1857, he released a book entitled *The Impending Crisis of the South: How to Meet It.* In it, Helper argued that slavery kept jobs from workers of European descent and also economically crippled the South.

Northerners embraced the book and the Republican party even adopted it as a campaign document. Few noticed Helper's unsound scholarship, nor did they pay attention to his lack of concern for enslaved Africans. Helper wanted to aid poor whites, not improve the lives of Africans. The book offended Southerners, who banned it. North Carolina shut the doors on Helper, who spent the rest of his life in the North.

Bringing abolition south. As controversy swirled around the Dred Scott decision and Helper's book, Daniel Worth arrived in North Carolina. Worth, a native of Guilford County, had moved to Indiana, where he became a Methodist minister. In 1857, he decided to serve churches in his home state. Worth opposed slavery and preached to both people of European descent and enslaved Africans. Few people objected to Worth's activities. Worth won many friends with his warm humor and good will.

In late 1859, Worth's fortunes changed. That October, North Carolinians received bone-chilling news. John Brown had struck again, this time at **Harpers Ferry,** Virginia (now West Virginia). Here Brown seized a federal **arsenal,** or weapons depot, and sent word for enslaved Africans to join him in a rebellion. Instead, federal troops arrived at Harpers Ferry under the command of Colonel Robert E. Lee.

As Brown marched off to trial and death by hanging, the people of North Carolina regarded Worth with suspicion. A judge and jury found Worth guilty of inciting enslaved Africans. Worth got a year's prison sentence, but his friends posted bond and helped him escape from North Carolina.

A Republican in the White House. In 1860, the Republican party picked Abraham Lincoln as its candidate for President. Two years earlier, Lincoln had run against Stephen Douglas for the Senate seat in Illinois. Although Lincoln lost that race, his speeches won national attention. In words that foreshadowed the future, Lincoln declared, "A house divided against itself cannot stand. I believe this government cannot last forever, half slave and half free. I do not expect the house to fall—but I do expect it will cease to be divided."

In 1860, the political nightmare long dreaded by the South came true. Lincoln became President. Although he received only 39 percent of the popular votes, he gained a majority of votes in the electoral college. No Southern state voted for him nor did Kentucky or Missouri.

Hinton Rowan Helper grew up near Mocksville. Because of negative reaction to his book on the part of the people of North Carolina, Helper left the state and never returned. He died at the age of 80, friendless and impoverished.

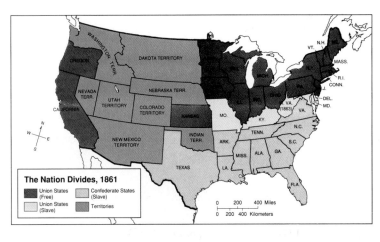

Maps Matter

This map shows the two sides in the Civil War. ■ *To Do:* Which states joined the Confederacy? How many Union states were there? Which of them were slaveholding states?

North Carolina governor John W. Ellis strongly supported secession. When President Lincoln's secretary of war called for troops from North Carolina to help force South Carolina back into the Union, Ellis told him that he would "get no troops from North Carolina."

During the campaign, the South had warned it would secede if Lincoln won. On December 20, 1860, South Carolina led the march out of the Union. One by one, Southern states formed a new nation: the **Confederate States of America.** Jefferson Davis of Mississipi became president.

North Carolina did not rush to secede. Many people loved the Union. Also, North Carolina was not a strong slaveholding state. Some 361,522 Africans lived there, but 30,463 were free. In addition, only about 4,065 people out of a population of European descent that numbered 629,932 owned more than 20 slaves. As a result, the people of North Carolina felt little sympathy for the brash actions of their neighbors. They chose to follow a policy of "watch and wait." Most hoped Lincoln would find a solution to the crisis.

The Confederacy broke the uneasy calm. In April 1861, South Carolina soldiers fired on federal troops stationed at **Fort Sumter,** an island overlooking Charleston Harbor. The act shocked many people in North Carolina, but they were more shocked by Lincoln's actions. The President telegraphed states still in the Union and requested that each one supply the United States Army with troops. Civil war had come to the United States.

Some North Carolinians felt betrayed by Lincoln. Others felt patriotism for the South. A few wanted to support the Union. In the end, most people sided with the Confederacy. Explained a one-time Union supporter named Jonathan Worth,"I think the South is committing suicide, but my lot is cast with the South. . . . I intend to face the breakers [waves of war] manfully and go down with my companions." On May 20, 1861, North Carolina became the last Southern state to leave the Union.

Think Twice

1. How did each of the following events enflame sectional divisions? (a) the Dred Scott decision, (b) Hinton Helper's book, (c) John Brown's raid on Harpers Ferry, (d) the election of Lincoln.
2. Why did the people of North Carolina delay leaving the Union?
3. Jonathan Worth believed North Carolina might have stayed in the Union if Lincoln had not called for troops. Do you think Lincoln had any other choice?

Chapter 15 Review

Choose from the following menu of activities.

Think Back: Main Ideas

Sectionalism has been one of the continuing themes in United States history. To evaluate whether the sectional debate over slavery made civil war inevitable, answer the following questions.

1. What were some of the ways in which the North and the South differed from each other in the mid-1800s?
2. What were some of the factors that helped bind the sections together?
3. How did newly acquired lands in the West contribute to sectional rivalries?
4. At what point did compromise break down in the sectional conflicts?
5. If you had the power to rewrite the script of history, what solutions would you have tried to avoid the Civil War?
6. Why do you think that North Carolina was the last state to join the Confederacy?

Maps Matter

The enslaved African population of North Carolina was not evenly distributed. In fact, slave ownership fueled sectional divisions within the state. To speculate on how various parts of North Carolina might have reacted to the issue of secession, refer to the map on page 210. Then answer the questions that follow.

1. How do you think a person in Brunswick County might have felt about the election of Lincoln in 1860? Why?
2. Do you think a person in Macon County might have been as eager to join the Confederacy as someone in Jones County? Explain.
3. In general, which part of the state had the most to gain by Confederate victory in the Civil War—east or west? Explain.

Word Wizard

Review the definition of each term below. Then write a question for which each term is the answer.

annexation   abolition   spiritual
secede   slave codes   arsenal

Working Cooperatively

Working in small groups, study the life of abolitionist Frederick Douglass, Sojourner Truth, or Henry Highland Garnett. Use your group's findings to produce a brief skit depicting a dramatic incident in that person's life.

Curriculum Connection

Below are some lyrics taken from a spiritual composed by enslaved Africans in Missouri. Read these lyrics carefully, and then answer the questions that follow.

O, gracious Lord! When shall it be,
That we poor souls shall be free;
Lord, break them slavery powers—
Will you go along with me?
Lord break them slavery powers.
Go sound the jubilee!

1. What request are the enslaved people making in the spiritual?
2. Slave owners often whipped or locked up enslaved Africans for singing spirituals such as this. Why do think this was the case?
3. How could this spiritual be used to disprove arguments by people such as John C. Calhoun who claimed slavery was "a good"?

Learning through Literature

Freedom Train: The Story of Harriet Tubman, by Dorothy Sterling
The House of Dies Drear, by Virginia Hamilton
My Folks Don't Want Me To Talk About Slavery, edited by Belinda Hurmence
Sojourner Truth and the Struggle for Freedom, by Edward Beecher Claflin

Chapter **16** Fighting the Civil War

The Civil War was costly for both sides.

As states joined the Confederacy, they took over federal forts and arsenals in their territory. Most Union commanders surrendered quietly. For a time, it seemed as though the Southern states might be allowed to form a separate country in peace. That idea went up in the smoke of the bombardment of Fort Sumter and was given a death blow by Lincoln's call for troops to put down the rebellion.

During the four long years of war that followed these events, the nation suffered as brother met brother, cousin met cousin on the battlefields. Since the war was fought almost entirely on Southern soil, the Confederate states suffered the most damage. Both Union and Confederacy, however, lost thousands of young men, cut down in the prime of their lives.

Confederate troops fire on Fort Sumter ▶

Think Ahead

When the war began, many people thought of it as a war over states' rights—particularly the right of states to form their own country. That idea changed, however, and in the end, the war had also become a war to end slavery. Read to find out how that came about. Also find out how the Confederacy lost after seeming to be winning for the first two years of the war.

1 Weighing Advantages

With the taking of Fort Sumter, both the Union and the Confederacy geared for war, although neither side expected the war to last long. The first Union soldiers were recruited for just three months; North Carolina's for six months.

Union resources. Although each side had certain advantages, Union resources were clearly superior. The Union had an experienced government in place and established trade links with foreign nations. It had 23 states (24 after West Virginia became a separate state in 1863), while the Confederacy only had 11. The Union's population was more than twice as large as the Confederacy's population.

The Union also had 80 percent of the nation's factories and mills, so it could produce large amounts of war supplies. In addition, the Union had better transportation—more roads, canals, and railroads to move goods and soldiers.

Confederate advantages. The Confederacy had a number of outstanding military leaders. General Robert E. Lee, who eventually led the Confederate army, was considered the nation's best military leader.

Since the Confederacy did not plan to invade the North, it had only to defend itself on land its soldiers knew well. Moreover, Confederate soldiers clearly knew what they were fighting for—their homes, the land, and their loved ones. The Union's stated goal—to preserve the Union—was more abstract.

RESOURCES OF NORTH AND SOUTH, 1860		
	North	**South**
Population	22,700,000	9,000,000*
Railroads (miles)	21,700	9,000
Value of manufactures	$1,000,000,000	$156,000,000
Corn (bushels per year)	717,000,000	316,000,000
Iron (tons per year)	480,000	31,000
* Including 3,500,000 enslaved persons		

Tables Teach

Of the items on this table, the North and South were most nearly alike in miles of railroads, yet the North had more than twice as many miles of railroads. What other general statement can you make about the items on this table?

Gathering armies. At the beginning of the war, more men flocked to volunteer than either side believed it would ever need. As the war dragged on, however, both sides had to **draft** soldiers. Each side required men between the ages of

*I*n 1860, North Carolina had an African American population of about 362,000, of whom about 30,000 were free. Although not allowed to serve as soldiers, these people, free and enslaved, took part in raising crops to support the soldiers. They worked building forts, mining coal, and elsewhere. Many Confederate officers were attended throughout the war by young enslaved African men from home. Many African American families helped white families survive while the men were at war. ■ *To Do*: Why do you think the enslaved Africans didn't rebel against their owners? Why didn't more of those serving their officer masters slip away in the fighting? Why did free African families help white families?

18 and 35 (later 17 and 50) to sign up for military service.

Not everyone was required to serve, however. In the Confederacy, men who owned 20 or more enslaved Africans were excused from the draft. In the North, a man could pay the government $300 to be excused, or he could pay someone to go in his place. People on both sides grumbled that it was a "rich man's war and a poor man's fight."

At first, neither side let African Americans, free or enslaved, serve as soldiers. Lincoln feared that the slave-holding Union states would secede if he allowed African Americans into the army. Yet many found other ways to help—as cooks, scouts, spies, supply-wagon drivers. Later on, Lincoln changed his stand, and before the war ended, 186,000 African Americans had served in the Union army. Fearful of a revolt if enslaved Africans were armed, the Confederacy did not allow them into the army until March 1865. Since the war ended in April, few African Americans served in the Confederacy.

As in the Revolution, some women disguised themselves as men and hurried off to battle. As many as 400 women fought as soldiers, while other women served as messengers or spies. Harriet Tubman, a brave conductor on the Underground Railroad, was also a daring Union spy. Although many people thought it was improper for women to treat sick men, over 3,000 women, including Tubman, served as nurses. Clara Barton's experiences as a nurse in the war led her to found the American Red Cross. Women who stayed behind also had heavy responsibilities managing homes, farms, and plantations and keeping factories and shops open. Without these women, the war could not have gone on.

After 1863, African Americans were allowed to serve as soldiers in the Union army. However, their pay was less than that of white soldiers and they served in separate units under white officers. About half the 186,000 African American soldiers in the Union army were runaways from Confederate states, a fourth were from Union slave-holding states, and the rest were from free states.

North Carolina's share of troops. North Carolina furnished the Confederacy with troops equal to nearly a fifth of the state's total white population. And of the approximately 129,000 white men between ages 20 and 60, an estimated 96 percent served in the Confederate army. These troops made up more than one sixth of the army, a large part since there were 11 Confederate states. During the war, the state lost about 40,000 men — a little less than half in battle, the rest to disease.

W.M.Allison

Across Cultures

*B*efore the war, it was thought improper for women to act as nurses outside their immediate family. A few women, like Clara Barton, ignored that attitude. Soon it became obvious that women were desperately needed as thousands of wounded filled the hospitals, overwhelming the poorly equipped doctors and male nurses. The Union eventually set up a nurses training program under Dr. Elizabeth Blackwell, the first American woman to graduate from medical school. ■ *To Do:* Find out more about this courageous woman and make a report about her. Choose your own format for the report—a series of captioned illustrations, a skit, a written narrative, or some other format.

When Clara Barton heard of the shortage of nurses, she loaded an ox cart with medical supplies and headed for the battlefields.

Think Twice

1. Name at least two advantages each side had when the Civil War started.
2. Why might it be easier to fight for your home and loved ones rather than for an abstract goal such as preserving the Union?
3. Why were people opposed to the military draft?
4. Why were African Americans not at first allowed to serve as soldiers (a) in the Confederate army? (b) in the Union army?
5. Name at least three ways women served in the war.

2 On the Battlefields

After Fort Sumter, one of President Lincoln's first acts was to order a blockade of all Southern ports. This action would make it difficult for the South to sell cotton to Europe and buy weapons, medicines, and other supplies.

The war's first battle.   The Union army made its first big move in July 1861, when it set out from Washington, D.C., to capture the Confederate capital of **Richmond,** Virginia, 100 miles away. Sightseers from Washington, traveling in carriages and carrying picnic lunches, followed after the troops to watch what they expected to be a quick victory for the Union.

The Union army met Confederate troops at Manassas Junction, Virginia, only 30 miles from Washington. The untrained Northern troops fought bravely but were no match for the Confederate army. In the end, Union soldiers fled the battlefield only to find the way blocked by panicked sightseers. In their rush to get away, the sightseers overturned wagons and carriages. Horses fell. The road to Washington was jammed for hours.

Tightening the blockade.   The **Battle of Manassas** showed both sides that the war would not be over as soon as they had thought. As the months passed, the Union tightened

General Thomas "Stonewall" Jackson earned his nickname by holding his Confederate regiment "like a stone wall" against the Union soldiers at Manassas.

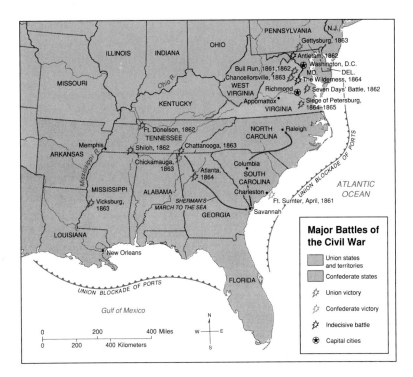

Maps Matter

The map on this page shows more battles than this chapter can describe.
■ *To Do:* In an encyclopedia or another reference book, find out about one such battle. Write a paragraph or two describing the battle's significance.

Major Battles of the Civil War

- Union states and territories
- Confederate states
- ☆ Union victory
- ☆ Confederate victory
- ☆ Indecisive battle
- ✵ Capital cities

its blockade. In 1862, the Union navy gained control of the Mississippi River from its mouth to New Orleans. Trade at the port of New Orleans came to a standstill, closing the Confederacy's most important western gateway for goods and supplies.

Meanwhile the Confederate armies in the East had prevented Union forces from taking Richmond and had won several battles. In September 1862, General Robert E. Lee planned to surprise the Union army by surrounding Washington, D.C., thereby cutting off the more northerly states from the capital and bringing the slave state of Maryland into the Confederacy.

Lee's plan might have worked, but a Union soldier found a copy of the plan that had fallen from a Confederate general's pocket. Because of this lucky find, Union General George McClellan knew exactly what route Lee's army planned to take.

On September 17, 1862, Lee's outnumbered army faced the Union forces in the **Battle of Antietam** near Sharpsburg, Maryland. As the two armies clashed, the tide of battle flowed back and forth in the bloodiest day of fighting in the Civil War. At least 6,000 soldiers were killed and 17,000 wounded. Although neither side won a clear victory, Lee's army did withdraw into Virginia.

The Emancipation Proclamation. After Antietam, Lincoln decided that the Union's best interests would be

Confederate General Robert E. Lee gallantly led his army against the Union at Antietam Creek.

Abraham Lincoln was President during one of the most troubling times of the nation's history.

served by adding the end of slavery to its goals for the war. He therefore issued the **Emancipation Proclamation.** To *emancipate* means to "free from slavery." This proclamation, or announcement, stated that on January 1, 1863, all enslaved persons in the Confederate states would be freed. Lincoln purposely didn't include the slave-holding Union states in the proclamation for fear that they would join the Confederacy if he did.

Since the Union had no control over the Confederate states, the proclamation had little effect on slavery there. However, it did have three important effects. First, it gave new heart to many Union soldiers and supporters. For many, abolishing slavery was a more sympathetic goal than preserving the Union. Second, African American soldiers were now allowed into the Union army. Third, it gained European support, particularly from the British, who had abolished slavery in the 1830s.

Most people in North Carolina who supported the war did so because they felt they were fighting for states' rights and freedom from the federal government's oppression. A fight to maintain slavery was a different matter to a people who were largely nonslaveholders. After the proclamation, many soldiers began to grumble, not only because they might be fighting to preserve slavery, but also because they did not have enough food, clothing, and shelter. Families at home were suffering, too. Goods were scarce, prices were high, and they needed help on their farms. Further, they had lost loved ones to battle and disease.

A new phase of the war. After Antietam, victory slowly shifted toward the Union. But in July 1863, Lee made a last try at cutting off Washington from the Northern states. As his army advanced, one unit stumbled upon Union troops at Gettysburg, Pennsylvania, before Lee was fully ready to attack. The ensuing battle raged for three days. A Union soldier described one of the last attacks of Confederate troops trying to take a hill at a cemetery:

Primary Source

Holes like graves were gouged in the earth by exploding shells. The flowers in bloom upon the graves at the Cemetery were shot away. Tombs and monuments were knocked to pieces, and ordinary gravestones shattered in rows. If a constellation . . . had exploded above our heads, it would have scarcely been more terrible than this iron rain of death furiously hurled upon us.

— *"Letter of Union soldier"*

Finally, the Union army turned back Lee's fiercely attacking troops and defeated them. Lee retreated toward Richmond.

One day after the **Battle of Gettysburg,** Union General Ulysses S. Grant captured Vicksburg on the Mississippi River after a blockade of months had left the Confederates there without rations. Since Vicksburg was the last Confederate stronghold on the river, Grant's victory cut off the western Confederate states from the eastern states, preventing the shipping of food, supplies, and soldiers from the West.

The fighting Tar Heels. During the first two years of the war, the Confederate forces won many battles in Virginia. Troops from North Carolina were involved in most of the action and were highly praised for their bravery. Once, after a battle in which Virginia troops fled but North Carolinians stood fast, General Lee said, "God bless the Tar Heel boys," giving rise to the state's nickname.

In 1863 and 1864, North Carolina troops were deeply involved in the fighting that took place in Virginia, as well as in the fateful Battle of Gettysburg. In that battle, one North Carolina regiment drove farther north in the face of heavy enemy fire than any other troops. Over 4,000 of the more than 15,000 Confederate troops killed at Gettysburg were North Carolinians.

Union General Ulysses S. Grant won important battles at Vicksburg and Appomattox Court House, Virginia

Sherman's objective on his march was to cause such massive destruction that the Confederacy would have no chance of extending the war. When people objected to his destruction of civilian property, he is said to have responded, "War is hell." (After the war, Sherman stated that he never said this.)

Think as a Geographer

Geography isn't just mountains and rivers. It also includes what is called economic geography, which deals with the number and kinds of resources a place has. ■ *To Do*: Remembering what you learned about the South's military skill and the North's resources, explain why the short war would have been to the South's advantage, while a long war was to the North's advantage.

A few months after Gettysburg, Lincoln visited the battlefield to dedicate it as a national cemetery for fallen soldiers. He spoke briefly, but his powerful Gettysburg Address has become a classic speech, memorized by generations of schoolchildren.

Sherman's march to the sea. The battles of Gettysburg and Vicksburg marked the turning point in the war. After Vicksburg came Chattanooga, Tennessee, where Union forces under Grant and General William T. Sherman again prevailed. From Tennessee, Sherman began what is one of the best known events of the Civil War—his long, destructive march to the sea. From Tennessee south through Georgia and north into the Carolinas, Sherman's troops stormed across the South, burning crops, looting homes, ripping up railroad tracks, and wrecking trains. The cities in his path, including Atlanta and Savannah, Georgia, fell in flames, driving thousands of women and children from their homes.

While Sherman was cutting off the lower South, Grant, now commander of all the Union's forces, moved steadily against Lee's forces in Richmond. Grant's larger and better equipped army finally drove the desperate Confederates from their capital. As Lee's soldiers retreated, they carried on a running battle with the pursuing Union forces. Grant's army finally cornered Lee's army at the village of **Appomattox Court House,** Virginia. There Lee surrendered. It was the death blow to the Confederacy.

The Gettysburg Address

*F*OUR SCORE AND SEVEN YEARS AGO, *our fathers brought forth on this continent a new nation conceived in liberty and dedicated to the proposition that all men are created equal.*

Now we are engaged in a great civil war, testing whether that nation—or any nation, so conceived and so dedicated—can long endure.

We are met on a great battlefield of that war. We have come to dedicate a portion of that field as a final resting place for those who here gave their lives that that nation might live.

It is altogether fitting and proper that we should do this.

But, in a larger sense, we cannot dedicate, we cannot consecrate, we cannot hallow, this ground. The brave men, living and dead, who struggled here have consecrated it, far above our poor power to add or detract.

The world will little note nor long remember what we say here, but it can never forget what they did here.

It is for us, the living, rather, to be dedicated, here, to the unfinished work which they who fought here have thus far so nobly advanced. It is rather for us to be here dedicated to the great task remaining before us—that from these honored dead we take increased devotion to that cause for which they gave the last full measure of devotion; that we here highly resolve that these dead shall not have died in vain; that this nation, under God, shall have a new birth of freedom; and that government of the people, by the people, for the people shall not perish from the earth.

Grant and Lee shake hands at Appomattox. Later, tattered Southern veterans wept as they took leave of their beloved commander. Elated Union soldiers cheered, but were silenced by Grant's stern admonition, "The war is over; the rebels are our countrymen again."

Lee's surrender.   The two generals met on April 9, 1865, at a farmhouse in the village to discuss the terms of surrender. Grant wrote generous terms, allowing Confederate soldiers to return to their homes and, at Lee's request, letting them keep their horses and mules for the spring plowing. After the agreement was signed, Lee walked out onto the porch of the farmhouse. Three times he slowly struck the gloved palm of his left hand with his right fist. Then he mounted his horse. Grant saluted by raising his weather-beaten hat. Lee lifted his tailored hat in response and rode off. After four years, the bloody war was finally over.

Lincoln's assassination.   The Union celebrated its victory, but the celebrations were sadly cut short. On April 14, 1865, an actor named John Wilkes Booth shot Lincoln in the back of the head while he was attending a play. The President died early the next morning. He was succeeded by Vice President Andrew Johnson.

Think Twice
1. Why was the Battle of Manassas a surprise to both sides?
2. Why did Lee want to surround Washington, D.C.?
3. Why was the Emancipation Proclamation important even though it had no immediate effect on slavery?
4. Sherman's march did not end at the sea. Look at the map on page 223 and find out where he went after leaving the coast at Savannah.

Zebulon B. Vance
John N. Maffitt
Fort Fisher
Jefferson Davis
Albemarle
Gilbert Elliott
Robert F. Hoke
Joseph E. Johnston
Battle of Bentonville
casualty

3 North Carolina in the War

After Lincoln's call for troops, most North Carolina Unionists accepted the idea of secession and put their efforts into defending the state and preparing it for war. In the words of Zebulon B. Vance, who would succeed Ellis as governor, "if war must come, I preferred to be with my own people. If we had to shed blood, I preferred to shed Northern rather than Southern blood. If we had to slay, I had rather slay strangers than my own kindred."

Preparing for war.   Even before North Carolina seceded, Governor Ellis ordered state troops to take over three federal forts in the state. All three surrendered quietly. The state also took over the United States Mint at Charlotte and the arsenal at Fayetteville. At the same time, the state bought horses from Kentucky and saddles and harnesses from New Orleans. Powder works and arsenals were created.

Getting supplies during the war.   When the war started, only a few men in North Carolina knew how to make swords and bayonets, but they soon trained others to do so. A company in Raleigh made coverings for bullets, while factories to make rifles, uniforms, and shoes were built at several places around the state. Foundries made cannons from melted down church bells and scrap iron.

In 1862, Governor Vance persuaded the state to buy four steamships and send agents abroad to sell cotton and buy supplies for soldiers. Privately owned ships soon joined the state's steamships in running the Union blockade. Together they brought in everything from medicines and farm tools to military supplies, needles, and cloth. Expert

North Carolina's people raised money for the war effort in many ways. The advertisement above is for a reading of Shakespeare's works to benefit the state's troops.

READINGS
FROM
SHAKSPEARE AND OTHER POETS!

This evening, at 7 o'clock, in the COMMONS HALL,

MRS. HEAVLIN OF GRANVILLE,

Who has high testimonials of her skill and attainments, will read from Shakspeare and other authors. The audience may expect a treat of the highest order. Mrs. H's object is a benevolent one; it being her purpose to appropriate the proceeds of these readings to the benefit of our brave soldiers who are fighting our battles.

Tickets can be had at the Bookstores of Messrs. Turner and Pomeroy, and at Mr. Pescud's Drug store. Price 50 cents.
Raleigh, N. C., Nov. 20, 1861.

A Narrow Escape

One evening, Captain John Maffitt was about 10 miles from Wilmington, headed for home, and cautiously picking his way through the Union blockade. Lights on shore were out as usual, to avoid helping the crews on Union ships see any Confederate vessels. As Maffitt's ship neared shore, he strained to see what lay ahead in the dark. Dimly he recognized two Union warships on either side of the channel. He decide to dash through, hoping to escape being seen. Then came the hissing sound of a rocket flare going up. He had been discovered! Abrubtly a voice from a speaking trumpet ordered,"Heave to, or I will sink you."

"Ay, Ay, sir!" Maffitt responded. Loudly he ordered, "Stop the engines." The crew feared the worst, but Maffitt knew that the ship's momentum had carried it beyond the enemy, who was sending over a boarding party. The gruff voice sounded again, this time just behind the blockade runner. "Back your engines, sir, and stand by to receive my boat."

Maffitt whispered to his engineer, "Full speed ahead, sir, and open wide your throttle-valve!" In the darkness, the Union captains couldn't tell that the ship wasn't really backing. When they did realize, the Union gunners couldn't fire without hitting their own men.

Quick thinking and skillful sailing had saved the blockade runner. And a lucky thing it was. If hit, the cargo of 900 barrels of gunpowder might have blown the ship out of the water. Instead, the ship was soon anchored under the friendly guns of the fort protecting Wilmington.

---

tailors cut most of the cloth, which was then sent out to be sewn into uniforms by women around the state. In this way, North Carolina not only clothed its own troops but also sold many uniforms to other states.

Despite the blockade runners' best efforts, the state ran critically short of many goods. Factories needed parts and oil for machinery. Iron for railroads was in short supply, and the price of household necessities rose sky-high.

Blockade runners. With the Union blockade in place, foreign ships would not enter Southern ports. As a result, European manufacturers shipped goods to the West Indies, where Confederate ships from Wilmington, Charleston, and Savannah picked them up. In exchange, Confederate ships carried cotton, which could be bought cheaply in the South and sold for high prices to Europeans. The only hitch in this profitable trade was getting past the blockade.

Ingenious captains soon found ways to elude the Union ships. Starting out from Wilmington at the darkest time of night, the low-decked vessels, painted as near the color of the water as possible, sailed along the coast so as not to present a silhouette against the sky. As they approached the Union ships, they put on speed, usually managing to escape capture.

Gibralter of the South. The friendly guns that protected Maffitt's ship (See box, above.)were those of **Fort Fisher**, a huge earthwork in the shape of an L at the mouth of the Cape Fear River. Largely designed by Colonel William Lamb and under his command since July 4, 1862, it

Captain John Newland Maffitt ran the blockade many times, bringing in much needed supplies for North Carolina and the Confederacy.

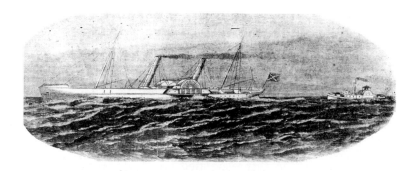

The Union blockade presented a great challenge to Confederate ships. Shown to the right are blockade runners off the coast at Wilmington.

The inside of Fort Fisher, Gibralter of the South, under attack. The nickname comes from a fortified rocky peninsula at the western end of the Mediterranean Sea, which withstood invaders for hundreds of years at a time.

protected shipping and kept Wilmington's port open longer than any other Confederate port.

Fort Fisher withstood many attempts to take it, including one in December 1864. At that time, a strong Union fleet approached the fort, exploding an old Union ship packed with 185 tons of gunpowder just 200 yards from the walls. This attempt to destroy the fort failed, as did the heavy bombardment that followed. A few days later, another attempt failed.

Finally on January 12, 1865, just three months before the end of the war, Union ships began a bombardment of the fort that lasted for three days. Then the shelling stopped, and sailors and marines scrambled from every ship, attacking the fort from all directions. One group managed to get in and overcome the heavily outnumbered Confederates in several hours of hand-to-hand combat.

Vance and the Confederacy. One man, Governor Zebulon Vance, greatly influenced North Carolina's relationship with the Confederate government. It was his energy and ability that made possible the organization and direction of the state's independent-minded people. People came to love him, not only for his charm and his stock of funny stories, but because of the way he defended the state's interests. He was the driving force that kept the state's troops and people supplied during the war. He spent his best efforts in keeping courts and schools open and railroads running. Vance was intent on protecting the state's citizens against arbitrary actions by the Confederate government and never gave that government his full support.

Vance often disagreed with Confederate policies and wrote long letters to President Davis, stating his objections to the Confederate government's actions. Vance felt that the Confederate government neglected North Carolina's defense. He resented the absence of North Carolinians in the government as well as the failure of the Confederate army to appoint North Carolina officers to high-ranking positions. The governor suspected that his former Unionist position or the fact that the state waited so long to secede was responsible for these conditions.

The Union in northeastern North Carolina. After Manassas, Union leaders turned their attention to the Outer Banks of North Carolina. The state stationed some steamers in the area but needed troops to help defend the coast. When the Confederate government refused to send any, the state quickly built several forts on the Outer Banks. One, Fort Hatteras, fell to Union forces in August 1861, and the others were soon abandoned. The Union then sent a massive force to take Roanoke Island, capturing the island

Confederate President Jefferson Davis was hesitant to name North Carolinians to his cabinet or to recommend them for promotion to high military rank.

The railroad bridge at Kinston was one of the targets of a Union raid.

The Union fleet attacked Confederate forts on Roanoke Island.

Lieutenant Gilbert Elliott designed and built the *Albemarle.*

in February 1862. The island became a base from which much of eastern North Carolina was taken. Elizabeth City and New Bern fell into Union hands by March, and Fort Macon was captured the next month.

From New Bern and elsewhere, the Union launched raids on the eastern towns and cities: Plymouth, Murfreesboro, Tarboro, Washington, Kinston, Goldsboro, and Rocky Mount. On their raids, Union troops wreaked havoc—burning railroad bridges; damaging the tracks; burning mills, houses, and barns; slaughtering livestock; and raiding smokehouses. Confederate forces tried but were unable to regain control of the area, although some towns changed hands several times.

The *Albemarle.*   At about the same time as the Battle of Gettysburg, work began in North Carolina on a special ironclad ship called the *Albemarle.* Designed and built under the supervision of nineteen-year-old Gilbert Elliott, a native of Elizabeth City, the ship was powered by a train engine and had an 18-foot prow that could be used to ram other vessels. Since iron was scarce, the men working on the project had to scavenge for material—old pots, useless railroad rails, even nuts and bolts—that could be melted down and made into armor and fittings.

While the *Albemarle* was under construction, two separate Confederate forces had been trying unsuccessfully to retake cities in eastern North Carolina. Finally, North Carolina General Robert F. Hoke, the commander of the attacking

The *Albemarle* was constructed at Edwards Ferry in Halifax County.

forces, asked for the help of the *Albemarle*. Although the ship was not finished, it was sent to the aid of troops trying to retake Plymouth. It set out with a small boat bearing a portable forge in tow. Workmen scrambled over the ship, trying to make it at least halfway usable.

The *Albemarle* arrived late at night. Downstream, ahead of the *Albemarle*, two Union steamers loomed in the dark. Lashed together with long planks and chains, they meant to catch the *Albemarle* between them so it could be battered and sunk. The *Albemarle's* crew, however, sailed the ship close to shore and then turned and rammed one of the steamers. With a large hole in its side, the steamer promptly sank. After a brief fight in which enemy fire just bounced off the *Albemarle's* ironclad sides, the second steamer fled. Two days later, Hoke's land forces finished the job of retaking Plymouth.

During the spring and summer of 1864, the *Albemarle* remained such a threat to Union control of the coastal waters that the Union fleet made an all-out effort to destroy

The Union repeatedly tried to destroy the *Albemarle*.

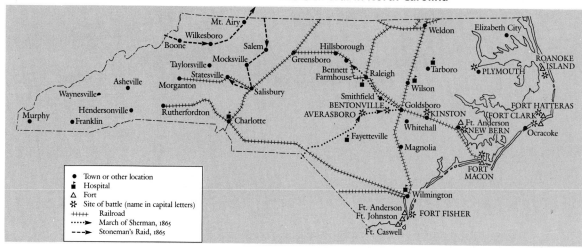

The Civil War in North Carolina

Map legend:
- ● Town or other location
- ■ Hospital
- △ Fort
- ✳ Site of battle (name in capital letters)
- +++++ Railroad
- •••••► March of Sherman, 1865
- – – –► Stoneman's Raid, 1865

Maps Matter

On March 28, 1865, Union General George Stoneman moved from Tennessee into western North Carolina. At the town of Boone, he began a rapid series of raids, destroying public, private, and military property as Sherman had done on his march. ■ *To Do*: Find Stoneman's route on the map. Where does he leave the state? What towns does he go through when he comes back into North Carolina?

the ship. Bombarded and rammed and with its smokestack full of holes, the ship still evaded capture. Finally it fell victim to a torpedo placed directly under it. Without the *Albemarle* to protect it, Plymouth was soon retaken. Shortly thereafter, Hoke and his men went to Virginia to aid the forces struggling to defend Richmond. Soon Union forces again took over northeastern North Carolina, remaining in control until the war ended a few months later.

Sherman in North Carolina. General Sherman knew that before the war there were many Unionists in North Carolina. Hoping that he might receive help from some of them, Sherman ordered that raids on private property were to stop when the troops crossed into the state from the south in March 1865. However, he didn't foresee one temptation his men would face and gave no instructions about it.

In North Carolina, his soldiers found tall, stately pines with strips of bark removed so that rosin could be collected to make turpentine. Where the bark was stripped, rosin had oozed out. When touched with a lighted match, the rosin flared up, quickly engulfing the whole tree in spectacular flames. Officers could not control the soldiers, who ran from tree to tree, setting the forest afire to watch the awe-inspiring sight. The soldiers' madness destroyed vast tracts of longleaf pines.

Tables Teach

On which side were the most people killed? Which had the most wounded and missing?

CASUALTIES IN THE BATTLE OF BENTONVILLE

	Killed	Wounded	Missing
Confederate	239	1,694	673
Union	304	1,112	221
Total	543	2,806	894

In North Carolina, as in other states, Sherman encountered resistance from Confederate troops. North Carolina's bloodiest battle of the war took place in the village of Bentonville near Goldsboro. Here, on a Sunday morning in March 1865, Confederate troops under General Joseph E. Johnston met an advance party of Sherman's troops and drove them back. The **Battle of Bentonville** continued on Monday as more of Sherman's men arrived. Vastly outnumbered, the Confederates still fought on and on. When the rest of Sherman's army arrived on Tuesday, the Confederates finally were forced to retreat. Total **casualties**—killed, wounded, and missing men—on both sides were 4,243.

Before Sherman reached Raleigh, both sides received news of Lee's surrender. Reluctantly President Davis authorized General Johnston to surrender to Sherman. To ease the burden on the war-torn state, Sherman asked his men to release horses, mules, livestock, and whatever else was available to the people of North Carolina so that they could begin planting crops.

A Civil War reenactment at the Bentonville Battleground State Historic Site is shown below.

General Johnston surrendered to Sherman at the farmhouse of James Bennett a few miles west of Durham.

The devastation of North Carolina. Shortages of many goods during the war caused great hardship. Salt for preserving food was in short supply. Coffee all but disappeared and sugar was scarce. Near the end, as cloth also became scarce, people went into their attics for old clothes to wear again. They made draperies into clothing, and hospitals used rugs as blankets.

Agriculture declined during the war as broken tools could not be replaced and the people who worked the farms were off at the fighting. Rail fences and barns fell into disrepair. Union troops used fence rails and sometimes whole buildings for firewood.

Bridges and public buildings had been destroyed in the fighting. Railroad tracks had been torn up. Worse, thousands of young men had died. Hardly a family in the state was untouched by the loss of life.

Think Twice

1. Describe at least three ways in which North Carolina prepared itself for war and kept itself supplied during the war.
2. Why was Fort Fisher important?
3. Why was Governor Vance often at odds with Jefferson Davis?
4. How did the Union gain access to northeastern North Carolina?
5. Why do you think the soldiers at Bentonville kept fighting even though vastly outnumbered?

Chapter 16 Review

Choose from the following menu of activities.

Think Back: Main Ideas

1. One side's advantage is the other side's disadvantage. Reread the sections "Union resources" and "Confederate advantages." Then state four advantages for one side as disadvantages for the other. For example, "The Union had an experienced government in place" would be matched by "The Confederacy had to form a new government."

2. Why do you think a person owning 20 or more enslaved Africans was excused from the draft?

3. Lincoln planned the Emancipation Proclamation several months before issuing it. His advisers thought he should wait until the Union won a major battle before doing so. Although neither side won a clear victory at Antietam, he decided it was enough of a victory to serve the purpose. Why do you think he was advised to wait? (Remember who was winning in the first two years of the war.)

4. Other Confederate commanders surrendered weeks after Lee did, but the war was essentially over at the time of Lee's surrender. In a few sentences, explain why. Use these words in your explanation: *Vicksburg, west, east, lower South, Sherman, Richmond.*

5. Governor Vance was a Unionist before the war but, as you have read, decided to fight with his own people. Many other people on both sides had to make a similar decision. In fact, at times families had a son on each side in a battle. Suppose you had to make such a choice. What would you do? Give reasons for the choice you make.

Maps Matter

Using the map on page 223, name and locate the capital city of the Confederacy and the capital city of the Union. How does the location of these cities help explain why much of the fighting took place in the Virginia-Maryland region?

Word Wizard

The Gettysburg Address contains a number of words whose meaning you may not know. Reread the speech, looking for the words listed below. Define each word as it is used in the speech. Use a dictionary as needed.

score, conceived, dedicated, proposition, consecrate, hallow, detract, devotion, vain, perish

Working Cooperatively

Before the war, Jefferson Davis was a strong believer in states' rights. He felt that the federal government was too powerful and that states should be making their own decisions in certain matters such as slavery. When he became president of the Confederacy, he found himself trying to form a strong central government that would be united in its war effort. The people he had to work with were the leaders of states that had seceded because of a belief in states' rights. Working in groups, research and write a report on the problems Davis faced and his relationships with officials such as Governor Vance.

Curriculum Connection

Use the information in the table on page 234 to make a bar or pictograph showing Union and Confederate casualties at the Battle of Bentonville.

Learning through Literature

Red Badge of Courage, by Stephen Crane
Jubilee, by Margaret Walker
Marching On, by James Boyd
Phantom of the Blockade, by Stephen W. Meader
Spy for the Confederacy: Rose O'Neal Greenhow, by Jeannette Nolan
The Ghost Battalion, by Manly Wade Wellman

Chapter 17 A Troubled Peace

The South suffers after its defeat.

People in both the North and the South mourned the great losses they had suffered in the war. A quarter of a million Southerners had died. The North had lost one third of a million. Many were eager to put the war behind them. However, the suffering was not yet over for the South. Much of the region was in ruins. Thousands of people, both African Americans and those of European descent, were hungry and homeless.

North Carolina waits for readmittance.

With the end of the war, North Carolina's government collapsed. Governor Vance took refuge in Statesville with friends but was soon arrested and sent to prison in Washington. With the governor gone, a Union general, John McA. Schofield, took command of North Carolina. He placed other generals in charge of each of the three sections—west, central, and east. President Andrew Johnson wanted his native state to return to the Union as rapidly as possible. However, there was no constitutional provision for the return of a state to the Union. In fact, since the North maintained that the right of secession did not exist, it may seem strange that North Carolina was regarded as out of the Union when the war ended in 1865. Since Congress was not in session at the end of the war, it was up to the President to make arrangements for the return of the states to the Union.

Cartoon showing President Johnson mending Uncle Sam's war-torn coat. ▶

Think Ahead

The end of the war brought new misery to Southerners. Read about the struggle and humiliation that North Carolina and other Southern states faced as they tried to rejoin the Union. Find out how they were finally successful.

1 Restoring the Union

Two years before his death and the war's end, President Lincoln had worked out a plan for the **Reconstruction**, or rebuilding, of the South. Unlike some people in the government, Lincoln wanted to "bind up the nation's wounds," not to make them worse. He also wanted to achieve a "just and lasting peace."

Lincoln's plan for Reconstruction. Lincoln announced his plan for handling the defeated states on December 8, 1863. In his **Proclamation of Amnesty and Reconstruction**, Lincoln offered a full pardon to all but a very few Southerners involved in the war. To be pardoned, citizens of the former Confederate states would have to take an oath of loyalty to the Constitution. They also would have to agree to abolish slavery. A Confederate state could take its place in the Union and in Congress when the number of its citizens equal to 10 percent of the state's voters in 1860 had taken the oath and organized a government.

The South suffered great damage during the Civil War. Richmond, Virginia, the capital of the Confederacy, was in ruins when the war ended.

Johnson in support of Lincoln's plan. When Lincoln was assassinated, Vice President Andrew Johnson took over as President. Like Lincoln, Johnson wanted to forgive the South and bring it back into the Union as quickly as possible. He outlined his Reconstruction program in the months after he took office.

Johnson's Reconstruction plan was similar to Lincoln's but was stricter in some ways. Johnson asked that Confederate citizens take oaths of loyalty to the Union. As soon as 10 percent of the voters in a state had sworn to be loyal to the Union, they would be allowed to form a new government. They could choose their own lawmakers, but they could not elect anyone who had been a Confederate leader. Some of

Andrew Johnson was born in Raleigh. The son of poor parents, he had no formal schooling and started life as a tailor. He moved to Tennessee and served in the state legislature and in Congress. He was the only Southern senator to support the Union after the Civil War began. As Vice President in 1865, he succeeded to the presidency when Lincoln was assassinated.

the high-ranking Confederates had to get a special pardon from the President. Each state had to repeal all secession laws. In addition, new state governments had to approve the Thirteenth Amendment, passed in 1865, which outlawed slavery in the United States. They also had to write new state constitutions and agree not to repay Confederate war debts.

Although Johnson's plan was stricter than Lincoln's, Johnson did not enforce it strictly. He failed to look closely at the records of the new governments "reconstructed" under his presidency. For example, Mississippi, although readmitted to the Union, did not **ratify**, or approve, the Thirteenth Amendment.

North Carolina and Johnson's plan. On May 29, 1865, Johnson chose W.W. Holden as provisional governor of North Carolina until the state was admitted back into the Union. Holden had converted to Unionism during the war and supported a peace movement. He was a strong supporter of the President's plan for Reconstruction. Holden, however, had many enemies. It was said that he changed his mind so many times that no one knew where he stood on any question.

In his new position, Holden appointed more than 3,000 people to state and local offices. He also called for an election of delegates to a convention in Raleigh in October 1865. That convention repealed the Ordinance of Secession, declared slavery abolished, provided for an election to be held in November for governor, legislators, and congressmen, and decided that the state's war debts would not be paid.

Anger over Black Codes. Many members of Congress were upset with Johnson's handling of Reconstruction. They felt that the South was not being punished enough. The final blow came when Southern states passed **Black Codes**—laws that strictly limited the freedom of formerly enslaved people. These laws said that freed Africans could not own guns or meet together after sunset. In addition, they could be put in prison if they had no jobs. At least one state, South Carolina, said that freed Africans could practice no other trade except that of a farmer or a servant. Many members of Congress, as well as ordinary citizens of the Union, felt that if such laws were allowed to stand, the Civil War had accomplished nothing, and Union soldiers had died in vain.

Think Twice

1. What were Lincoln's plans for Reconstruction?
2. What was Johnson's Reconstruction program?
3. (a) How did Johnson's plan differ from Lincoln's? (b) In what ways was it similar?

2 Congress Takes Over

Most of Johnson's opponents in Congress were Republicans, but some were more radical than others. The Radical Republicans wanted to protect the rights of the formerly enslaved Africans and punish the former Confederate states. They also thought that freedmen should get the vote, not only because this was just, but also because they might vote for Republican candidates. Moderate Republicans agreed on the need to protect the rights of the formerly enslaved, but they were less anxious to punish the South. Both groups of Republicans, however, were dissatisfied with Johnson's Reconstruction. They believed that the President did not have the power to make rules for Reconstruction. Only Congress had that authority. As a result, in 1867, the Republicans set up a committee entitled the **Joint Committee on Reconstruction.** It was made up of members of both houses. The Joint Committee's task was to draw up a Reconstruction plan to replace Johnson's.

The extension of the Freedmen's Bureau.   The first measure recommended by the Joint Committee on Reconstruction was a new **Freedmen's Bureau Bill**, which Congress passed in February 1866. It extended the life of the Freedmen's Bureau, an agency set up in March 1865, to help people in the South. The Freedmen's Bureau supplied food, medicine, and other emergency aid to both white and African American Southerners. It also helped the formerly enslaved to start a new life by providing them with an education. The following passage describes the importance of education to young and old alike.

Primary Source

> *Whatever else the freedmen lacked, there was in them a fierce hunger for knowledge. They believed, as perhaps no other people had believed so fervently that knowledge would make them truly free, for had not their masters taken great pains to withhold it from them? Before freedom, "stealing learning" was a crime for which they could be whipped; now it held the magic of the rainbow after a violent storm.*

> —*Pauli Murray*, Proud Shoes

The clash between Johnson and Congress.   Johnson refused to sign the new Freedmen's Bureau Bill because it gave the Bureau the power to try in military courts cases against a person interfering with the civil rights of African Americans. Johnson believed the local courts should handle such questions.

When the war ended, the Freedmen's Bureau built schools in the South for the formerly enslaved of all ages. A large number of Northerners, formerly active abolitionists, moved to the South to teach African Americans.

The Republicans tried to impeach Johnson for several high crimes and misdemeanors in office. This drawing shows President Johnson receiving a summons of impeachment from the sergeant-at-arms of the Senate.

In June 1866, Congress passed the **Fourteenth Amendment** to the Constitution and offered it to the southern states for ratification—even though Southerners had not been represented in the Congress that wrote it. The Fourteenth Amendment defined United States citizenship in a way that included African Americans.

President Johnson encouraged the Southern states to oppose the Fourteenth Amendment. Then he declared open war against the Republicans in Congress. He actively campaigned against them in the Congressional elections of 1866. The voters, however, did not agree. When the ballots were counted, the Republicans held two thirds of the seats in both the House and the Senate.

Congress in control. With such an outpouring of support, the Republicans took control of Reconstruction. On March 2, 1867, they passed a Reconstruction act that returned former Confederate states to military rule. The new act divided the ten "unreconstructed" states into military districts. The army once again took charge.

Before the army could leave and civilian rule could be restored, the people of the ex-Confederate states had to elect delegates to conventions and write new state constitutions. Male African Americans over the age of 21 were to be given the vote. However, former office holders in the Confederacy could not vote or run for office. Moreover, each new state government had to approve the Fourteenth Amendment.

Because Johnson disapproved of Congress's plans and actions, he vetoed bills Congress suggested and ignored laws Congress passed. Finally, Congress had had enough. In February 1868, they voted to **impeach** the President. *Impeach* means "to charge someone with wrongdoing." If the person who is so charged is found guilty, he or she may be removed from office. When the final voting took place, however, Johnson remained President by a single vote.

Republican President Ulysses S. Grant in power. In 1868, the Republicans helped to elect Ulysses S. Grant—a President with whom they could work. The votes of Southern African Americans played an important part in the Republican victory. That encouraged Republicans to go further in securing suffrage for African Americans.

In February 1869, the Republican-dominated Congress passed the **Fifteenth Amendment** to the Constitution, which said states could not deny anyone the vote "on account of race, color, or previous condition of servitude." States that still had not complied with Congress's Reconstruction requirements had to ratify the Fifteenth as well as the Fourteenth Amendment. However, the Fifteenth Amendment had its greatest effect in the North, where most states still denied the vote to African Americans.

The conflict over Reconstruction in North Carolina.
The struggle over Reconstruction between Johnson and Congress spilled over into North Carolina. Congress, about to establish its own plan for Reconstruction, refused seats to North Carolina senators and representatives chosen by the state's General Assembly.

Despite such problems, the General Assembly went on with its work. It ratified the Thirteenth Amendment ending slavery. It also heard complaints from people who were angry that federal soldiers were still in the state. There were reports of their interfering in elections. Activities of the Freedmen's Bureau also caused concern. Many people believed the Bureau made unrealistic promises to African Americans about what the government would do for them.

Meanwhile, Holden had changed his political views. He no longer supported the President's plan of Reconstruction, but instead backed the much harsher program being discussed in Congress. He also favored suffrage for African Americans. In 1866, Holden went to Washington to discuss with some Republicans the creation of a state political party in North Carolina. In March 1867, the Republican party was organized in North Carolina.

In 1867, as you have read, Congress ended presidential Reconstruction and began its own plan. North Carolina was occupied by federal troops. The state's government was declared provisional and could at any time be changed or even abolished. Until North Carolina followed Congress's requirements for readmittance to the Union, it had a dual government: Governor Worth and a federal general, Daniel E. Sickles, commander of the Second Military District.

Jonathan Worth, a former Whig and prewar Unionist, easily defeated W.W. Holden in the November 1865 race for governor.

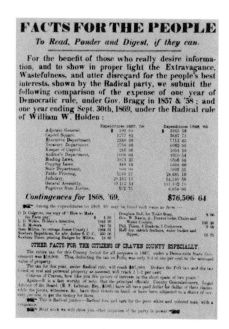

This political advertisement was directed against the Holden administration.

Think Twice

1. How did the views of Radical and moderate Republicans differ in 1865?
2. Explain the rights African Americans gained from the Fourteenth and Fifteenth Amendments.
3. What laws did Republicans enact after they took control of Reconstruction?
4. Why do you think Holden changed his views about Reconstruction and began to support Congress's plan?

3 Reconstruction in the South

Between 1867 and 1870, all the old states of the Confederacy adopted constitutions acceptable to Congress. However, for a large number of white Southerners, the trials of Reconstruction were far from over. For them, the first elected governments of those "reconstructed" states were almost as unacceptable as the military governments they replaced.

Newcomers in Southern government.   Republican Reconstruction brought many new people into the government. A few were Northerners, known as **carpetbaggers** because they often carried suitcases made of carpeting. It was not a friendly nickname. After they stuffed their bags with whatever they could steal, Southerners said, the carpetbaggers would return to the North. Most new government officials, however, were Southerners. These Republicans were called **scalawags** by their enemies, who believed that anyone who worked for the new governments was a crook or a traitor.

African Americans also took part in the new governments. Many served in state legislatures. Two African American men from Mississippi, Hiram Revels and Blanche K. Bruce, were elected to the United States Senate. There were African American lieutenant governors in Louisiana, Mississippi, and South Carolina. Although some African Americans were poorly prepared for their political duties, others had received a good education in Canada or in the North and were very able officials.

During Reconstruction, 14 African Americans were elected to the House and to the Senate. Among the first were (left to right) Senator Hiram Revels of Mississippi (who was elected to the seat previously occupied by Jefferson Davis), and Congressmen Benjamin Turner of Alabama; Robert De Large of South Carolina; Josiah Walls of Florida; Jefferson Long of Georgia; and Joseph Rainey and R. Brown Elliot from South Carolina.

Changes in state governments. The new Republican state governments brought many changes to the South. They started public school systems. They rebuilt vast areas that were destroyed in the war. They also tried to lay the basis for further economic growth. For example, they appropriated large amounts of tax money to help railroad companies lay track throughout the South. Government in the South also became more democratic, since planters no longer controlled state government. Poor people, both African American and white, had larger roles in political life.

Resistance to change. Many white Southerners did not like the changes that came to the South under Reconstruction. State governments were spending a lot of money, and taxes were high. Critics of the government accused the Republicans of corruption. Also, Confederate army veterans resented the fact that they had no say in the new governments, while African Americans did.

A few people in the South resorted to violence. In 1866, a group of young ex-Confederates got together in Pulaski, Tennessee, and started a secret society known as the **Ku Klux Klan.** The Klan, which spread rapidly throughout the South, hoped to use intimidation to return political power to white men. Dressed in white robes and hoods, the Klan members attacked and even killed African Americans, as well as whites who helped African Americans.

A new constitution for North Carolina. In 1867, in compliance with Congress's requirements for readmittance to the Union, North Carolina held its election for delegates to a state convention. However, many of the prewar leaders of the state were ineligible to vote under Congress's guidelines. In addition, the Conservatives were not well organized, and many who might have voted did not bother to register.

As a result, in the election of 1867, 107 of the 120 delegates elected were Republicans. Among them were 18 carpetbaggers and 15 African Americans. Other delegates included native-born whites, most of whom had never been elected to office. Some former Whigs as well as Democrats became Republicans and were elected. Among them were former Confederate officers and members of prominent families, as well as Holden.

Delegates to the convention met in Raleigh from mid-January to mid-March 1868 and drew up a revised state constitution that, according to Congress's decree, included the following provisions. North Carolina would remain a member of the United States with no right to secede. Slavery, of course, was specifically prohibited. Universal manhood suffrage, regardless of race, was guaranteed. The new constitution also included changes in the structure of

Ku Klux Klan members usually wore long white robes, tall pointed hats, and masks to hide their identity and to instill terror in their victims. Riding on horseback and heavily armed, Klan members paid "night visits" to African Americans as well as whites who helped African Americans. Hundreds of African Americans were murdered by members of the Klan.

Nearly 500,000 African Americans voted for the first time in the 1868 presidential election. Their votes helped to elect Republican Ulysses S. Grant as President.

Across Cultures

*I*n 1868, when a new constitution was being drawn up for North Carolina, some members of one committee asked why women should not be allowed to vote. However, no one seemed to pay any attention to the remark.
■ *To Do*: Why do you think African American males were given the vote, yet not women?

all three branches of government; the establishment of free public schools for everyone between the ages of 6 and 21 regardless of race; provisions for funding the railroads; and progressive guidelines for the care of the poor and other unfortunates. Before citizens could vote on the constitution, however, the military required a new registration of voters. This was to clear the books of anyone not eligible to vote because of his participation in the war.

The Klan in North Carolina. The people of North Carolina felt that they had lost everything. Their cause was lost, as well as the lives of so many of their sons. Their state's economy was destroyed, and the new constitution only added to their misery. They no longer had control of their government. As a result, some people decided to find a way to break the Republican hold on their state government. They thought the quickest way was to scare African Americans, who were voting for the Republicans, away from the polls.

The elections for new state and county officials and congressmen were being held at the same time that the people were voting on the revised constitution. It was during this bitter election campaign that the Ku Klux Klan made its first appearance in North Carolina. At first, Klan activities were meant to be only harmless scare tactics, but violence soon occurred.

Despite the Klan, however, the Republicans claimed a clear victory. William Woods Holden was elected governor in 1868. His party also carried 58 of the 89 counties in the state. Conservatives elected just one judge, a solicitor, and one congressman.

The return of North Carolina to the Union. With a majority in the General Assembly, Holden's followers quickly ratified the Fourteenth Amendment and elected two Republican senators to Congress. Satisfied with the state's new constitution, Congress finally permitted North Carolina's congressmen and senators to take their seats. On July 20, 1868, North Carolina was accepted once again as a member of the Union.

Think Twice

1. Describe three new groups of people elected to Southern state governments during Reconstruction.
2. Name at least one positive change that occurred as a result of the new state governments.
3. List and explain the major changes made in North Carolina's new state constitution of 1868.

4 The End of Reconstruction

People, Places, Terms

Wyatt Outlaw
John W. Stephens
George W. Kirk
Kirk-Holden War
Rutherford B. Hayes

The period between 1868 and 1871 when Holden and the Republicans were in power came to be known as a period of "pillage and plunder" in North Carolina. Many of Holden's friends and fellow Republicans were involved in dishonest dealings. These scandals were widely publicized by the Conservative press. This, along with the fact that 20 African American men and a large number of carpetbaggers were in the General Assembly, stirred up many Conservatives. They began to seek ways to end what they considered to be an oppressive and corrupt government and to return control of North Carolina to the Conservatives.

The spread of terror in North Carolina.   Under Governor Holden, some members of the General Assembly and Republican businessmen grew rich. Funds that were intended for building and repairing the railroads found their way into the hands of dishonest legislators and railroad officials. Bribery, fraud, and other underhanded dealings were not uncommon in Holden's administration.

Conservatives, frustrated by their lack of political power and desperate to regain control of state government, turned to the Ku Klux Klan. Klan members broke up political meetings. They frightened African Americans as well as others who supported the Republican party. Verbal and written threats, whippings, and even murder were used to scare away the Republican vote. The Klan was so successful that the Republicans lost control of 13 counties within a few months. Only Alamance and Caswell counties went over to the Republican's side.

As the 1870 election neared, the Klan stepped up its terrorism in these two counties. Near midnight on February 26, 1870, in Graham, the county seat of Alamance, a large band of robed horsemen went to the home of African American Republican leader Wyatt Outlaw. Outlaw was abducted and taken to the town square, where he was hanged from a tree within a hundred feet of the courthouse. In nearby Caswell County, Republican leader John W. Stephens, a white man, was murdered by the Klan in May 1870.

The Kirk-Holden War.   Governor Holden reacted swiftly after Stephens's murder. In 1869, the General Assembly passed an act that allowed the governor to place counties under martial law if he thought life and property were in danger. In 1870, Holden used this act to call out the militia. He placed it under the command of Colonel George W. Kirk

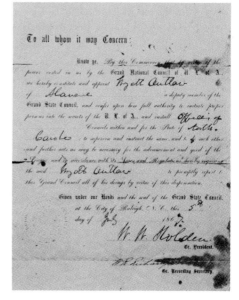

This document appointing Wyatt Outlaw to the Grand State Council of the Union League was signed by W.W.Holden as Grand President. The Union League, which African Americans were encouraged to join, was a society that supported the Republican party. Originally, it was organized in 1862 to raise Union morale at the time of Confederate victories. Later political activities of the Union League helped to spark the formation of the Ku Klux Klan.

W.W.Holden was elected governor of North Carolina in 1868. He was impeached in 1871 because of his "high crimes and misdemeanors in office." Although Holden was the second governor in the United States to be impeached, he was the first to be convicted.

from Tennessee. Kirk had led Union troops on raids into western North Carolina during the war. He now led a small army of untrained men ranging in age from 15 to 70 years into Alamance and Caswell counties. There he arrested over 100 men, including a few prominent citizens, who were suspected of being Klan members. Kirk kept them prisoner at his camp. When the men petitioned for their release on the grounds that they were being held unlawfully, Governor Holden ignored them. Finally, a federal judge ordered most of the prisoners freed. The judge ruled that they were being held without due process of law, which violated the recently adopted Fourteenth Amendment.

The **Kirk-Holden War,** as this episode was called by the governor's opponents, came to a quick end. In an election in August, the Conservatives took control of the General Assembly. The Klan had achieved its goal. In September, Holden disbanded the militia.

The Conservatives in control.   Conservatives began suggesting that Holden be impeached for his actions in Alamance and Caswell counties. A short while before Christmas of 1870, the House of Representatives prepared eight charges against the governor. In a trial that lasted from February 2 to March 23, 1871, Holden was convicted on six of the eight offenses and removed from office. Former Governor Vance commented that "it was the longest hunt after the poorest hide I ever saw."

In 1875, a constitutional convention was held. The election of delegates was very close. There were 58 Democrats, 58 Republicans, and 3 independents. Some of the amendments proposed and adopted by a vote of the people set a one-year residency requirement for voting; required non-discriminatory racial segregation in the

Up from Slavery

Booker T. Washington was born into slavery in 1856. As a young boy, he had a strong desire to learn, but it was against the law for anyone to teach a slave to read or write. In 1863, Lincoln issued the Emancipation Proclamation. Freedom changed Washington's life. He learned to read. He then spent every spare minute studying.

In 1881, Washington founded one of the most famous industrial schools of all times—Tuskegee Institute in Alabama. Booker T. Washington devoted his life to the school. When he died in 1915, Tuskegee Institute had more than a hundred buildings, taught 38 trades, and employed almost 200 teachers.

public schools; gave the legislature power to revise or abolish the form and power of county and township government; and simplified the amendment process for the future. These amendments helped to restore some of the power the legislature had lost after the Civil War.

Conservatives, anxious to elect their own governor, nominated Civil War Governor Zebulon B. Vance in 1877. When Vance won, many people in the state rejoiced. It was said that the state had been "redeemed," and that "home rule" had been restored.

A united nation. By 1876, the United States was a united nation again. In 1877, President Rutherford B. Hayes withdrew the army from the Southern states. The South, however, still suffered the scars of the Civil War.

Most Southerners were poor. The region made little progress in farming, and factories and businesses did not thrive. Some gifted Southerners, who might have helped the South, gave up and headed North to look for better opportunities.

In addition, by 1877, Republicans had lost interest in helping African Americans. The formerly enslaved people were on their own. Southern African Americans, stripped of many of the rights they had gained, now faced new struggles. Many moved North. Yet there too they were treated as if they were not equal to whites. Not until the 1960s, a century after the Civil War, did African Americans begin to win the fight against discrimination.

Think as a Geographer

As you have read, many African Americans left the South after the Civil War. Some fled the region to escape the vengeance of the Klan. Others went in search of better opportunities. ■ *To Do:* Use newspapers and other sources to identify shifts in population due to war. What are some of the results of these population shifts? What do you think are some of the changes and challenges a family faces when forced to move to a new location?

Think Twice

1. Why did the period during which Holden was governor become known as the time of "pillage and plunder"?

2. What role did the Ku Klux Klan play in restoring power to the Conservatives in North Carolina?

3. Describe the Kirk-Holden War.

4. Do you think Reconstruction was successful? Explain why or why not.

Chapter 17 Review

Choose from the following menu of activities.

Think Back: Main Ideas

This chapter describes the Reconstruction plans of Abraham Lincoln, Andrew Johnson, and the Republican Congress in power after the Civil War. Make a chart explaining how each plan proposed to deal with the following people or groups.

1. Ordinary citizens of the ex-Confederacy
2. Confederate officials and army officers
3. African Americans
4. The former Confederate states in resuming their place in the Union

Graphs Teach

This line graph shows how North Carolina's population gradually became more urban. Refer to the graph in answering the questions following it.

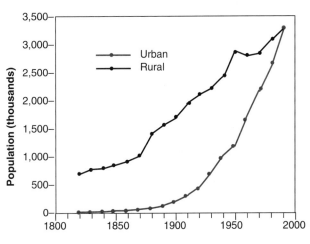

Rural and Urban Populations, 1820–2000

1. (a) How many people lived in rural North Carolina in 1900? (b) How many people lived in urban parts of the state that same year?
2. In 1930, did more people live in rural or urban areas?

3. During what years were the urban and rural populations nearly the same?
4. Which population grew more rapidly between the years 1950 and 1990—urban or rural?

Word Wizard

1. Look up *scalawag* and *carpetbagger* in the dictionary. What can you tell about the history of each of these words?
2. Use a dictionary to find the definitions of *radical* and *moderate*. How do the definition of these words describe the two types of Republicans found in Congress after the Civil War?

Working Cooperatively

Get together in groups of three to five. Imagine that you are a group of senators trying to come up with a plan for Reconstruction. Write a plan that includes a policy for dealing with the readmission of Southern states into the Union, the treatment of Confederate officers and officials, and the treatment of formerly enslaved people.

Curriculum Connection

Pretend you are one of these people: a newly freed African American, a carpetbagger, or a former officeholder in the Confederacy. Write a letter to a relative outside the South. In your letter, describe your view of the Reconstruction Act of 1867.

Learning through Literature

Our Words, Our Ways, by Sally Buckner
Black Hood, by Thomas Dixon
Stubborn Heart, by Frank G. Slaughter
A Fool's Errand and *Bricks Without Straw,* by Albion W. Tourgée

Growth in the State and Nation

1859 First successful oil well in the United States is drilled.

1863 Work begins on transcontinental railroad. Rockefeller begins Standard Oil Company.

1865 Carnegie starts his first company.

1867 Peabody establishes school fund for South.

Many educational reforms included **1868** in new state constitution.

1869 Transcontinental railroad is completed.

Board of Immigration is founded. **1874**

Constitutional Convention increases **1875** power of state legislature.

Vance is elected governor. **1876**

1876 Bell invents the telephone. Centennial Exposition in Philadelphia.

North Carolina ranks seventh in **1881** illiteracy in the United States.

1887 National Farmers' Alliance is formed.

1890 Congress passes Sherman Antitrust Act.

1892 Populist Party is formed.

1897 First underground train opens in Boston.

1903 Ford builds his first car. Wright Brothers make first airplane flight.

What's Ahead

Chapter **18**
Preparing for a New Century

Chapter **19**
Signs of Improvement in North Carolina

Chapter 18

Preparing for a New Century

The Industrial Revolution takes hold in the United States.

In 1876, many Americans attended the Centennial Exposition in Philadelphia to celebrate the nation's one hundredth birthday. At this fair, inventors displayed the newest machines and products. For the first time, many people saw Alexander Graham Bell's telephone, an elevator, a bicycle, and a typewriter. The main attraction, however, was a huge steam engine towering almost four stories high. It supplied the power for about 8,000 pieces of equipment at the fair.

These and other machines invented in the mid-1800s caused a revolution in the way Americans lived and worked. Soon the nation was in the midst of an **Industrial Revolution**—a time of great and rapid changes, when people switched from making goods by hand to manufacturing goods with power-driven machines.

Centennial Exposition in Philadelphia, 1876 ▶

Think Ahead

After the Civil War, the growth of industry dramatically changed how people lived in every part of the United States. These changes helped launch the nation into the twentieth century. Read about the Industrial Revolution and its impact on cities and farms.

1 The Rise of Industry in the United States

During the Industrial Revolution, two new industries—railroads and steel—grew especially quickly and hastened the growth of other industries. With railroad lines linking all parts of the nation, raw materials could easily be carried from the countryside to factories in the cities. Factory products could be traded in cities as distant from each other as Sacramento and Boston. As steelmaking improved, steel mills produced huge quantities of strong low-cost metal that was used for building railroads and skyscrapers as well as for making factory machines and other products.

The railroad coast to coast.   Ever since the 1840s, when railroad builders began constructing tracks in the United States, many Americans had been dreaming about a railroad that would cross the continent. Such a railroad— the **transcontinental railroad**—would connect the Atlantic and Pacific coasts of the country. However, the project raised many questions. What was the best route? Who could complete such a huge task? Who would pay for it?
    In 1862, Congress stepped in and passed a law giving the task of building the transcontinental railroad to two companies—the Union Pacific and the Central Pacific.

People, Places, Terms

Industrial Revolution
transcontinental railroad
Andrew Carnegie
emigrate
corporation
stockholder
refine
John D. Rockefeller
monopoly
Alexander Graham Bell
Thomas Alva Edison
patent
Henry Ford
assembly line

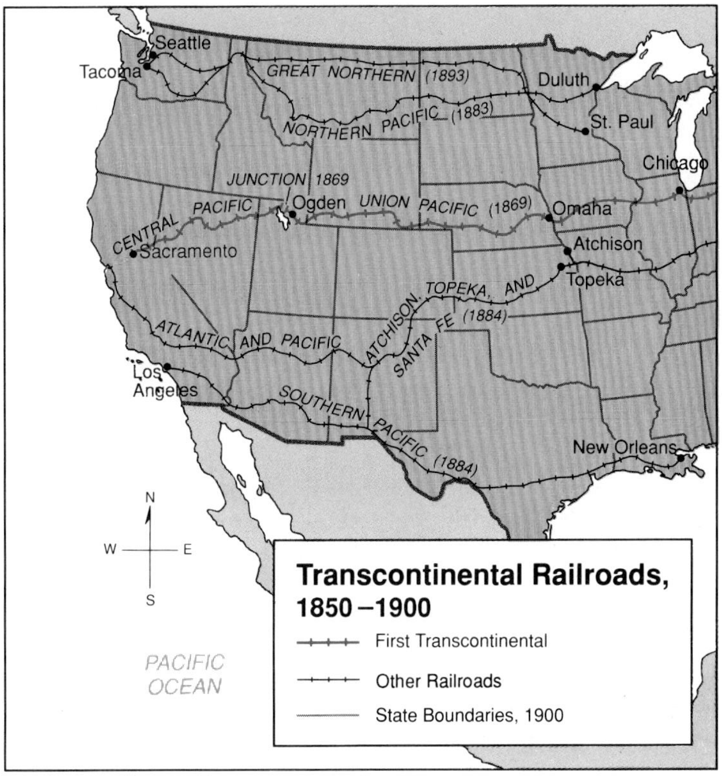

Maps Matter

The transcontinental railroad connected cities throughout the United States. ■*To Do:* What cities were connected by the transcontinental railroad? What cities were connected by other railroads that followed?

Transcontinental Railroads, 1850–1900

+++ First Transcontinental

+++ Other Railroads

— State Boundaries, 1900

The Union Pacific would start at the eastern end in Omaha, Nebraska, and lay tracks westward. The Central Pacific would start at the western end in Sacramento, California, and build eastward. The two companies would meet somewhere along the route and join their tracks into a single railroad line across the continent.

Congress promised to lend each company $16,000 for each mile of track built on level land and $48,000 for each mile of track built in the mountains. Congress also gave land along the tracks to each company. The companies could sometimes earn more money by selling some of this land to settlers.

Building the railroad. The work began in 1863, when the Union Pacific hired about 10,000 men. Some had served as soldiers in the Civil War. Others were immigrant farmers from Ireland and other countries. The company also hired sharpshooters to ward off attacks from Native Americans, who were still fighting to protect their way of life on the plains.

To build tracks eastward, workers faced the heat of burning deserts and the cold of freezing slopes in the high mountains. As a result, the Central Pacific had trouble getting workers. To compensate for this shortage, the company brought in thousands of Chinese who were willing to do the work. Some of these workers were already living in the West, but many more came directly from China.

The Golden Spike

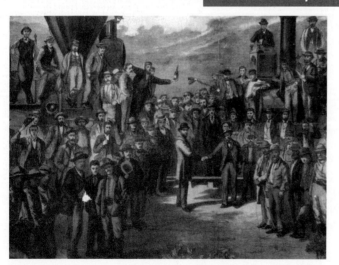

Six years after the work began on the transcontinental railroad, the westbound and eastbound tracks finally approached each other at Promontory Point near Ogden, Utah. The Union Pacific had built 1,086 miles of track across the Great Plains and the rugged Rocky Mountains. The Central Pacific, building through the desert and over the towering Sierra Nevada, had finished 689 miles of track.

On May 10, 1869, company crews and officers celebrated the meeting of East and West. The officers of each company hoisted a silver hammer to strike down a golden spike that would fasten the last pieces of adjoining track and complete the transcontinental railroad. Telegraph operators flashed the news to a waiting nation: "One, two, three, done!" Citizens celebrated with parades and speeches. To highlight the success, the Liberty Bell in Philadelphia tolled loudly.

Using money to make money. In part because railroads used so much steel, the steel industry grew quickly. Steel, which is made from iron ore, is harder than iron and easier to shape. As a result, steel railroad tracks were tougher than the old iron tracks and lasted 20 times longer. Steel also made better locomotives and stronger bridges.

A business leader who entered the steel industry at this time of great growth could make a fortune. Andrew Carnegie was such a person. Born in Scotland, Carnegie and his family **emigrated** to the United States. This means that they left their homeland for another country. Carnegie's family was too poor to send him to school. As a result, he went to work in a cloth factory as a bobbin boy, changing the spools of thread on the machines that wove the thread into cloth. By the time he was 18, Carnegie became a clerk for the Pennsylvania Railroad and learned much about the business from his boss, Thomas Scott.

Scott showed Carnegie how to use his savings to make money. On Scott's advice, Carnegie bought stock in various companies. A stock is a share of a business. The businesses in which Carnegie bought stocks were **corporations**—businesses owned by many people. People who own stock in corporations are called **stockholders.** If the businesses make money, the stockholders get a share of the profits.

In 1865, with some partners, Carnegie set up his own companies to build bridges and make equipment needed by railroads. Carnegie was so successful in this business that before long he became a millionaire.

In the 1870s, Carnegie built the most up-to-date steel mill in the world. Using an improved way of making steel, Carnegie was able to produce steel at a low cost. With this lower price, more manufacturers could use steel for tools, equipment, and buildings. Because the demand for steel increased greatly, Carnegie grew richer.

The discovery of black gold. One of the most important new industries after 1860 began with the accidental discovery of oil. In western Pennsylvania, workers were drilling wells several hundred feet deep to bring up salt water. Often an oily substance, which the drillers found troublesome, reached the surface with the salt water. Then Benjamin Silliman, Jr., a Yale professor, took a sample of the oil. He tested it and proved it had many uses, such as lighting lamps and greasing machinery.

Drillers began digging in Pennsylvania for this valuable new resource—sometimes called black gold. In 1859, Edwin L. Drake drilled the first successful oil well in Titusville, Pennsylvania. Many drillers tried their luck, but

Across Cultures

When Andrew Carnegie left Scotland with his family, he was thirteen years old. What do you think he was thinking and feeling as he left his native country for America? ■ *To Do*: Write a journal entry of a young emigrant who is about to leave his or her native land for America in the 1800s. Then write a second entry of a young emigrant leaving his or her native land for America today.

In the 1850s, a new process—developed independently by William Kelly in Kentucky and Sir Henry Bessemer in Great Britain—used a blast of air to remove impurities from iron. The process allowed for cheaper production of steel.

only a few struck steady wells or oil gushers. Even those lucky drillers who found crude oil did not necessarily get rich quickly. Crude oil, which comes directly from the earth, is costly to **refine,** or prepare for use. As a result, most drillers did not make much money from their wells.

Rockefeller's rise to riches in the oil industry. John D. Rockefeller, a young businessman in Ohio, realized that refining was important to the oil industry. He hoped that if he built and controlled oil refineries, he would make a fortune.

In 1863, Rockefeller entered the oil business with four partners. They built a refinery the first year. Seven years later, Rockefeller bought out his partners and organized the Standard Oil Company. Under Rockefeller's management, the company built new refineries and bought refineries from other companies. By the 1880s, the Standard Oil Company controlled 90 percent of the refining industry. If drillers found a new oil field, they had almost no choice but to sell the crude oil to the Standard Oil Company to be refined. If people wanted kerosene to light lamps or grease to lubricate machinery, they had to buy these products from the Standard Oil Company. The company had nearly a **monopoly** on oil, and Rockefeller acquired a fortune of almost one billion dollars.

Communicating by wire. Another new industry, telecommunications, developed as a result of an invention. Working with hearing-impaired children, Alexander Graham Bell came to believe he could invent a machine that would let one person talk to another person who was far away. After working for three years, Bell invented the telephone in 1876.

At first, Bell had trouble finding users for his telephone. People were fascinated by his invention, but they thought of it only as a toy, wonderful but not very useful. They were proven wrong when Bell set up a company that developed a network of phones nationwide. By 1900, three fourths of the small farmers in the United States had telephones. Because of Bell's telephone, a whole new system of communication was established across the country—and later around the world. Thus, an important new industry developed because of an invention.

Edison's sparks of inventions. The most productive inventor between 1860 and 1900 was Thomas Alva Edison. For each of his inventions, Edison obtained a **patent,** which is a document that legally protects an inventor from having his or her invention copied by others. Over his lifetime, Edison took out 1,093 patents—more than any other person in United States history. Because of his inventions, Edison was called the Wizard of Menlo Park, since his laboratory was in Menlo Park, New Jersey. Edison's goal was to invent useful things. His inventions—including the phonograph, motion picture camera, light bulb, and electric power plant—started many new industries.

Ford's new way of manufacturing. Another important inventor, Henry Ford, moved to Detroit, Michigan, to get a job and to work on his idea for a horseless carriage—a vehicle that would run on its own power. In 1903, Ford completed his first car. He called it a quadricycle, meaning a four-wheeled vehicle. It could move forward but not backward. Still, the engine Ford built worked well. It used gasoline—a fuel refined from oil—for power.

Ford was not only an inventor, he was also an industrialist. He wanted to produce many cars to sell, so he set up an automobile factory. In his factory, he used Eli Whitney's idea of interchangeable parts. That is, he built machines to turn out car parts that fit as well on one car as on another. However, Ford took the idea of interchangeable parts one step further. In Ford's factory, each worker placed a single part on the frame of a car as it passed by on a moving belt. This way of making goods is called an **assembly line.** At the beginning of the line, the frame of a car stood alone. At the end, after each worker had put a part in place, the car was complete. By 1914, Ford's factories were producing 146 cars per hour—one car about every 25 seconds.

Think as a Historian

*W*ho were some important inventors who lived after Thomas Edison? ■ *To Do*: Use an encyclopedia or another resource to find out about one important inventor of the twentieth century. Then explain the importance of that person's invention or inventions.

Think Twice

1. Describe the building of the first transcontinental railroad.
2. How did steelmaking change between 1850 and 1900?
3. Why are the growth of railroads and steelmaking examples of the Industrial Revolution in America?
4. (a) Explain how Thomas Edison, John D. Rockefeller, Alexander Graham Bell, and Henry Ford changed the way people lived. (b) In your opinion, which man made the most important contribution to a changing way of life? Explain your opinion.
5. You have read about some benefits of industry. What problems might have been created by the growth of industry?

Workers on an assembly line are seen here putting together wheels for Model T cars.

257

2 Industry and Reform

The growth of industry in the late 1800s turned the United States into an industrial giant. From city to countryside, industry and invention changed the way Americans lived. As new mills, mines, and factories opened, workers were in high demand. Growing companies advertised at home and abroad for workers. Thousands of men, women, and children answered the call.

Newcomers arrive in the cities. Two major groups of newcomers poured into the already crowded **urban** areas, or cities, to find jobs. One group was the sons and daughters of American farmers. Before 1860, most Americans lived on farms. However, over the years, booming city factories had attracted thousands of farm families. The young women and men of these farm families found life in **rural** areas, or the countryside, hard. Urban life seemed to offer them new opportunities and an escape from endless farm work.

At the same time, another group of newcomers joined the flood of people settling in the cities. **Immigrants**, or people who leave their homelands to settle in another country, came to the United States to work in factories and mines. They came looking for jobs and a better life. For immigrants, the United States was the land of opportunity.

Until the 1880s, most immigrants came to America from countries in western Europe, such as Great Britain,

The Gilded Age

Mark Twain and Charles Dudley Warner wrote a satirical novel, *The Gilded Age*, about the pursuit of wealth in the years of rapid industrial growth in the United States. This period—from about 1869 to 1899—is sometimes called the Gilded Age. The word *gild* means "to cover with a thin coating of gold."

Why was this term appropriate? The lives of new American millionaires were often characterized by greed, corruption, and excess. For example, Andrew Carnegie, shown on the left, built a mansion that included solid gold plumbing fixtures. George W. Vanderbilt built a $5 million mansion on more than 130,000 acres in Asheville, North Carolina. At one lavish party given during the Gilded Age, the guests found rare black pearls in their oysters. The lifestyles of the wealthy, who profited from oil, railroad, meat-packing, and steel businesses, contrasted sharply with those of poor workers.

Norway, and Germany. After the 1880s, many more people came from eastern and southern Europe. These immigrants had left Poland, Russia, Austria-Hungary, Italy, Greece, and Turkey. Between 1865 and 1900, over 12 million immigrants settled in the United States. Very few of them settled in North Carolina or other Southern states, however, because there were few jobs for them.

Immigrants Arriving in the United States, 1860–1909

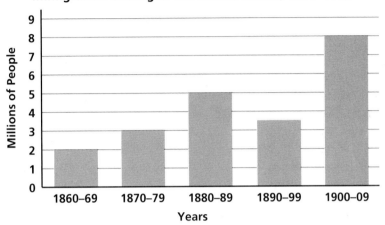

Graphs Teach

A bar graph shows increases and decreases over a certain period of time. This bar graph tells how many immigrants arrived in the United States in the decades between 1860 and 1910. In what decade did the fewest people arrive? In what decade did the most people come?

Labor unions are formed.   Newcomers to cities—whether from rural America or Europe—could find work. They poured hot steel in a steel mill, installed car parts on an assembly line, or made tools in a shop powered by electricity. Other people worked as sales clerks, office workers, electricians, and train conductors. Millions of city dwellers held jobs that did not even exist before 1860.

Whatever the job, conditions were often unhealthy. Factories had poor lighting and stale air. The workday was ten or more hours long, and some people worked six or seven days a week. To meet the demand for steel, workers in steel mills generally worked 12 hours a day, 7 days a week. In addition, many of the machines were dangerous. Although workers were injured or killed in accidents, companies were not required to follow safety rules or to help support injured workers or their families.

To solve these problems, workers united together to form **labor unions**. A labor union is an organization of workers that helps its members receive higher wages and have better working conditions. Factory owners listened to these groups of employees because if they all stopped working, a factory would have to shut down.

Congress tries to reform business.   Standard Oil was just one of several companies that grew to giant size in the late 1800s. Many, like Standard Oil, were monopolies that

Across Cultures

Millions of immigrants from all over the world arrived in the United States in the late 1800s.
■ *To Do*: Think of a neighbor, friend, or family member who came to America from another country. Ask this person about his or her experiences. Find out where this person came from, why he or she left, and how he or she adjusted to a new life in the United States.

controlled all or nearly all of the sales of a product or service. Under such conditions, a consumer had little choice but to pay whatever the company charged for goods or services. In 1890, reformers persuaded Congress to pass the Sherman Antitrust Act, a law that made it illegal for large companies to control an entire industry. The reformers wanted to encourage competition among several companies so that consumers would have a better chance of getting the lowest possible prices.

John D. Rockefeller owned Standard Oil Company. In this political cartoon, he snips off the competing rosebuds in order to perfect his own company's flower.

Women join the work force. In the late 1800s, new industries created job opportunities for women. Some women worked in factories and department stores, while others learned to type or to work as telephone operators. Although women did the work, they had no legal right to the money that they earned. Most married women turned money over to their husbands. Unmarried women usually gave their wages to their fathers. Although women were helping build the country, they did not have laws to protect them.

Think Twice

1. What two groups of newcomers moved to cities in the 1800s?
2. Why did workers form labor unions?
3. What was the Sherman Antitrust Act?
4. How were women affected by the Industrial Revolution?
5. Identify one positive and one negative change that resulted from the growth of industry in the late 1800s.

Life in the City and Country

People, Places, Terms

tenement
Jane Addams
settlement house

Before the Industrial Revolution, the United States was a nation of farmers. By 1890, however, the United States was becoming a nation of factory workers. More and more people were moving from farms to cities and towns.

Although cities in the United States offered opportunities, the steady arrival of new workers presented many problems. Overcrowded cities did not have enough housing, clean water, police, or fire fighters. These problems had to be solved by individual citizens—builders, reformers, and workers—as well as by city governments.

Families live in tenements. With the flood of newcomers to cities, finding a place to live became difficult. Few families could afford a house of their own. Most, especially immigrant families, shared rooms or apartments in crowded, run-down parts of the city. Perhaps as many as one fourth lived in city **tenements**, large buildings in which people crowded together to live. Many tenements were in need of repair and had no windows to let in sunlight and fresh air.

In spite of these conditions, many city dwellers had little choice but to live in tenements. Workers wanted to live

Immigrants often had to live in crowded tenements. What few possessions did this immigrant family have? Although tenements were dismal, conditions outside were equally poor. Dark, narrow alleys were filled with garbage.

261

While she operated Hull House, Jane Addams cared for and read to hundreds of immigrant children.

This photo shows workers putting together steel beams for a skyscraper.

within walking distance of jobs, and there was no room for more housing to be built. Jacob Riis, himself a Danish immigrant, wrote a book about tenement life in New York City. Read the passage from his book that follows.

Primary Source

Take a look into this Roosevelt Street alley; just about one step wide, with a five-story house on one side that gets its light and air—God help us for pitiful mockery!—from this slit between brick walls. There are no windows in the wall on the other side; it is perfectly blank. The fire escapes of the long tenement fairly touch it; but the rays of the sun, rising, setting, or at high noon, never do.

— JACOB RIIS, How the Other Half Lives

In most cities, people tried to help those living in tenements. One such person was Jane Addams. In Chicago, she and a friend founded a kind of community center known as a **settlement house**. At Hull House, Addams and her supporters helped newcomers to face challenges and have a better life. They set up English classes, started reading and cooking clubs, and began a kindergarten so that working mothers could leave their children.

Builders ease the housing problem. A change that eased overcrowding was a new kind of building. As early as the 1880s, people could build many-storied buildings by means of a steel framework. When steel prices dropped, builders began to put up tall buildings to provide more living and office space. This kind of building—a skyscraper—seemed to touch the clouds.

City services increase. Cities had to tackle the effects of overcrowding. As the population swelled, cities faced water shortages, danger of fires, and more crime. Cities also needed good transportation to help people get around the city.

To provide enough water for so many people, New York City had large reservoirs built outside the city. A system of pipes brought stored water from the reservoirs to houses, apartment buildings, and office buildings in the city. Before long, many other cities had built reservoirs.

Most cities had volunteer fire departments, but there were not enough fire fighters. Because these volunteers had other jobs, it often took a long time for them to hear about a fire. Once they arrived, little was left but burned rubble. Over time, some full-time fire fighters were hired.

As cities grew in population, crime began to increase. Regular police departments were formed. At first, the police officers were on duty only during the day, but large cities soon hired officers to be on duty day and night.

To allow housing to spread out, officials hired companies to build and operate public transportation. The first transportation system was made up of streetcars that ran on tracks and were pulled by horses. Later, wires strung above the streets provided power to run electric streetcars. Because streetcars added to the traffic of horses, carts, wagons, and walkers on bustling streets, tracks were sometimes built above the ground. In 1897, the first underground train, the subway, opened in Boston.

Think as a Historian

The rapid growth of cities during the Industrial Revolution created problems. ■ *To Do*: Compare city life in the late 1800s with city life today. You may want to read a national newspaper or watch a television news broadcast to find out about contemporary urban life. What are the differences? What are the similarities?

To relieve street overcrowding in cities, railroad and streetcar tracks were built above ground, as shown in this picture of New York City. In some cities, tracks also stretched for miles deep below the ground.

Farm life changes.   During the Industrial Revolution, people who stayed on the farm may not have been able to get all of the new products and public services that city dwellers enjoyed. However, improved farming tools and equipment did make farm work a little easier. Farmers were able to produce more crops to feed and clothe the growing nation.

American farmers took advantage of new products and farming methods that were developed in the late 1800s. They used commercial fertilizers to nourish worn-out soil. New harvesting equipment helped farmers use larger areas of land to raise more grain. Plow horses were replaced by steam-driven tractors, and the steel plow helped farmers in the plains cut through thick sod.

Since farm families were often isolated from one another, new forms of communication and transportation helped reach across the miles in many rural areas. Telephones linked farmers to towns and cities. In 1898, the postal service began rural free delivery of mail to people living in the country.

With the first cars, invented in the 1890s, farmers could make more frequent trips to town and visit faraway friends and relatives. Rural roads, which were not paved, were improved in the late 1800s. The railroad made long-distance travel and transportation of goods and supplies easier.

In this photograph, farmers in Colorado are shown using a steam tractor and a belt-driven threshing machine to harvest wheat in the late 1800s.

Think Twice

1. How did Jane Addams help newcomers?
2. How did builders help improve housing in cities?
3. How did cities solve three problems related to overcrowding?
4. What is one change that improved farm life in the late 1800s?

Chapter 18 Review

Choose from the following menu of activities.

Think Back: Main Ideas

Explain how each of the following contributed to the Industrial Revolution.

1. Transcontinental railroad
2. Steel
3. Discovery of oil
4. New manufacturing methods
5. Three specific inventors or industrialists

The Industrial Revolution affected people throughout the United States. For each group listed below, write a sentence that describes how the ways of life of that group changed in the late 1800s.

6. The sons and daughters of farmers.
7. Immigrants from eastern Europe.
8. American millionaires.
9. Workers in factories.
10. Women workers in the city.

Maps Matter

Use the map of transcontinental railroads on page 253. If you need help naming the states, refer to the map of the United States in the atlas section of your book.

1. Through which states did the first transcontinental railroad pass on its route between Omaha and Sacramento?
2. Through which states did the Southern Pacific pass?

Word Wizard

1. The prefix *trans* means "across" as in the word *transcontinental*. Think of other words that contain this prefix. Then write the meaning of each word.
2. Henry Ford's *quadricycle* was a vehicle with four wheels. The prefix *quad* means "four." Replace the prefix *quad* with different prefixes to come up with words to describe vehicles with one, two, and three wheels.

Working Cooperatively

With three to five classmates, research an invention of the late 1800s. Find out about one invention mentioned in the chapter—subway, automobile, fertilizer—or another of your choice. Divide the tasks of discovering why this invention was important, who invented it, and how it changed life in the city or the country.

In this chapter, you read about corporations and monopolies. Two other types of businesses are single ownership and partnership. Working in groups of three to five people, research the advantages and disadvantages of the four forms and prepare a chart showing the advantages and disadvantages of each.

Curriculum Connection

In 1903, a poem by Emma Lazarus was engraved on the base of the Statue of Liberty. Read these lines from the poem. Then answer the questions that follow.

. . . Give me your tired, your poor,
Your huddled masses yearning to breathe free,
The wretched refuse of your teeming shore.
Send these, the homeless, tempest-tost to me,
I lift my lamp beside the golden door!

1. Who are the tired, poor, huddled masses?
2. What do you think the "golden door" is?
3. Do you think that Americans today might make the same invitation to people from other countries? Why or why not?

Learning through Literature

Spotlight on Iron and Steel, by Mark Lambert
Faster Than a Horse: Moving West with Engine Power, by Suzanne Hilton
Boy Life on the Prairie, by Hamlin Garland
How the Other Half Lives, by Jacob Riis

Signs of Improvement in North Carolina

The Industrial Revolution affects life in North Carolina.

The revolution that had begun in the early 1800s reached North Carolina as well as other parts of the nation. Farmers used new inventions to help them grow higher yields of crops. In turn, two important cash crops—cotton and tobacco—helped spur the growth of industry in the state. In the late 1800s, textile mills turned out cotton, and tobacco factories produced cigarettes. As workers left the countryside to live in towns where they could learn new skills, traditional ways of life in North Carolina began to change.

Education improves.

During the Civil War, much of the state's progress in education came to a halt. However, in the late 1800s and early 1900s, North Carolina's schools once again began to show significant improvements in materials and instruction. Tar Heels could take pride once again in their educational system.

Wilmington Harbor ▶

Think Ahead

The rise of industry in the United States had an important impact on North Carolina. Find out how the Industrial Revolution and other changes in politics, farming, and education helped North Carolina to regain its confidence and prosperity.

1 Industry in North Carolina

People, Places, Terms

George A. Gray
R.J. Reynolds
Washington Duke
James B. Duke
High Point

In Chapter 17, you read how Conservatives (or Democrats as they were called after the mid-1870s) regained control of the General Assembly and the governorship from the Republicans. The amendments passed as a result of the Constitutional Convention of 1875 helped strengthen the General Assembly's control of state affairs. Although the Democrats in the Assembly did little to help western farmers, they gained the farmers' support by playing on racist fears of African American control if the Republicans were allowed to return to power.

While Democratic control did little for the farmers and actually hurt the situation of African Americans, it did provide a certain amount of political stability, which allowed for stability in other aspects of life in the state and provided a climate in which industry could grow.

Rebuilding industries.   Although North Carolina was mainly an agricultural state, it did have a number of industries, most of them small operations. A few of them survived the war; others were rebuilt using funds that people had either hidden away or invested abroad or in the North before the war. In some cases, community members pooled their resources to start businesses. Only a few industries were begun by newcomers from the North.

Although it came a little more slowly to North Carolina and other Southern states, the Industrial Revolution made

Flights of Fancy

A high point of the Industrial Age took place on North Carolina's Outer Banks. On December 17, 1903, brothers Orville and Wilbur Wright made the first airplane flight. The flight lasted a mere 12 seconds and covered a distance of about 100 feet, but this event changed transportation forever.

The brothers had tested their ideas with kites and gliders before they flew their flying machine—a lightweight, gasoline-powered airplane—on Kill Devil Hill. Despite the success of the Wrights, some Americans mocked them and did not believe them. However, their invention, shown on the left, slowly changed how people traveled.

This Charlotte textile mill was typical of countless others that opened in the Piedmont area of the state in the late 1800s and early 1900s.

Richard Joshua Reynolds (1850–1918) worked for his father's Virginia tobacco factory until 1874, when he moved to Winston to establish his own firm among the growing industrialists in North Carolina. His R.J. Reynolds Tobacco Company became one of the nation's leading producers of tobacco products.

its influence felt. Mills and factories were powered first by water, then steam, and finally by electricity. New machines were introduced and factories increased in output, variety, and quality. With electric lighting, they could operate at night. Improved transportation, especially by rail, helped the growth of industry as well.

The textile industry.   One of the first industries to regain strength after the war was the textile industry, which had never really been wiped out. Not only was there a demand for the product, but the raw material, cotton, was grown nearby and there were many trained workers in need of jobs. Between the late 1860s and the early 1890s, many old mills were revived and new ones established. In some instances, prewar reputations for quality, as in the case of the Holt family's mills in Alamance County, ensured a demand from the North for cloth.

Other families associated with textiles before the war built or rebuilt factories as well. Such families included the Ramseurs, Battles, Cannons, Moreheads, and Fries. A few people new to the business succeeded in creating new factories. A true rags-to-riches story was that of George Alexander Gray, who began work in a mill at age 10 and was assistant superintendent by 19. By hard work and thrift, together with mechanical skill, he progressed steadily, and by the time of his death in 1912, he was president of 16 mills.

In 1860, the state had had 39 cotton mills; by 1880, there were 10 more. In the 1890s, Northerners recognized the importance of this growing industry and began building and operating mills in the state. By 1900, 177 mills provided employment for 30,000 workers who produced goods worth $28 million each year. North Carolina was producing more cotton textiles than any other Southern state except South Carolina.

The tobacco industry. During the war, Union soldiers discovered the bright leaf smoking tobacco grown in some northern counties. Later, after they reached home, they wrote back for more. With a growing demand for their product, tobacco makers began to expand operations and consolidate small factories into larger ones. In the Salem area, several families began production, and they were soon joined by R.J. Reynolds, who moved across the line from his Virginia farm a few miles away.

It was Durham, however, that became the most flourishing center of tobacco production. When tobacco farmer Washington Duke returned from the war to his farm near Durham, he had just 50 cents in his pocket. He and his sons Ben and Buck (James B.) gathered up some tobacco leaves that Union soldiers had overlooked, crushed them, and packaged them in small cloth bags to sell. Driving a wagon pulled by two old mules, they soon sold all they had. With the money they earned, they built a small log building for processing tobacco. As the Dukes continued to grow, they introduced cigarettes to North Carolina and the South, promoting the newfangled invention with heavy advertising. The Dukes also were the first to use machines to make cigarettes. From their small beginnings, the Dukes created the American Tobacco Company, the largest in the world. In 1908, the company had such a monopoly that an antitrust suit was filed against it, and the company was forced to split into four companies in 1911.

The furniture industry. Before the war, a few furniture makers produced limited quantities of high quality pieces in North Carolina. The Swicegood family in the Davidson-Forsyth County area produced fine furniture for three generations, and Thomas Day, a free African American in Milton, was famous for his popular styles and good quality. Some of his massive pieces are still in existence in homes and in the University of North Carolina's literary societies' halls.

The first factory to produce quantities of furniture was started by three men from **High Point**—Ernest A. Snow, John H. Tate, and Thomas F. Wrenn. In 1889, the three men pooled their life savings (about $3,000 each) to create the

The cigarette machine allowed production to increase greatly.

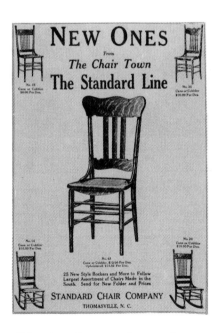

This advertisement shows why Thomasville became known as the "Chair town of the South." North Carolina's forests supplied lumber for furniture factories that began to spring up in the Piedmont section about 1889.

RURAL AND URBAN POPULATION IN NORTH CAROLINA 1880–1900		
Year	Rural	Urban
1880	1,345,000	55,000
1890	1,502,000	116,000
1900	1,707,000	187,000

Tables Teach

Tables present data in columns. A table may help you compare information or notice patterns. This table shows how North Carolina's population shifted in the late 1800s.
■ *To Do:* Did the rural population increase or decrease from 1880 to 1900? Did the urban population increase or decrease from 1880 to 1900? How many people lived in cities in 1900?

High Point Furniture Manufacturing Company. Their small factory was little more than a shed, but it was an immediate success. They made so much furniture the first year that Wrenn said, " I thought surely the whole world would soon be supplied . . . and from the amount of lumber we used I was positive that the forests of North Carolina were completely destroyed."

Many factors contributed to High Point's success. It had an excellent location, with good rail transportation, and was in the middle of the state's hardwood forests from which raw materials were available. Nearby were plenty of rural citizens who were anxious to work for steady wages. In addition, large numbers of people needed new furniture. Not only were young couples getting married and setting up housekeeping, but also older families had had no opportunity or money to buy furniture since before the war.

High Point's success encouraged others to start companies, and factories began to spring up all along the North Carolina Railroad and its feeder lines in that part of the state. To tap the national market, manufacturers began to pay more attention to quality, and soon the state had a reputation for fine furniture that continues to the present. As furniture grew in importance, related businesses grew—providing varnishes, stains, hinges, and other items needed by the furniture industry.

Soon after the war, sawmills appeared across the state to provide lumber for new homes, factories, railroad ties, and above all, furniture.

Towns grow. The building of mills and factories brought large numbers of rural people to the towns. Women and children as well as men worked for low wages, ten to twelve hours a day. Families lived in company-owned houses clustered around a mill and bought on credit from the company store whatever food, clothing, and supplies were necessary.

By 1900, six towns in the state had more than 10,000 people. These towns had electricity, running water, telephones, streetcars, and paved streets. Smaller towns grew as well, most noticeably in the Piedmont and mountain sections.

However, as you can see from the table on page 270, North Carolina remained largely rural. Although the urban population tripled between 1880 and 1900, the state was still 90 percent rural. As late as 1990, only 50.4 percent of the population was urban.

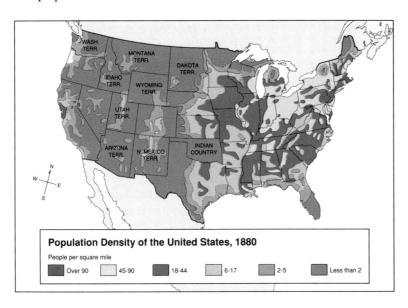

Population Density of the United States, 1880

People per square mile

Over 90	45-90	18-44	6-17	2-5	Less than 2

Think as a Geographer

*T*he Industrial Revolution caused the population to shift in North Carolina. Locate the table entitled North Carolina Counties in the North Carolina Resources section in the back of your text. ■ *To Do*: Identify the ten counties with the largest populations in 1990. Now look at the map entitled North Carolina Counties in the atlas section of your text. On the map, locate the ten counties that you identified. Do you see a pattern? For example, in what part or parts of North Carolina are the ten largest counties located?

Maps Matter

A population density map shows you how many people live in different areas. This map shows where people lived in the late 1800s. ■ *To Do:* Find North Carolina on the map. About how many people per square mile lived here in 1880? Which area of the state had the most people? Which area had the fewest?

Think Twice

1. Name one way in which North Carolinians funded the rebuilding of industry.
2. What impact did the Industrial Revolution have on industry in North Carolina?
3. What were the three main industries of North Carolina in the late 1800s?
4. As industry grew in North Carolina, so did banking. Why do you think this was so?
5. People's lives were largely controlled by the company they worked for. How would buying on credit from a company store contribute to this loss of freedom?

2 Farm Changes in North Carolina

After 1865, rural farmers in North Carolina faced many problems. Most of the 40,000 men who died in the war were from farms. As a result, the physical conditions of North Carolina farms deteriorated from neglect as fields were overrun by weeds or pines. The war also destroyed property—barns, rail fences, and houses. Seeds, which farmers usually saved from year to year, were not retained and were in short supply.

Freedmen and freedwomen.   One important result of the war—the end to the system of enslaved labor—brought about a far-reaching change in the basic labor system in North Carolina. At the end of the war, 350,000 enslaved African laborers were freed in the state. Many of these men and women moved away with their families, but many others stayed on the same farm or plantation where they had worked before. Farmers hired these men and women as well as other laborers who did not own land but needed jobs. A new relationship between employer and worker soon developed.

Tenant farmers and sharecroppers.   After the war, many people were left without money or land, but they had the skills needed to grow crops. At the same time, landowners had land but little money to pay wages. The result was the rise of the systems of **tenant farming** and **sharecropping.** Under these systems, people who did not own land lived and worked on farms that belonged to someone else. A tenant rented the land, provided the labor, and purchased some of the necessary resources such as seeds, fertilizer, and equipment. A sharecropper, however, usually provided only labor—his own and sometimes that of his family. In exchange for their work, these laborers received

This engraving from a North Carolina bank note shows a farm laborer taking a break from harvesting wheat.

a share of the crop or part of the income from the crop. In North Carolina, sharecroppers outnumbered tenants by five to one. By 1880, more than one third of the farms in the state were operated under one system or the other.

The systems had many disadvantages. Life was difficult for the workers, and their standard of living was low. Tenants often moved from one farm to another. As a result, people rarely felt settled in a community, and their children seldom attended school on a regular basis. In addition, crops were not rotated according to good farming practices. Fields eroded and the land lost its fertility. Nonetheless, these farming arrangements did provide a way for large numbers of landless people to earn a bare living. A few people even earned enough to buy farms of their own.

NUMBER AND SIZE OF NORTH CAROLINA FARMS 1860–1900		
Year	Number	Average Size (in acres)
1860	72,203	316
1870	93,565	212
1880	157,609	142
1890	178,359	127
1900	225,000	101

Tables Teach

After the war, many plantations and larger farms were divided as families sold off their property.
■ *To Do:* Study the table on this page to learn about farm division in North Carolina from 1860 to 1900. What happened to the number of farms in North Carolina during this period? What happened to the average size of farms in the state?

Economic factors. For North Carolina farmers, the difficult years following the Civil War were made worse by four economic forces that farmers could not control. First, crop prices remained the same or declined, leaving the farmers' income low and uncertain. Secondly, the cost of seeds, fertilizer, tools, and equipment was high, forcing farmers to pay high prices to produce their crops. High land tax was a third economic factor affecting the farmer. Because businesses and railroads were exempt from paying certain taxes, the burden to finance the government fell more heavily on landowners. Finally, most farmers had to borrow money, and they had to pay high rates of interest. These factors hindered farmers in their efforts to recover after the war.

Progress and changes in crop production. In an attempt to improve their conditions, some farmers tried to change the crops they were growing to those that would yield a larger profit. Before the war, many small farmers who owned land practiced subsistence farming by producing almost everything they needed. After the war, these

Think as a Historian

*B*etween 1890 and 1895, George Washington Vanderbilt, grandson of railroad tycoon Cornelius Vanderbilt, built the lavish Biltmore Estate in the mountains of Asheville. George was not just a rich landowner, however, and he and his wife Edith had an impact on the lives of the people in the area. ■ *To Do:* With the help of your school or local librarian, find out about the activities of these two important North Carolinians.

This advertisement, published in *The Progressive Farmer* in May 1889, advertised tobacco grown by Farmer's Alliance members. Members also joined together to buy large amounts of fertilizer and to manufacture shoes. Why do you think members tried to work together?

farmers turned to growing cash crops—mainly cotton and tobacco. By planting cotton and tobacco instead of grain, fruit, and garden vegetables, farmers hoped to earn enough money to improve their condition and pay off their debts.

Agricultural production in the state soon reached prewar levels. By 1870, North Carolina was producing as much cotton and oats as ever, and by 1880, three times as much cotton was ginned compared to 20 years earlier. Smaller amounts of some products, such as flax, cheese, and sweet potatoes were produced because the state was raising cotton and tobacco in larger amounts.

United States farmers face problems. Many farms in the state and nation were without electricity, running water, and mail delivery. New farming methods and machinery did help increase crop production, yet the increased supply drove prices down. Beginning in 1873, wheat, cotton, and corn prices steadily dropped. By the 1890s, cotton sold for less than it cost farmers to grow.

Farmers not only received less money for their crops, but they also had to buy expensive machinery and supplies. They had to pay high railroad fees to transport goods from state to state. Farmers wanted to sell their extra crops in other countries, but laws prevented them from selling in foreign markets.

Many farmers could not keep up with these rising costs and ended up losing their farms. While industry grew across the country, farms in the western and southern parts of the country were failing. An editor described this confusing national situation when he wrote the following passage in a North Carolina farm journal in 1887.

Primary Source

> *The railroads have never been so prosperous, and yet agriculture languishes. The banks have never done a better or more profitable business, and yet agriculture languishes. . . . Towns and cities flourish and "boom" and grow and "boom," and yet agriculture languishes. . . . Salaries and fees were never so temptingly high and desirable, and yet agriculture languishes.*

— The Progressive Farmer

Farmers join the National Farmer's Alliance. Some frustrated farmers decided to fight back. They began to organize in order to fight for higher prices and a stronger voice in the government. In North Carolina, more than 100,000 farmers had joined the **National Farmer's Alliance** by 1888.

AMOUNT OF COTTON AND TOBACCO PRODUCED IN NORTH CAROLINA 1860–1900		
Year	Bales of Cotton	Pounds of Tobacco
1860	145,000	33,000,000
1870	145,000	11,000,000
1880	390,000	27,000,000
1890	360,000	36,000,000
1900	460,000	128,000,000

Tables Teach

You can read a table to compare information or to find patterns. This table compares how much cotton and tobacco was grown in North Carolina between 1860 and 1900. Did cotton production increase or decrease from 1890 to 1900? Did tobacco production increase or decrease from 1880 to 1900? Why did farmers face difficult times then?

Although the National Farmer's Alliance was not a political organization, some leaders did encourage gaining control of state governments in order to help farmers. Members regularly voted in elections and began to elect farmers to both state and national offices. Members of the National Farmer's Alliance hoped that these representatives would support laws that protected farmers.

The Populist party is formed. By 1891, the National Farmer's Alliance had about two million members. As a result of their success in electing many senators, representatives, and officers of state government in 1890, Alliance men decided to form a new political party. The People's party, also called the **Populist party,** sought to unite working people in factories and on farms and wanted reforms that would help these people. The party wanted to set up a new kind of income tax and it also wanted people to have a greater say in their government.

The Populist party held its national convention in February 1892. Delegates chose a candidate for President, but Democrat Grover Cleveland won the presidential election. The Populists later joined with Republicans to try to defeat their political opponents—Democrats—but the Populist party died out by 1896.

Leonidas L. Polk was a leader of the "farmers' revolt" in North Carolina and in the nation. He became president of the National Farmer's Alliance in 1889. To support America's farmers, he also published a magazine, *The Progressive Farmer.*

Think Twice

1. Why did the basic labor system change after the war?
2. (a) Explain the difference between a tenant farmer and a sharecropper. (b) What were the advantages and disadvantages of these systems of farming?
3. Why did farmers join the National Farmer's Alliance?
4. What new political party was formed in the early 1890s?

3 The Late Bell Rings

Before the Civil War, North Carolina had made great progress in education. In 1839, the General Assembly passed the first public school law that created school districts and called for the establishment of a primary school in each district. However, by the end of the war, the number of public schools in the state had greatly declined. It was not until the late 1860s that the people of North Carolina began to take public education seriously once again.

Taking education seriously.   In the late 1860s, the state began to renew its commitment to education. A Republican administration, sympathetic to education, was elected. In addition, the new constitution of 1868 created the Office of Superintendent of Public Instruction—a leader to be elected by the people. The 1868 constitution also required that the legislature and county commissioners provide funding "by taxation and otherwise" for a system of free public schools. The schools were required to stay open for at least four months each year for all students between the ages of 6 and 21.

By 1870, there were 1,400 schools in the state, enrolling 50,000 children. A serious problem facing all of these students was the lack of proper textbooks. The Bible or New Testament was often the only reading material in the classroom. Two texts—Webster's *Blue Back Spelling Book* and Wiley's *North Carolina Reader*—left over from prewar days, were still widely used.

This photograph shows the interior of an 1870s one-room schoolhouse that has been relocated to the Charles B. Aycock Birthplace State Historic Site near Fremont.

More progress in city schools than county schools. In 1867, George Peabody—a wealthy merchant from Massachusetts—established a fund to assist schools in the South. The fund gave financial assistance to schools that could raise matching funds. Since city schools could raise money more easily than county schools, they received more money for public education. As a result, city schools were able to lengthen their school year, build new schools, and offer special courses.

Progress at last. When Charles B. Aycock was elected governor in 1901, little progress had been made in the state's education system since the 1870s. Of the 660,000 children of school age in 1900, only about two thirds were even enrolled, and less than half of them attended on a regular basis. Twenty-three counties had cotton mills where many children under age 14 worked long hours without ever going to school. These conditions appalled the new governor and he set about popularizing his ideas for improvement.

During Aycock's term, the General Assembly adopted some new education measures. It increased the amount of money for education and revised the way the money was distributed, so that rural schools could begin to catch up with city schools. Later, in 1907, the Assembly passed a rural high school law, and within a year nearly 160 new high schools opened in 81 of the state's 98 counties. At about the same time, the school year was extended from 4 to 6 months. Later, many small rural school districts were consolidated into larger units, whose combined resources allowed for better materials and instruction. To make consolidation work, children were transported to school at public expense. By the late 1920s, North Carolinians could take pride in the progress of their schools. Unfortunately, the improvements did not apply to all schools. Those for African Americans were largely inferior. As you will learn in Chapters 22 and 23, it was not until the 1950s and 1960s that education for African Americans improved.

Think Twice

1. What had happened to public education in North Carolina by the end of the war?
2. (a) What did the state do in the late 1860s to try to rebuild the education system? (b) What was the result?
3. Why did city schools make more progress than county schools?
4. Name two improvements in education that occurred during or after Aycock's term as governor.

Across Cultures

*I*n both the North and the South, schools were separate for African Americans and other Americans. In the South, this practice was upheld by law. In theory the schools were separate but equal, but this was seldom true. Usually the schools for African Americans received far less funding and had to make do with very little equipment and with fewer teachers than other schools.
■ *To Do:* Think about most white people's attitudes toward African Americans in the 1800s, and consider what you learned in Chapter 17 about the activities of the Ku Klux Klan. Then explain why this inequality in education was allowed to exist for so long.

Charles B. Aycock (1859–1912) was a newspaper editor, a lawyer, and a school administrator before he became governor in 1901.

Chapter 19 Review

Choose from the following menu of activities.

Think Back: Main Ideas

1. What were the main industries of North Carolina in the late 1800s?
2. How did the farm labor system change after the Civil War?
3. Why did many farmers have trouble making ends meet in the late 1800s?
4. Why was the National Farmer's Alliance formed?
5. What contribution did Charles Aycock make to education in North Carolina?

Maps Matter

During the Industrial Revolution, many people in the United States moved to cities. Use the map on page 271 to answer these questions.

1. Which areas of the country had the most people per square mile in 1880?
2. Which areas of the country had the fewest people per square mile in 1880?
3. Name two cities that had more than 90 people per square mile in 1880.

Word Wizard

1. *Populist* comes from a Latin word that means "the people." Can you think of some other words that have the same Latin origin?
2. In the 1880s, North Carolina ranked seventh in the nation in illiteracy. Find out what the term *illiteracy* means.

Working Cooperatively

Work with a group of three to five classmates to find out the effects of the Industrial Revolution on the environment. Choose one innovation, such as the automobile or electricity, and list all the ways you can think of that this innovation has affected the environment. Then use reference materials to find out more about the impact the innovation has had. Present your findings in an illustrated report, a bulletin-board display, or by a method of your own choosing.

For town or city dwellers, here is another activity. Find out what your town was like in the late 1800s. Was it a mill town, or was the area still rural at that time? When did it start to grow? Where did people live? Where was the mill (or mills) located? What shops or businesses were there? Present your findings in a method of your own choosing.

Curriculum Connection

1. Use a stopwatch or a watch with a second hand to time 12 seconds and see how long the first Wright brothers' flight lasted. Measure 100 feet to see the distance of the flight.
2. Use the information from one of the tables in this chapter to make a circle or bar graph.
3. Find the percent of the population that was urban in each of the three years shown on the table on page 270. To do that, you must add the rural and urban populations to get the total population, then divide the urban population by the total. Round your answer to the nearer one hundredth. Next drop the decimal point to express the figure as a percent. For example, .054 would round to .05, which is 5 percent.

Learning through Literature

The Sky Is Falling, by Barbara Corcoran
No Promises in the Wind, by Irene Hunt
Windmills, Bridges, and Old Machines: Discovering Our Industrial Past, by David Weitzman
Purslane, by Bernice Kelly Harris

The Twentieth Century

NORTH CAROLINA

Time Line

THE UNITED STATES

NORTH CAROLINA	Year	THE UNITED STATES
	1898	Spanish-American War begins.
	1914	Panama Canal opens.
Over 85,000 men from North Carolina join the armed forces. **1917**	1917	United States enters World War I on the side of the Allies.
	1920	Nineteenth Amendment
Highway Act is passed. **1921**	1921	U. S. Congress passes law limiting immigration.
	1924	Native Americans gain the right to vote.
	1929	Stock market decline leads to start of Great Depression.
Hundreds of banks and savings and loan associations close in North Carolina crippling the state's economy. **1930**		
	1933	President Roosevelt announces New Deal.
	1939	World War II begins in Europe.
Defense boom helps pull North Carolina out of the Depression. **1941**	1941	The United States enters World War II.
	1945	World War II ends.
Rocket research begins at Topsail Island. **1947**	1947	Puerto Rico becomes a commonwealth.
	1950	Korean War starts.
	1957	Vietnam War begins.
	1959	Alaska and Hawaii become states.
	1969	United States astronauts walk on moon.
	1973	United States withdraws from Vietnam.

What's Ahead

Chapter 20
A New Century Begins

Chapter 21
A Rise from the Depths

Chapter 20

A New Century Begins

The world shrinks in the twentieth century.

As the United States grew larger and more powerful in the twentieth century, the world seemed to be growing smaller. News and people traveled faster and farther than ever before as a result of inventions made during the Industrial Revolution. Advances in communication—radio and the telephone—let people throughout the world know almost instantly what was happening elsewhere around the globe. Advances in transportation meant that people in different countries were hours, not weeks, away from one another.

The United States takes a role in world affairs.

As a result of this shrinking world, Americans became more aware of conflicts and events around the world. The nation soon found itself involved in **international** affairs. *International* means "relating to many nations." Although some people in the United States were uncomfortable with this new role, most citizens expected the government to protect them and their business interests in Europe, Asia, Africa, and Australia. As the United States began to take an active role in conflicts and events in other countries, the nation began to emerge as a twentieth-century world power.

A pamphlet cover advertising the 1904 World's Fair held in St. Louis ▶

Think Ahead

The Industrial Revolution in the 1800s helped our nation to grow strong and prosper. Through war and trade, the United States became a leading world power in the twentieth century. Discover how the people of the United States and North Carolina faced challenges as they moved into a new century.

1 Becoming a World Power

People, Places, Terms

international
Commodore George Dewey
Theodore Roosevelt
imperialism
commonwealth
expansionist
Queen Liliuokalani
Panama Canal

By the early 1900s, the United States was one of the richest nations in the world. Each year thousands of ships loaded with steel, machinery, and other goods left United States ports and sailed to countries in all parts of the world. The people of the United States also started businesses in other countries. Although many United States citizens liked taking a leading role in international affairs, they did not relish the idea of being dragged into quarrels in other parts of the world.

A war with Spain. In 1895, the island of Cuba, just 90 miles off the coast of Florida, revolted against Spanish rule. Dozens of United States reporters poured into Havana, the capital of Cuba, to report on the fighting. As fighting continued, people in the United States read the shocking accounts of the conflict. They urged Congress and the President to help free Cuba of Spanish rule.

At first, the United States tried to stay out of the revolution. However, on the night of February 15, 1898, an American battleship blew up in the harbor of Havana, Cuba. The *Maine* had been sent to Cuba to protect United States citizens from the fighting. When the ship exploded, more than 250 of those aboard were killed. Although to this day no one knows the cause of the explosion, the event led the United States to declare war on Spain on April 24, 1898.

The Spanish thought the United States would invade Cuba. Instead, the United States struck first in the Pacific. On April 30, a United States fleet in the Pacific steamed to the Philippines, islands in Pacific ruled by Spain. On May 1, 1898, the fleet, led by Commodore George Dewey, captured or destroyed every Spanish ship in the harbor of Manila, the Philippine capital.

Victory in Cuba. While Dewey was fighting in the Philippines, more than 17,000 professional and volunteer United States soldiers sailed toward Cuba. Theodore Roosevelt, one of the volunteers, led a group known as the Rough Riders. The Rough Riders, which included cowboys, lumberjacks, and Native Americans, charged up San Juan Hill near Santiago, Cuba, and took the Spanish fortifications there. Although the United States was not thoroughly prepared for war, it had enough soldiers, guns, and supplies to defeat the Spanish.

By the middle of August 1898, the United States had won the war. At the peace talks, Spain freed Cuba. Spain also turned over the island of Guam in the Pacific and

This *New York Journal* article was published two days after the tragic sinking of the *Maine*. The account, which was exaggerated and included opinions instead of facts, is an example of yellow journalism. The aim of yellow journalism was to sell more copies of the paper.

Queen Liliuokalani was the last queen of Hawaii. She tried to limit the influence of foreigners in Hawaii during her brief two-year rule.

Across Cultures

*A*merican writer Mark Twain expressed his reaction to imperialism with these words: "Shall we go on conferring our Civilization upon the People that Sit in Darkness, or shall we give those poor things a rest?" ■ *To Do*: Based on this excerpt, do you think Twain supported or opposed imperialism? Explain your answer.

Puerto Rico in the West Indies to the United States. In addition, Spain sold the Philippines to the United States for $20 million.

The debate over the treaty.   The United States Senate had to approve the treaty the President had worked out with Spain. Some senators believed that the United States had no right to take over other lands. Others pointed out that Great Britain, Germany, and other nations were taking over land in Africa and Asia as well as islands in the Pacific. They wanted the United States to do the same.

One person who disagreed with the Philippine takeover was Senator Carl Schurz. In a speech he delivered in 1899, Senator Schurz expressed his reaction to **imperialism,** or the policy of conquering and ruling other lands.

Primary Source

We are told that our industries are gasping for breath; that we are suffering from over-production; that our products must have new outlets, and that we need colonies and dependencies the world over to give us more markets. More markets? Certainly. But do we, civilized beings, indulge in the absurd and barbarous notion that we must own the countries with which we wish to trade?

— *SENATOR CARL SCHURZ, "A reaction to imperialism"*

The people of Puerto Rico and the Philippines were also alarmed over United States control of their lands. Throughout the years, each group dreamed of independence. Their dreams were realized in the 1940s. In 1946, the Philippines became an independent nation. One year later in 1947, Puerto Rico became a **commonwealth.** A commonwealth is a political unit, such as a state or nation. In Puerto Rico, the citizens have their own governor and their own lawmakers. The main difference between Puerto Rico and a state is that Puerto Ricans do not have any representation in the United States Congress.

Expanding the nation.   In 1867, Secretary of State William H. Seward arranged for the United States to buy Alaska from the Russians for $7,200,000, or less than two cents an acre. Some United States citizens thought it was foolish to buy a land of ice and snow, while others talked of a land rich in timber, fish, and furs. **Expansionists,** or those who favored taking over land outside of the country, won the debate. In 1959, almost 100 years after Seward's purchase, Alaska became the nation's 49th state.

During the 1880s, many United States business people had settled in the Hawaiian Islands. Hoping to sell Hawaiian sugar to the United States, many of these business people started sugar plantations. By 1890, these planters owned most of the farmland in Hawaii. Hawaiians led by their ruler—Queen Liliuokalani (lih LEE uh WOH kuh LAHN ee)—fought to limit foreign power over Hawaii. However, in 1893, United States settlers, led mostly by plantation owners, revolted against Hawaii's queen. Aided by American troops, the settlers won the revolt. Five years later in 1898, President William McKinley made Hawaii a territory of the United States. About 60 years later, in 1959, Hawaii became the nation's 50th state.

A shortcut between oceans. As trade grew with Pacific islands, the United States needed to replace the long, dangerous route around South America with a faster, safer route through Central America. The Spanish, French, British, and Americans had talked of building a canal across Central America's Isthmus of Panama for years. The distance across the isthmus is only 50 miles. However, the land was covered with thick rain forests, tall mountains, and swamps filled with disease-carrying mosquitoes.

Still, many people dreamed of a canal that would connect the Atlantic to the Pacific. The French started one in the 1800s but diseases such as malaria and yellow fever killed too many workers. Then, in 1903, the United States offered to buy a 10-mile-wide strip of land at the Isthmus

Maps Matter

A map can show how political boundaries change. This map shows you what new territories the United States gained between 1867 and 1899. ■ *To Do:* Use the map to answer these questions. What territories were gained in the Pacific? What territory was gained northwest of the United States? What territory was gained to the southeast?

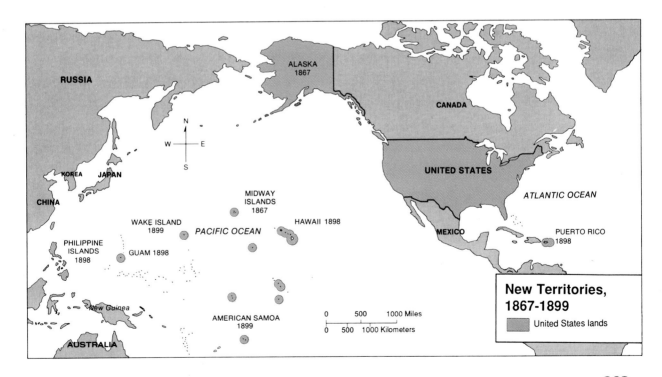

New Territories, 1867-1899
United States lands

To dig the 50-mile-long Panama Canal, workers cut through 9 miles of solid rock and built dams to slow raging rivers. They moved millions of tons of dirt during 10 years of construction.

of Panama. Colombia, which ruled Panama, refused to sell the land. After Panama won independence from Colombia later that year, the United States and Panama signed a treaty. The United States agreed to pay Panama $10 million then and $250,000 yearly for land on which the canal would be built. The first ship passed through the **Panama Canal** on August 15, 1914. (In 1974, 71 years after the United States purchased the Canal Zone, the United States agreed to transfer control of the Canal to Panama on December 31, 1999.)

By the early 1900s, the United States was conducting world trade and acquiring lands far from its own shores. World events could not help but affect the United States. Americans worried about trading partners in Europe, where trouble was brewing.

Think Twice

1. Why did the United States declare war on Spain in 1898?
2. What lands did Spain turn over to the United States in 1898?
3. (a) Name two territories that the United States acquired in the late 1800s. (b) How was each acquired?
4. Why was the Panama Canal important to the United States?
5. In the 1800s and early 1900s, there were many debates concerning United States expansion. Summarize the different viewpoints in these debates. Include views expressed concerning the Philippines, Puerto Rico, Alaska, and Hawaii.

2 World War I

People, Places, Terms

Central Powers
Allied Powers
League of Nations
neutral
communism

Throughout the late 1800s and early 1900s, the industrial nations of the world competed for raw materials and customers. They raced to see who could build the biggest navy and the strongest army. Each nation also tried to build as large an empire as possible. The competition enflamed old hatreds and sparked new ones. It led to many small wars and, in time, to the largest war in history—World War I.

The start of the war. On June 28, 1914, a 19-year-old Serbian student shot and killed Archduke Franz Ferdinand, the heir to the throne of Austria-Hungary. The student hoped his act would start a revolution among the Slavs in the Austro-Hungarian Empire. Like many other Slavs, he wanted Serbia to become a homeland for all Slavic people, including those in the Austrian Empire.

The Austrian emperor was outraged. Immediately he declared war on Serbia. Germany, Austria's most powerful ally, was quickly drawn into the fighting. Russia, an ally of Serbia, also prepared for war. In no time at all, sides were drawn. One side, called the **Central Powers,** included Austria-Hungary, Germany, the Ottoman Empire, and, after 1915, Bulgaria. The other side, called the **Allied Powers,** included Serbia, France, Great Britain, Russia, Japan, and, later, Italy. In 1917, the United States entered the war on the side of the Allies.

A war of the people. In the past, most wars were fought by professional soldiers. World War I was different. When it began, thousands of eager young men volunteered to fight. Those who could not fight worked for the war at home. Women took the place of men in factories, offices, and shops. As a result of the work women did during World War I, many people changed their viewpoint that only men could handle certain jobs.

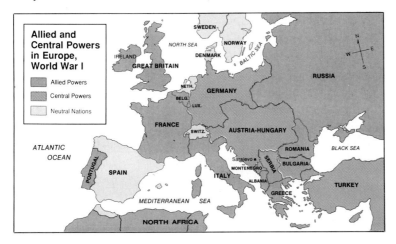

Allied and Central Powers in Europe, World War I

Allied Powers
Central Powers
Neutral Nations

Maps Matter

This map helps you see the balance of power during World War I.
■ *To Do:* Which European countries joined the Allied Powers? Which joined the Central Powers? Which remained neutral?

To prepare North Carolina citizens for combat, military training camps were established at Camp Greene in Charlotte (shown at right), at Camp Polk in Raleigh, and at Camp Bragg near Fayetteville. North Carolina shipyards manufactured ships for use in the war. Other factories in the state made gun shells, uniforms, wagon wheels, and airplane propellers.

North Carolina contributions. Like people from other states, the people of North Carolina also did their share for the war effort. For example, Josephus Daniels of North Carolina served as Secretary of the Navy. Walter Hines Page of North Carolina served as ambassador to Great Britain, and North Carolinian David Houston served as Secretary of Agriculture. Ordinary citizens of North Carolina also contributed to the war effort by working in war-related industries and serving in the Red Cross. The people of North Carolina raised more than $140 million in funds to help pay for war expenses. Over 85,000 men from North Carolina joined the armed forces. The United States Thirtieth Division was almost totally comprised of North Carolina soldiers.

New inventions. During World War I, countries used all the advances of the Industrial Revolution to invent new weapons and to make older ones more deadly. The machine gun, invented in the 1860s and refined over the years, fired so rapidly that soldiers could not protect themselves against the hail of bullets. The machine gun forced both sides to dig trenches where men could lie low to escape the deadly fire. Within these trenches, soldiers on both sides lived for months at a time. They were plagued by constant gunfire and diseased rats. The following passage is from a novel that tells about World War I through the eyes of an 18-year-old German soldier who fought in the trenches.

Primary Source

Towards morning, while it is still dark, there is some excitement. Through the entrance rushes in a swarm of fleeing rats that try to storm the walls. Torches light up the confusion. Everyone yells and curses and slaughters. The madness and despair of many hours unloads itself in this outburst. Faces are distorted, arms strike out, the beasts scream; we stop just in time to avoid attacking one another.

— ERICH MARIA REMARQUE, All Quiet on the Western Front

Eat less

and let us be thankful that we have enough to share with those who fight for freedom

UNITED STATES FOOD ADMINISTRATION

During World War I, Herbert Hoover launched a successful campaign to get Americans to produce more food and to consume less.

Poison gas and tanks, two other new inventions, also added to the brutality of the war. For the first time in history, airplanes were used to bomb battlegrounds. Yet after several years of desperate fighting, neither side seemed to be winning. Many people wondered if the war would ever end.

The turning point of the war. In 1917, a series of events finally brought the war to an end. It began in February of 1917, when the Russian people—weary of war, death, and starvation—revolted against the tsar, or emperor, of Russia. A few days later, the tsar surrendered. On November 7, 1917, a new Russian government was established. That government signed a peace treaty with Germany. As a result, Germany and Austria no longer had to fight in the east. They could send more troops to fight the Allies in the west.

With the Russians gone, many Germans thought that victory would soon be theirs. They were wrong. Shortly after the start of the Russian Revolution, the United States decided to enter the war on the side of the Allies.

By June of 1918, American troops were arriving in France at the rate of 250,000 a month. By August, they were helping to push the Germans farther and farther east. The German people had enough. Like the Russians, they too refused to fight any longer. On November 9, 1918, the German kaiser gave up his throne and Germany became a republic. Two days later, the Germans signed an agreement ending the war.

Making peace. In January of 1919, representatives from 27 nations met in Paris to write a peace agreement. The losers of the war were not invited. After months of bargaining, the treaty was finally completed. Because it was signed in the palace of Versailles, it is known as the Treaty of Versailles.

The treaty placed all the blame for the war on Germany. As a result, Germany was forced to give up its colonies and pay for the costs of the war. The Austro-Hungarian Empire was divided into several small countries. The same was true of the Ottoman Empire.

At the peace conference, President Woodrow Wilson called for a **League of Nations** that would settle conflicts without war. However, many United States citizens believed that their country's best hope for peace was to stay **neutral.** A neutral nation does not take sides. In the end, the United States refused to join the League and sign the treaty. It worked out a separate treaty with Germany and its allies several years later.

Changes in Russia. While the peacemakers debated, the Russians were in the middle of a civil war. Many different groups battled for control of the country. By 1920, Vladimir

Think as a Geographer

*D*uring World War I, the Germans and the Allies fought each other from long trenches dug into the ground to protect soldiers from enemy fire. These trenches, called the Western Front, stretched for 600 miles from the North Sea to the Swiss border. In time, the land between the trenches became a scarred desert. ■ *To Do:* The Western Front is an example of how people use or change land during war. Identify modern-day examples of the effects of war on land and water. Write a paragraph describing your findings.

Ilyich Ulianov (better known as Lenin), leader of a radical group called the Bolsheviks, had won. Soon after, Lenin and the Bolsheviks changed the name the country to the Union of Soviet Socialist Republics or the Soviet Union. The Bolsheviks set up a new kind of government based on the ideas of Karl Marx. He had lived in Germany about a hundred years before.

Marx favored **communism,** a system in which the people own all land, factories, and businesses. *Communism* means "common" or "belonging to all." In a Communist system, power is supposed to rest with the people. However, in the Soviet Union, only people who belonged to the Communist party had any say in government.

This painting by Sir William Open is called "The Signing of the Peace in the Hall of Mirrors, Versailles, 28 June 1919."

Think Twice

1. How did the conflict between Serbia and the Austro-Hungarian Empire draw the whole world into war?
2. In what two ways did World War I differ from earlier wars?
3. List at least three contributions made by the people of North Carolina to the war effort.
4. Describe two events that took place in 1917 that finally brought the war to an end.
5. (a) What was the League of Nations? (b) Why did the United States refuse to join it?
6. The people of Germany were outraged by the Versailles Treaty of 1919. (a) Why were the Germans outraged? (b) Do you agree with the idea of severely punishing the losing side in a war? Why or why not?

The Progressive Movement

People, Places, Terms

progressives
Ida Tarbell
Robert La Follette
initiative
referendum
direct primary
graduated income tax
Prohibition
Cameron Morrison
Harriet Berry

About 1900, a new wave of reform began in the nation. The new reformers were called **progressives**. Most progressive reformers came from cities, but they received important support from farmers. Many business people and politicians were progressives of one sort or another. The progressive movement was more complicated than populism because not all progressives stood for the same reforms. Nor were they all members of the same political party.

Progressives did tend to have some things in common. They were generally white, native-born, middle-class Americans with college degrees. They wanted government to play an active role in public life, and they had great faith in people's ability to study and solve problems. As a result, they created many commissions of experts to study public problems and to help govern the cities, the states, and the nation.

Progressivism's roots go back to the 1800s, and it is still an important force, but its heyday was the early 1900s. Some of the reforms you read about earlier, such as women's suffrage, measures dealing with life in city tenements, and help for immigrants were part of the progressive movement.

Muckrakers. Among those with the progressive spirit were some novelists and some reporters who wrote articles for magazines such as *McClure's, Cosmopolitan,* and *Colliers.* These writers investigated unethical and illegal practices in industry, government, and society. Although President Theodore Roosevelt gave them the name muckrakers because he felt they were overzealous in their pursuit of wrongdoing, it was an unfair nickname. Muckrakers generally did very careful research, and their publishers did rigorous fact-checking.

One of the best known muckrakers was Ida Tarbell, whose "History of Standard Oil" was published in *McClure's* in 18 installments between November 1902 and the spring of 1904. In the series, Tarbell traced the beginnings of the oil industry and its takeover by John D. Rockefeller. She found much to admire in Standard Oil, but she also sympathized with the owners of small companies destroyed by Rockefeller. Finding many of his methods unacceptable, she wrote that when people acquire as much power as Rockefeller had, they use that power "to oppress and defraud the public."

Other muckrakers wrote on different topics—Lincoln Steffens on corruption in city and state government; David

Ida Tarbell's "History of Standard Oil" doubled the readership of *McClure's.*

Another reform, the secret ballot, came into use at different times in different states. Here voters in Boston are using it in 1889. It came into use in North Carolina in 1929. The idea of the secret ballot was to reduce vote buying, since the purchaser could not tell whether he was getting what he paid for.

G. Phillips on the control of senators by railroads and other monopolies; John Spargo on the abuses of child labor; Upton Sinclair on the filth and disease in the meatpacking industry. These and other muckrakers presented the public with the problems, but what were the solutions? As Steffens had discovered, local and state governments were often controlled by political bosses or by corrupt business interests. So long as that remained true, the people had little influence on public policy. As a result, progressive reformers looked for ways to increase the power of the people.

The Wisconsin reforms.   One of the most important progressive reformers was Robert La Follette, the governor of Wisconsin. Finding that the state's government was largely controlled by the railroads and banks, "Battling Bob" supported measures that increased the power of the people. He fought for the initiative, the referendum, and the direct primary. In the **initiative,** voters themselves may propose new laws and force their state legislature to vote on them. Under the **referendum,** laws may be placed on the ballot so that the people can vote on them directly instead of letting the legislature make the decisions. The **direct primary** is a special election in which voters who claim membership in one of the political parties choose their party's candidates for office, rather than allowing the politicians to choose. Other reforms under La Follette included a commission to regulate railroad rates and banks; tax laws in which corporations paid a fairer share of state taxes; a **graduated income tax** in which the amount of tax paid was increased according to the size of a person's income; and laws to regulate working conditions and to make employers responsible for employee safety on the job.

The Wisconsin ideas spread.   Progressive government spread to other states and even to the federal level. Reforms varied by state, but all eventually adopted more democratic measures and some legislation aimed at social concerns such as working conditions and aid to the poor. At the national level, reforms resulted in several new amendments to the Constitution. In 1913, the Sixteenth Amendment introduced the graduated income tax. In the same year, direct election of senators became the law of the land under the Seventeenth Amendment. In 1919, the manufacture, sale, import, or export of alcoholic beverages became illegal under the Eighteenth Amendment. (This amendment was repealed by the Twenty-first Amendment in 1933.) Finally, in 1920, the Nineteenth Amendment gave women the right to vote nationwide.

Progressivism in North Carolina. In North Carolina, progressivism's roots go back at least as far as the Populists' attention to farmers' concerns. In the late 1800s, despite the Democratic party's protection of railroads and big business, there were hints at least of the social and economic reforms of the twentieth century. The state began, in 1885, to pay pensions to "disabled and destitute" veterans of the Civil War and to widows of soldiers. During the 1870s and 1880s, the state also created or supported previously established orphanages and institutions for the mentally ill.

Reform in North Carolina in the twentieth century underwent some advances and some setbacks. In Chapter 19, you read about the educational reforms under Governor Aycock. On the other hand, the state took a step backward when it revised the voting laws to make it almost impossible for most African Americans to vote. **Prohibition** (the banning of alcoholic beverages) was implemented in North Carolina in 1908, 11 years before the Eighteenth Amendment became law.

Farmers' lives were largely unchanged, but after a slow and rocky start, labor unions in the state managed to reduce the workweek to 55 hours, improve working conditions in mills, and provide aid to the poor in company towns. The state enacted rather weak laws regulating child labor in 1903 and 1907. These were strengthened in 1913 and 1919. Finally, in 1933, a federal law abolished child labor altogether.

Across Cultures

John Thomas Scopes was a high school teacher in Tennessee who in 1925 was brought to trial for violating the state law against teaching the theory of evolution. The trial attracted nationwide attention. ■ *To Do:* Find out what religious and political issues caused differences of opinion on this case in the nation and in North Carolina.

Wages at the mills were low, so whole families often had to work. These men, women, and children worked at West Monbo Manufacturing on the Catawba River in Catawba County.

Cameron Morrison was governor from 1921 to 1925.

The state's first association to promote women's suffrage was organized in 1894. In 1897, to the surprise of the all-male Assembly, Senator J. L. Hyatt of Yancey County introduced a women's suffrage bill. His fellow legislators probably applauded when it was sent to a committee on insane asylums (now called mental health institutions), where it died. Women continued to fight for their cause, but made little headway with the Assembly. Finally, by the summer of 1920, only one more state's approval was needed for the ratification of the Nineteenth Amendment to the United States Constitution. Both the Tennessee and North Carolina legislatures held special sessions to consider the matter. True to form, the North Carolina Assembly declined to approve the amendment, and Tennessee became the last state to ratify it.

Under Cameron Morrison, who was governor from 1921 to 1925, the state made some important strides. Largely because of the work of Harriet Morehead Berry of the North Carolina Geological and Economic Survey, legislation was passed to greatly improve the road system in the state. During Morrison's term, the overcrowded colleges and universities were expanded and improvements were made in institutions for the mentally ill, in schools for the hearing impaired and visually impaired, and in other institutions. The state Board of Health received an increase in funding, as did public schools. Morrison also tried to improve race relations in the state.

Think Twice

1. What did muckrakers do?
2. Explain the terms *initiative* and *referendum*.
3. Identify Ida Tarbell, Robert La Follette, Harriet Berry, and Cameron Morrison.
4. Name two reforms implemented in North Carolina.
5. Two ideas basic to progressivism were reform and more power to the people. How were the two linked?

4 The Roaring Twenties

People, Places, Terms

civil rights
discrimination
consumer goods
credit
interest

Following World War I, distrust of other nations emerged in the United States. This distrust led to shutting off foreign ideas, limiting immigration, and challenging the patriotism and rights of fellow United States citizens. However, when postwar distrust began to lift, life became brighter for many citizens. The Roaring Twenties brought Americans good times and great changes.

The fear of Communists. Some Americans feared that, like Russia, the United States would be taken over by Communists (sometimes called the Reds). The so-called Red Scare made headlines in 1919 and 1920, when several political and business leaders around the country became the targets of terrorist bombings. Some Americans believed that these actions were the work of Communist revolutionaries. Although only a few thousand people in the United States favored communism, some Americans felt that the country was at great risk.

Using the bombs as an excuse, some groups of Americans began accusing citizens they disliked of being Communists. By 1925, most Americans had become disgusted with those who accused innocent people of being Communists. The Red Scare ended as citizens realized that Communists in the United States did not threaten the American way of life.

In the Roaring Twenties, young women known as flappers felt free to try new styles. These people are doing a popular dance called the Charleston.

This photograph shows Native Americans in Florida voting for the first time.

Setting immigration limits. Some Americans feared that immigrants would spread communism or take jobs away from American workers. In 1921, Congress passed a law in order to limit immigration. This law set the total number of immigrants that could come to the United States each year. It also set the number of immigrants allowed to enter from each different country. Newcomers from Asian countries, such as Japan or China, were totally barred. For the first time in United States history, the flood of immigrants slowed to a trickle.

Citizenship for Native Americans. At the same time that the country shunned Communists and immigrants, some groups of Americans were fighting for their rightful place in society. Native Americans, African Americans, and women sought more rights.

During the war, thousands of Native Americans volunteered to fight even though they did not have to. They were not United States citizens. Once the war had ended, Native Americans felt that they deserved full citizenship and **civil rights.** Civil rights are those rights that are guaranteed by the Constitution, including the right to vote. With the help of Kansas Senator Charles Curtis, Native Americans gained the right to vote in 1924.

Civil rights for African Americans. Many African Americans also fought bravely in Europe or had held factory jobs in the United States during World War I. Yet they faced **discrimination** when the war ended. *Discrimination* means "treating people differently because of their race, beliefs, or heritage." Many were fired from their wartime jobs, and African American soldiers returning from the war could not find work. Moreover, African Americans could not live wherever they wanted, and their children often could not attend schools of their choice. The NAACP—National Association for the Advancement of Colored People—helped African Americans gain civil rights by bringing cases of discrimination to state and federal courts. The NAACP also fought for laws that would give equal rights to all Americans.

Voting rights for women. Women's groups were among those who fought for equal rights during the 1920s. The struggle among women for equal rights had begun years before. Yet by 1900, women had gained suffrage in only a few states. Spurred by early leaders, such as Elizabeth Cady Stanton and Susan B. Anthony, increasing numbers of women began taking up the cause of suffrage.

By 1914, 13 states had granted women the right to vote in state elections, but it took more speeches, marches, pamphlets, and newspaper articles to convince the United States government to give women across the country the right to vote. That right was granted in 1920 by the Nineteenth Amendment to the Constitution.

The beginning of the consumer age. During the Roaring Twenties, businesses and industries boomed, providing jobs and good wages for workers. Factories produced goods for prosperous Americans to buy. The nationwide demand for factory-made **consumer goods** grew, leading to an economic boom. Consumer goods are products made for use by the average person. Factories poured out a flood of washing machines, electric irons, vacuum cleaners, and toasters. Ready-made dresses and suits, cosmetics, soaps, and toothpaste filled store racks and shelves.

Think as a Historian

Women finally gained suffrage when the Nineteenth Amendment was adopted in 1920. ■ *To Do*: Compare the opportunities of women in the 1920s with the opportunities of women today. You may wish to use newspaper clippings, an encyclopedia, or another reference book to find out how opportunities for women have changed or stayed the same.

The Good Roads State

North Carolinian Harriet Morehead Berry, shown at left, was called the "best woman politician in the state" in 1921. A leader in the "good roads" movement, she lobbied for laws that would create a state system of paved roads, publicized the plan, and raised money for the North Carolina Good Roads Association.

North Carolina Governor Cameron Morrison also supported the idea of a good roads program. Thanks to his and to Berry's efforts, the Highway Act of 1921 was passed. A state highway commission was created to take control of state roads, to build new routes, and to maintain over 5,000 miles of highways. Soon paved roads crisscrossed the state, connecting towns and cities.

In the 1920s, department stores carried hundreds of consumer goods from which people could choose.

The automobile took the biggest share of the consumer market. From 1919 to 1929, the number of cars in the United States rose from 7 million to 23 million. As people bought more cars, automobile factories expanded and hired more workers. Factories supplying car parts or materials—such as steel, tires, and glass—also grew, creating a need for more workers and more plants.

Not only did the automobile industry create more factory jobs, but it also spurred the building of new roads and highways. Along these roads and highways, new businesses—gas stations, repair shops, and restaurants—mushroomed. In all, the automobile helped create jobs for more than four million people.

Buy now, pay later. Where did Americans get the money for consumer products? Many earned good wages, and some used their savings. Others went into debt.

In the 1920s, more and more Americans were buying on **credit**—that is, they paid a small part of the total price of a car or a radio each month until it was paid for in full. The amount they paid each month included an extra charge called **interest.** People were spending more money than they actually earned.

The Roaring Twenties was a prosperous time for many. Many Americans believed that the good times were endless. Yet in the 1930s, the economic bubble would finally burst.

Think Twice

1. What was the Red Scare?
2. Why did Congress pass laws to limit immigration?
3. What three groups fought to win civil rights in the 1920s?
4. How did the automobile lead to the growth of businesses?
5. Explain why the 1920s were called the Roaring Twenties.

Chapter 20 Review

Choose from the following menu of activities.

Think Back: Main Ideas

During the twentieth century, the United States became a world power. Answer the questions about the new role of the nation.

1. Name three ways the United States extended its borders in the 1800s and early 1900s.
2. (a) What event sparked the beginning of World War I? (b) How did the United States' role during the war increase its prestige and political influence around the world?
3. Name at least two conditions investigated by muckrakers.
4. What did the initiative, referendum, and direct primary reforms have in common?
5. Why did reformers want a graduated income tax rather than the same tax rate for all?
6. Assume you must vote on (a) the Eighteenth Amendment and (b) the Nineteenth Amendment. How you will vote? Why?
7. How did the United States become a leader in social trends and reforms during the Roaring Twenties?

Maps Matter

In the 1800s, the United States acquired new territories. Refer to the map on page 283 to answer the following questions.

1. About how many miles is Hawaii from the United States mainland?
2. About how many miles is Puerto Rico from the United States mainland?
3. Alaska has a strategic location. Between which two countries is it located?

Word Wizard

1. *International* is made up of the prefix *inter-* + *national*. *Inter-* means "among or between." Can you think of other words that begin with this prefix?

2. Look up the words *credit* and *interest* in a dictionary. Copy the definitions that best match the use of these words in this chapter.

Working Cooperatively

Work in a group of three to five students. Have each person choose one of the following topics: radio, jazz, silent movies, flappers, the Harlem Renaissance, or another aspect of culture in the Roaring Twenties.

After each person researches his or her chosen topic, have the group come together to create a collage of the Roaring Twenties. Include appropriate illustrations, poems, sayings, cartoons, song lyrics, and other representative items that convey the spirit of the Roaring Twenties. Display your group's collage in the classroom.

As an additional activity, do some research on strikes and other actions of labor unions in the state and in the nation in the late 1800s.

Curriculum Connection

During the Spanish-American War of 1898, many soldiers died as a result of malaria and yellow fever. The threat of these diseases also prevented the building of the Panama Canal for many years. Use an encyclopedia to find out about one of these diseases: how it is spread, what its effects are, who discovered its cause, how it is treated, and so on. If you choose to focus on malaria, research recent outbreaks and the problems scientists are having in treating the disease with conventional methods. Use your findings to write a column for a medical newsletter.

Learning through Literature

All Quiet on the Western Front, by Erich Maria Remarque

Khaki Wings, by Milton Dank

The Great Gatsby, by F. Scott Fitzgerald

Chapter 21

A Rise from the Depths

Americans face an economic crisis.

In the late 1920s, a new song climbed to the top of the radio charts: "How the Money Rolls In!" In March 1929, when President Herbert Hoover took the oath of office, he asserted: "I have no fears for the future of our country. It is bright with hope." Yet within months, the nation plunged into the worst economic crisis in its history. By the 1930s, Americans sadly sang a new tune: "Buddy Can You Spare a Dime?" Amid the suffering, Franklin Delano Roosevelt won the presidency. He pushed through legislation that reached into every state. North Carolina was no exception. Tar Heels joined with other Americans to pull themselves up by their bootstraps and weather the economic storm.

The United States leads the free world.

In the 1940s, the United States found itself entangled in a second world war. Wartime production ended economic hardship. However, the war brought new sorrows as Americans died in battle in Europe and Asia. When the war ended, the United States emerged as the strongest democratic nation in the world. It faced a Communist bloc of nations led by another superpower—the Soviet Union.

Sending a new ship, the *U.S.S. North Carolina*, out to sea ▶

Think Ahead

In the 1930s and 1940s, the United States successfully met two huge challenges—a great economic disaster and a second world war. As you read through this chapter, list actions taken by the United States and North Carolina to overcome both crises.

1 From Boom to Bust

People, Places, Terms

Wall Street
stock
depression
Franklin Delano Roosevelt
New Deal
Hundred Days
O. Max Gardner

In 1929, the stock market on New York City's **Wall Street** teemed with action. "The sky's the limit," said investors. Many people believed the prices of **stocks,** or shares in a company, would rise forever. As a result, even taxicab drivers and waitresses "dabbled in the market." Most people bought stocks on margin. That is, they put down a little money, placed the rest on credit, and walked away thinking soaring prices would pay off the loan. For a while, the tactic worked. With everybody buying and few people selling, stocks did keep going up—far beyond their actual worth.

In September, prices inched down slightly. "There's a crash coming," predicted financial expert Roger W. Babson. Most people laughed. Then, on Wednesday, October 23, 1929, prices plunged. Within hours, investors lost more than $5 billion. The next day, panic set in. On what has become known as Black Thursday, people rushed to sell their stocks. Those who could not sell rushed to their banks to withdraw money to cover debts. Then, as thousands of banks shut down, many people lost everything. Economic boom had turned to economic bust.

Searching for answers. Americans suddenly found themselves in the midst of a **depression**, or sharp downswing in the economy. The depression that began in 1929 seemed to have no bottom. Things went from bad to worse. As banks failed, other businesses shut down. Unemployment crept upward. Because people had less money to spend, factories cut back on production. Then they laid off workers. The result was higher unemployment and even less consumer spending. Soon some factories closed entirely. The chain of events produced such economic hardship that the period has become known as the Great Depression, or simply the Depression.

North Carolina in the Depression. No matter what the cause, the Great Depression touched nearly everyone. In North Carolina alone, 194 banks and 438 savings and loan associations closed between 1930 and 1933. As a result, many North Carolinians lost their homes and their businesses. Without the help of banks, rural families throughout the state could not keep their farms afloat.

Large numbers of rural people moved into North Carolina's mill towns hoping to find work. But the Depression crippled the state's tobacco, furniture, and textile industries. Few people could afford new furniture or clothes. The tobacco industry limped along, but only by offering its

Tenant farmers, such as this man from Chatham County, were hit especially hard by the Depression. Why do you think tenant farmers suffered more than most other Americans?

299

Thousands of Dust Bowl families like this one learned to live out of trucks, alongside roads, or anywhere they might stop for a rest.

products at a greatly reduced price. All over North Carolina, mills either shut down, laid off workers, or slashed wages.

Relatives did their best to take in jobless family members, but people in both town and country often went to bed hungry. Families lived for weeks off cornmeal mush, fatback, or collard or pokeweed greens. Driven to desperation, otherwise honest parents stole to feed and clothe their children. They broke into smokehouses, took milk off front porches, and raided gardens. A woodpile or clothesline proved too tempting for someone whose children shivered at home. Not since the Civil War had North Carolinians and other Southerners faced such shortages.

Broken hopes and dreams.   Despite these hardships, North Carolina fared better during the Depression than did some other states. In 1932, for example, a drought hit the Great Plains. Crops withered and died in the field. Topsoil turned to dust. By the following spring, winds whipped across the Plains, stirring up huge clouds of dirt in a vast Dust Bowl that covered parts of Texas, Colorado, Kansas, and Oklahoma. So devastating were the dust storms that thousands of families piled their belongings on top of cars and trucks and headed west to California. Unfortunately, few found full-time work there. Instead, many huddled together in refugee camps, living on the edge of starvation.

Jobless workers in the cities fared little better. One woman described Chicago as "a place of broken hopes and dreams." Here, as in other major cities, homeless workers built shacks out of discarded lumber, boxes, and metal. They nicknamed these shantytowns Hoovervilles, after President Hoover.

Hoover, who took office in 1929, tried to ease the Depression. But he resisted pouring massive government aid into programs for the jobless. Instead, he focused on restarting businesses. Some Americans called Hoover's plan a "breadline for business." By 1932, Hoover despairingly said, "We are at the end of our string." Many Americans agreed as a wave of hopelessness spread across the nation.

A new deal.   As the 1932 presidential election neared, the confident voice of Franklin Delano Roosevelt, or FDR, boomed across the air waves. Roosevelt—Governor of New York—promised change. "It is common sense to take a method and try it," said Roosevelt. "If it fails, admit it frankly and try another. But above all try something."

Nobody was sure exactly what Roosevelt would try. However, the words of one speech fired the public imagination. Said Roosevelt, "I pledge you, I pledge myself, to a new deal for the American people." In 1932, voters swept Roosevelt into office.

On March 4, 1933, millions of Americans sat glued to their radios to hear Roosevelt's inaugural address. "This great nation," vowed Roosevelt, "will endure as it has endured, will revive and will prosper." He then said, "The only thing we have to fear is fear itself." A few days later, Roosevelt took to the airwaves again. In the first of many "fireside chats," Roosevelt told Americans that he had ordered a four-day bank holiday. When the banks reopened, said Roosevelt, they would have the support of Congress. "I can assure you," continued the new President, "that it is safer to keep your money in a reopened bank than under the mattress."

With these words, Roosevelt announced the first program of what became known as the **New Deal**. Others soon followed. On March 9, Roosevelt called Congress into a special session that lasted 100 days. During the so-called **Hundred Days,** the President sent 15 bills to Congress. Congress voted all of them into law. Some of them are listed in the chart below.

Tables Teach

Congress passed many laws during the New Deal. These are some of the most important ones. Which laws tried to correct causes of the Great Depression? Which laws tried to help farmers? Which laws are still in effect today?

ROOSEVELT'S NEW DEAL			
Program	**Initials**	**Dates**	**Goal**
Civilian Conservation Corps	CCC	1933–1942	Controlled erosion; employed young men to plant trees, set up parks, build bridges
Tennessee Valley Authority	TVA	1933–	Built dams to provide electricity for seven Southern states, including North Carolina
Federal Emergency Relief Administration	FERA	1933–1938	Offered direct relief to jobless workers
Agricultural Adjustment Administration	AAA	1933–1936	Paid farmers not to plant crops so that prices would rise
National Recovery Administration	NRA	1933–1935	Oversaw labor codes that protected wages, prices, and working conditions
Public Works Administration	PWA	1933–1939	Provided jobs through construction of schools, aircraft carriers, and ports
Federal Deposit Insurance Corporation	FDIC	1933–	Protected savings accounts in all federally approved banks
Securities and Exchange Commission	SEC	1934–	Regulated the stock exchange
Federal Housing Administration	FHA	1934–	Insured loans for mortgages
Rural Electrification Administration	REA	1935–	Offered loans to bring electricity to rural farming communities, including some in North Carolina
National Labor Relations Board	NLRB	1935–	Regulated and protected unions
Works Progress Administration	WPA	1935–1942	Provided work for jobless writers, artists, and musicians; extended jobs to men and women through construction of hospitals, schools, and airports
Social Security Act	SSA	1935–	Set up pensions and unemployment insurance for workers; provided aid to the disabled

President Roosevelt contracted polio as an adult. Although he was wheelchair-bound or wore painful leg braces, FDR's forceful presence and iron will carried the nation through some of its most difficult years.

Rocky Mount Home Demonstration Club canning during the Depression.

Not everyone agreed with the New Deal. Roosevelt's projects cost the government billions of dollars. Some of the projects did not work. The Supreme Court ruled five laws, including the NRA (see chart), unconstitutional. Other laws, such as the Social Security Act, survived Court challenges and have continued into the present. However, even today, many people debate the costliness of the policy of direct federal aid to the people started under FDR.

Despite criticism of the New Deal, countless Americans saw FDR and his wife Eleanor as a ray of hope in otherwise bleak times. Eleanor Roosevelt made it her special task to reach out to minorities. She personally invited such leading African Americans as singer Marian Anderson to the White House. FDR appointed more African Americans to federal offices than had any other President before him. In the end, Americans of all racial and ethnic backgrounds voted FDR into office a record four times.

Relief in North Carolina.   North Carolinians took action even before the New Deal. Under the leadership of Governor O. Max Gardner, the state introduced a "Live at Home" program. It encouraged farmers to grow more food for themselves and less for sale. Government agents also traveled around the state showing people how to can and preserve foods. Within two years, the amount of land devoted to cotton declined by 536,000 acres, while the production of corn increased by 10 million bushels.

This Civilian Conservation Corps camp was at Globe in Caldwell County.

During these difficult years, churches and nonprofit agencies such as the Community Chest and Salvation Army took action, too. They provided temporary shelters and hot meals, especially for children. Hospitals, notably the Baptist Hospital in Winston-Salem and Duke Hospital in Durham set aside beds for those unable to pay for medical care.

When Roosevelt ran for office in 1932, Tar Heels gave him 497,566 votes to 208,344 for Hoover. Like the rest of the nation, North Carolina soon felt the effects of the New Deal. The Civilian Conservation Corps set up 61 camps in North Carolina. Young men dressed in olive drab uniforms planted trees, reclaimed eroded land, built hiking trails, and did other work for the state. The National Youth Administration (NYA) provided funds to help hundreds of North Carolina students pay for college through part-time jobs. The North Carolina Symphony received a grant from the Works Progress Administration (WPA) to play public concerts. Another WPA project hired interviewers to collect state folklore, including the stories of formerly enslaved Africans. Electricity came to rural parts of North Carolina through the Rural Electrification Administration (REA).

These are but a sampling of the programs put into effect in North Carolina and the rest of the nation. Some ended when the economy improved. Others have continued into the present. However, none of the New Deal programs successfully ended the Depression. Economic recovery finally came with the outbreak of another world war.

Think as a Historian

*F*ranklin Roosevelt brought many changes to United States government. One was his unprecedented election to a fourth term of office. ■ *To Do:* Read the Twenty-second Amendment at the back of the book. What are the provisions of this amendment? Do you agree with this amendment? Why or why not?

Think Twice

1. What hardships did the Depression bring to North Carolina?
2. How did Roosevelt's approach to the Depression differ from that of Hoover?
3. What actions did North Carolina take to relieve the Depression?

2 World War II

"There's a Paramount Picture probably around the corner. See it and you'll be out of yourself, living someone else's life." This was the promise made by one movie studio in the 1930s. Americans by the millions took up the offer. For just a little while, they escaped from the problems of everyday life into the fantasies created by Hollywood. Americans sat on the edge of their seats as a huge gorilla named King Kong climbed up New York's Empire State Building. They roared at the slapstick comedy of the Marx Brothers—Harpo, Chico, and Groucho. They relived the 1920s as Edward G. Robinson and James Cagney played the parts of tough-guy gangsters.

By the end of the 1930s, however, new faces began to appear on the movie screens. Amid the fantasies, newsreels flickered the rumblings of war. Americans watched goose-stepping German soldiers saluting Adolf Hitler. They saw crowds of Italians cheering Benito Mussolini. Americans grew increasingly uncomfortable with the actions of these two **dictators,** or rulers who exercise absolute control over their countries.

The sounds of war. With memories of World War I not yet faded, many Americans supported **isolationism,** or a policy of staying out of the affairs of other nations. By the 1930s, however, the world was linked in many ways. The Depression, for example, was just one part of a global economic slump. Shortages and unemployment existed worldwide. Most European nations, never fully recovered from World War I, could not supply the needs of their own people, much less buy or sell goods on the world market. This situation hurt the United States because other countries could no longer afford to buy its products.

In the desperate years of the Depression, leaders emerged in Italy, Germany, and Japan who fed on people's fears or held out dreams of glory. Recalling the greatness of ancient Rome, Mussolini promised Italians a new empire. Hitler ranted and raved over Germany's defeat in World War I, reminding people of the humiliating terms of the Versailles Treaty. Hitler also stirred up dangerous racial hatreds by falsely blaming the Jews for Germany's problems. In Japan, Emperor Hirohito and his military supporters not only talked of glory, but also set out to claim it. In 1933, Japan boldly seized Manchuria and several other parts of Asia. World leaders protested, but nobody moved to stop Japan.

Japan's success at aggression encouraged Italy and Germany. In 1935, Mussolini ordered Italian troops to invade the African nation of Ethiopia. That same year, Hitler, in defiance of the Versailles Treaty, rearmed Germany and sent troops into the Rhineland. Again, the world protested. But nobody took action. A year later, in 1936, Germany and Italy signed a pact creating the Rome-Berlin Axis, or partnership.

Peace at what price?   Few nations, including the United States, wanted war in the 1930s. Hitler, however, created a political party called the Nazis that depended upon the raw use of power. In a campaign of ethnic hatred, Hitler set out to destroy European Jews. Nazi soldiers herded thousands of Jewish men, women, and children into prisons called **concentration camps,** where they were starved, tortured, and killed by the thousands each day. By 1945, the Nazis had managed to wipe out more than six million Jews in what people call a **holocaust,** or terrible destruction of human life. Millions of others were sent to join the Jews in the death camps, including opponents of the Nazis, labor leaders, Roman Catholics, Gypsies, and even the disabled.

At first, the world knew little of these horrible crimes against humanity. Instead, people watched helplessly as Hitler stormed into Austria and then Czechoslovakia. Although Hitler promised to take no more land after that, he was only buying time to make a deal with the Soviet Union. The Soviet Union practiced communism, an economic system in which the government owns and operates all aspects of the economy. While Hitler and the Soviet dictator Joseph Stalin had no love for each other, they did have a common desire — conquest of Poland. In 1939, the two leaders signed a secret agreement to divide Poland between them. In exchange, Stalin promised not to stop Hitler from rolling over western Europe.

The world in flames.   On September 1, 1939, Hitler attacked Poland. Two days later, England and France declared war on Germany. Hitler then unleashed what he called a *blitzkrieg,* or lightning war, against Europe. He threw his full military force — cannons, tanks, airplanes, and armed troops — into battle. A startled world saw nation after nation fall in northern and western Europe until England stood alone. There, British Prime Minister Winston Churchill vowed, *We shall fight on the beaches, we shall fight on the landing grounds, we shall fight in the fields, and in the streets, we shall fight in the hills; we shall never surrender.*

While Hitler rolled over Europe, Japan pushed into Asia. In 1940, Hirohito joined the Axis. Around the world, nations took sides, but the United States wavered. At first,

Thousands of Jews in Poland were rounded up and sent to Nazi prison camps.

Spark Matsunaga of Hawaii was among the Nisei who fought in World War II. So was Daniel K. Inouye, who went on in 1963 to become the first Japanese American member of the Senate. Matsunaga later won election to the Senate, too.

■ *To Do*: Write a speech that either Inouye or Matsunaga might have delivered to persuade Congress to compensate Japanese Americans who were imprisoned during World War II.

Maps Matter

This map shows the nations involved in World War II. ■ *To Do:* Which nations remained neutral in the war? Countries on three continents came under Axis control. Which three were they?

FDR bowed to isolationists. However, he urged Americans to examine their consciences closely. "This nation will remain a neutral nation," said Roosevelt, "but I cannot ask that every American remain neutral in thought as well. . . . "

The year 1941 proved to be a turning point in the war. In June, Hitler broke his pact with Stalin and plowed across Soviet borders. On December 7, 1941, American sailors at **Pearl Harbor**, Hawaii, awoke to the sounds of screaming sirens. They rushed to the decks of their ships to see the sky filled with Japanese planes. In a matter of minutes, Japanese bombs sank many ships and claimed about 2,500 American lives. On December 8, 1941, the United States entered the war. Most of the world was in flames.

A time of fear. Pearl Harbor drove home the horrors of modern warfare. With the development of the airplane, the oceans no longer shielded the United States from attack. Suddenly some Americans saw danger everywhere. Fear was strongest along the Pacific Coast. Here people believed they would be the next target for Japanese bombs. Some looked with suspicion at the many Japanese Americans who lived there, afraid they might be spies.

To quiet fears, FDR ordered the army to round up some 120,000 Japanese Americans and move them to inland prison camps. Nearly five decades later, in 1988, the federal government officially apologized for the unfair treatment of Japanese American citizens. An act of Congress gave $20,000 to each living person who had been confined in the prison camps.

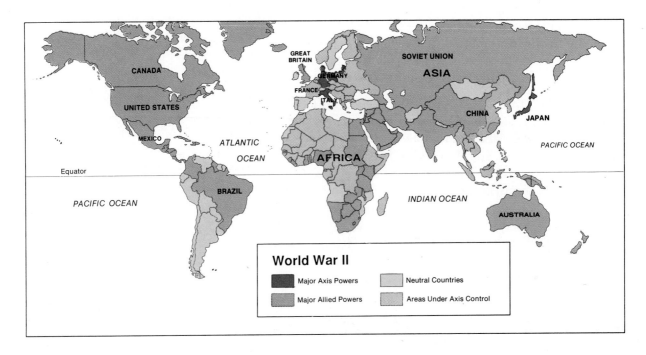

World War II

- ■ Major Axis Powers
- ■ Major Allied Powers
- ■ Neutral Countries
- ■ Areas Under Axis Control

Gearing up for war. Despite challenges to their loyalty, some 33,000 **Nisei,** or second-generation Japanese Americans, signed up to fight in the war. Millions of other Americans joined them, and by the war's end, some 15 million American men and women of every race, creed, and national background had served in the military. At least one member of nearly every family in the United States reported for duty. Those who remained at home threw their full support behind the war effort.

North Carolina became involved in the conflict almost from the start. Tar Heels called the waters off Cape Hatteras "Torpedo Junction" because of German submarine activity there. Time and again, the submarines fired on oil tankers sailing out of the Gulf of Mexico. Burning oil slicks became a common sight. Regional hospitals in North Carolina set up special burn units to take care of badly injured sailors. When the bodies of four British sailors washed ashore at Ocracoke, Tar Heels buried them in a cemetery still maintained today by the United States Coast Guard.

North Carolina also had more military installations than almost any other state. Millions of fighting troops trained at bases such as the ones on the map below. Some Allied soldiers also received special training in North Carolina.

As in other states, the defense boom helped pull North Carolina out of the Depression. Nearly $2 billion of the more than $10 billion in federal contracts for war materials went to North Carolina. Shipyards at Elizabeth City, New Bern, and Wilmington built submarine chasers, minesweepers,

Think as a Geographer

*I*nformation in the text and on the map show some of North Carolina's contributions to the war.
■ *To Do:* Working individually or in small groups, draw a poster showing how North Carolina used its human and natural resources to help the nation achieve victory in World War II.

Maps Matter

This map shows the distribution of military bases in North Carolina during World War II. ■*To Do:* Why might German submarines prowl North Carolina waters? Compare this map with the county map at the back of the book. Were any military bases or POW camps in your county? If so, which ones?

World War II Military Installations

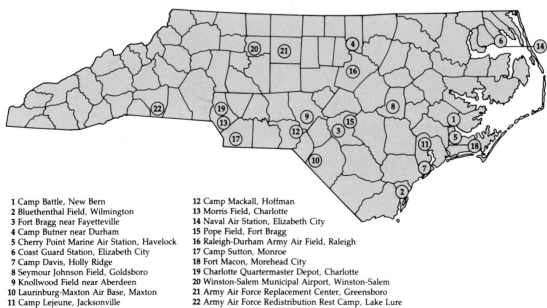

1 Camp Battle, New Bern
2 Bluethenthal Field, Wilmington
3 Fort Bragg near Fayetteville
4 Camp Butner near Durham
5 Cherry Point Marine Air Station, Havelock
6 Coast Guard Station, Elizabeth City
7 Camp Davis, Holly Ridge
8 Seymour Johnson Field, Goldsboro
9 Knollwood Field near Aberdeen
10 Laurinburg-Maxton Air Base, Maxton
11 Camp Lejeune, Jacksonville
12 Camp Mackall, Hoffman
13 Morris Field, Charlotte
14 Naval Air Station, Elizabeth City
15 Pope Field, Fort Bragg
16 Raleigh-Durham Army Air Field, Raleigh
17 Camp Sutton, Monroe
18 Fort Macon, Morehead City
19 Charlotte Quartermaster Depot, Charlotte
20 Winston-Salem Municipal Airport, Winston-Salem
21 Army Air Force Replacement Center, Greensboro
22 Army Air Force Redistribution Rest Camp, Lake Lure

A paratrooper getting ready to jump at Fort Bragg during World War II. At this time, the Air Force was part of the other services. However, the Department of Defense soon made the Air Force a separate military service. Why do you think officials took this action?

and merchant ships. Textile mills produced everything from sheets to parachutes for the troops.

Both factories and farms mobilized for war. Some manufacturers converted from peacetime goods to such things as rockets, bomb clusters, and radar equipment. Lumber for barracks, bunks, and boxes also came from North Carolina. So did stone for roads, mica for insulation, and tungsten for hardening steel. W. Kerr Scott, the state's commissioner of agriculture, also praised farmers for their output of "food, feed, and fibre." Throughout the war, North Carolina ranked either third or fourth in farm output.

On the home front. Nearly one million men and women helped fill North Carolina's defense contracts. As in World War I, women worked alongside men in manufacturing, construction, and other jobs formerly limited to men. Some positions required women to wear slacks for safety reasons, marking the start of a new fashion that has lasted to this day.

To deal with labor shortages, North Carolina took unusual measures. Although few people knew it at the time, the Defense Department opened some prisoner-of-war camps in North Carolina. The state used these prisoners for such labor as harvesting cotton and peanuts.

Throughout the state, Tar Heels reached out to help men and women overseas. They joined with other Americans in buying war bonds. Money raised by the sale of bonds in North Carolina purchased 14 ambulance planes—more than any other state. North Carolina, like other states, distributed ration books, or books of coupons provided by the federal government to deal with wartime shortages. **Rationing** ensured that everyone got a fair share of scarce items such as shoes, gasoline, rubber and metal products, and foods such as coffee, meat, sugar, and butter. To contribute to the war effort, some people planted Victory gardens and supported recycling drives. Others wore canvas shoes instead of leather. In this way, they made sure that the fighting troops received the supplies they needed.

Breaking the Axis. The rush of fresh United States troops helped turn the course of the war. Around 361,000 men and women from North Carolina served in the armed forces—258,000 in the Army, 90,000 in the Navy, and 13,000 in the Marines. Women did not serve in active combat, but they took positions as drivers, aircraft mechanics, parachute riggers, aerial gunnery instructors, and nurses. Dr. Margaret O. Craighill of Southport was one of the first women to receive the rank of major in the Army Medical Corps.

Most North Carolinians saw action along European fronts. The Allies had decided to crush Germany and Italy, then Japan. From 1942 to 1944, airplanes pounded away at Nazi strongholds. Then on June 6, 1944—known by the code name **D-Day**—the Allies launched a massive invasion of Nazi-occupied Europe. Some 130,000 Allied soldiers under the command of United States General Dwight D. Eisenhower landed on the beaches of Normandy in France. From there, they fought their way east. The Soviets, who joined the Allies after Hitler's attack, pushed west. Meanwhile, other troops landed in North Africa and still others went into Italy. By May 1945, the Allies were within reach of Hitler. Rather than surrender, Hitler killed himself.

The war in Europe ended, but not the horror. As Soviet and Allied troops entered Nazi-occupied territory, especially in eastern Europe, they uncovered the Nazi death camps. The Nazi leaders who ran the camps were charged with war crimes against the human race. At the war's end, most were tried and convicted at what became known as the **Nuremberg Trials** in Germany.

A deadly cloud over Japan. With Europe in ruins, defeat of Japan fell largely to the United States. Efforts to drive the Japanese from islands in the Pacific led to some of the bloodiest battles of the war. The Japanese, however, refused to surrender. President Harry S Truman, who took over after the death of FDR in 1945, faced a difficult decision. The United States possessed a terrible new weapon of war—the atom bomb. Should he fight on in the Pacific at a great loss of life? Or should he drop the bomb and end the war quickly?

On August 6, 1945, the world learned Truman's decision. A single plane dropped a single bomb on the military base city of Hiroshima, Japan. A huge mushroom cloud appeared in the sky as the city melted under the bomb's full force. When the Japanese did not surrender, the United States dropped a second bomb on Nagasaki. On August 11, the Japanese surrendered. World War II drew to a close, and a new and deadly atomic age opened.

Hiroshima after the atom bomb. (Inset) The atom bomb being tested. How did this new weapon change the nature of modern warfare?

Think Twice

1. How did dictators take power in Europe and Asia?
2. How did World War II begin?
3. Why did the United States delay entry into the war?
4. How did North Carolinians contribute to the war effort?
5. What factors played a role in Truman's decision to drop the atom bomb on Japan?
6. Some experts say that World War II shattered United States isolationism forever. Do you agree or disagree? What arguments support your answer?

People, Places, Terms

Cold War
atomic fallout
totalitarian
satellite
arms race
containment
Sputnik I

3 The Cold War

In 1947, a research team set up camp on Topsail Island in the Outer Banks. Topsail was small, but it suited the needs of the research team perfectly. Tucked away between the Intracoastal Waterway and the Atlantic Ocean, this isolated island was safe from prying eyes. On Topsail, researchers began work on a secret rocketry project.

United States officials believed that when Soviet troops marched into Germany, they seized many of the scientists who had worked on rocketry projects. However, the United States had its experts, too, including German-born scientist Albert Einstein. The Topsail project was part of a government plan to beat the Soviets into space. This race into space was part of the **Cold War**—the war without bullets—between the United States and the Soviet Union that developed after World War II.

Searching for peace. As World War II ended, people could see that the stakes for peace were high. Development of the atom bomb changed international relations forever. No nation in the world could hope to escape **atomic fallout,** or the tiny radioactive particles carried by global wind currents after an atomic explosion. Shortly before the end of World War II, President Truman, recognizing dangers posed by atomic weapons, suggested the creation of a new international peacekeeping organization—the United Nations. Commented Truman, "If we do not want to die together in war, we must live together in peace."

In April 1945, fifty nations met in San Francisco. There they drew up the United Nations Charter.

Primary Source

We the people of the United Nations determined
to save succeeding generations from the scourge [suffering]
*   of war, which twice in our lifetime has brought untold*
*   sorrow to mankind, and*
to reaffirm faith in fundamental human rights, in the
*   dignity and worth of the human person, in the equal*
*   rights of men and women and of nations large and small,*
*   and*
to establish conditions under which justice and respect for . . .
*   international law can be maintained, and*
to promote social progress and better standards of life in
*   larger freedom.*

— "Preamble to the United Nations Charter"

In the midst of war, the United Nations Charter held out a ray of hope for future peace. However, sharp differences soon emerged between the Soviet Union and United States. As the Soviet Union encouraged the spread of communism, the United States saw itself as the guardian of democracy for all.

A war without bullets.   The wartime alliance between the United States and the Soviet Union broke down as soon as Germany surrendered. When the Soviets occupied Eastern Europe, Stalin had promised to hold democratic elections. Instead, he set up **totalitarian** governments that controlled all aspects of life. An "iron curtain," said Winston Churchill, had descended across Europe. The invisible curtain kept democracy from reaching the ring of **satellites,** or nations ruled by another country, that the Soviets had set up around their western border.

In 1947, after an international conference, President Truman confided his thoughts about Stalin to his daughter Margaret: "There is no difference in totalitarian or police states, call them what you may, Nazi, Fascist [Mussolini's party], Communist. . . . The attempt of Stalin . . . to fool the world . . . is just like Hitler's and Mussolini's [lies]. . . "

With the breakdown of the wartime alliance came the Cold War between the United States and the Soviet Union and its satellites. Each side entered into a deadly **arms race,** producing vast stores of weapons. The Soviet Union did not possess the atom bomb until the end of the decade, but this fact did not lessen United States fears.

Turning up the heat.   To prevent the Soviets from getting a foothold in other parts of the world, Truman offered a massive package of aid to war-torn nations. United States aid helped strengthen the nations of Western Europe— those European governments outside Soviet control. United States aid kept Turkey and Greece free as well. Truman called his actions **containment,** a policy aimed at stopping the spread of communism.

A showdown between the Americans and Soviets took place in Germany. The Soviets refused to give up lands occupied in the war. As a result, in 1948, the world saw the creation of two Germanys—democratic West Germany and Communist East Germany. The conflict did not stop there, though. The capital of Germany, Berlin, sat right in the middle of East Germany. As a result, it too was divided.

In 1949, the Soviets cut off all supply routes through East Germany into West Berlin. Truman acted swiftly, ordering a massive airlift into the divided city. The constant flight of United States planes into West Berlin forced the Soviets to back down.

President Harry S Truman is shown here addressing a session of the United Nations.

When the Soviets fired *Sputnik I* (above) into orbit, they fueled United States ambition to aim even higher—a shot at the moon.

The situation grew more tense as the 1950s began. In late 1949, the Soviets exploded their first atom bomb. In 1957, they created a new kind of **satellite**—an information-gathering instrument that circled Earth in outer space. News of *Sputnik I,* as the satellite was called, confirmed United States fears about Soviet knowledge of rocketry. Another shock wave followed in 1959 when Fidel Castro set up Communist rule in Cuba.

The United States did not sit idly by. The Presidents who followed Truman continued the policy of containment. They also stepped up the space race begun at Topsail. President John F. Kennedy announced that the nation would place humans on the moon by 1969—a goal that the nation kept.

Kennedy also backed Cuban exiles who tried unsuccessfully to launch an invasion to topple Castro. The failed incident at the Bay of Pigs embarrassed the United States and encouraged the Soviets to set up missile bases in Cuba. When the United States discovered the missiles, Kennedy ordered ships to seal off the island. For days, the world held its breath as the United States and the Soviet Union teetered on the edge of war. In the end, the Soviets pulled out the missiles. In describing the Cuban missile crisis, Secretary of State Dean Rusk said to reporters, "Remember when you report this, that eyeball to eyeball, they [the Soviets] blinked first."

The Korean War. In the 1950s and 1960s, events took a serious turn in Asia. A civil war in China had resulted in the creation of the People's Republic of China. Its Communist leader, Mao Zedong, backed Communist rebellions elsewhere in Asia. Sometimes Mao had the support of the

A Hero from North Carolina

Some 543,000 Americans served in the Vietnam War. Of this number, 46,397 lost their lives in combat. Included in the casualties were 1,282 North Carolinians. Thousands of troops also spent time in horrible North Vietnamese prison camps. Most heroically refused to lend their support to Communists, who sought to discredit the United States. One of the heroes who stood firm was Air Force Captain Norman Alexander McDaniel of Fayetteville.

McDaniel fell into North Vietnamese hands in 1966 when his plane was shot down. He spent nearly seven years as a prisoner of war, or POW. As an African American, McDaniel received special treatment. The North Vietnamese knew about racial troubles in the United States. As a result, they pushed McDaniel to tell African American soldiers not to fight. "I would tell them no," McDaniel later recalled, "This is not a black-white war. We're in Vietnam trying to help the South Vietnamese." For such remarks, the North Vietnamese beat McDaniel and denied him food. McDaniel's love of the United States and his religious faith helped him to survive. In the 1980s, African American reporter Wallace Terry interviewed McDaniel and other African Americans who served in Vietnam. Terry told their stories in a best-selling book entitled *Bloods,* a name of racial pride taken by many African Americans who had served in the war.

Soviets. Sometimes the two nations quarreled. Nonetheless, the prospect of two huge Communist powers in control of a continent gravely concerned the United States.

Crises developed in two divided nations—Korea and Vietnam. The division of Korea had taken place when the Soviets refused to give up lands in the north at the end of World War II. The result was a Communist-backed North Korea and a United States-backed South Korea. In 1950, the North Koreans launched an invasion to unite the Koreas. The United Nations sent in troops from 15 nations to help the South Koreans, while the People's Republic supplied troops to the North Koreans. During the three-year conflict, 876 North Carolinians lost their lives. In the end, neither side claimed victory. Korea remains divided.

Bitterness over the Korean War split Americans apart. Some favored use of the atom bomb. Others felt the United States should not involve itself in outside conflicts. When the nation later intervened in Vietnam, this debate grew.

The war in Vietnam. At the end of World War II, the Vietnamese successfully rebelled against their French rulers. However, conflicts between Communist and anti-Communist forces led to civil war—and another divided nation. In the mid-1960s, it seemed that Communist North Vietnam might take over South Vietnam. President Lyndon B. Johnson decided to send United States troops into South Vietnam. Johnson expected a quick victory. Instead the Vietnam War dragged on for years and caused deep divisions among Americans.

When the United States finally withdrew from Vietnam in 1973, South Vietnam fell to Communist control. The experience of Vietnam again forced Americans to reexamine the price of intervening in conflicts around the world. Some wondered if the United States would ever again enter a world conflict in defense of democracy. The answer came, as you will see in Chapter 22, when the United States led United Nations troops in the Persian Gulf War of 1991.

Vietnam Memorial on Capitol Square, Raleigh.

Think Twice

1. What were the goals of the United Nations?
2. Why did President Truman start a policy of containment?
3. How did each of the following nations become divided: Germany, Korea, Vietnam?
4. Why did the Americans undertake a space race?
5. Imagine you are an adviser to the President in either the Korean War or the Vietnam War. What are the pros and cons of using the atom bomb in either conflict? What advice would you offer?

Chapter 21 Review

Choose from the following menu of activities.

Think Back: Main Ideas

North Carolina played an important role in helping the United States meet some of its gravest challenges of the 1900s. To assess the state's contribution during these difficult years, answer the following questions.

1. How did North Carolina encourage self-help in dealing with the Great Depression?
2. How did each of the following groups of North Carolinians help the United States achieve victory in World War II: (a) farmers, (b) manufacturers, (c) soldiers, (d) women?
3. Why did North Carolinians take pride in the rocketry experiments on Topsail Island?
4. How did events in Korea and Vietnam affect North Carolina?

Maps Matter

To study United States involvement in world affairs during the period covered by this chapter, complete the following activities.

1. Skim through the chapter and make a list of all the places or events outside the United States that touched Americans during the years 1929–1973. After each place or event, write a sentence explaining its significance.
2. Next, turn to the world map at the back of the book. Find the location of each of the places or events in your list. Based on your map study, write a generalization about United States involvement in world affairs during the period covered. (Remember, a generalization is a true statement based upon the available facts.)

Word Wizard

Review the definition of each term below. Then write a question in which each term is the answer.

depression	communism	satellite
totalitarian	dictators	cold war
holocaust	arms race	

Working Cooperatively

During the Depression, Governor O. Max Gardner turned to the Brookings Institution in Washington, D.C., for advice on how "to promote increased efficiency and economy in the . . . affairs of the State." This independent organization investigated and analyzed conditions in North Carolina and prepared suggestions for improvement. Working in small groups, find out what the institution proposed and present your findings to your class.

Curriculum Connection

Read these lyrics from a song about the Dust Bowl entitled "Goin' Down the Road." Then answer the questions that follow.

I'm goin' where the dust storms never blow,
I'm goin' where the dust storms never blow,
I'm goin' where the dust storms never blow, Lord, Lord,
And I ain't gonna be treated thisaway.

I'm lookin' for a job with honest pay,
I'm lookin' for a job with honest pay,
I'm lookin' for a job with honest pay, Lord, Lord,
And I ain't gonna be treated thisaway.

I can't live on cornbread and beans,
I can't live on cornbread and beans,
I can't live on cornbread and beans, Lord, Lord,
And I ain't gonna be treated thisaway.

1. What conditions during the Great Depression is the songwriter protesting?
2. What evidence in this chapter supports the accuracy of the song's lyrics?
3. Imagine you are the songwriter. Write a letter to President Roosevelt describing the plight of people fleeing the Dust Bowl.

Learning through Literature

Farewell to Manzanar, by Jeanne Wakatuski Houston
Unhailed Heroes, Stories of Vietnam Veterans, by Manteo High School Students

Building for the Future

1953 Commission on the Reorganization of State Government is created.

1954 *Brown* v. *Board of Education of Topeka, Kansas*

1955 Montgomery bus boycott

1956 Pearsall Plan

1956 United States Supreme Court rules segregation on public transportation unconstitutional.

1960 African Americans stage "sit-in" in Greensboro.

1963 North Carolina Fund is created.

1963 Martin Luther King, Jr., leads rally against segregation in Washington, D.C.

1964 King receives Nobel Peace Prize. Civil Rights Act.

1969 Charlotte ordered to integrate schools.

1969 NASA lands people on the moon.

1970 Executive Organization Act

1971 Environmental Policy Act

1972 United States Congress passes Equal Rights Amendment but states fail to approve it.

1974 Susie Marshall Sharp is first woman to serve as chief justice of North Carolina Supreme Court.

1974 United States Supreme Court orders schools to provide bilingual education for children who do not speak English.

1977 *Voyager 2* spacecraft is launched.

1981 Commission on the Future of North Carolina is created.

1981 NASA's first space shuttle, *Columbia*, is launched. Sandra Day O'Connor becomes the first woman in the United States Supreme Court.

1983 Henry E. Frye becomes first African American on state Supreme Court.

1990 Census results require state to reorganize congressional districts.

1990 Gulf War begins as Iraq invades Kuwait.

1991 United States soldiers attack Iraqi forces.

What's Ahead

Chapter 22
The United States and the World in the Twentieth Century

Chapter 23
North Carolina Today

Chapter 22

The United States and the World in the Twentieth Century

The twentieth century was a time of great change.

After World War II, the United States entered a period of rapid growth, both in population and in industry. More people than ever before enjoyed the fruits of this growth—a home in the suburbs, a car or even two cars, modern appliances. Even so, millions of people did not share in this new prosperity. Some coal mines in Appalachia gave out. As a result, people there had no jobs and lived in extreme poverty. People in inner cities—many of whom were Hispanics and African Americans—also faced hardship as businesses and jobs moved to the suburbs.

The second half of the twentieth century saw many other changes as well. Women's roles changed at home and at work. African Americans and other groups made significant gains in their struggle for the right to equal treatment under the law. Technological innovations made important changes in everything from the way food is cooked to the way war is waged.

Astronaut on the moon's surface ▶

Think Ahead

As you read about the changes in the twentieth century, think about the ways these changes affect your life.

1 Twentieth-Century Trends

In the twentieth century, the nation began changing in some new and unexpected ways. American cities grew, extended by sprawling suburbs into the countryside. At home and at work, men and women filled new roles.

New industries. By the end of World War II, the United States had become the world's leading industrial nation. As new industries developed, new kinds of jobs opened up. A trend that had begun in the early 1900s continued, as fewer and fewer people worked in agriculture or in small businesses and more began working for large companies. After 1945, the nation's economy began to shift from manufacturing industries to service industries. Instead of producing goods, many people worked as scientists, doctors, nurses, repair persons, computer programmers, and the like.

Women in the work force. After the 1960s, the number of women workers rose sharply. By the 1980s, well over half of America's women held jobs outside the home. Women entered new industries and held a greater variety of jobs than ever before. While most working women still held low-paying jobs, more and more women began entering professions as doctors, lawyers, engineers, and so on. A few true pioneers became construction workers, airplane pilots, fire fighters, and police officers. Women also began to play a greater role in government, winning state and national offices.

A nation of consumers. After World War II, Americans entered the most prosperous time in their history. During the war, factories had expanded to make weapons, airplanes, and other war materials. After the war, these plants switched to making peacetime products—cars, radios, appliances, and clothing. After 1945, the number of such consumer goods produced in the nation doubled every ten years. This growth, with the increase in services, gave Americans the most comfortable life-style in the world.

After the war, the buying power of the average American worker more than doubled. Workers rushed to make up for wartime sacrifices by buying goods to make their lives easier and more fun. Later, as women entered the workforce in greater numbers, they provided a new market for consumer goods. Since many families had more money, children's buying power increased. Makers of such items as jeans, athletic shoes, and transistor radios made huge profits from young shoppers.

In 1981, President Reagan named the first woman, Sandra Day O'Connor, to serve on the Supreme Court.

T he post-war home-building boom set off a chain reaction of producing and buying. Builders needed lumber and tools. New and growing towns had to build new streets and schools. ■ *To Do*: What other products can you think of that would be needed? How might the building of suburban shopping malls be related to the building boom?

Levittown, one of the first housing developments after World War II, was built using mass production techniques.

World markets and competition. For decades after the war, the United States dominated the world market for manufactured goods and agricultural products. However, as other nations rebuilt their factories, they began to offer sharp competition to United States industries. Often these nations could offer goods more cheaply than manufacturers at home could. The balance shifted from exporting goods to importing goods. American manufacturers are still scrambling to meet global competition for clothing, cars, cameras, and electronic goods.

New homes in the suburbs. With changes in the work force came changes in living conditions. Early in the century, Americans moved from farms to cities, where growing industries were located. After World War II, improvements in transportation allowed many workers to move outside the cities to the suburbs and commute to their jobs by car or train. Meanwhile, other Americans—including many African Americans and Hispanics—moved into the cities looking for greater opportunities and prosperity for themselves.

To provide homes for the millions of couples who moved to the suburbs to raise their children, builders put up houses quickly and cheaply. In the late 1940s, one builder, William Levitt, built 17,000 homes on former potato fields on Long Island, New York. By 1990, more Americans lived in the suburbs than in cities.

Changing population. At the end of World War II, husbands and wives were reunited, and sweethearts married. In prosperous peacetime, many couples started

families, touching off a baby boom that added greatly to the United States population. As you will read below, thousands of immigrants arrived, swelling the population even more. Between 1950 and 1970, the population grew by more than 50 million people.

Americans have always been on the move. Each year about one fifth of the nation's people move—for better job opportunities, lower taxes, sunnier weather. Some head for the Sunbelt, others for the Pacific and Rocky Mountain states, leaving the Northeast and the North Central states.

Immigrants. Laws passed in the 1920s limited or banned immigration from some countries. Under those laws, for example, only 100 Chinese immigrants could settle in the United States each year, yet thousands could come from Western European countries. During the 1960s, Congress passed a new immigration law, which still limited the total number of immigrants, but no longer played favorites among countries. The law also made immigration easier for **refugees**—people who flee their own country out of fear of being persecuted or killed for their political beliefs.

Today about 80 percent of immigrants come from Latin America and Asia. They include Cuban refugees escaping from the Communist dictatorship in their country and Central Americans leaving countries torn by years of civil war. More recently, boat loads of people have come from the French-speaking Caribbean island of Haiti, where a military coup toppled the elected government in 1991.

Asians come from many different countries—India, China, South Korea, the Philippines, and the countries of Southeast Asia. Many are Vietnamese who fled after the Communists took over in the mid-1970s. Others have come seeking refuge from the unrest in the nearby countries of Cambodia, Laos, and Thailand.

***

Graphs Teach

These two graphs compare immigration in the past with immigration in the future. ■ *To Do*: What is happening to the number of immigrants from Europe? Add the figures for all the Latin American areas on the second graph, and then make a general statement about the source of immigration in the future.

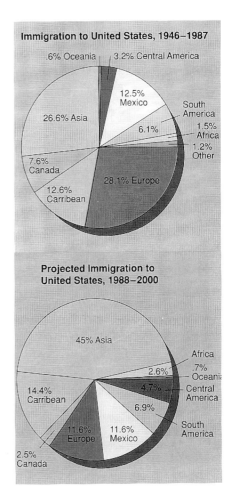

Think Twice

1. What is the difference between manufacturing industries and service industries?
2. How have roles for women and men changed in the twentieth century?
3. What are consumer goods?
4. What is the origin of most of today's immigrants?
5. How do you think life-styles will change in the next 50 years?

The Struggle for Human Rights

People, Places, Terms

segregate
Rosa Parks
Brown v. *Board of Education of Topeka*
Martin Luther King, Jr.
bilingual education
Equal Rights Amendment

Most African Americans did not share in the post-war prosperity. For them, prejudice limited opportunities for education and jobs. In many parts of the country, African Americans were denied their civil rights. Some Southern states had laws making it almost impossible for most African Americans to vote. Many states, particularly in the South, had laws that **segregated** African Americans from other Americans. African Americans had to go to separate schools, eat at separate restaurants, and sit in separate parts of buses and trains. Restrooms and water fountains were also separate. Usually, the facilities for African Americans were inferior to those provided for other Americans. African Americans who dared to challenge these conditions often risked injury to themselves or their property—or even death.

Challenging segregation. Despite the danger, many African Americans took courageous steps to challenge segregation. The parents of a young African American girl, Linda Brown, took one such step when they decided to send their daughter to an all-white school near their home in Topeka, Kansas. School officials turned Linda away, but her parents, aided by lawyers from the NAACP (National Association for the Advancement of Colored People),

Rosa Parks is shown below as she enters the Montgomery County Courthouse.

The Montgomery Bus Boycott

African Americans challenged other state laws. One of these was the Alabama law that required African Americans to sit at the back of a bus and to give up their seats to white riders if the bus became crowded. In 1955, Rosa Parks, Executive Secretary of the Alabama NAACP and a respected member of the African American community, boarded a bus in Montgomery, Alabama, after a long, tiring day. She sat in the first row of the "colored" section. When the bus filled up, the driver ordered her to give up her seat to a white man. Parks refused, and the driver had her arrested. Parks took her case to court.

The day after Parks was arrested, leaders of the African American community called a meeting. They decided that the time was right to execute a long-planned boycott of the city's buses. For more than a year, while the lawyers debated, the city's African Americans walked to work or formed carpools. With its nearly empty buses rumbling along the streets, the bus company steadily lost money. Finally, in 1956, the Supreme Court decided that segregation in public transportation is unconstitutional. On December 21, 1956, the boycott leaders boarded a Montgomery bus and, in a symbolic gesture, sat in the front.

fought for their rights. The case, **Brown v. Board of Education of Topeka,** went all the way to the Supreme Court, which in 1954 ruled that segregation in public schools is unconstitutional.

Winning a court case was one thing; making sure that the decision was carried out was another. Some communities quietly integrated their schools. In others, when African American students tried to attend white schools they faced angry crowds. Federal troops had to protect the students from the threatening mobs. Some communities even tried to close their schools rather than integrate them.

The March on Washington.   One of the leaders of the Montgomery boycott was a young African American minister from Georgia named Martin Luther King, Jr. A believer in nonviolent methods, King led many protests against segregation. The largest took place in August 1963, when more than 200,000 Americans joined a rally in Washington, D.C., urging Congress to pass civil rights laws. King's stirring speech at the rally moved the audience and the nation.

Primary Source

I have a dream that one day on the red hills of Georgia, the sons of former slaves and the sons of former slave owners will be able to sit together at the table of brotherhood. . . . I have a dream that my four little children will one day live in a nation where they will not be judged by the color of their skin but by the content of their character.

— MARTIN LUTHER KING, JR., *"Speech at the March on Washington"*

Martin Luther King, Jr. addressed the crowd at the March on Washington in August 1963.

Native Americans from the Southwest, joined by others on their route, walk to the nation's capital to protest treaty violations.

In 1964, King received the Nobel Peace Prize for his leadership in bringing equal rights to all people. Four years later, he was shot and killed in Memphis, Tennessee—a victim of the violence he had always opposed. The nation mourned the loss of a great leader.

The work of King and other Americans brought about many changes. During the 1960s, Congress passed several new laws, making it illegal to deny anyone a job or the right to vote because of his or her ancestors, race, or sex. Only integrated schools could receive federal funds, and companies that did not offer all workers an equal chance to get ahead could no longer do business with the federal government and faced other limits as well.

Hispanic Americans. People who come from Spanish-speaking countries—or whose parents or ancestors did—are Hispanic Americans. The two largest groups of Hispanic Americans in the United States are Mexican Americans and Puerto Ricans. Like African Americans, Hispanics have faced problems getting good jobs, education, and housing.

In 1974, one group of Hispanic Americans won an important victory. The Supreme Court ruled that schools must provide **bilingual education** for children who do not speak English. In other words, schools must teach those children in their own language as well as in the English language.

Native Americans. Native Americans suffered unique kinds of injustices. Once they had been able to use all the continent's land and resources, but by the 1880s, most Native Americans had been forced onto reservations by the United States government. Today about half the Native Americans in the country live on or near a reservation. Many live in poverty.

In the 1960s, Native Americans began to demand better opportunities and to protest unfair treatment. By the 1970s, several court decisions forced the United States government to honor old treaties, either by paying the Native Americans for their lost land or by returning the land to them.

Women and the Equal Rights Amendment.   Women gained the right to vote by 1920, yet as late as the 1960s, they did not have many of the same opportunities as men. Employers paid women workers only about half as much as men, and women were excluded from many careers. The Civil Rights Act of 1964 had forbidden unequal treatment based on sex. As with African Americans, however, the law did not wipe out all inequalities.

Many women hoped a constitutional amendment would help end unequal treatment based on sex. Although Congress passed the **Equal Rights Amendment** (ERA) in 1972, not enough states approved it. Opponents claimed the ERA would destroy the traditional American family, result in women serving in combat, and otherwise harm women. Though the ERA wasn't approved, Congress did pass laws guaranteeing equal job opportunities for women and men, as well as equal pay for equal work.

Older Americans.   In recent times, older Americans have worked to end unequal treatment based on age. They have formed groups—such as the American Association of Retired People and the Gray Panthers—to fight for their goals. As a result of their efforts, Congress raised the age at which people must retire from 65 to 70. Older Americans continue to fight for equal treatment in hiring and other concerns.

Physically challenged Americans.   Physically challenged Americans have also demanded equal opportunities. In the 1970s, Congress stated that people cannot be denied jobs for which they are qualified just because they are physically challenged. Physically challenged people must be given equal educational opportunities, and public buildings must be accessible to physically challenged people. That is, they must have such things as ramps for wheelchairs and Braille numbers on elevator buttons.

Special parking spaces near ramps allow the physically challenged access to public places.

Think Twice

1. How did new laws and court rulings help African Americans, Hispanics, and Native Americans?
2. What goals did older Americans and disabled Americans work for?
3. Why is it that not all Americans have the same opportunities, despite laws forbidding unequal treatment?

3 Frontiers of Science and Technology

The need for new technology during World War II produced a number of discoveries and inventions. Among them were radar, jet engines, synthetic materials, and the atom bomb. From such inventions came others—such as antibiotics and new vaccines—that have revolutionized life in the United States and around the world.

The Space Age.   As you have read, the United States beefed up its space research after the launching of *Sputnik I.* To meet the challenge to American space technology, the federal government created **NASA,** the National Aeronautics and Space Administration. Over the next decade, NASA trained astronauts, developed a space capsule, and ran test flights.

In July 1969, NASA achieved one of its major goals—to be the first to land humans on the moon. As astronaut Michael Collins orbited the moon in the spacecraft *Apollo 11,* Neil Armstrong and Edwin Aldrin, Jr. set the landing craft—the *Eagle*—on the moon. "That's one small step for a man," said Armstrong as he stepped on lunar soil, "but one giant leap for mankind."

During the next twenty years, NASA concentrated on the development of **space shuttles,** spacecraft that could return to earth under their own power. NASA launched its first shuttle—*Columbia*—in 1981. Later the shuttle *Challenger* carried into space the first American woman astronaut—Sally Ride—as well as the first African American astronaut—Guy Bluford. A chilling reminder of the dangers of space missions came in 1986, when the *Challenger* exploded seconds after lift-off, killing all seven crew members.

Over the years, NASA spacecraft have been sending a variety of scientific data back to Earth. Satellites provide weather information, help in mapping the earth, and are also used in transmitting television, radio, and telephone signals. Astronauts on the various shuttles have run numerous scientific experiments and have recorded the effects of weightlessness and radiation on people, animals, and plant life.

One of the most ambitious projects is the *Voyager 2,* which was launched on a journey of billions of miles in 1977. After sending back pictures of Jupiter, Saturn, and Uranus, *Voyager 2* reached Neptune in 1989. From there, it left the solar system and headed toward the stars. It has enough fuel to keep it going beyond the year 2000.

The 1988 launch of the shuttle *Discovery* was the first after the *Challenger* explosion in 1986.

Communications.   Some of the most significant changes in technology occurred in communications. Telephone answering machines, cordless phones, computerized calling, fax machines, and cellular phones have all become part of our lives within the past few decades.

One of the most dramatic breakthroughs of the post-World War II years was television. In 1945, most Americans had never seen a TV. By 1960, almost every family had one. TV became the nation's main source of information and entertainment. The world shrank as people watched the news—transmitted live by satellite—of the *Challenger* explosion in 1986, the fall of the Berlin Wall in 1989, and the Gulf War in 1991.

Developed in the 1940s, the computer came into its own during the 1980s. Computers store, recall, and process large amounts of information. Today they affect almost every area of our lives—reading labels in stores; sending mail to its proper destination; controlling working parts in car, bus, train, and aircraft engines; and helping people make airline reservations, run factories, and keep accounts. Computers are used in telephone systems and in printing books, magazines, and newspapers. Scientists use them to predict weather patterns and to solve complex problems.

Medical advances.   New technology and research have greatly changed medicine. Once-feared diseases such as polio and scarlet fever can be cured or prevented with the use of new drugs and vaccines. More powerful microscopes, miniaturized equipment, and lasers allow surgeons to perform delicate operations on the brain and other parts of the body. Heart pacemakers and organ transplants save thousands of patients and allow them to live more normal lives. Tiny, insect-sized robots will soon travel in the body, monitoring blood pressure and aiding the body's natural systems.

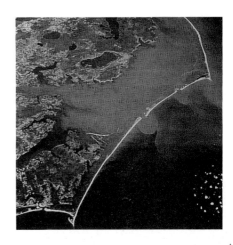

Satellite images are used in mapmaking and in weather forecasting. Shown here is a satellite image of the Outer Banks.

Think Twice

1. Who were the first humans on the moon?
2. What kind of information do satellites provide?
3. Name three ways people use computers.
4. Describe something that you wish someone would invent.

People, Places, Terms

George Bush
AIDS
recession
Soviet Union
Mikhail Gorbachev
glasnost
Berlin Wall
free enterprise system
Persian Gulf
Saddam Hussein

4 America and the World

In 1988, Republican George Bush, Vice President under Ronald Reagan, was elected President. During his term as President, the nation faced many worrisome problems at home—illegal drugs, a growing AIDS epidemic, a sluggish economy. Great changes occurred in the Soviet Union and in Eastern Europe, and the United States went to war in the Persian Gulf region.

The war on drugs.   Illegal drug use was not new to the 1980s or even to the twentieth century, but it was growing at an alarming rate. Bush proposed an all-out war on drugs with an $8 billion program. Much of the money was to be used in trying to prevent the smuggling of drugs from Colombia and Panama and other Latin American countries rather than in education to prevent drug use or in programs to help users quit. Money was also to go to local drug enforcement agencies to help catch those who sell the drugs on the streets. So far, the program has had little or no effect. When smugglers or dealers are caught, others are ready to take their place, lured by the huge profits.

AIDS.   First identified in the late 1970s, **AIDS**—*Acquired Immune Deficiency Syndrome*—is caused by a deadly virus that attacks the body's ability to fight disease. Scientists have found a few drugs that seem to be of some help in treating the disease, so AIDS patients are now living a little longer. No one has found a cure or a vaccine to prevent AIDS, though, and many people are concerned that the federal government is not spending enough money on AIDS research. As of May 31, 1991, nearly 180,000

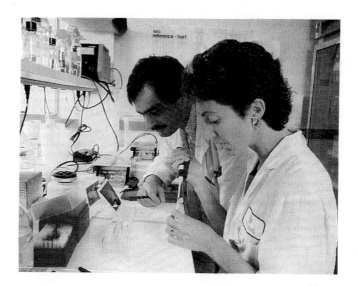

Researchers are seeking a cure for AIDS. Worldwide, the disease is growing even faster than it is in the United States. The World Health Organization predicts that 40 million people will be infected by the virus by the year 2000.

Americans had the disease. In 1990 alone, AIDS killed over 24,000 Americans, a 13 percent increase over the year before.

Recession.   Another challenge of the Bush years was the **recession,** or downturn in the nation's economy. Some companies went out of business; others cut back production and laid off workers. People were out of work for so long that their unemployment benefits were running out. To help these people, Congress voted to extend the time that benefits would be paid. As of the spring of 1992, the recession showed little sign of ending.

A new era in the Soviet Union.   In March 1985, a new leader, Mikhail Gorbachev, took power in the **Soviet Union.** For years, the Soviet Union had been spending vast amounts of money on weapons and its armed forces. Since 1979, it had been helping the Communist rulers of Afghanistan fight rebels who were trying to take over the government there. Meanwhile, the Soviet Union's economy was in dire straits. There were shortages of everything from milk to cars. Few people could afford to buy anything beyond the barest necessities, and even those who had money could not find goods on the shelves of the nation's stores.

Gorbachev decided that money should be diverted from the military to the needs of the people. Accordingly, he ordered the withdrawal of troops from Afghanistan and cut back on the number of troops stationed in Eastern Europe. At home, he instituted a policy of **glasnost,** or openness, which encouraged Soviet citizens to discuss ways of revitalizing their society. This was a huge breakthrough, since all previous Communist leaders had severely punished those who spoke against the government. Under Gorbachev, elections were opened up so that voters had more choice in candidates for the Soviet Union's legislative body.

Under communism, a central agency controlled agriculture and industry. The agency told factories and farms how much to produce, what wages to pay workers, and what prices to charge customers. Since the agency often failed to recognize what people wanted, large supplies of some goods sat unwanted on store shelves while others were unavailable. Workers had no reason to work harder, because they received the same wage no matter what they did. Gorbachev tried to give local managers greater control over their farms and factories and encouragied them to rely on profits rather than government funding to operate their businesses.

Eastern Europe.   From time to time, revolts against Communist rule had erupted in Eastern European countries. Each revolt was suppressed with the aid of

Mikhail Gorbachev started great changes in the Soviet Union, changes that echoed around the world.

Soviet troops. When Gorbachev declared that the Soviet Union would no longer interfere in the affairs of these nations, Communist governments toppled, one by one. One of the most dramatic events was the fall of the **Berlin Wall.** Erected in 1961 to keep East Germans from fleeing their country, it had become a symbol of the Cold War. On November 9, 1989, the gates in the wall were opened, and thousands of East Germans poured into West Berlin. Jubilant Berliners danced, sang, and chanted, "The Wall is gone! The Wall is gone!" The Cold War was all but over.

The changes in Eastern Europe and the Soviet Union have not been smooth. All 15 republics in the Soviet Union have become independent nations. Civil war broke out in Yugoslavia, and ethnic clashes erupted in some of the former Soviet republics. Czechoslovakia split into two nations peacefully. In Eastern Europe and in the former republics, switching from controlled economies to free economies will take time and cause hardship. People need to learn whole new ways of thinking and behaving. In addition, these changes have caused ripples in the United States.

Germans are jubilant at the opening of the Berlin Wall.

Ripples in the United States. With the end of the Cold War, United States military spending could be cut greatly. While people rejoiced at the reduced threat of war, they soon realized that their own lives would be directly affected. Plants that produced weapons cut back on production and laid off workers. Scientists were also affected as funds for research and development shrank. When the government began closing military bases at home, stores in the towns around the bases lost thousands of dollars worth of business, and the civilians who had jobs on the bases were out of work.

On the other hand, American businesses have huge new markets for their products and services in the newly opened countries. As people there begin to earn more money, they will be eager to spend it on goods that were unavailable under Communist rule. Already one fast-food chain has built a restaurant in Moscow. On opening day, huge crowds appeared, eager for their first taste of American hamburgers and French fries.

The Gulf War. While democracy was spreading across Eastern Europe and the Soviet Union, a new threat to world peace arose in the **Persian Gulf** region. The ruler of Iraq, one of the countries on the Gulf, was a ruthless dictator named Saddam Hussein. Like Hitler in the 1930s, Hussein had plans to bring the people and resources of neighboring nations under his control. In the summer of 1990, Hussein chose as a target the tiny but oil-rich nation of Kuwait. In a surprise attack on August 2, 1990, Iraqi forces invaded Kuwait and overwhelmed the nation's outnumbered defenders.

World leaders feared that an Iraqi takeover of Kuwait would endanger both world peace and world oil supplies. Led by the United States and the Soviet Union, the United Nations demanded that Iraq withdraw. Since Hussein showed no signs of withdrawing, the United Nations in November 1990 authorized its members to "use all necessary means" to see that Iraq left Kuwait, giving Iraq until January 15, 1991 to withdraw.

Perhaps Hussein thought the United Nations was bluffing, or perhaps he thought his military strength was great enough to prevail. At any rate, Iraqi forces remained in Kuwait. On January 16, 1991, United States forces, joined by United Nations allies, began an air attack on Iraq from Saudi Arabia, a Gulf country that borders on both Iraq and Kuwait. For a month, bombs and missiles pounded targets in Iraq and Kuwait, aiming at communications centers, bridges, air bases, nuclear power plants, and chemical-weapons plants, as well as the

Before invading Kuwait, Saddam Hussein spent eight years (1980–1988) trying to conquer neighboring Iran. Iraq gained a small amount of territory, but paid a huge price in casualties: 120,000 killed and 300,000 wounded.

The Middle East has long been a troubled region. Conflicts between Arabs and Jews, between the Kurdish people and the various governments of the lands in which they live, and between other ethnic groups have histories that go back hundreds, even thousands of years. Part of the conflict is based on religious differences, part on the struggle for territory. ■ *To Do*: Research one conflict in the area and give a brief written description of it. Make a map showing the territory involved.

enemy's tanks, artillery, troops, and missile launchers. In February, ground forces joined the attack, rolling across the desert into Iraq and Kuwait. After 100 hours of heavy ground fighting, the war was over. Iraqi forces were defeated, and Kuwait was free.

An interdependent world. The Persian Gulf crisis underscored the need for global cooperation. As the century draws to a close, planet Earth is more than ever a fragile place. To survive, people must be aware of that fragility and recognize their common interests.

While Armstrong and Aldrin were exploring the moon on that July day in 1969, Michael Collins watched the gleaming sphere of Earth from the window of his spacecraft. As the craft drifted silently above the moon's surface, he reflected on the meaning of his mission.

Primary Source

> I really believe that if the political leaders of the world could see their planet from a distance of 100,000 or 200,000 miles, their outlook would be fundamentally changed. Those all-important borders and their noisy arguments would be suddenly silenced. The tiny globe would continue to turn, serenely ignoring its subdivisions, presenting a united front that would cry out for united understanding.

—MICHAEL COLLINS, *"Thoughts while hovering over the moon"*

Think Twice

1. How effective has the war on drugs been?
2. Why is AIDS such an alarming problem?
3. What is a recession?
4. How did the Soviet Union become more democratic under Gorbachev?
5. How has the fall of communism and the end of the Cold War affected the United States?
6. Why were world leaders concerned about Iraq's invasion of Kuwait?

Chapter 22 Review

Choose from the following menu of activities.

Think Back: Main Ideas

1. Name two ways in which you are a consumer of (a) goods, (b) services.
2. As women's roles changed, so too did men's. From what you know about the world around you, name one way men's roles have changed (a) at home, (b) at work.
3. In 1896, in the case of *Plessey* v. *Ferguson,* the Supreme Court ruled that segregation of railroad facilities was legal as long as the facilities were equal. The doctrine of "separate but equal" was used to justify segregation in all areas. In the Linda Brown case, the Court overturned that idea, but not because the facilities were unequal. Think what the Court's reasoning might have been. Then check your ideas in a reference book.
4. How would you try to persuade a friend to vote for or against the ERA?
5. Television is faulted for many reasons— portraying idealized families that no real family could hope to be like, encouraging violence in young people, giving false importance to sex and romantic love, luring students away from books and learning. Do you agree with any of these charges? If so, explain why. If you think TV has redeeming qualities, write about them instead.
6. When people think of drug abuse, they usually think of crack cocaine and other illegal drugs. However, people abuse legal substances too. Do you know what the two most common of these substances are? If not, find out in a reference book or ask your school nurse.

Maps Matter

1. Find old maps of Europe and Asia and compare them to the world map in the back of your book. (a) Into what countries has Czechoslovakia split? (b) Yugoslavia? (c) The Soviet Union?
2. On outline maps of Europe and Asia, label these new countries. You may draw or trace the maps if outline maps aren't available.
3. Make a list of the countries around the Persian Gulf or label them on a map you have drawn or traced.

Word Wizard

1. AIDS is an acronym. Acronyms are made from the first letter or letters of a series of words. List any acronyms you know and give the words that they come from. If you don't know any, find out what these stand for: NATO, SEATO, SADD, SCUBA, UNICEF.
2. Some acronyms have become so common that they are no longer spelled in capitals. Find out what the acronyms radar, sonar, and laser stand for.

Working Cooperatively

Work in small groups to do research and prepare an illustrated report on any of the following: (1) Events in the Civil Rights movement of the 1960s, such as freedom rides and voter registration drives, (2) Space exploration, (3) Robotics, (4) AIDS.

Curriculum Connection

Do some research on lasers. Find out how they work and what they can do.

Learning through Literature

Space Shots, Shuttles, and Satellites, by Melvin Berger
Contributions of Women: Medicine, by Demerris C. Ranahan
Breakthrough: Women in Politics, by Barbara Williams
Sun Power: The Story of Solar Energy, by Madeleine Yates

Chapter 23

North Carolina Today

The United States changes in the twentieth century.

As the Age of Technology dawned in the United States, science and technology brought about a revolution in travel, communication, business, and medicine. Although changes brought by technology were largely positive, the growth of industry led to increased pollution and a faster pace of life. Americans had to learn new skills to keep up with this rapidly changing world.

North Carolina also undergoes great changes.

Against the dizzying backdrop of changes in the nation as a whole, the face of North Carolina also changed. New industries appeared, the population increased, and new challenges and opportunities emerged. Some of the people of North Carolina had difficulty in adjusting to changing ways of life. However, North Carolina's leaders took charge in helping the state's citizens go forward into a new century.

The Great Seal of the State of North Carolina ▶

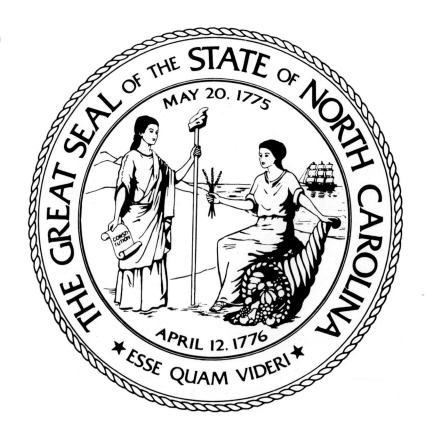

Think Ahead

The twentieth century was a time of change in the United States. Americans faced great challenges and new opportunities. Find out about the social, political, and economic changes that have taken place in North Carolina in the twentieth century. Read about what lies ahead for the state in the next century.

1 The Civil Rights Movement in North Carolina

People, Places, Terms

Pearsall Plan
busing
sit-in

The Constitution guarantees civil rights for all citizens of the United States. Yet some groups of people face discrimination. In North Carolina, African Americans and women have struggled to gain equal rights. Each of these groups has worked to bring about social change in the state.

African Americans fight school segregation.   Because North Carolina's schools were segregated by state law, African Americans were forced to attend schools that were designated for them. In the 1950s, African Americans began to fight for the right to attend the same elementary schools, high schools, and universities that other people of North Carolina attended.

The first attempts at integrating schools in North Carolina began in March 1951. A court order required the University of North Carolina to admit African Americans to its law, graduate, and medical schools. Yet many African Americans in North Carolina did not gain equal opportunities for education until the United States Supreme Court decided *Brown* v. *Board of Education of Topeka* on May 15, 1954. (See Chapter 22.)

The Pearsall Plan is adopted.   In 1955, the North Carolina General Assembly passed a resolution against the Supreme Court's decision. The resolution claimed that school integration would never work in the state.

To delay the process of integration, Thomas J. Pearsall drafted an amendment to the state constitution. His plan allowed local schools to close—by majority vote—rather than integrate. The plan also permitted the state legislature to give tuition money to parents who preferred to have their children attend private schools. The **Pearsall Plan,** adopted in July 1956, was not put into practice but did help quiet the outcry in North Carolina against the Supreme Court decision.

While North Carolina's leaders continued to resist, the slow process of school integration began in 1957. African American children were reassigned in three city school systems. By the fall of 1960, less than one tenth of one percent of North Carolina's African American students were enrolled in integrated schools. To speed up the process of integration throughout the nation, Congress passed a Civil Rights Act in 1964, allowing federal funds for education to be withheld if discrimination continued.

As a result of laws passed in the 1950s and 1960s, public schools in North Carolina gradually became integrated.

The Greensboro "Coffee Party" accomplished its goal. The event drew attention to the plight of African Americans and the need for reform. Soon African Americans had equal access to hotels, restaurants, parks, theaters, and transportation.

Busing helps integrate schools. To end discrimination, the NAACP brought lawsuits against many schools that refused to integrate. In 1969, Judge James B. McMillan ordered the Charlotte school system in Mecklenburg County to integrate, even if it meant **busing** students from one school district to another as a means to do so.

Judge McMillan's decision was appealed to the United States Supreme Court in 1970 but was upheld in 1971. Busing students to different schools became a powerful tool for integration in North Carolina as well as in other states throughout the nation.

African Americans resist discrimination. Not only were African Americans told where to go to school, but they were also expected to live together in certain areas and to sit in certain seats on buses and trains. Some African Americans resisted these unfair practices by a means of peaceful protest called **sit-ins**.

On February 1, 1960, four African American students who attended North Carolina Agricultural and Technical College in Greensboro staged a sit-in. David Richmond, Franklin McCain, Joseph McNeil, and Ezell Blair, Jr., attempted to order coffee at a lunch counter in Woolworth's. Although they were refused service, the four men remained in their seats until the restaurant closed. They returned the next day and were joined by other African Americans. This event, known as the Greensboro "Coffee Party," covered by national news media, sparked the beginning of widespread sit-ins across the country.

African Americans enter state politics. During the years of integration, prominent African Americans held office in state government. In 1968, Reginald A. Hawkins

ran for governor but lost the election. Henry E. Frye was elected to North Carolina's General Assembly in 1968 and in 1983 became the first African American elected to the North Carolina Supreme Court. In 1969, Howard N. Lee became mayor of Chapel Hill.

Throughout the twentieth century, African Americans in North Carolina served in both houses of the General Assembly, on city councils, on county boards of commissioners, as district attorneys, and in other positions in state and local government.

Women in North Carolina seek equal rights. As you have read, the Assembly refused to ratify the Nineteenth Amendment. Nevertheless, in 1919, a woman had been appointed to a state office, and women began to vote in 1920 after the amendment became law. Governor James B. Hunt, Jr., strongly supported the Equal Rights Amendment to the United States Constitution, which, you may remember, was presented to the states in 1972. North Carolina's Assembly did not approve the amendment, but women in the state have made significant strides in the struggle for equal rights.

The civil rights movement led to social change in North Carolina. African Americans, women, and others were affected. These social changes helped spur reforms in state government.

Henry E. Frye was the first African American to be elected to the North Carolina legislature in the twentieth century.

Think Twice

1. Why did North Carolina's schools begin to integrate?
2. What was the Pearsall Plan?
3. What was the Greensboro "Coffee Party"?
4. What was the purpose of the Equal Rights Amendment?
5. How has the civil rights movement personally affected you?

2 Changes in North Carolina's Government

During the twentieth century, many changes took place in North Carolina. These changes—population growth, the rise of business, and the growth of new educational and cultural opportunities for all citizens—created the need to modernize state government. The state's leaders sought to reorganize and reform government in order to better meet the needs of the people.

The state government is reorganized. In 1953, North Carolina's General Assembly created the Commission on the Reorganization of State Government. During a 16-year period, the commission studied various subjects, including the General Assembly itself, licensing boards, public records management, and management of water resources and state land. Reporting regularly to the General Assembly, the commission issued recommendations on nearly every aspect of state government.

In 1967, Governor Dan K. Moore called for a study to find out how the state constitution could be revised and updated to reflect the changes that had occurred in North Carolina. The 25 members of the North Carolina State Constitution Commission did not alter the basic structure of the constitution or change the bill of rights. However, the commission did make some recommendations.

As a result of the commission's recommendations, the General Assembly drafted an act to amend the state constitution in 1969. The Executive Organization Act, approved on November 3, 1970, reduced the number of

The commission recommended building a new facility for North Carolina's government. The State Legislative Building, completed in 1963, was the first building in the United States devoted solely to the legislative branch of government.

state administrative departments from over 350 to fewer than 25 and authorized the governor to reorganize these departments with the legislature's approval. The reorganization took place between 1971 and 1973.

The North Carolina Fund creates new opportunities. In July 1963, Governor Terry Sanford announced the creation of the North Carolina Fund. His plan was to help people in the state break the cycle of poverty. With more than $9 million donated by several charitable organizations, Governor Sanford and the directors of the North Carolina Fund established community programs that would help the poor.

The programs created by the North Carolina Fund were staffed by local leaders and college students who were called North Carolina Volunteers. These programs included a farmers' cooperative, a School Improvement Program to help adults read and write and to bring art and literature to children, and an artisans' cooperative to help people sell traditional crafts. The North Carolina Fund, a model for both the national War on Poverty and the Peace Corps, was dissolved in 1968, after its goal of ending poverty in specific local areas was accomplished.

A two-party system arises. North Carolina has traditionally been a Democratic state. Yet for the first time since 1896, North Carolinians elected a Republican governor in 1972. Governor James E. Holshouser, Jr., continued the reorganization of state government, expanded the community college and state park systems, opened rural health facilities, and created an office of Minority Business Enterprise.

In 1977, Democrat James B. Hunt, Jr., succeeded Governor Holshouser. During Governor Hunt's first term in office, an amendment to the state constitution—permitting the

Governor Terry Sanford wanted North Carolina "to move into the mainstream of America." He supported innovative educational programs, including Operation Second Chance, the Governor's School for Gifted Children, and the School for the Arts.

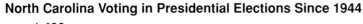

North Carolina Voting in Presidential Elections Since 1944

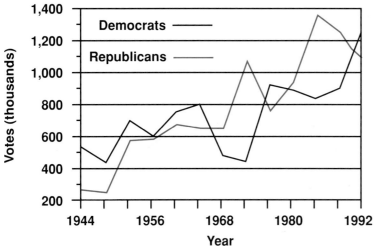

Democrats ——
Republicans ——

Votes (thousands)

1,400
1,200
1,000
800
600
400
200

1944   1956   1968   1980   1992

Year

Graphs Teach

This line graph compares the number of votes cast in North Carolina for past Presidential candidates in both political parties. In what year did the largest number of people vote for a Democrat? In what year did the largest number vote for a Republican? About how many votes did the 1988 Republican candidate get in North Carolina?

337

Governor Martin was born in Georgia. Before being elected governor of North Carolina, he was a professor of chemistry at Davidson College, a member of the Mecklenburg County board of commissioners, and a member of Congress.

governor to serve two consecutive terms—was approved. In 1981, Governor Hunt became the first governor in modern times to succeed himself for a second full term.

In 1984, Republican James G. Martin was elected governor. He also served two terms. With members of their party twice holding the state's highest office, Republicans filled many other posts in the government as well. Their success encouraged many who had long hoped for a workable two-party system for North Carolina. From this point on, slates of candidates from both political parties appeared on election ballots.

The state's congressional districts are redefined.

Every ten years, the federal government takes a **census**, or a count of the population. The census is used to determine how many members a state can have in the House of Representatives. Following the 1990 census of North Carolina's population, the state had to undergo **redistricting**, or changing congressional districts to reflect changes in population. Under federal guidelines, each congressional district in a state must contain approximately the same number of people.

A legislative committee was appointed to determine the new congressional districts in North Carolina. Because new districts must be drawn to increase the likelihood that one or more members of minority groups will be elected, the committee's first plan was rejected by federal officials. African Americans, scattered around the state, did not make up a majority in any district. To correct this problem, the new Twelfth Congressional District—winding from Durham to Charlotte like a long snake—was created.

The government of North Carolina was streamlined to keep pace with changes in the state. What other changes would the people of North Carolina face? New problems and possibilities—from stopping pollution to planning research facilities—surfaced in the twentieth century.

Think Twice

1. What was the result of the study conducted by the Commission on the Reorganization of State Government?
2. What was the purpose of the North Carolina Fund?
3. Which of these political parties—Democrat or Republican—has traditionally been in power in North Carolina?
4. Why did North Carolina undergo redistricting in 1990?
5. Which reform in state government was most effective? Why?

Twentieth-Century Trends in North Carolina

People, Places, Terms

Research Triangle Park
acid rain
erosion

Some of the changes that took place in the nation in the twentieth century were mirrored in North Carolina. Certain economic, political, and social trends developed in the state. These trends presented challenges as well as opportunities for many of the people of North Carolina.

Business and industry grow. North Carolina's primary industries—textiles, tobacco, and furniture—continued to grow in the twentieth century. Textile mills today turn out towels, carpets, fabric for automobiles, clothing, and other products. The state's cigarette and furniture manufacturers earn billions of dollars each year.

While established industries continue to grow, new businesses have taken root in North Carolina. During the 1980s, factories in the state began to produce machinery for use on farms, in mines, in oilfields, in food processing, in textile mills, and in printing. The production of electronic equipment such as telephones, computers, telegraphs, and television equipment also increased in the 1980s. Other diverse businesses, such as a cosmetics firm, a publishing company, and a national airline, moved to the state.

Both new and established businesses employ skilled workers. However, robots and other machines do some of the work that people in factories once did by hand. Computers are widely used to plan and design products and production equipment. The use of new technology has provided job opportunities for many people in the state.

Maps Matter

This map shows you where the major manufacturing areas in North Carolina are located. ■*To Do:* Use the map on this page to answer these questions. What are three kinds of manufacturing in North Carolina? What is made in the western part of the state near the Tennessee border? In which part of the state is most of the manufacturing located?

Major Manufacturing Areas in North Carolina

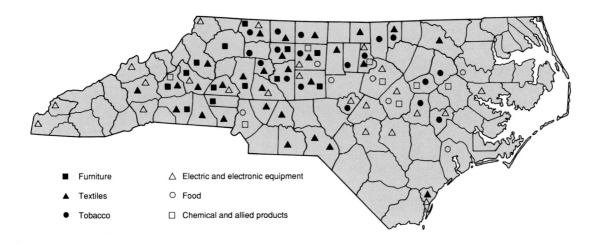

■ Furniture △ Electric and electronic equipment

▲ Textiles ○ Food

● Tobacco □ Chemical and allied products

The National Humanities Center in the Research Triangle Park attracts scholars from across the nation as well as from around the world. They engage in an exchange of ideas, research, and writing in the fields of history, biology, literature, sociology, and politics. (*Courtesy of JoAnn Sieburg-Baker, Photographer, Charlotte*)

The Research Triangle Park is planned. During the 1950s, leaders in North Carolina discussed the possibility of bringing together research and industry in a national research institute that would benefit the entire state. This dream became a reality when the first building at the **Research Triangle Park** was completed in 1961.

The Research Triangle Park was built on more than 5,000 acres near the campuses of Duke University in Durham, North Carolina State College in Raleigh, and the University of North Carolina at Chapel Hill. Tenants, including hundreds of private businesses from all over the world and state and federal agencies, study and develop new medicines, means of communication, and solutions to worldwide problems. Researchers examine such topics as urban transportation systems, long-range weather forecasting, and the process of aging.

Writer V. S. Naipaul visited the Research Triangle Park in the 1980s. He describes the park in the following passage:

Primary Source

To the east, in North Carolina, was the area known as the Research Triangle, bounded by the university campuses of Chapel Hill, Raleigh, and Durham, where over a period of almost thirty years a big industrial park of seventy-five hundred acres had been created: thirty thousand new jobs there, poor North Carolina pineland landscaped into the discreetest kind of industrial garden.

— *V. S. NAIPAUL,* Turn in the South

Think as a Geographer

*T*he wooded site for the Research Triangle Park in North Carolina was carefully chosen.
■ *To Do*: Look at the state map in the atlas at the back of your text. Find the Raleigh, Chapel Hill, and Durham area. Why do you think the planners of the park selected this location? What advantages does this location offer?

The people of North Carolina protect the environment.
To help protect North Carolina's environment, the General Assembly created the Environmental Management Commission in 1973. State leaders hoped to stop or prevent the effects of air and water pollution and soil and coastal erosion. They also hoped to preserve the state's natural resources for enjoyment and use in the twenty-first century.

In the late 1970s and 1980s, scientists in North Carolina found that **acid rain** was killing spruce, balsam, and fir trees in the mountains. Harmful chemicals in the air were being carried to the earth by rainfall. State and federal laws were passed to control the release of smoke and harmful fumes into the air, and state leaders have sought to prevent air and water pollution by discussing the problem with governors of neighboring states.

Another problem facing North Carolina is **erosion,** or the slow wearing away of the soil and sand. In 1971, the Environmental Policy Act was passed to regulate land use. Other laws prevent builders from allowing loose soil or mud to wash into streams. To prevent beach erosion along the Outer Banks, some communities build fences, replace sand, and plant grass or other plants to anchor the sand.

Despite strong objections raised by those concerned about the environment, several nuclear power plants were constructed in the eastern and central parts of the state. The disposal of harmful nuclear waste and other chemical wastes is a serious problem in the state today.

Transportation improves in the state. North Carolina has a modern transportation system. People can travel to and from the state on highways, trains, airplanes, and boats. The system allows goods to be carried efficiently in and out of North Carolina.

The "good roads" program of the early twentieth century gave North Carolina an extensive network of highways. New super highways—some six and eight lanes wide— have been built, greatly reducing travel time across the state. Automobiles, buses, and trucks serve most communities.

Railroads continue to carry freight and passengers across the state. Regional airports serve the nation, and some airports offer direct flights to Europe. Barges, fishing boats, and pleasure craft use the Intracoastal Waterway—a system of canals, channels, and rivers and sounds.

Opportunities for higher education increase. Beginning in the 1950s, opportunities for higher education increased in North Carolina. Many community and private colleges, technical institutes, and industrial education centers were established. In addition, enrollment at established colleges

This spruce forest high on Mount Mitchell in the Appalachians is a victim of acid rain. The top of Mount Mitchell is receiving 200 pounds of sulfates each year, more than ten times the amount that the soil can handle naturally.

One group of Asian refugees in North Carolina are the Hmong, who lived near the Laos-North Vietnam border. ■ *To Do*: Use an encyclopedia or other reference books to research the culture of the Hmong. Find out about their language, customs, beliefs, and other aspects of their culture. Write an article about the Hmong for your school newspaper.

increased, and new buildings were constructed. Special training programs were created to provide employees of new businesses with the skills that they needed.

In the 1960s, the General Assembly brought state colleges under the management of the University of North Carolina, set aside funds for public education, and created new educational programs. By the 1980s, more than half a million students were enrolled in North Carolina's community colleges. However, less than 15 percent of people in the state over the age of 25 had completed four or more years of college.

The state's population changes. New industries and improved transportation have attracted new citizens to North Carolina. According to the 1990 census, the state population has increased by more than one million people since 1980. While North Carolina has always been considered a rural state, the rural population is now slightly less than the urban population. This population shift can be explained in part by the new United States Census Bureau definition of *urban* to include towns with as few as 2,500 people.

Many of North Carolina's new citizens are immigrants from Asia. Some of these immigrants have opened shops to sell native foods. Others work as skilled tailors and seamstresses, in tobacco factories, or on farms. A great number of Asian immigrants are refugees who fled during the Vietnam War. These new citizens have learned English, found jobs, and begun to share their culture with the communities in which they live.

As North Carolina continues to grow and change in the late twentieth century, the future seems bright. What will life be like in the state in the year 2000? The state's leaders are studying the trends of today in order to plan for the future.

Think Twice

1. (a) What three industries have continued to grow in North Carolina? (b) What are two new industries that developed in North Carolina in the 1980s?
2. (a) What is the Research Triangle Park? (b) Where is it located? (c) What is the purpose of the park?
3. What are two environmental problems facing the state?
4. In what two ways has the population in North Carolina changed since 1980?
5. Choose one twentieth-century trend that you have read about in Unit 9. Evaluate whether this trend has had a negative or a positive impact on North Carolina.

4 The State Looks to the Future

People, Places, Terms

community
rehabilitate

With the year 2000 fast approaching, the people of North Carolina must think about what life in their state will be like in the twenty-first century. What goals would they like to reach? What problems must they solve? The state's leaders are preparing for the future, hoping to build on the solid foundation of the past.

What will life be like in 2000?   In anticipation of the problems and prospects of the twenty-first century, Governor James B. Hunt, Jr., created the Commission on the Future of North Carolina on June 1, 1981. Governor Hunt announced his plans with the following:

Primary Source

> Our task today is to anticipate and prepare for the North Carolina our children will encounter tomorrow. . . . We must take responsibility for making the world what we want it to be, for ourselves and for our children. And that requires looking into the future now. Looking at the future can help us anticipate changes and make decisions. It can help prepare us for what lies ahead and put us in the driver's seat, to chart the course for North Carolina.

— GOVERNOR JAMES B. HUNT, JR., "Speech on Commission on the Future of North Carolina"

The purpose of the commission was to carry out a project known as NC 2000. The commission called upon experts in the state for advice, held public meetings, and prepared a long questionnaire to find out about the needs and hopes of citizens. The information gathered by the commission helped give leaders a glimpse of the state's future.

For two years, the governor's commission studied a variety of issues that concerned the people of North Carolina. Members examined what the people need, how to reach the long-term goals of the economy, how to protect natural resources, and how to preserve the unique aspects of their community. The result of their two-year study was a 310-page book called *The Future of North Carolina, Goals and Recommendations for the Year 2000.*

What do the people need?   The governor's commission found that North Carolinians were concerned with education, health, housing, and poverty. The report suggested ways of improving conditions in each of these areas.

James B. Hunt, Jr., was elected governor of North Carolina in 1976 and served two terms (1977 – 1985). He was elected again in 1992 and took office January 1993.

This worker tests synthetic fabric for colorfastness at a dye plant in Albemarle.

The textile industry is one of the state's primary businesses. At this factory, workers fit hosiery over metal forms before it is heat treated.

To improve education, the commission recommended that public schools be sufficiently supported, offering all citizens the chance for a good education. The commission also called for the use of qualified teachers, the creation of programs to train new workers, and the establishment of day-care for young children.

To improve citizens' health, the commission recommended regulating harmful substances to which workers are exposed and increasing health care for elderly, poor, and rural residents. In addition, the commission sought better public education in order to reduce infant deaths and preventable diseases.

The commission examined ways to improve housing. The report proposed that more affordable housing for all citizens be provided and that poor housing be upgraded. As commission members studied the problem of poverty, they found that the ill, children, the elderly, and the physically challenged needed more aid. They also found that women and minority groups needed training and job-placement programs to help them find better employment.

How will the economy grow? The commission established 15 economic goals to be met in North Carolina by the year 2000. Most of these goals related to creating and supporting a climate in which regional and statewide business would flourish.

Specific ideas given by the commission would help small and large businesses, industry, agriculture, and fisheries grow. To support business growth, the commission suggested improving public transportation, exploring new energy sources, and developing new communication networks. The report predicted that different manufacturing fields such as chemicals, machinery, and electronic equipment would grow in the new century.

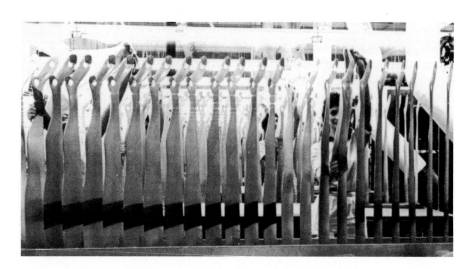

This photograph of Charlotte shows different kinds of communities within the city.

How can natural resources be conserved? The commission gave guidelines for protecting the state's environment. Their report recommended that immediate action be taken to clean air and water pollution, stop soil erosion, and conserve energy. The commission urged preservation of the natural landscape, including plants and animals, through careful planning, restricted land and water use, and better public education. While the commission supported giving citizens more access to natural areas, they also recognized the need for resource management.

What kind of community will exist in North Carolina? There is a strong sense of **community** in the towns and cities of North Carolina. *Community* means "a group of people living in a given locale who share some common activities, attitudes, and interests." To maintain this sense of community, the commission created a list of ten goals.

Among the goals were renewing and improving business areas, reducing crime, and **rehabilitating**, or restoring, rundown areas. Schools, recreation areas, parks, and libraries should be supported and maintained. Also, cultural differences should be recognized and celebrated.

While the NC 2000 project was far from complete, this in-depth report helped leaders take a critical look at the state. If the recommendations are addressed, then North Carolina's children can look forward to a rewarding future.

Think Twice

1. What is one need that should be met for citizens by 2000?
2. How could state leaders help business grow in the future?
3. What is one way to protect the environment for the future?
4. How can community life be preserved beyond this century?
5. Imagine North Carolina in 2050. What will life be like?

Chapter 23 Review

Choose from the following menu of activities.

Think Back: Main Ideas

During the twentieth century, North Carolina changed in different ways. Name at least two changes that have occurred in the following areas:

1. Social life in North Carolina
2. Politics in the state
3. Economic conditions in the state

Maps Matter

North Carolina boasts several important fields of manufacturing. Refer to the map on page 339 to answer these questions.

1. What is currently the largest type of manufacturing in North Carolina?
2. What is currently the smallest type of manufacturing in the state?
3. In which part of the state is little or no manufacturing located?

Word Wizard

1. *Sit-in* and *acid rain* are both compound nouns made up of two separate words. Make a list of other compound nouns that you know.
2. Now that you have completed a study of North Carolina from its early days to the present, make a list of adjectives that you would use to describe this proud state in our nation.

Working Cooperatively

1. Imagine that you have been invited to the Research Triangle Park. With a group of three to five classmates, brainstorm a list of worldwide problems that you might like to solve. Choose one problem, and have each member of your group propose a solution. Have members of your group vote on the most innovative solution.
2. Work with three to five classmates. Have each member of your group write one or two questions about the future. For example, you might ask: *What health issue most needs to be solved by 2000?* Then work with other groups to make a class questionnaire. Distribute copies to other students, collect their completed questionnaires, and analyze their answers for a report about the future.

Curriculum Connection

1. In Chapter 7, you read about some of the earliest religious groups in North Carolina, most of which were Christian. Although never very numerous, Jews and Roman Catholics have lived in the state since colonial days. In this century, Moslems and Hindus have arrived as well. Do some research on the influence religion has had on the state or nation. How have people's beliefs affected economic, social, or political life? For example, how has religion affected social reform?
2. Using an encyclopedia or your science text, research the causes and effects of one environmental problem that faces North Carolina—soil or coastal erosion, air or water pollution, acid rain, hazardous waste disposal—or another of your choice. Make a diagram to illustrate this cause-effect relationship.
3. Find out about the electronics industry that developed in North Carolina in the twentieth century. Use an encyclopedia, a high-tech magazine, or another resource to research this industry. What products are made? How are they made? Why are these products important?

Learning through Literature

The Lake at the End of the World, by Caroline Macdonald

Ludie's Songs, by Dirlie Herligy

Thinking Machines, by Isaac Asimov

North Carolina Resources

Dogwood

Cardinal

State Government Chart

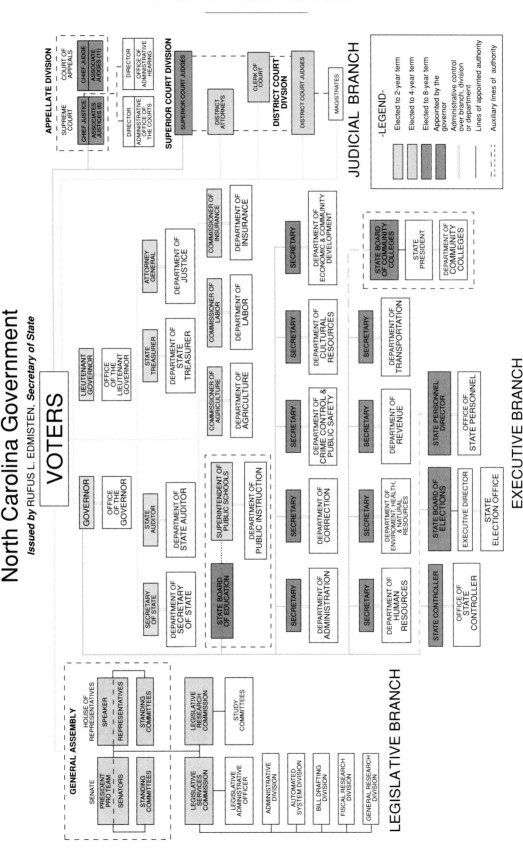

ORGANIZATIONAL CHART OF
North Carolina Government

Issued by RUFUS L. EDMISTEN, *Secretary of State*

VOTERS

APPELLATE DIVISION

- SUPREME COURT
  - CHIEF JUSTICE
  - ASSOCIATES JUSTICES (6)
- COURT OF APPEALS
  - CHIEF JUDGE
  - ASSOCIATE JUDGES (11)
- DIRECTOR ADMINISTRATIVE OFFICE OF THE COURTS
- DIRECTOR OFFICE OF ADMINISTRATIVE HEARING

SUPERIOR COURT DIVISION
- SUPERIOR COURT JUDGES
- DISTRICT ATTORNEYS

DISTRICT COURT DIVISION
- CLERK OF COURT
- DISTRICT COURT JUDGES
- MAGISTRATES

JUDICIAL BRANCH

-LEGEND-
- Elected to 2-year term
- Elected to 4-year term
- Elected to 8-year term
- Appointed by the governor
- Administrative control over branch, division or department
- Lines of appointed authority
- Auxiliary lines of authority

EXECUTIVE BRANCH

- GOVERNOR — OFFICE OF THE GOVERNOR
- LIEUTENANT GOVERNOR — OFFICE OF THE LIEUTENANT GOVERNOR
- SECRETARY OF STATE — DEPARTMENT OF SECRETARY OF STATE
- STATE AUDITOR — DEPARTMENT OF STATE AUDITOR
- STATE TREASURER — DEPARTMENT OF STATE TREASURER
- SUPERINTENDENT OF PUBLIC SCHOOLS — DEPARTMENT OF PUBLIC INSTRUCTION
- STATE BOARD OF EDUCATION
- ATTORNEY GENERAL — DEPARTMENT OF JUSTICE
- COMMISSIONER OF AGRICULTURE — DEPARTMENT OF AGRICULTURE
- COMMISSIONER OF LABOR — DEPARTMENT OF LABOR
- COMMISSIONER OF INSURANCE — DEPARTMENT OF INSURANCE
- SECRETARY — DEPARTMENT OF ADMINISTRATION
- SECRETARY — DEPARTMENT OF CORRECTION
- SECRETARY — DEPARTMENT OF CRIME CONTROL & PUBLIC SAFETY
- SECRETARY — DEPARTMENT OF CULTURAL RESOURCES
- SECRETARY — DEPARTMENT OF ECONOMIC & COMMUNITY DEVELOPMENT
- SECRETARY — DEPARTMENT OF HUMAN RESOURCES
- SECRETARY — DEPARTMENT OF ENVIROMENT, HEALTH, & NATURAL RESOURCES
- SECRETARY — DEPARTMENT OF REVENUE
- SECRETARY — DEPARTMENT OF TRANSPORTATION
- STATE CONTROLLER — OFFICE OF STATE CONTROLLER
- STATE BOARD OF ELECTIONS — EXECUTIVE DIRECTOR — STATE ELECTION OFFICE
- STATE PERSONNEL DIRECTOR — OFFICE OF STATE PERSONNEL
- STATE BOARD OF COMMUNITY COLLEGES — STATE PRESIDENT — DEPARTMENT OF COMMUNITY COLLEGES

LEGISLATIVE BRANCH

GENERAL ASSEMBLY
- SENATE
  - PRESIDENT PRO TEAM
  - SENATORS
  - STANDING COMMITTEES
- HOUSE OF REPRESENTATIVES
  - SPEAKER
  - REPRESENTATIVES
  - STANDING COMMITTEES
- LEGISLATIVE RESEARCH COMMISSION
  - STUDY COMMITTEES
- LEGISLATIVE SERVICES COMMISSION
  - LEGISLATIVE ADMINISTRATIVE OFFICER
  - ADMINISTRATIVE DIVISION
  - AUTOMATED SYSTEM DIVISION
  - BILL DRAFTING DIVISION
  - FISCAL RESEARCH DIVISION
  - GENERAL RESEARCH DIVISION

Governors of the State of North Carolina[1]

		Home County
1776–80	Richard Caswell	Dobbs (now Lenoir)
1780–81	Abner Nash	Craven
1781–82	Thomas Burke	Orange
1782–84	Alexander Martin	Guilford
1784–87	Richard Caswell	Dobbs (now Lenoir)
1787–89	Samuel Johnston	Chowan
1789–92	Alexander Martin	Guilford
1792–95	Richard Dobbs Spaight	Craven
1795–98	Samuel Ashe	New Hanover
1798–99	William R. Davie	Halifax
1799–1802	Benjamin Williams	Moore
1802–05	James Turner	Warren
1805–07	Nathaniel Alexander	Mecklenburg
1807–08	Benjamin Williams	Moore
1808–10	David Stone	Bertie
1810–11	Benjamin Smith	Brunswick
1811–14	William Hawkins	Warren
1814–17	William Miller	Warren
1817–20	John Branch	Halifax
1820–21	Jesse Franklin	Surry
1821–24	Gabriel Holmes	Sampson
1824–27	Hutchins G. Burton	Halifax
1827–28	James Iredell	Chowan
1828–30	John Owen	Bladen
1830–32	Montfort Stokes	Wilkes
1832–35	David L. Swain	Buncombe
1835–36	Richard Dobbs Spaight, Jr.	Craven
1836–41	Edward B. Dudley	New Hanover
1841–45	John M. Morehead	Guilford
1845–49	William A. Graham	Orange
1849–51	Charles Manly	Wake
1851–54	David S. Reid	Rockingham
1854–55	Warren Winslow	Cumberland
1855–59	Thomas Bragg	Northampton
1859–61	John W. Ellis	Rowan
1861–62	Henry T. Clark	Edgecombe
1862–65	Zebulon B. Vance	Buncombe

1. Elected by joint ballot of both houses of the legislature for one-year terms during the period 1776–1835; elected by the qualified voters for two-year terms, 1836–68; and elected by the voters for four-year terms since 1868.

1865	William W. Holden[2]	Wake
1865–68	Jonathan Worth	Randolph
1868–71	William W. Holden[3]	Wake
1871–74	Tod R. Caldwell	Burke
1874–77	Curtis H. Brogden	Wayne
1877–79	Zebulon B. Vance	Mecklenburg
1879–85	Thomas J. Jarvis	Pitt
1885–89	Alfred M. Scales	Rockingham
1889–91	Daniel G. Fowle	Wake
1891–93	Thomas M. Holt	Alamance
1893–97	Elias Carr	Edgecombe
1897–1901	Daniel L. Russell	Brunswick
1901–05	Charles B. Aycock	Wayne
1905–09	Robert B. Glenn	Forsyth
1909–13	William W. Kitchin	Person
1913–17	Locke Craig	Buncombe
1917–21	Thomas W. Bickett	Franklin
1921–25	Cameron Morrison	Mecklenburg
1925–29	Angus W. McLean	Robeson
1929–33	O. Max Gardner	Cleveland
1933–37	J. C. B. Ehringhaus	Pasquotank
1937–41	Clyde R. Hoey	Cleveland
1941–45	J. Melville Broughton	Wake
1945–49	R. Gregg Cherry	Gaston
1949–53	W. Kerr Scott	Almance
1953–54	William B. Umstead	Durham
1954–61	Luther H. Hodges	Rockingham
1961–65	Terry Sanford	Cumberland
1965–69	Dan K. Moore	Jackson
1969–73	Robert W. Scott	Alamance
1973–77	James E. Holshouser, Jr.	Watauga
1977–85	James B. Hunt, Jr.[4]	Wilson
1985–93	James G. Martin	Iredell
1993–	James B. Hunt, Jr.	Wilson

2. Appointed by President Andrew Johnson under his plan of Reconstruction.

3. Impeached and removed from office in 1871; he was succeeded by the lieutenant governor, Tod R. Caldwell.

4. An amendment to the state constitution during Hunt's administration permitting a governor to succeed himself for a second four-year term made it possible for him to serve two terms.

North Carolina Counties

Name	Date of Formation	Named For	County Seat	Land Area in Sq. Miles	1990 Population
Alamance	1849	Probably of Indian origin	Graham	431	108,213
Alexander	1847	William J. Alexander	Taylorsville	260	27,544
Alleghany	1859	Indian origin	Sparta	235	9,590
Anson	1750	Admiral George Anson, Baronet	Wadesboro	532	23,474
Ashe	1799	Samuel Ashe	Jefferson	426	22,209
Avery	1911	Waighstill Avery	Newland	247	14,867
Beaufort	1712	Duke of Beaufort	Washington	828	42,283
Bertie	1722	James and Henry Bertie	Windsor	699	20,388
Bladen	1734	Martin Bladen	Elizabethtown	875	28,663
Brunswick	1764	Town of Brunswick	Bolivia	855	50,985
Buncombe	1791	Edward Buncombe	Asheville	656	174,821
Burke	1777	Thomas Burke	Morganton	507	75,744
Cabarrus	1792	Stephen Cabarras	Concord	364	98,935
Caldwell	1841	Joseph Caldwell	Lenoir	472	70,709
Camden	1777	Earl Camden	Camden	241	5,904
Carteret	1722	Sir John Carteret	Beaufort	531	52,556
Caswell	1777	Richard Caswell	Yanceyville	426	20,693
Catawba	1842	Catawba Indians	Newton	400	118,412
Chatham	1771	William Pitt, Earl of Chatham	Pittsboro	683	38,759
Cherokee	1839	Cherokee Indians	Murphy	455	20,170
Chowan	1668	Chowan Indians	Edenton	173	13,506
Clay	1861	Henry Clay	Hayesville	215	7,155
Cleveland	1841	Benjamin Cleveland	Shelby	464	84,714
Columbus	1808	Christopher Columbus	Whiteville	937	49,587
Craven	1705	William, Earl of Craven	New Bern	696	81,613
Cumberland	1754	William, Duke of Cumberland	Fayetteville	653	274,566
Currituck	1668	Indian word	Currituck	262	13,736
Dare	1870	Virginia Dare	Manteo	382	22,746
Davidson	1822	William Lee Davidson	Lexington	552	126,677
Davie	1836	William R. Davie	Mocksville	265	27,859
Duplin	1750	Thomas Hay, Viscount Dupplin	Kenansville	818	39,995
Durham	1881	Town of Durham	Durham	291	181,835
Edgecombe	1741	Richard Edgecumbe	Tarboro	505	56,558
Forsyth	1849	Benjamin Forsythe	Winston-Salem	410	265,878
Franklin	1779	Benjamin Franklin	Louisburg	492	36,414
Gaston	1846	William Gaston	Gastonia	357	175,093
Gates	1779	Horatio Gates	Gatesville	341	9,305

Name	Date of Formation	Named For	County Seat	Land Area in Sq. Miles	1990 Population
Graham	1872	William A. Graham	Robbinsville	292	7,196
Granville	1746	John Carteret, Earl Granville	Oxford	531	38,345
Greene	1799	Nathanael Greene	Snow Hill	265	15,384
Guilford	1771	Francis North, Earl of Guilford	Greensboro	650	347,420
Halifax	1759	Earl of Halifax	Halifax	725	55,516
Harnett	1805	Cornelius Harnett	Lillington	595	67,822
Haywood	1808	John Haywood	Waynesville	554	46,942
Henderson	1838	Leonard Henderson	Hendersonville	374	69,285
Hertford	1760	Earl of Hertford	Winton	354	22,523
Hoke	1911	Robert F. Hoke	Raeford	391	22,856
Hyde	1705	Governor Edward Hyde	Swanquarter	613	5,411
Iredell	1788	James Iredell	Statesville	574	92,931
Jackson	1851	Andrew Jackson	Sylva	491	26,846
Johnston	1746	Gabriel Johnston	Smithfield	792	81,306
Jones	1779	Willie Jones	Trenton	473	9,414
Lee	1907	Robert E. Lee	Sanford	257	41,374
Lenoir	1791	William Lenoir	Kinston	400	57,274
Lincoln	1779	General Benjamin Lincoln	Lincolnton	299	50,319
McDowell	1842	Joseph McDowell	Marion	442	35,681
Macon	1828	Nathaniel Macon	Franklin	517	23,499
Madison	1851	James Madison	Marshall	449	16,953
Martin	1774	Josiah Martin	Williamston	463	25,078
Mecklenburg	1763	Princess Charlotte of Mecklenburg	Charlotte	527	511,433
Mitchell	1861	Elisha Mitchell	Bakersville	222	14,433
Montgomery	1779	Richard Montgomery	Troy	491	23,346
Moore	1784	Alfred Moore	Carthage	699	59,013
Nash	1777	Francis Nash	Nashville	540	76,677
New Hanover	1729	House of Hanover	Wilmington	199	120,284
Northampton	1741	Earl of Northampton	Jackson	536	20,798
Onslow	1734	Arthur Onslow	Jacksonville	767	149,838
Orange	1752	William V of Orange	Hillsborough	400	93,851
Pamlico	1872	Pamlico Sound	Bayboro	337	11,372
Pasquotank	1668	Indian tribe	Elizabeth City	227	31,298
Pender	1875	William D. Pender	Burgaw	871	28,855
Perquimans	1668	Indian tribe	Hertford	247	10,447
Person	1792	Thomas Person	Roxboro	392	30,180
Pitt	1761	William Pitt, Earl of Chatham	Greenville	652	107,924

Name	Date of Formation	Named For	County Seat	Land Area in Sq. Miles	1990 Population
Polk	1855	William Polk	Columbus	238	14,416
Randolph	1779	Peyton Randolph	Asheboro	788	106,546
Richmond	1779	Duke of Richmond	Rockingham	474	44,518
Robeson	1786	Thomas Robeson	Lumberton	949	105,179
Rockingham	1785	Marquis of Rockingham	Wentworth	567	86,064
Rowan	1753	Matthew Rowan	Salisbury	511	110,605
Rutherford	1779	Griffith Rutherford	Rutherfordton	564	56,918
Sampson	1784	John Sampson	Clinton	946	47,297
Scotland	1899	Scotland	Laurinburg	319	33,754
Stanly	1841	John Stanly	Albemarle	395	51,765
Stokes	1789	John Stokes	Danbury	452	37,223
Surry	1771	County of Surrey, England	Dobson	537	61,704
Swain	1871	David L. Swain	Bryson City	528	11,268
Transylvania	1861	Latin words	Brevard	378	25,520
Tyrrell	1729	Sir John Tyrrell	Columbia	390	3,856
Union	1842	County made from parts of two others	Monroe	637	84,211
Vance	1881	Zebulon B. Vance	Henderson	254	38,892
Wake	1771	Margaret Wake Tryon	Raleigh	834	423,380
Warren	1779	Joseph Warren	Warrenton	429	17,265
Washington	1799	George Washington	Plymouth	348	13,997
Watauga	1849	Watauga River	Boone	313	36,952
Wayne	1779	Anthony Wayne	Goldsboro	553	104,666
Wilkes	1778	John Wilkes	Wilkesboro	757	59,393
Wilson	1855	Louis D. Wilson	Wilson	371	66,061
Yadkin	1850	Yadkin River	Yadkinville	336	30,488
Yancey	1833	Bardett Yancey	Burnsville	312	15,419

Total Land Area in Sq. Miles	48,718
Total 1990 Population	6,628,637

Population of North Carolina

Year	Total Population[1]	Urban	Rural	Percent Urban	African Americans Free	African Americans Slave
1675	4,000					
1700	10,720					
1710	15,120					
1729	35,000					
1752	100,000					
1765	200,000					
1786	350,000					
1790	393,751				4,975	100,572
1800	478,103				7,043	133,296
1810	555,500				10,266	168,824
1820	638,829	12,502	626,327	2.0	14,612	205,017
1830	737,987	10,455	727,532	1.4	19,543	246,462
1840	753,409	13,310	740,109	1.8	22,732	245,817
1850	869,039	21,109	847,930	2.4	27,463	288,548
1860	992,622	24,554	968,068	2.5	30,463	331,059
1870	1,071,361	36,218	1,035,143	3.4	391,650	
1880	1,399,750	55,116	1,344,634	3.9	531,277	
1890	1,617,947	115,759	1,502,190	7.2	561,018	
1900	1,893,810	186,790	1,707,020	9.9	624,469	
1910	2,206,287	318,474	1,887,813	14.4	697,843	
1920	2,559,123	490,370	2,068,753	19.2	763,407	
1930	3,170,276	809,847	2,360,429	25.5	918,647	
1940	3,571,623	974,175	2,597,448	27.3	981,298	
1950	4,061,929	1,238,193	2,823,736	30.5	1,047,353	
1960	4,556,155	1,801,921	2,754,234	39.5	1,116,021	
1970	5,082,059	2,285,168	2,796,891	45.0	1,126,478	
1980	5,881,766	2,823,180	3,058,586	48.0	1,318,857	
1990	6,628,637	3,337,778	3,290,859	50.4	1,456,323	

1. Only estimates are available for the period before 1790; thereafter, official United States census returns are cited.

North Carolina's Twenty-five Largest Cities, 1970–1990

	Population		
	1990	*1980*	*1970*
Charlotte	395,934	314,447	241,420
Raleigh	207,951	150,225	122,830
Greensboro	183,521	155,642	144,076
Winston-Salem	143,485	131,885	133,683
Durham	135,611	100,831	95,438
Fayetteville	75,695	59,507	53,510
High Point	69,496	63,380	63,229
Asheville	61,607	53,583	57,929
Wilmington	55,530	44,000	46,169
Gastonia	54,732	47,333	47,322
Rocky Mount	48,997	41,283	34,284
Greenville	44,972	35,740	29,063
Cary	43,858	21,763	7,686
Goldsboro	40,709	31,871	26,960
Burlington	39,498	37,266	35,930
Chapel Hill	38,719	32,421	26,199
Wilson	36,930	34,424	29,347
Jacksonville	30,013	17,056	16,289
Kannapolis	29,696	*	*
Hickory	28,301	20,757	20,569
Concord	27,347	16,942	18,464
Kinston	25,295	25,234	23,020
Salisbury	23,087	22,677	22,515
Havelock	20,268	17,718	3,012
Lumberton	18,601	18,241	16,961

* Not incorporated as a city until after 1980 census

Atlas

Countries of theWorld

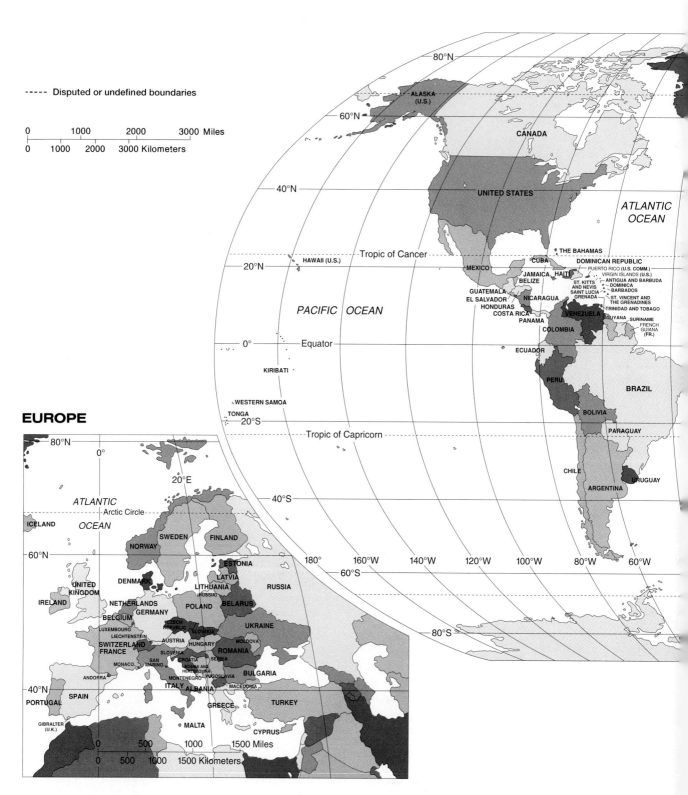

---- Disputed or undefined boundaries

0   1000   2000   3000 Miles
0   1000   2000   3000 Kilometers

80°N

ALASKA (U.S.)

60°N

CANADA

40°N

UNITED STATES

ATLANTIC OCEAN

Tropic of Cancer

20°N   HAWAII (U.S.)

THE BAHAMAS

CUBA

DOMINICAN REPUBLIC

MEXICO

PUERTO RICO (U.S. COMM.)
VIRGIN ISLANDS (U.S.)

JAMAICA HAITI

BELIZE

ANTIGUA AND BARBUDA
DOMINICA
BARBADOS

ST. KITTS
AND NEVIS
SAINT LUCIA

GUATEMALA
EL SALVADOR
HONDURAS

NICARAGUA

ST. VINCENT AND
THE GRENADINES

GRENADA

TRINIDAD AND TOBAGO

PACIFIC OCEAN

COSTA RICA
PANAMA

VENEZUELA
GUYANA
SURINAME

COLOMBIA

FRENCH
GUIANA
(FR.)

0°   Equator

ECUADOR

KIRIBATI

PERU

BRAZIL

WESTERN SAMOA

TONGA

BOLIVIA

20°S

Tropic of Capricorn

PARAGUAY

CHILE

URUGUAY

ARGENTINA

180°   160°W   140°W   120°W   100°W   80°W   60°W

60°S

80°S

EUROPE

80°N   **0°**

20°E

ATLANTIC

Arctic Circle

ICELAND   OCEAN

60°N

NORWAY   SWEDEN   FINLAND

ESTONIA

DENMARK

LATVIA

LITHUANIA

RUSSIA

UNITED
KINGDOM

IRELAND

(RUSSIA)

NETHERLANDS   POLAND   BELARUS

BELGIUM   GERMANY

UKRAINE

LUXEMBOURG
LIECHTENSTEIN

CZECH
REPUBLIC   SLOVAKIA

SWITZERLAND   AUSTRIA   HUNGARY   MOLDOVA

FRANCE

SLOVENIA   ROMANIA

MONACO   SAN
MARINO   CROATIA   SERBIA

ANDORRA   BOSNIA AND
HERZEGOVINA

MONTENEGRO   YUGOSLAVIA   BULGARIA

ITALY   ALBANIA   MACEDONIA

40°N

PORTUGAL   SPAIN

GREECE   TURKEY

GIBRALTER
(U.K.)

MALTA

CYPRUS

0   500   1000   1500 Miles
0   500   1000   1500 Kilometers

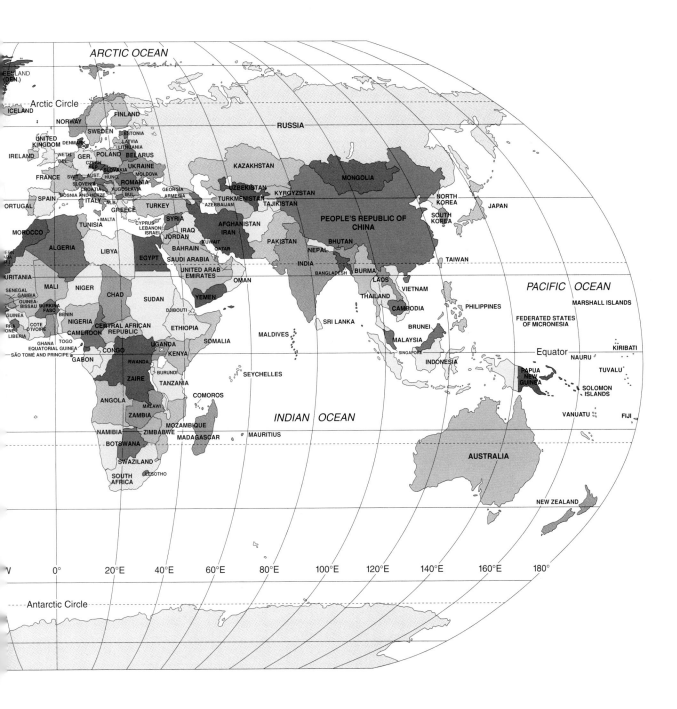

ARCTIC OCEAN

EELAND
(DEN.)

Arctic Circle

ICELAND

NORWAY FINLAND

SWEDEN ESTONIA

UNITED DENMARK LATVIA
KINGDOM NETH. LITHUANIA

IRELAND BEL. POLAND BELARUS
GER. CZECH
REP. SLOVAKIA UKRAINE

FRANCE SWIT. AUST. HUNG. MOLDOVA
SLOVENIA ROMANIA

CROATIA YUGOSLAVIA GEORGIA
SPAIN BOSNIA AND HERZE. ARMENIA
ITALY ALB. BUL.

ORTUGAL GREECE TURKEY

CYPRUS SYRIA
MALTA LEBANON
TUNISIA ISRAEL IRAQ

MOROCCO JORDAN
KUWAIT
ALGERIA LIBYA BAHRAIN
QATAR

EGYPT SAUDI ARABIA

URITANIA UNITED ARAB
EMIRATES OMAN

SENEGAL MALI NIGER
GAMBIA CHAD SUDAN
GUINEA- BURKINA
BISSAU FASO
GUINEA BENIN
RRA TOGO DJIBOUTI
ONE COTE NIGERIA
LIBERIA D'IVOIRE CENTRAL AFRICAN ETHIOPIA
GHANA REPUBLIC
EQUATORIAL GUINEA CAMEROON
SÃO TOMÉ AND PRINCIPE UGANDA
GABON CONGO KENYA
RWANDA
BURUNDI
ZAIRE
TANZANIA

ANGOLA

ZAMBIA MALAWI

MOZAMBIQUE
NAMIBIA ZIMBABWE
BOTSWANA MADAGASCAR

SWAZILAND
SOUTH LESOTHO
AFRICA

RUSSIA

KAZAKHSTAN

UZBEKISTAN KYRGYZSTAN MONGOLIA
TURKMENISTAN TAJIKISTAN
AZERBAIJAN

NORTH
KOREA JAPAN

AFGHANISTAN PEOPLE'S REPUBLIC OF SOUTH
IRAN CHINA KOREA

PAKISTAN BHUTAN
NEPAL
TAIWAN
INDIA
BANGLADESH BURMA
YEMEN LAOS PACIFIC OCEAN
THAILAND VIETNAM
MARSHALL ISLANDS
CAMBODIA PHILIPPINES
SRI LANKA FEDERATED STATES
BRUNEI OF MICRONESIA
MALDIVES MALAYSIA KIRIBATI
SINGAPORE Equator NAURU
INDONESIA TUVALU
PAPUA
SEYCHELLES NEW SOLOMON
GUINEA ISLANDS
COMOROS VANUATU FIJI

INDIAN OCEAN

MAURITIUS

AUSTRALIA

NEW ZEALAND

V 0° 20°E 40°E 60°E 80°E 100°E 120°E 140°E 160°E 180°

Antarctic Circle

359

United States: Political

KEY

⊛ National capital
— National boundary
★ State or provincial capital
— State or provincial boundary

0   500 Miles

0   100 Miles

PACIFIC OCEAN

HAWAII
(U.S.)

Growth of the United States, 1783–1853

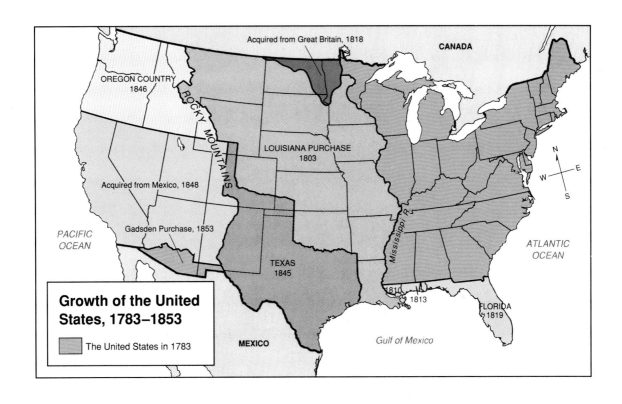

Acquired from Great Britain, 1818

CANADA

OREGON COUNTRY
1846

ROCKY MOUNTAINS

LOUISIANA PURCHASE
1803

Acquired from Mexico, 1848

Gadsden Purchase, 1853

PACIFIC
OCEAN

Mississippi R.

ATLANTIC
OCEAN

TEXAS
1845

1810
1813

FLORIDA
1819

N
W   E
S

Growth of the United States, 1783–1853

The United States in 1783

MEXICO

Gulf of Mexico

The Regions of the United States

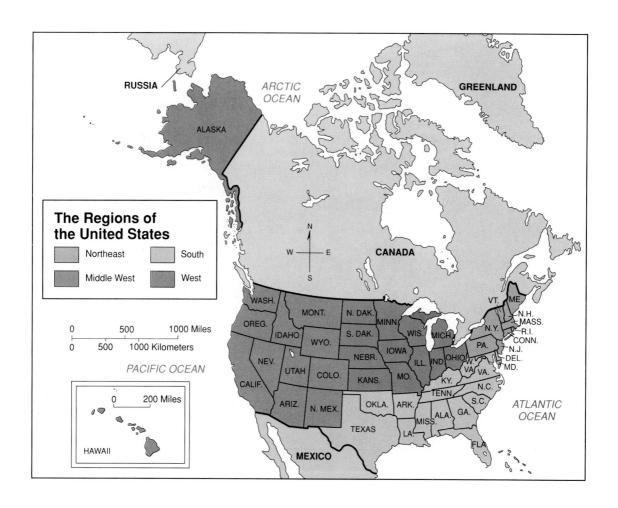

The Regions of the United States

- Northeast
- Middle West
- South
- West

RUSSIA

ARCTIC OCEAN

GREENLAND

ALASKA

CANADA

N
W · E
S

| 0 | 500 | 1000 Miles |

| 0 | 500 | 1000 Kilometers |

PACIFIC OCEAN

0 · 200 Miles

HAWAII

WASH.

OREG.

IDAHO

MONT.

WYO.

N. DAK.

S. DAK.

MINN.

WIS.

MICH.

VT. ME

N.H.

MASS.

N.Y.

R.I.

CONN.

N.J.

PA.

DEL.

MD.

NEV.

UTAH

COLO.

NEBR.

IOWA

ILL. IND OHIO

W.V.

VA. VA.

KY.

TENN

N.C.

CALIF.

ARIZ.

N. MEX.

KANS.

MO.

OKLA.

ARK.

S.C.

GA.

MISS.

ALA.

TEXAS

LA.

FLA.

ATLANTIC OCEAN

MEXICO

The South: Land Use and Resources

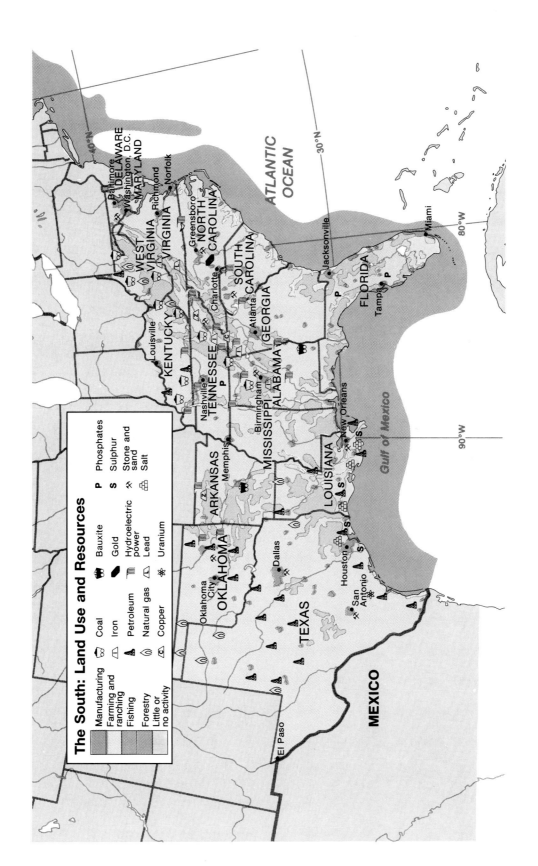

North Carolina: Physical/Political

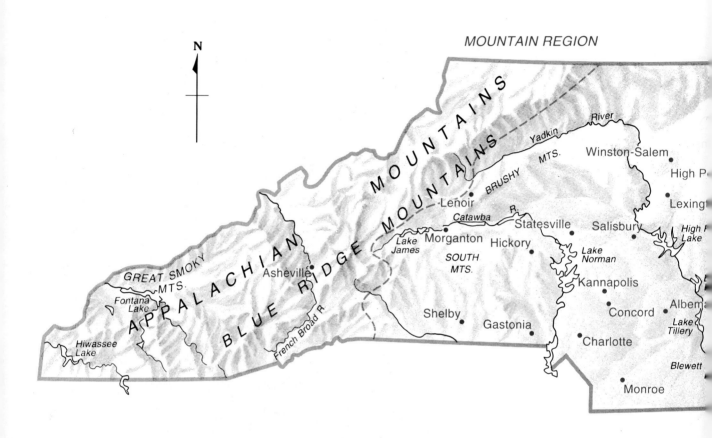

N

MOUNTAIN REGION

APPALACHIAN MOUNTAINS

BLUE RIDGE MOUNTAINS

GREAT SMOKY MTS.

BRUSHY MTS.

Yadkin River

Winston-Salem

High P

Lexing

Lenoir

Catawba R.

Statesville

Salisbury

High
Lake

Lake
James

Morganton

Hickory

SOUTH
MTS.

Asheville

Lake
Norman

Fontana
Lake

Kannapolis

Albem

French Broad R.

Shelby

Gastonia

Concord

Lake
Tillery

Hiwassee
Lake

Charlotte

Blewett

Monroe

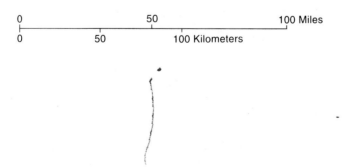

0   50   100 Miles

0   50   100 Kilometers

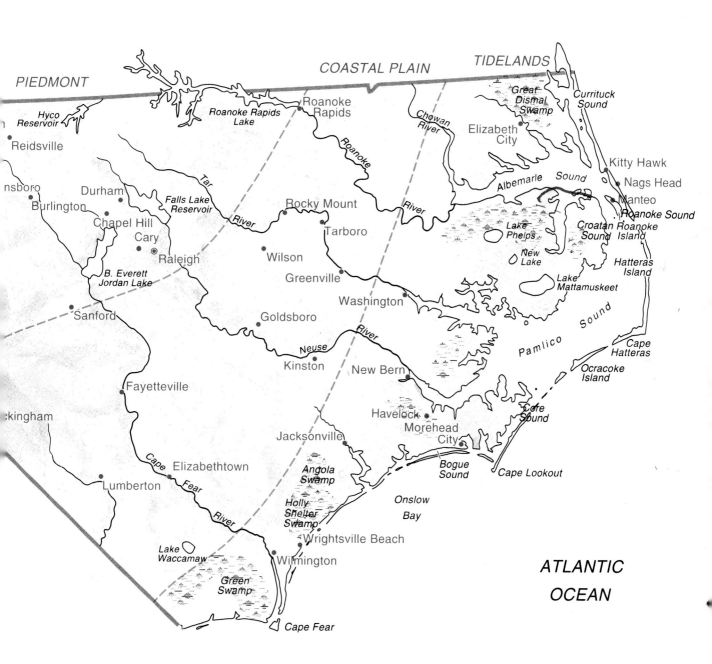

PIEDMONT

COASTAL PLAIN

TIDELANDS

Hyco
Reservoir

Reidsville

nsboro

Durham

Burlington

Chapel Hill
Cary

B. Everett
Jordan Lake

Raleigh

Sanford

:kingham

Fayetteville

Falls Lake
Reservoir

Roanoke Rapids
Lake

Tar

River

Rocky Mount

Tarboro

Wilson

Goldsboro

Neuse

Kinston

River

Roanoke
Rapids

Roanoke

River

Chowan
River

Great
Dismal
Swamp

Elizabeth
City

Albemarle

Sound

Lake
Phelps

New
Lake

Currituck
Sound

Kitty Hawk

Nags Head

Manteo

Roanoke Sound

Croatan Roanoke
Sound Island

Hatteras
Island

Lake
Mattamuskeet

Washington

Greenville

New Bern

Pamlico

Sound

Cape
Hatteras

Ocracoke
Island

Havelock

Morehead
City

Core
Sound

Elizabethtown

Lumberton

Cape

Fear

River

Jacksonville

Angola
Swamp

Holly
Shelter
Swamp

Bogue
Sound

Cape Lookout

Onslow
Bay

Lake
Waccamaw

Green
Swamp

Wrightsville Beach

Wilmington

Cape Fear

ATLANTIC

OCEAN

North Carolina Counties

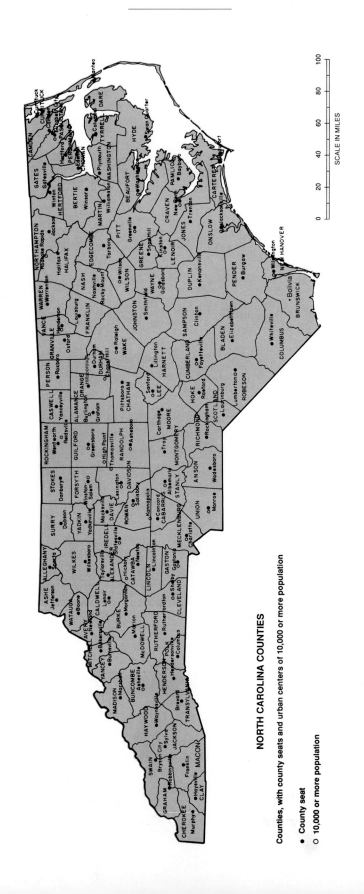

NORTH CAROLINA COUNTIES

Counties, with county seats and urban centers of 10,000 or more population

- • County seat
- ○ 10,000 or more population

Citizenship Handbook

Documents from American History

The Declaration of Independence

In Congress, July 4, 1776

By the summer of 1776, many American colonists felt that for their good and the good of their children, they had to break away from the British government and rule themselves. Delegates from the 13 colonies met in Philadelphia to decide what to do. There, Thomas Jefferson wrote the Declaration of Independence to explain to the world why Americans should separate from Britain. On July 4, 1776, the delegates voted to approve the Declaration of Independence.

The Declaration stated that all people are entitled to certain human rights—the right to life, liberty, and the pursuit of happiness. People, it said, also have the right to choose their government. That government must protect the rights of the people it governs. The Declaration then listed the abuses of the king. Finally, the men who signed the Declaration pledged themselves and everything they had to the cause of independence.

The Unanimous Declaration of the Thirteen United States of America

When in the course of human events, it becomes necessary for one people to dissolve the political bands which have connected them with another, and to assume among the powers of the earth, the separate and equal station to which the laws of Nature and of Nature's God entitle them, a decent respect to the opinions of mankind requires that they should declare the causes which impel them to the separation.

We hold these truths to be self-evident, that all men are created equal, that they are endowed by their Creator with certain unalienable rights, that among these are life, liberty and the pursuit of happiness. That to secure these rights, governments are instituted among men, deriving their just powers from the consent of the governed,—That whenever any form of government becomes destructive of these ends, it is the right of the people to alter or to abolish it, and to institute new government, laying its foundation on such principles and organizing its powers in such form, as to them shall seem most likely to effect their safety and happiness. Prudence, indeed, will dictate that governments long established should not be changed for light and transient causes; and accordingly all experience hath shown, that mankind are more disposed to suffer, while evils are sufferable, than to right themselves by abolishing the forms to which they are accustomed. But when a long train of abuses and usurpations, pursuing invariably the same object evinces a design to reduce them under absolute despotism, it is their right, it is their duty, to throw off such government, and to provide new guards for their future security.—Such has been the patient sufferance of these Colonies; and such is now the necessity which constrains them to alter their former systems of government. The history of the present King of Great Britain is a history of repeated injuries and usurpations, all having in direct object the establishment of an absolute tyranny over these States: To prove this, let facts be submitted to a candid world.

He has refused his assent to laws, the most wholesome and necessary for the public good.

He has forbidden his Governors to pass laws of immediate and pressing importance, unless suspended in their operation till his assent should be obtained; and when so suspended, he has utterly neglected to attend to them.

He has refused to pass other laws for the accommodation of large districts of people, unless those people would relinquish the right of representation in the legislature, a right inestimable to them and formidable to tyrants only.

He has called together legislative bodies at places unusual, uncomfortable, and distant from the depository of their public records, for the sole purpose of fatiguing them into compliance with his measures.

He has dissolved Representative Houses repeatedly, for opposing with manly firmness his invasions on the rights of the people.

He has refused for a long time, after such dissolutions, to cause others to be elected; whereby the legislative powers,incapable of annihilation, have returned to the people at large for their exercise; the State remaining in the mean time exposed to all the dangers of invasion from without, and convulsions within.

He has endeavoured to prevent the population of these States; for that purpose obstructing the laws for naturalization of foreigners; refusing to pass others to encourage their migrations hither, and raising the conditions of new appropriations of lands.

He has obstructed the administration of justice, by refusing his assent to laws for establishing judiciary powers.

He has made judges dependent on his will alone, for the tenure of their offices, and the amount and payment of their salaries.

He has erected a multitude of new offices, and sent hither swarms of officers to harass our people, and eat out their substance.

He has kept among us, in times of peace, standing armies without the consent of our legislatures.

He has affected to render the military independent of and superior to the civil power.

He has combined with others to subject us to a jurisdiction foreign to our constitution, and unacknowledged by our laws; giving his assent to their acts of pretended legislation:

For quartering large bodies of armed troops among us:

For protecting them, by a mock trial from punishment for any murders which they should commit on the inhabitants of these States:

For cutting off our trade with all parts of the world:

For imposing taxes on us without our consent:

For depriving us in many cases, of the benefits of trial by jury:

For transporting us beyond seas to be tried for pretended offenses:

For abolishing the free system of English laws in a neighbouring province, establishing therein an arbitrary government, and enlarging its boundaries so as to render it at once an example and fit instrument for introducing the same absolute rule into these colonies:

For taking away our charters, abolishing our most valuable laws, and altering fundamentally the forms of our governments:

For suspending our own legislatures, and declaring themselves invested with power to legislate for us in all cases whatsoever.

He has abdicated government here, by declaring us out of his protection and waging war against us.

He has plundered our seas, ravaged our coasts, burnt our towns, and destroyed the lives of our people.

He is at this time transporting large armies of foreign mercenaries to complete the works of death, desolation and tyranny, already begun with circumstances of cruelty and perfidy scarcely paralleled in the most barbarous ages, and totally unworthy the head of a civilized nation.

He has constrained our fellow citizens taken captive on the high seas to bear arms against their country, to become the executioners of their friends and brethren, or to fall themselves by their hands.

He has excited domestic insurrections amongst us, and has endeavoured to bring on the inhabitants of our frontiers, the merciless Indian savages, whose known rule of warfare is an undistinguished destruction of all ages, sexes and conditions.

In every stage of these oppressions we have petitioned for redress in the most humble terms: Our repeated petitions have been answered only by repeated injury. A prince, whose character is thus marked by every act which may define a tyrant, is unfit to be the ruler of a free people.

Nor have we been wanting in attentions to our British brethren. We have warned them from time to time of attempts by their legislature to extend an unwarrantable jurisdiction over us. We have reminded them of the circumstances of our emigration and settlement here. We have appealed to their native justice and magnanimity, and we have conjured them by the ties of our common kindred to disavow these usurpations which, would inevitably interrupt our connections and correspondence. They too have been deaf to the voice of justice and of consanguinity. We must, therefore, acquiesce in the necessity which denounces our separation, and hold them, as we hold the rest of mankind, enemies in war, in peace friends.

WE, THEREFORE, the Representatives of the United States of America, in General Congress, Assembled, appealing to the Supreme Judge of the world for the rectitude of our intentions, do, in the name, and by authority of the good people of these Colonies, solemnly publish and declare, That these United Colonies are, and of right ought to be FREE AND INDEPENDENT STATES; that they are absolved from all allegiance to the British Crown, and that all political connection between them and the State of Great Britain, is and ought to be totally dissolved; and that as free and independent States, they have full power to levy war, conclude peace, contract alliances, establish commerce, and to do all other acts and things which independent States may of right do. And for the support of this Declaration, with a firm reliance on the protection of Divine Providence, we mutually pledge to each other our lives, our fortunes and our sacred honor.

John Hancock.

Button Gwinnett	Thos. Nelson jr.	Geo Read
Lyman Hall	Francis Lightfoot Lee	Tho M:Kean
Geo Walton.	Carter Braxton	Wm. Floyd
Wm. Hooper	Robt. Morris	Phil. Livingston
Joseph Hewes,	John Adams	Frans. Lewis
John Penn	Robt. Treat Paine	Lewis Morris
Edward Rutledge.	Elbridge Gerry	Richd. Stockton
Thos. Heyward Junr.	Step. Hopkins	Jno Witherspoon
Thomas Lynch Junr.	William Ellery	Fras. Hopkinson
Arthur Middleton	Benjamin Rush	John Hart
Samuel Chase	Benja. Franklin	Abra Clark
Wm. Paca	John Morton	Josiah Bartlett
Thos. Stone	Geo Clymer	Wm: Whipple
Charles Carroll of Carrollton	Jas. Smith.	Saml. Adams
George Wythe	Geo. Taylor	Roger Sherman
Richard Henry Lee	James Wilson	Saml. Huntington
Th: Jefferson	Geo. Ross	Wm. Williams
Benja. Harrison	Caesar Rodney	Oliver Wolcott
		Matthew Thornton

Setting Up a Government

Starting here, you can read the Constitution of the United States just as it was written in 1787. Some parts of the Constitution, however, are no longer in effect. They have been changed by later amendments. These parts of the Constitution appear in *italic* type. Beside the Constitution, inside the gray block, are explanations that will help you with your reading.

Constitution of the
United States of America

PREAMBLE

WE THE PEOPLE of the United States, in order to form a more perfect Union, establish justice, insure domestic tranquility, provide for the common defense, promote the general welfare, and secure the blessings of liberty to ourselves and our posterity, do ordain and establish this Constitution for the United States of America.

ARTICLE I

SECTION 1.   All legislative powers herein granted shall be vested in a Congress of the United States, which shall consist of a Senate and House of Representatives.

SECTION 2.   The House of Representatives shall be composed of members chosen every second year by the people of the several States, and the electors in each State shall have the qualifications requisite for electors of the most numerous branch of the State Legislature.

No person shall be a representative who shall not have attained to the age of twenty-five years, and been seven years a citizen of the United States, and who shall not, when elected, be an inhabitant of that State in which he shall be chosen.

PREAMBLE

The Preamble says that the people have the power to set up the government. It also tells why they set up a new government: (1) to bind the states together, (2) to see that everyone is treated fairly by the laws, (3) to keep peace in the country, (4) to defend the country against foreign enemies, (5) to work for the good of all the people, and (6) to give the people freedom for generations to come.

ARTICLE I MAKING LAWS
Section 1. Congress

Lawmaking power   The power to make laws belongs to Congress. But Congress can make only those laws permitted by the Constitution. Congress has two parts—the Senate and the House of Representatives.

Section 2. The House of Representatives

Choosing members   Members of the House of Representatives are elected from each state every two years. Anyone a state allows to vote for members of the state legislature must also be allowed to vote for members of the House of Representatives.

Who may be a representative   A representative must be at least 25 years of age, must have been a United States citizen for at least 7 years, and must live in the state he or she represents.

371

Representatives *and direct taxes* shall be apportioned among the several States which may be included within this Union, according to their respective numbers, *which shall be determined by adding to the whole number of free persons, including those bound to service for a term of years, and excluding Indians not taxed, three-fifths of all other persons.* The actual enumeration shall be made within three years after the first meeting of the Congress of the United States, and within every subsequent term of ten years, in such manner as they shall by law direct. The number of representatives shall not exceed one for every thirty thousand, but each State shall have at least one representative; and until such enumeration shall be made, the State of New Hampshire shall be entitled to choose three, Massachusetts eight, Rhode Island and Providence Plantations one, Connecticut five, New York six, New Jersey four, Pennsylvania eight, Delaware one, Maryland six, Virginia ten, North Carolina five, South Carolina five, and Georgia three.

When vacancies happen in the representation from any State, the Executive authority thereof shall issue writs of election to fill such vacancies.

The House of Representatives shall choose their Speaker and other officers; and shall have the sole power of impeachment.

SECTION 3. The Senate of the United States shall be composed of two senators from each State, *chosen by the legislature thereof,* for six years and each senator shall have one vote.

Immediately after they shall be assembled in consequence of the first election, they shall be divided as equally as may be into three classes.

Representation based on population   The number of representatives each state has in the House of Representatives is based on the number of people living in the state. At the time the Constitution was written, taxes were collected by each state government to be paid to the United States government. These taxes were also based on the number of people living in the state. This rule was changed later as far as income taxes were concerned. The rules for counting the number of people living in a state also changed. Today all the people living in each state are counted. Slavery is against the law today. Indians are citizens, so they are now counted. Congress must count the number of people in the states every ten years. No matter how few people a state has, it gets at least one representative. Since 1929, the total size of the House of Representatives has been set at 435.

Filling vacancies   A vacancy exists when a representative dies or resigns before his or her term has ended. Then the state's governor must call for a special election to replace the representative.

Choosing officers; impeachment   Members of the House of Representatives choose their own leaders. Their leaders include a Speaker, or chairperson. Only the House of Representatives has the power of impeachment. That is, the House of Representatives may bring charges of serious misbehavior against any official of the United States government.

Section 3. The Senate
Choosing members   Each state has two senators. Each senator serves a six-year term and has one vote. Before 1913, senators were chosen by state legislatures. Since then, senators have been chosen by the voters of each state.

Three groups of senators   During the first years under the Constitution, senators were divided into three groups. One group served for six

The seats of the senators of the first class shall be vacated at the expiration of the second year, of the second class at the expiration of the fourth year, and of the third class at the expiration of the sixth year, so that one-third may be chosen every second year; and if vacancies happen by resignation, or otherwise, during the recess of the legislature of any State, the executive thereof may make temporary appointments until the next meeting of the legislature, which shall then fill such vacancies.

No person shall be a senator who shall not have attained to the age of thirty years, and been nine years a citizen of the United States, and who shall not, when elected, be an inhabitant of that State for which he shall be chosen.

The Vice President of the United States shall be President of the Senate, but shall have no vote, unless they be equally divided.

The Senate shall choose their other officers, and also a President pro tempore, in the absence of the Vice President, or when he shall exercise the office of President of the United States.

The Senate shall have the sole power to try all impeachments. When sitting for that purpose, they shall be on oath or affirmation. When the President of the United States is tried, the Chief Justice shall preside: And no person shall be convicted without the concurrence of two thirds of the members present.

Judgment in cases of impeachment shall not extend further than to removal from office, and disqualification to hold and enjoy any office or honor, trust or profit under the United States: but the party convicted shall nevertheless be liable and subject to indictment, trial, judgment and punishment, according to law.

years; one group served for four years; one group served for two years. In this way, their terms did not end at the same time. All senators are now elected for six-year terms. However, only one third are chosen at a time.

Who may be a senator   A senator must be at least 30 years of age, must have been a United States citizen for at least nine years, and must live in the state that he or she represents.

President of the Senate   The Vice President of the United States is the president, or chairperson, of the Senate. However, the Vice President can vote only when there is a tie vote.

Other officers   Members of the Senate choose all their other leaders. One of these, the President pro tempore, is the chairperson when the Vice President is absent. *Pro tempore* means "for a time."

Impeachment trials   The Senate holds a trial for any official impeached by the House of Representatives. The official is found guilty if two thirds of the senators present vote him or her guilty. If the President of the United States is on trial, the Chief Justice of the United States acts as chairperson of the Senate. The Chief Justice is the highest official on the Supreme Court.

Punishment   If an official is found guilty in an impeachment trial, the Senate can order the official out of office. The Senate can also order that the person never serve in the government again. After being put out of office, the person can be tried in a regular court for the crimes that the Senate has already judged.

SECTION 4. The times, places and manner of holding elections for senators and representatives, shall be prescribed in each State by the legislature thereof; but the Congress may at any time by law make or alter such regulations, *except as to the places of choosing senators.*

The Congress shall assemble at least once in every year, *and such meeting shall be on the first Monday in December, unless they shall by law appoint a different day.*

SECTION 5. Each house shall be the judge of the elections, returns and qualifications of its own members, and a majority of each shall constitute a quorum to do business; but a smaller number may adjourn from day to day, and may be authorized to compel the attendance of absent members, in such manner, and under such penalties as each house may provide.

Each house may determine the rules of its proceedings, punish its members for disorderly behaviour, and, with the concurrence of two-thirds, expel a member.

Each house shall keep a journal of its proceedings, and from time to time publish the same, excepting such parts as may in their judgment require secrecy; and the yeas and the nays of the members of either house on any question shall, at the desire of one-fifth of those present, be entered on the journal.

Neither house, during the session of Congress, shall, without the consent of the other, adjourn for more than three days, nor to any other place than that in which the two houses shall be sitting.

SECTION 6. The senators and representatives shall receive a compensation for their services, to be ascertained by law, and paid out of the Treasury of the United States. They shall in all cases,

Section 4. Elections and Meetings of Congress

How elections are held The states may make rules about elections to Congress. But Congress may change state election laws. As a result of later changes, both senators and representatives are chosen by the people.

Meetings of Congress Congress must meet at least once a year. A later amendment changed the beginning of each session from the first Monday in December to January 3.

Section 5. Rules of Congress

How Congress is organized Both the House of Representatives and the Senate can set rules for membership. Each can keep out any newly elected member who does not meet those rules. Neither the House nor the Senate can carry out official business unless there is a quorum—that is, unless more than half the members are present. If there is no quorum, members adjourn, or end their meeting for the day. Both houses may use penalties to force absent members to attend.

Rules of Congress Each house of Congress may make its own rules. Each may punish members who do not obey those rules. In both houses, a member can be expelled, or required to leave, by two thirds of those present.

Journal of meetings of Congress Each house must keep a record of what goes on at its meetings, and from time to time those records must be published. But members may decide to keep some things secret. How members vote on a question is published only if one fifth of the members there agree to do so.

Ending a meeting of Congress Neither house may adjourn, or end a meeting, for more than three days or move to another city unless the other house agrees.

Section 6. What Members of Congress Can and Cannot Do

Pay and privileges of members Members of both houses are paid out of the United States

except treason, felony and breach of the peace, be privileged from arrest during their attendance at the session of their respective houses, and in going to and returning from the same; and for any speech or debate in either house, they shall not be questioned in any other place.

No senator or representative shall, during the time for which he was elected, be appointed to any civil office under the authority of the United States, which shall have been created, or the emoluments whereof shall have been increased during such time; and no person holding any office under the United States, shall be a member of either house during his continuance in office.

SECTION 7.   All bills for raising revenue shall originate in the House of Representatives; but the Senate may propose or concur with amendments as on other bills.

Every bill which shall have passed the House of Representatives and the Senate, shall, before it become a law, be presented to the President of the United States; if he approves he shall sign it, but if not he shall return it, with his objections to that house in which it shall have originated, who shall enter the objections at large on their journal, and proceed to reconsider it. If after such reconsideration two thirds of that House shall agree to pass the bill, it shall be sent, together with the objections, to the other House, by which it shall likewise be reconsidered, and if approved by two thirds of that House, it shall become a law. But in all such cases the votes of both Houses shall be determined by yeas and nays, and the names of the persons voting for and against the bill shall be entered on the journal of each House respectively. If any bill shall not be returned by the President within ten days (Sundays excepted) after it shall have been presented to him, the same shall be a law, in like manner as if he had signed it, unless the Congress by their adjournment prevent its return, in which case it shall not be a law.

Treasury. The amount they are paid is decided by law. Members cannot be arrested at meetings of Congress or on their way to and from meetings unless they are suspected of treason, serious crimes, or disturbing the peace. They cannot be punished for anything they say in their meetings except by other members of their house.

Holding other official positions   No one can become a member of Congress without giving up other national positions. No member can take a position in the national government if that position was created, or the pay for that position was increased, while the member served in Congress.

Section 7. Ways of Passing Laws
Taxes   Only the House of Representatives may propose a law for raising money. But the Senate has the right to make changes in such proposals.

How a bill becomes a law   After a bill, or proposed law, has passed both houses of Congress, it must be sent to the President. If the President signs the bill, it becomes law. If the President does not approve of the bill, he or she may veto it—that is, refuse to sign it. The President then sends the bill, with a list of reasons stating why he or she does not approve of it, to the house that passed it first. The members of that house vote on the bill again. If two thirds pass it a second time, it is sent to the other house, along with the President's reasons for not wanting it to be law. If two thirds of that house also favor the bill, it becomes law. The President's reasons for not wanting the law must be published. The records of Congress must also show how each member voted. The President has ten days (not counting Sundays) to consider a bill. If the President takes longer, the bill becomes law without his or her signature as long as Congress has not adjourned in the meantime. If Congress has adjourned, the unsigned bill does not become law. This is known as a pocket veto.

Every order, resolution, or vote to which the concurrence of the Senate and House of Representatives may be necessary (except on a question of adjournment) shall be presented to the President of the United States; and before the same shall take effect, shall be approved by him, or being disapproved by him, shall be repassed by two thirds of the Senate and House of Representatives, according to the rules and limitations prescribed in the case of a bill.

SECTION 8. The Congress shall have power to lay and collect taxes, duties, imposts and excises, to pay the debts and provide for the common defense and general welfare of the United States; but all duties, imposts and excises shall be uniform throughout the United States.

To borrow money on the credit of the United States;

To regulate commerce with foreign nations, and among the several States, and with the Indian tribes;

To establish a uniform rule of naturalization, and uniform laws on the subject of bankruptcies throughout the United States;

To coin money, regulate the value thereof, and of foreign coin, and fix the standard of weights and measures;

To provide for the punishment of counterfeiting the securities and current coin of the United States;

To establish post offices and post roads;

Actions that need the President's approval Any action that needs the approval of both the House and the Senate must also be sent to the President for approval the same way that bills are. The only exceptions are votes to adjourn Congress.

Section 8. Powers of Congress

Taxing the people Congress may raise taxes in order to pay the nation's debts, defend the nation, and provide for the good of all the people. Those taxes must be the same throughout the United States.

Borrowing money Congress may borrow money to run the national government.

Trade relations Congress may control trade, transportation, communication, and related matters with other countries, among the states, and with Indian groups.

Becoming a citizen and paying debts Congress decides how citizens of foreign countries can become citizens of the United States. Congress may make laws for the whole country concerning the treatment of those who cannot pay their debts.

Coining money Congress may coin, or make, money and say how much it is worth. It may also put a value on foreign money. Congress also has the power to set weights and measures so they will be the same everywhere.

Punishment for making fake money Congress may pass laws to punish those who make false bonds, stamps, or money.

Rules concerning mail Congress may set up post offices and build the roads over which the mail travels.

To promote the progress of science and useful arts, by securing for limited times to authors and inventors the exclusive right to their respective writings and discoveries;

To constitute tribunals inferior to the Supreme Court;

To define and punish piracies and felonies committed on the high seas, and offenses against the law of nations;

To declare war, grant letters of marque and reprisal, and make rules concerning captures on land and water;

To raise and support armies, but no appropriation of money to that use shall be for a longer term than two years;

To provide and maintain a Navy;

To make rules for the government and regulation of the land and naval forces;

To provide for calling forth the militia to execute the laws of the Union, suppress insurrections and repel invasions;

To provide for organizing, arming, and disciplining the militia, and for governing such part of them as may be employed in the service of the United States, reserving to the States respectively, the appointment of the officers, and the authority of training the militia according to the discipline prescribed by Congress;

To exercise exclusive legislation in all cases whatsoever, over such district (not exceeding ten miles square) as may, by cession of particular States, and the acceptance of Congress, become the seat of the Government of the United States, and to exercise like authority over all places purchased by the consent of the legislature of the

Protecting people's work Congress may help science, industry, and the arts by making laws that protect the works of authors, composers, artists, and inventors. These laws would punish other people who try to copy the original work without permission.

Setting up lower courts Congress may set up national courts that have less authority than the Supreme Court of the United States.

Laws in places outside the United States Congress may decide what acts committed at sea are a crime and how they are to be punished. It may also make laws about crimes in which foreign countries and foreign citizens are involved.

Declaring war Congress, and only Congress, may declare war. Until 1856, it could also set rules about warfare carried on by private citizens. Such warfare is no longer allowed.

Supporting armed forces Congress may raise and support armed forces. It cannot, however, provide money for the army for more than two years at a time. Congress may also make rules for the organization and control of the armed forces.

Rules about militia Congress may call out militias to enforce national laws, put down rebellions, and drive out invaders. Militias are groups of citizen-soldiers in the various states. Congress may organize the militias, furnish weapons to them, and make rules for them while they are in the service of the United States. Each state may appoint officers of its militia, but it must train the militia as Congress directs.

Control of the capital Congress may make all the laws for governing the District of Columbia, which includes the national capital. Congress shall govern all places bought from the states for use as forts, arsenals, navy yards, and public buildings.

State in which the same shall be, for the erection of forts, magazines, arsenals, dock-yards, and other needful buildings;—And

To make all laws which shall be necessary and proper for carrying into execution the foregoing powers, and all other powers vested by this Constitution in the Government of the United States, or in any department or officer thereof.

SECTION 9. The migration or importation of such persons as any of the States now existing shall think proper to admit, shall not be prohibited by the Congress prior to the year one thousand eight hundred and eight, but a tax or duty may be imposed on such importation, not exceeding ten dollars for each person.

The privilege of the writ of habeas corpus shall not be suspended, unless when in cases of rebellion or invasion the public safety may require it.

No bill of attainder or ex post facto law shall be passed.

No capitation, or other direct, tax shall be laid, unless in proportion to the census or enumeration herein before directed to be taken.

No tax or duty shall be laid on articles exported from any State.

No preference shall be given by any regulation of commerce or revenue to the ports of one State over those of another: nor shall vessels bound to, or from, one State, be obliged to enter, clear, or pay duties in another.

No money shall be drawn from the Treasury; but in consequence of appropriations made by law; and a regular statement and account of the receipts and expenditures of all public money shall be published from time to time.

Changing laws of the Constitution   Congress may make any laws needed to carry out the powers given to the government of the United States by the Constitution. This part of the Constitution is known as the elastic clause, because it can be stretched to fit the changing needs of the nation.

Section 9. Powers Denied Congress

Tax on slaves   Before 1808, Congress could not outlaw the slave trade. But it could tax the people who brought slaves into the country. The tax could not be more than ten dollars for each slave.

Writ of habeas corpus   Only when the country is in danger from a rebellion or invasion can Congress keep courts from issuing writs of habeas corpus. A writ of habeas corpus forces a jailor to bring a prisoner to court so that a judge can decide whether that person is being held lawfully.

Punishing individuals   Congress can never pass a law punishing a particular person. Congress cannot pass a law punishing people for doing something that was lawful at the time they did it.

Direct taxes   Congress cannot set a capitation, or direct tax on individuals, except in proportion to population figures. The only exception is the income tax. Congress may not tax goods sent from one state to another.

Trade taxes   Congress may not favor one state or city over the others in matters of trade. Ships from any state may enter the ports of any other state without paying charges.

Spending government money   Congress cannot spend government money without passing a bill for that purpose. An account of all money taken in and spent must be made public.

No title of nobility shall be granted by the United States: And no person holding any office of profit or trust under them, shall, without the consent of the Congress, accept of any present, emolument, office, or title, of any kind whatever, from any King, Prince, or foreign State.

SECTION 10. No State shall enter into any treaty, alliance, or confederation; grant letters of marque and reprisal; coin money; emit bills of credit; make any thing but gold and silver coin a tender in payment of debts; pass any bill of attainder, ex post facto law, or law impairing the obligation of contracts, or grant any title of nobility.

No State shall, without the consent of the Congress, lay any imposts or duties on imports or exports, except what may be absolutely necessary for executing its inspection laws: and the net produce of all duties and imposts, laid by any State on imports or exports, shall be for the use of the Treasury of the United States; and all such laws shall be subject to the revision and control of the Congress.

No State shall, without the consent of Congress, lay any duty of tonnage, keep troops, or ships of war in time of peace, enter into any agreement or compact with another State, or with a foreign power, or engage in war, unless actually invaded, or in such imminent danger as will not admit of delay.

ARTICLE II
SECTION 1. The executive power shall be vested in a President of the United States of America. He shall hold his office during the term of four years, and, together with the Vice President, chosen for the same term, be elected, as follows:

Each State, shall appoint, in such manner as the legislature thereof may direct, a number of electors, equal to the whole number of senators and representatives to which the State may be entitled in the Congress; but no senator or

Official titles Congress may not create titles such as that of lord, duchess, or count. No national official can accept a title, gift, or position from another country without the permission of Congress.

Section 10. Powers Denied to the States
What states cannot do No state can make treaties with foreign countries. No state can give private citizens permission to wage a war. No state can coin money. These powers belong to the national government. Like the national government, a state government may not punish people for things that were lawful when they did them, and it may not grant titles of nobility.

States' power to charge inspection fees A state cannot tax goods entering or leaving the state without the permission of Congress. But states may charge an inspection fee. Any profit from that fee must go to the United States Treasury. Congress has the power to change state inspection laws.

More things states cannot do Unless Congress gives permission, no state may tax ships, keep troops other than a militia, or keep warships in peacetime. States cannot ally with other states or with foreign countries unless Congress agrees. States cannot go to war without the permission of Congress unless invaded or in such danger that delay is impossible.

ARTICLE II THE EXECUTIVE BRANCH
Section 1. President and Vice President
Terms of the President and Vice President The President of the United States enforces the nation's laws. The President serves a four-year term. The Vice President also serves for four years.

The selection of electors The President and Vice President are to be chosen by electors in each state. These electors are selected according to rules set by state legislatures. The electors from all the states form the electoral college. The

representative, or person holding an office of trust or profit under the United States, shall be appointed an elector.

The electors shall meet in their respective States, and vote by ballot for two persons, of whom one at least shall not be an inhabitant of the same State with themselves. And they shall make a list of all the persons voted for, and of the number of votes for each; which list they shall sign and certify, and transmit sealed to the seat of the Government of the United States, directed to the President of the Senate. The President of the Senate shall, in the presence of the Senate and House of Representatives, open all the certificates, and the votes shall then be counted. The person having the greatest number of votes shall be the President, if such number be a majority of the whole number of electors appointed; and if there be more than one who have such majority, and have an equal number of votes, then the House of Representatives shall immediately choose by ballot one of them for President; and if no person have a majority, then from the five highest on the list the said House shall in like manner choose the President. But in choosing the President, the votes shall be taken by States, the representation from each State having one vote; a quorum for this purpose shall consist of a member or members from two thirds of the States, and a majority of all the States shall be necessary to a choice. In every case, after the choice of the President, the person having the greatest number of votes of the electors shall be the Vice President. But if there should remain two or more who have equal votes, the Senate shall choose from them by ballot the Vice President.

The Congress may determine the time of choosing the electors, and the day on which they shall give their votes; which day shall be the same throughout the United States.

number of electors in each state Is equal to the number of representatives and senators the state has in Congress. No person who has a position in the national government may be an elector.

Duties of the electors The electors, meeting in their respective states, vote for President and Vice President on one ballot. Their votes are recorded and then sent to the President of the Senate, who counts them in front of both houses of Congress. The candidate with the highest number of electoral votes becomes President, and the one with the second highest total becomes Vice President. If there is a tie, or no candidate has a majority, the House of Representatives shall choose the President from the five candidates with the highest totals. In the balloting, each state has one vote. At least two thirds of the states must be present. The candidate who wins a majority of all states becomes President. The person who comes in second will be the Vice President. This section of the Constitution was changed by a later amendment.

Election day Congress can decide on what day electors are to be chosen and on what day they are to cast their ballots. Each day is to be the same throughout the United States. (The day set for choosing electors is the first Tuesday after the first Monday in November. The electors cast their ballots on the first Monday after the second Wednesday in December.)

No person except a natural born citizen, or a citizen of the United States, at the time of the adoption of this Constitution, shall be eligible to the office of President; neither shall any person be eligible to that office who shall not have attained to the age of thirty-five years, and been fourteen years a resident within the United States.

In case of the removal of the President from office, or of his death, resignation, or inability to discharge the powers and duties of the said office, the same shall devolve on the Vice President, *and the Congress may by law provide for the case of removal, death, resignation, or inability, both of the President and Vice President, declaring what officer shall then act as President, and such officer shall act accordingly, until the disability be removed, or a President shall be elected.*

The President shall, at stated times, receive for his services, a compensation, which shall neither be increased nor diminished during the period for which he shall have been elected, and he shall not receive within that period any other emolument from the United States, or any of them.

Before he enter on the execution of his office, he shall take the following oath or affirmation:— "I do solemnly swear (or affirm) that I will faithfully execute the office of President of the United States, and will to the best of my ability, preserve, protect and defend the Constitution of the United States."

SECTION 2. The President shall be Commander in Chief of the Army and Navy of the United States, and of the militia of the several States, when called into the actual service of the United States; he may require the opinion, in writing, of the principal officer in each of the Executive Departments, upon any subject relating to the duties of their respective offices, and he shall have power to grant reprieves and pardons for offenses against the United States, except in cases of impeachment.

Qualifications for President The President must be a citizen of the United States by birth or must have become a citizen by the time the Constitution was adopted. He or she must be at least 35 years old and must have lived in the United States for 14 or more years.

Who can take the place of the President If the President dies, resigns, or is unable to carry out the duties of the office, the Vice President becomes President. Congress can decide by law who becomes President when neither the President nor the Vice President can serve. This part of the Constitution was changed by a later amendment.

The President's salary The salary of a President cannot be raised or lowered during his or her term of office. The President cannot receive any other salary from national or state governments.

The President's oath of office Before starting a term of office, the President is to make a solemn promise to carry out faithfully the duties of President and to protect the government that was set up by the Constitution.

Section 2. Powers of the President

Military and civil powers The President is Commander in Chief of the armed forces of the United States. He or she is also the Commander in Chief of the state militias when they are called to national service. The President may order written reports from Cabinet officers about the work of their departments. The President may pardon people accused of crimes against the national government or delay their punishment. The President cannot, however, pardon or delay the punishment of an impeached government official.

He shall have power, by and with the advice and consent of the Senate, to make treaties, provided two thirds of the Senators present concur; and he shall nominate, and by and with the advice and consent of the Senate, shall appoint ambassadors, other public ministers and consuls, Judges of the Supreme Court, and all other officers of the United States, whose appointments are not herein otherwise provided for, and which shall be established by law: but the Congress may by law vest the appointment of such inferior officers, as they think proper, in the President alone, in the courts of law, or in the heads of departments.

The President shall have power to fill up all vacancies that may happen during the recess of the Senate, by granting commissions which shall expire at the end of their next session.

SECTION 3. He shall from time to time give to the Congress information of the state of the Union, and recommend to their consideration such measures as he shall judge necessary and expedient; he may, on extraordinary occasions, convene both houses, or either of them, and in case of disagreement between them, with respect to the time of adjournment, he may adjourn them to such time as he shall think proper; he shall receive ambassadors and other public ministers; he shall take care that the laws be faithfully executed, and shall commission all the officers of the United States.

SECTION 4. The President, Vice President and all civil officers of the United States, shall be removed from office on impeachment for, and conviction of, treason, bribery, or other high crimes and misdemeanors.

Making treaties and appointing officers The President can make treaties with foreign countries. At least two thirds of the Senators present must vote for each treaty before it becomes binding.

The President can appoint people to represent the United States in other countries, judges of the Supreme Court, and other government officials unless the Constitution says differently. In each case, a majority of the Senate must vote for the President's choice. Congress may pass laws giving the President, the courts, or heads of government departments the right to select people for less important government positions. The President may appoint individuals to fill open positions that occur when the Senate is not meeting. These temporary appointments come to an end at the close of the next session of the Senate.

Section 3. Duties of the President
Other presidential powers The President is to inform Congress from time to time about the condition of the country. Traditionally the President does so at the beginning of each session of Congress. The speech is called the State of the Union message. In it, the President recommends changes or improvements in government. In emergencies, the President may call meetings of the House of Representatives or the Senate or both. If the two houses of Congress disagree about the ending of a session, the President may end it. The President deals with representatives of other countries. It is the President's duty to see that the laws of the country are obeyed. The President signs official papers appointing individuals to jobs in the national government.

Section 4. Impeachments
Who can be impeached The President, Vice President, and other officials of the national government (except members of Congress and military officers) can be removed from office if they are accused of wrongdoing by the House of Representatives and then found guilty by the Senate.

ARTICLE III

SECTION 1. The judicial power of the United States, shall be vested in one Supreme Court, and in such inferior courts as the Congress may from time to time ordain and establish. The judges, both of the supreme and inferior courts, shall hold their offices during good behaviour, and shall, at stated times, receive for their services, a compensation, which shall not be diminished during their continuance in office.

SECTION 2. The judicial power shall extend to all cases, in law and equity, arising under this Constitution, the laws of the United States, and treaties made, or which shall be made, under their authority;—to all cases affecting ambassadors, other public ministers and consuls;—to all cases of admiralty and maritime jurisdiction;—to controversies to which the United States shall be a party;—to controversies between two or more States;—*between a State and citizens of another State;*—between citizens of different States,—between citizens of the same State claiming lands under grants of different States, and between a State, or the citizens thereof, and foreign States, citizens or subjects.

In all cases affecting ambassadors, other public ministers and consuls, and those in which a State shall be a party, the Supreme Court shall have original jurisdiction. In all the other cases before mentioned, the Supreme Court shall have appellate jurisdiction, both as to law and fact, with such exceptions, and under such regulations as the Congress shall make.

The trial of all crimes, except in cases of impeachment, shall be by jury; and such trial shall be held in the State where the said crimes shall have been committed; but when not committed within any State, the trial shall be at such place or places as the Congress may by law have directed.

ARTICLE III THE JUDICIAL BRANCH
Section 1. Judicial Power

Judges and what they can do The Supreme Court of the United States makes the final decisions in matters of law. Congress may set up other national courts with less power than the Supreme Court. Judges of all national courts hold office for life or until they are proved guilty of wrongful acts. Their salaries cannot be lowered while they are in office.

Section 2. Cases Heard in the United States Courts

Powers of the federal courts The national courts settle disputes that have to do with the Constitution, laws of the United States, treaties, and laws about ships and shipping. These courts also settle legal disputes between people of different states, disputes in which people of the same state claim land in other states, and disputes between a state or citizen of a state and a foreign country. Until a later amendment was passed, the national courts also settled disputes between a state and a citizen of another state.

Jurisdiction of the Courts If a representative of a foreign country or a state is involved in a dispute, the trial may go directly to the Supreme Court. All other cases described above are tried in a lower national court first. These cases are brought to the Supreme Court only if one of the parties objects to the decision of the lower court and appeals to the Supreme Court. After the case has been tried in the Supreme Court, there is no higher court to which either side may appeal.

Trial by jury for criminal cases Except for an impeached official, anyone accused of a crime by the national government has the right to a trial by jury. The trial must be held in the state where the crime was committed. If the crime took place outside of any state—at sea, for example—the trial is to be held in a place Congress has chosen by law.

SECTION 3. Treason against the United States, shall consist only in levying war against them, or in adhering to their enemies, giving them aid and comfort. No person shall be convicted of treason unless on the testimony of two witnesses to the same overt act, or on confession in open court.

The Congress shall have power to declare the punishment of treason, but no attainder of treason shall work corruption of blood, or forfeiture except during the life of the person attainted.

ARTICLE IV

SECTION 1. Full faith and credit shall be given in each State to the public acts, records, and judicial proceedings of every other State. And the Congress may by general laws prescribe the manner in which such acts, records and proceedings shall be proved, and the effect thereof.

SECTION 2. The citizens of each State shall be entitled to all privileges and immunities of citizens in the several States.

A person charged in any State with treason, felony, or other crime, who shall flee from justice, and be found in another State, shall on demand of the executive authority of the State from which he fled, be delivered up, to be removed to the State having jurisdiction of the crime.

No person held to service or labour in one State, under the laws thereof, escaping into another, shall, in consequence of any law or regulation therein, be discharged from such service or labour, but shall be delivered up on claim of the party to whom such service or labour may be due.

Section 3. Treason

Definition of treason Treason is carrying on war against the United States or helping the enemies of the United States. No one can be punished for treason unless two or more witnesses swear they saw the same act of treason or unless the accused person confesses to the crime in court.

Punishment for treason Congress can pass laws fixing the punishment for treason. However, the family of a person found guilty of treason cannot be punished in any way.

ARTICLE IV THE STATES AND THE NATION
Section 1. Official Acts of the States

Laws of other states Each state must respect the laws, records, and court decisions of all other states.

Section 2. Rights of Citizens of Other States

Rights of a person legally in another state Citizens of one state who move to or do business in another state have the same rights as citizens who live in that state.

Rights of a person illegally in another state A person accused of a crime in one state and found in another is to be returned for trial to the state in which the crime was committed. The request for the accused person's return must come from the governor of that state.

Rights of a slave illegally in another state Slaves did not become free by escaping to a state that did not allow slavery. Instead, they had to be returned to their owners. Because slavery is no longer legal, this part of the Constitution is no longer in effect.

SECTION 3. New States may be admitted by the Congress into this Union; but no new State shall be formed or erected within the jurisdiction of any other State; nor any State be formed by the junction of two or more States, or parts of States, without the consent of the legislatures of the States concerned as well as of the Congress.

The Congress shall have power to dispose of and make all needful rules and regulations respecting the Territory or other property belonging to the United States; and nothing in this Constitution shall be so construed as to prejudice any claims of the United States, or of any particular State.

SECTION 4. The United States shall guarantee to every State in this Union a republican form of Government, and shall protect each of them against invasion; and on application of the legislature, or of the executive (when the legislature cannot be convened) against domestic violence.

ARTICLE V

The Congress, whenever two thirds of both Houses shall deem it necessary, shall propose amendments to this Constitution, or on the application of the legislatures of two thirds of the several States, shall call a convention for proposing amendments, which, in either case, shall be valid to all intents and purposes, as part of this Constitution, when ratified by the legislatures of three fourths of the several States, or by conventions in three fourths thereof, as the one or the other mode of ratification may be proposed by the Congress; provided that no amendment which may be made prior to the year one thousand eight hundred and eight shall in any manner affect the first and fourth clauses in the Ninth Section of the First Article; and that no State, without its consent, shall be deprived of its equal suffrage in the Senate.

Section 3. New States and Territories

Adding new states   Congress has the right to add new states to the United States. No state can be divided to make a new state without the consent of Congress and the original state. No new state can be formed from parts of two or more states without the agreement of the legislatures of all the states involved and without the agreement of Congress.

National territory   Congress has the power to make rules about all government lands and property. Congress also may set up a government for any territory before it becomes a state.

Protecting the States   It is the duty of the national government to see that every state has a government in which the people rule and that each state is protected against invasion. If a state asks the national government for help in putting down a riot or other disturbance, the United States must provide that help.

ARTICLE V AMENDING THE CONSTITUTION

Changing the Constitution   The Constitution can be changed by amendment. There are two ways to propose an amendment. An amendment can be proposed (1) by the vote of two thirds of the Senate and two thirds of the House of Representatives or (2) by Congress, called together In a special convention. This happens when two thirds of all state legislatures have asked for the special convention. There are two ways in which the amendment may become part of the Constitution. The amendment becomes part of the Constitution when it is approved (1) by the legislatures of at least three fourths of the states or (2) by special conventions in at least three fourths of the states. Before 1808, no amendment could change the first and fourth clauses in Article 1, Section 9. No amendment may take away a state's right to have the same number of senators as other states unless the state affected agrees.

ARTICLE VI

All debts contracted and engagements entered into, before the adoption of this Constitution, shall be as valid against the United States under this Constitution, as under the Confederation.

This Constitution, and the laws of the United States which shall be made in pursuance thereof; and all treaties made, or which shall be made, under the authority of the United States, shall be the supreme law of the land; and the judges in every State shall be bound thereby, any thing in the Constitution or laws of any State to the contrary notwithstanding.

The senators and representatives before mentioned, and the members of the several State legislatures, and all executive and judicial officers, both of the United States and of the several States, shall be bound by oath or affirmation, to support this Constitution; but no religious test shall ever be required as a qualification to any office or public trust under the United States.

ARTICLE VII

The ratification of the conventions of nine States shall be sufficient for the establishment of this Constitution between the States so ratifying the same.

Done in convention by the unanimous consent of the States present the seventeenth day of September in the year of our Lord one thousand seven hundred and eighty seven and of the Independence of the United States of America the twelfth. In witness whereof we have here unto subscribed our names.

Go. Washington—*Presid't. and deputy from Virginia*

Attest William Jackson Secretary

ARTICLE VI THE SUPREME LAW OF THE LAND
Public debt   Loans made by Congress before the Constitution was adopted were to be paid.

Laws of the Constitution   The Constitution, the laws made by Congress as permitted by the Constitution, and treaties made by the United States are the highest laws of the United States. Judges must follow these laws even if state laws contradict them. All national government and state government officials must promise to uphold the Constitution and abide by it.

No religious requirements   Anyone who meets the requirements to hold a position in the United States government cannot be kept out of the position because of religion.

ARTICLE VII RATIFICATION
Accepting the Constitution   When nine states have held conventions and agreed to the Constitution, the government set up by this Constitution shall begin in those states. The states represented in the Constitutional Convention on September 17, 1787, agreed to the Constitution as a plan of government to be proposed to the states. (Only Rhode Island refused to take part in the Constitutional Convention. The other 12 states chose 65 delegates to the convention; 55 attended most of the meetings. The day the Constitution was signed, 43 delegates were present, but only 39 actually put their signatures on the document.)

New Hampshire	*Connecticut*	*New Jersey*
John Langdon	Wm. Saml. Johnson	Wil: Livingston
Nicholas Gilman	Roger Sherman	David Brearley.
		Wm. Paterson.
Massachusetts	*New York*	Jona: Dayton
Nathaniel Gorham	Alexander Hamilton	
Rufus King		

Pennsylvania
  B Franklin
  Thomas Mifflin
  Robt Morris
  Geo. Clymer
  Thos. FitzSimons
  Jared Ingersoll
  James Wilson
  Gouv Morris

Delaware
  Geo: Read
  Gunning Bedford jun
  John Dickinson
  Richard Bassett
  Jaco: Broom

Maryland
  James McHenry
  Dan of St Thos. Jenifer
  Danl. Carroll

Virginia
  John Blair—
  James Madison Jr.

North Carolina
  Wm. Blount
  Richd. Dobbs Spaight
  Hu Williamson

South Carolina
  J. Rutledge
  Charles Cotesworth
    Pinckney
  Charles Pinckney
  Pierce Butler

Georgia
  William Few
  Abr Baldwin

Amendments

The First Ten Amendments:
The Bill of Rights

1st Amendment: Religious and Political Freedom

Congress shall make no law respecting an establishment of religion, or prohibiting the free exercise thereof; or abridging the freedom of speech, or of the press; or the right of the people peaceably to assemble, and to petition the Government for a redress of grievances.

2nd Amendment: Right to Bear Arms

A well regulated militia, being necessary to the security of a free State, the right of the people to keep and bear arms, shall not be infringed.

3rd Amendment: Quartering of Soldiers

No soldier shall, in time of peace be quartered in any house, without the consent of the owner, nor in time of war, but in a manner to be prescribed by law.

4th Amendment: Searches and Seizures

The right of the people to be secure in their persons, houses, papers, and effects, against unreasonable searches and seizures, shall not be violated, and no warrants shall issue, but upon probable cause, supported by oath or affirmation, and particularly describing the place to be searched, and the persons or things to be seized.

5th Amendment: Rights of Those Accused of Crimes

No person shall be held to answer for a capital, or otherwise infamous crime, unless on a presentment or indictment of a Grand Jury, except in cases arising in the land of naval forces, or in the militia, when in actual service in time of war or public danger; nor shall any person be subject for the same offense to be twice put in jeopardy of life or limb; nor shall be compelled in any criminal case to be a witness against himself, nor be deprived of life, liberty, or property,

---

The First Ten Amendments:
The Bill of Rights

1st Amendment Congress cannot pass the following kinds of laws: laws that would establish an official religion; laws that would keep people from following any religion; laws that would prevent people from speaking freely or publishing their ideas and beliefs; laws that would stop people from meeting peacefully or from asking the government to right a wrong.

2nd Amendment Because the people have a right to have militias, Congress cannot stop people from keeping and carrying firearms.

3rd Amendment In peacetime, citizens cannot be forced to give either room or board to soldiers. In wartime, however, Congress may pass a law instructing citizens to give soldiers room and board.

4th Amendment A person's house or belongings cannot be searched or seized unless a warrant—an official order from a judge—gives permission to do so. A judge cannot issue a warrant unless there is sufficient evidence to indicate that doing so will aid in capturing a criminal. The warrant must describe the place that is to be searched and identify the persons or things that will be seized.

5th Amendment No person may be tried in a national court for a serious crime unless a grand jury has decided there is enough evidence against that individual to warrant a trial. The only individuals not covered by this rule are those serving in the armed forces in time of war or public danger. If a person has been tried in a national court and found innocent of a crime, he or she cannot be tried a second time for the same offense. However, if the offense is a crime under state law, the person can be tried for that offense

without due process of law; nor shall private property be taken for public use, without just compensation.

6th Amendment: Protection in Criminal Courts

In all criminal prosecutions, the accused shall enjoy the right to a speedy and public trial, by an impartial jury of the State and district wherein the crime shall have been committed, which district shall have been previously ascertained by law, and to be informed of the nature and cause of the accusation; to be confronted with the witnesses against him; to have compulsory process for obtaining witnesses in his favor, and to have the assistance of counsel for his defense.

7th Amendment: Civil Suits

In suits at common law, where the value in controversy shall exceed twenty dollars, the right of trial by jury shall be preserved, and no fact tried by a jury, shall be otherwise reexamined in any court of the United States, than according to the rules of the common law.

8th Amendment: Bails, Fines, Punishments

Excessive bail shall not be required, nor excessive fines imposed, nor cruel and unusual punishments inflicted.

9th Amendment: Other Rights of the People

The enumeration in the Constitution, of certain rights, shall not be construed to deny or disparage others retained by the people.

10th Amendment: Powers Kept by the States or the People

The powers not delegated to the United States by the Constitution, nor prohibited by it to the States, are reserved to the States respectively, or to the people.

in a state court. Also, if the offense injures another party, the person accused can be made to pay damages, even though innocent of a crime.

No person can be forced to say anything in national court that would help to prove his or her guilt.

No person can be executed, imprisoned, or fined except as a punishment after a fair trial.

The government cannot take a person's property for public use without paying a fair price for it.

6th Amendment A person accused of a crime must be tried promptly and in public. The trial is held in the district or state where the crime took place. The accused must be told what he or she is being tried for. The accused must be present when witnesses speak against him or her in court. The accused is entitled to call witnesses and to have the help of a lawyer.

7th Amendment In disputes over property that is worth more than $20, either party can insist on a jury trial or both can agree not to have a jury.

8th Amendment A person accused of a crime can get out of jail until the trial if he or she hands over a sum of money to the court. This money, called bail, is returned when the accused person appears at the trial. If the accused person fails to appear, the bail is lost. Courts cannot force the accused to pay unreasonably large amounts of bail. A person tried in a national court and found guilty cannot be punished with an unreasonably large fine or unreasonably long prison sentence. That person also cannot be punished in cruel or unusual ways—such as torture or branding.

9th Amendment The mention of certain rights in the Constitution does not mean that these are the only rights that people have. They still have rights that are not listed in the Constitution.

10th Amendment All of the powers that are not given by the Constitution to the national government and not denied to the states belong to the states or to the people.

Amendment XI: Suits against a State (1798)

The judicial power of the United States shall not be construed to extend to any suit in law or equity commenced or prosecuted against one of the United States by citizens of another State, or by citizens or subjects of any foreign State.

Amendment XII: Election of President and Vice President (1804)

The electors shall meet in their respective States, and vote by ballot for President and Vice President, one of whom, at least, shall not be an inhabitant of the same State with themselves; they shall name in their ballots the person voted for as President, and in distinct ballots the person voted for as Vice President, and they shall make distinct lists of all persons voted for as President, and of all persons voted for as Vice President, and of the number of votes for each, which lists they shall sign and certify, and transmit sealed to the seat of the government of the United States, directed to the President of the Senate;—The President of the Senate shall, in the presence of the Senate and House of Representatives, open all the certificates and the votes shall then be counted;—The person having the greatest number of votes for President, shall be the President, if such number be a majority of the whole number of electors appointed; and if no person have such majority, then from the persons having the highest numbers not exceeding three on the list of those voted for President, the House of Representatives shall choose immediately, by ballot, the President. But in choosing the President, the votes shall be taken by States, the representation from each State having one vote; a quorum for this purpose shall consist of a member or members from two-thirds of the States, and a majority of all the States shall be necessary to a choice. And if the House of Representatives shall not choose a President whenever the right of choice shall devolve upon them, before the fourth day of March next following, then the Vice President shall act as President, as in the case of the death or other constitutional disability of the President.—The person having

Amendment XI Citizens of the United States or of foreign countries cannot bring a law suit against a state in national courts.

Amendment XII Electors, or the elected officials who actually vote for President and Vice President, meet in the states they are from to cast separate ballots for President and Vice President. The President and Vice President cannot be from the same state. The ballots are recorded on two separate lists—one for President and one for Vice President. Each list is sent to the United States Senate, where the votes are counted in the presence of senators and representatives. The presidential candidate with the most electoral votes becomes President only is he or she has the majority of votes cast.

If not candidate has a majority, the House of Representatives selects the President from the three candidates with the highest number of votes. Each state has one vote. Two thirds of the states must be represented when the votes are cast. The candidate who receives a majority of the representatives' votes becomes President.

If the House of Representatives does not select a President before the date set for the President to take office, the Vice President is to act as President.

The vice presidential candidate who receives the majority of the electoral votes becomes Vice President. If no candidate has a majority, the Senate chooses between the two candidates with the largest number of electoral votes. Two thirds of all senators must be present for the voting. The winning candidate must receive the votes of more than half of all senators.

A person who does not have the qualifications to be President cannot be Vice President.

the greatest number of votes as Vice President, shall be the Vice President, if such number be a majority of the whole number of electors appointed, and if no person have a majority, then from the two highest numbers on the list, the Senate shall choose the Vice President; a quorum for the purpose shall consist of two-thirds of the whole number of Senators, and a majority of the whole number shall be necessary to a choice. But no person constitutionally ineligible to the office of President shall be eligible to that of Vice President of the United States.

Amendment XIII: Slavery Outlawed (1865)

SECTION 1. Neither slavery nor involuntary servitude, except as a punishment for crime whereof the party shall have been duly convicted, shall exist within the United States, or any place subject to their jurisdiction.

SECTION 2. Congress shall have power to enforce this article by appropriate legislation.

Amendment XIV: Civil Rights in the States (1868)

SECTION 1. All persons born or naturalized in the United States, and subject to the jurisdiction thereof, are citizens of the United States and of the State wherein they reside. No State shall make or enforce any law which shall abridge the privileges or immunities of citizens of the United States; nor shall any State deprive any person of life, liberty, or property, without due process of law; nor deny to any person within its jurisdiction the equal protection of the laws.

SECTION 2. Representatives shall be apportioned among the several States according to their respective numbers, counting the whole number of persons in each State, excluding Indians not taxed. But when the right to vote at any election for the choice of electors for President and Vice President of the United States, Representatives in Congress, the executive and judicial officers of a State, or the members of the legislature thereof, *is denied to any of the male inhabitants of such State, being twenty-one years of age, and citizens of the United States, or in any way*

Amendment XIII No person may be held in slavery. No person can be forced to work against his or her will except as punishment for a crime. This amendment was added shortly after the end of the Civil War.

Amendment XIV Any person born in the United States or who was born in another country and has become naturalized is a United States citizen. A citizen of the United States is also a citizen of the state in which he or she lives. No state can take away the rights of a United States citizen. No state can take away a person's life, freedom, or property except through the order of a court of law. All laws apply to each person in the same way.

All people, except Indians who do not pay taxes, are to be counted in order to determine how many representatives a state is to have in Congress. The number of representatives that a state has in the House of Representatives may be reduced according to the number of eligible voters that a state does not allow to vote. Members of a rebellion, if they are denied the right to vote, however, may be included in determining a state's number of representatives in Congress. This includes male citizens who fought against the United States during the Civil War.

abridged, except for participation in rebellion, or other crime, the basis of representation therein shall be reduced in the proportion which the number of such male citizens shall bear to the whole number of male citizens twenty-one years of age in such State.

SECTION 3. No person shall be a Senator or Representative in Congress, or elector of President and Vice President, or hold any office, civil or military, under the United States, or under any State, who, having previously taken an oath, as a member of Congress, or an an officer of the United States, or as a member of any State legislature, or an an executive or judicial officer of any State, to support the Constitution of the United States, shall have engaged in insurrection or rebellion against the same, or given aid or comfort to the enemies thereof. But Congress may by a vote of two-thirds of each house, remove such disability.

No person shall hold a United States office or a state office if he or she participated in or was a member of a rebellion against the United States. Nor may that person hold any office if he or she helped in a rebellion against or was an enemy of the United States. Congress may overrule this law and allow a person to hold office by a two-thirds vote of both the Senate and the House of Representatives.

SECTION 4. The validity of the public debt of the United States, authorized by law, including debts incurred for payment of pensions and bounties for services in suppressing insurrection or rebellion, shall not be questioned. But neither the United States nor any State shall assume or pay any debt or obligation incurred in aid of insurrection or rebellion against the United States, or any claim for the loss or emancipation of any slave; but all such debts, obligations and claims shall be held illegal and void.

Money that the United States borrowed for putting down a rebellion against the Union shall be repaid. But money borrowed to aid in a rebellion against the United States will not be paid by the United States.

SECTION 5. The Congress shall have power to enforce, by appropriate legislation, the provisions of this article.

Amendment XV: The Right of Black Americans to Vote (1870)
SECTION 1. The right of citizens of the United States to vote shall not be denied or abridged by the United States or by any State on account of race, color, or previous condition of servitude.

Amendment XV Neither the United States nor any state may keep a citizen from voting because of race or color or because that person was once a slave.

Amendment XVI: The National Income Tax (1913)

The Congress shall have power to lay and collect taxes on incomes, from whatever source derived, without apportionment among the several States, and without regard to any census or enumeration.

Amendment XVII: Direct Election of Senators (1913)

SECTION 1. The Senate of the United States shall be composed of two senators from each State, elected by the people thereof, for six years; and each senator shall have one vote. The electors in each State shall have the qualifications requisite for electors of the most numerous branch of the State legislatures.

SECTION 2. When vacancies happen in the representation of any State in the senate, the executive authority of such State shall issue writs of election to fill such vacancies: *Provided,* That the legislature of any State may empower the executive thereof to make temporary appointments until the people fill the vacancies by election as the legislature may direct.

SECTION 3. This amendment shall not be so construed as to affect the election or term of any senator chosen before it becomes valid as part of the Constitution.

Amendment XVIII: National Prohibition (1919)

SECTION 1. *After one year from the ratification of this article the manufacture, sale, or transportation of intoxicating liquors within, the importation thereof into, or the exportation thereof from the United States and all territory subject to the jurisdiction thereof for beverage purposes is hereby prohibited.*

SECTION 2. *The Congress and the several States shall have concurrent power to enforce this article by appropriate legislation.*

SECTION 3. *This article shall be inoperative unless it shall have been ratified as an amendment to the Constitution by the legislatures of the several States, as provided in the Constitution, within seven years from the date of the submission hereof to the States by the Congress.*

Amendment XVI Congress has the right to tax income. The amount of money the citizens of a state pay to the national government does not have to be in proportion to a state's population.

Amendment XVII Senators can now be elected directly by the people for 6 year terms. The Senate has 2 senators from each state. Each senator has 1 vote in Congress. Citizens who are allowed to vote for representatives may vote for senators.

If a senator cannot finish his or her term, the governor of that senator's state may appoint a replacement senator until an election is held.

Amendment XVIII One year after this amendment was ratified, people were not allowed to make, sell, or carry intoxicating drinks in the United States or its territories. It also became illegal to import or export such beverages.

Amendment XVIII is often referred to as the prohibition amendment. In 1933, it was repealed by Amendment XXI.

Amendment XIX: Women's Voting Rights (1920)

SECTION 1. The right of citizens of the United States to vote shall not be denied or abridged by the United States or any State on account of sex.

SECTION 2. Congress shall have power to enforce this article by appropriate legislation.

Amendment XX: Terms of Office (1933)

SECTION 1. The terms of the President and Vice President shall end at noon on the 20th day of January, and the terms of Senators and Representatives at noon on the 3d day of January, of the years in which such terms would have ended if this article had not been ratified; and the terms of their successors shall then begin.

SECTION 2. The Congress shall assemble at least once every year, and such meeting shall begin at noon on the 3d day of January, unless they shall by law appoint a different day.

SECTION 3. If, at the time fixed for the beginning of the term of President, the President elect shall have died, the Vice President elect shall become President. If a President shall not have been chosen before the time fixed for the beginning of his term, or if the President elect shall have failed to qualify, then the Vice President elect shall act as President until a President shall have qualified; and the Congress may by law provide for the case wherein neither a President elect nor a Vice President elect shall have qualified, declaring who shall then act as President, or the manner in which one who is to act shall be selected, and such person shall act accordingly until a President or Vice President shall have qualified.

SECTION 4. The Congress may by law provide for the case of the death of any of the persons from whom the House of Representatives may choose a President whenever the right of choice shall have devolved upon them, and for the case of the death of any of the persons from whom the Senate may choose a Vice President whenever the right of choice shall be devolved upon them.

Amendment XIX   This amendment gave women the right to vote in national and state elections.

Amendment XX   The President's and Vice President's terms in office now end at noon on January 20 instead of on March 4. The end of senators' and representatives' terms in office is noon on January 3. The people who are elected to any of these offices begin their new terms as soon as the people they are replacing finish their terms.

Congress must meet once a year beginning at noon on January 3, unless Congress legally decides to begin another day.

If the person elected President dies before the term starts, the person elected Vice President then becomes President.

If the person elected President does not meet the requirements for the presidency as stated in the Constitution, the newly elected Vice President acts as President until a new President is chosen.

Congress may decide what to do if neither the newly elected President or Vice President meets the requirements stated in the Constitution. Congress also has the power to pass a law deciding how to choose a Vice President if one of the candidates has died.

SECTION 5. Sections 1 and 2 shall take effect on the 15th day of October following the ratification of this article.

SECTION 6. This article shall be inoperative unless it shall have been ratified as an amendment to the Constitution by the legislatures of three-fourths of the several States within seven years from the date of its submission.

Amendment XXI: The End of Prohibition (1933)

SECTION 1. The eighteenth article of amendment to the Constitution of the United States is hereby repealed.

SECTION 2. The transportation or importation into any State, Territory, or possession of the United States for delivery or use therein of intoxicating liquors, in violation of the laws thereof, is hereby prohibited.

SECTION 3. This article shall be inoperative unless it shall have been ratified as an amendment to the Constitution by conventions in the several States, as provided in the Constitution, within seven years from the date of submission hereof to the States by the Congress.

Amendment XXII: Terms of Office of the President (1951)

SECTION 1. No person shall be elected to the office of the President more than twice, and no person who has held the office of President, or acted as President, for more than 2 years of a term to which some other person was elected President shall be elected to the office of the President more than once. But this Article shall not apply to any person holding the office of President when this Article was proposed by the Congress, and shall not prevent any person who may be holding the office of President, or acting as President during the term within which this Article becomes operative from holding the office of President or acting as President during the remainder of such term.

Amendment XXI Amendment XVIII is no longer in effect. Therefore, the national government may no longer outlaw the making, selling, or transporting of intoxicating drinks. However, any state, territory, or possession of the United States may outlaw alcoholic beverages.

Amendment XXII No person may be elected for more than 2 terms as President. If any person serves for more than 2 years in place of an elected President, that person may be elected President only once. In any case, no person may serve more than 10 years as President.

SECTION 2. This Article shall be inoperative unless it shall have been ratified as an amendment to the Constitution by the legislatures of three-fourths of the several States within 7 years from the date of its submission to the States by the Congress.

Amendment XXIII: Presidential Voting in the District of Columbia (1961)

SECTION 1. The District constituting the seat of Government of the United States shall appoint in such manner as the Congress may direct:

A number of electors of President and Vice President equal to the whole number of Senators and Representatives in Congress to which the District would be entitled if it were a State, but in no event more than the least populous State; they shall be in addition to those appointed by the States, but they shall be considered, for the purposes of the election of President and Vice President, to be electors appointed by a State, and they shall meet in the District and perform such duties as provided by the twelfth article of amendment.

SECTION 2. The Congress shall have power to enforce this article by appropriate legislation.

Amendment XXIV: Tax Requirements for Voting Outlawed (1964)

SECTION 1. The right of citizens of the United States to vote in any primary or other election for President or Vice President, for electors for President or Vice President, or for Senator or Representative in Congress, shall not be denied or abridged by the United States or any State by reason of failure to pay any poll tax or other tax.

SECTION 2. The Congress shall have the power to enforce this article by appropriate legislation.

Amendment XXV: Presidential Continuity (1967)

SECTION 1. In case of the removal of the President from office or of his death or resignation, the Vice President shall become President.

SECTION 2. Whenever there is a vacancy in the office of the Vice President, the President shall

Amendment XXIII Citizens living in the District of Columbia (Washington, D.C.) have the right to take part in the election of the President and Vice President. The District of Columbia may have as many votes in the electoral college as the state with the smallest population. Members of the District of Columbia's electoral college cast votes as described in Amendment XII.

Amendment XXIV No government—local, state, or national—may keep a citizen from voting for President, Vice President, or any member of Congress because that citizen has not paid his or her taxes.

Amendment XXV If the President is removed from office, dies, or resigns, the Vice President becomes President.

If the office of the Vice President is vacant, the President may name a Vice President. If a majority of both houses of Congress approves the choice, the person the President chooses becomes Vice President.

nominate a Vice President who shall take office upon confirmation by a majority vote of both Houses of Congress.

SECTION 3. Whenever the President transmits to the President pro tempore of the Senate and the Speaker of the House of Representatives his written declaration that he is unable to discharge the powers and duties of his office, and until he transmits to them a written declaration to the contrary, such powers and duties shall be discharged by the Vice President as Acting President.

SECTION 4. Whenever the Vice President and a majority of either the principal officers of the executive departments or of such other body as Congress may be law provide, transmit to the President pro tempore of the Senate and the Speaker of the House of Representatives their written declaration that the President is unable to discharge the powers and duties of his office, the Vice President shall immediately assume the powers and duties of the office as Acting President.

Thereafter, when the President transmits to the President pro tempore of the Senate and the Speaker of the House of Representatives his written declaration that no inability exists, he shall resume the powers and duties of his office unless the Vice President and a majority of either the principal officers of the executive department or of such other body as Congress may by law provide, transmit within four days to the President pro tempore of the Senate and the Speaker of the House of Representatives their written declaration that the President is unable to discharge the powers and duties of his office. Thereupon Congress shall decide the issue, assembling within forty-eight hours for that purpose if not in session. If the Congress, within twenty-one days after receipt of the latter written declaration, or, if Congress is not in session, within twenty-one days after Congress is required to assemble, determines by two-thirds vote of both Houses that the President is unable to discharge the powers and duties of his office,

If the President is unable to carry out the responsibilities of his or her office, the President must send a written statement to Congress. The Vice President then becomes acting President and takes on the responsibilities of the President. When the President is once again able to carry out the responsibilities of his or her office, the President must send another statement to Congress. If the Vice President and a majority of the Cabinet do not believe the President is able to take over the responsibilities of the presidency again, they must submit a statement saying so to Congress within four days of the President's announcement. Congress then has 48 hours to decide on the issue after receiving both statements.

the Vice President shall continue to discharge the same Acting President; otherwise, the President shall resume the powers and duties of his office.

Amendment XXVI: Right to Vote—Citizens over the Age of Eighteen (1971)

SECTION 1.   The right of citizens of the United States, who are 18 years of age or older, to vote shall not be denied or abridged by the United States or by any State on account of age.

SECTION 2.   The Congress shall have power to enforce this article by appropriate legislation.

Amendment XXVI   Neither the United States nor any state can keep a citizen eighteen years of age or older from voting because of age.

On Becoming a Citizen

The word citizen means a person who belongs to a country. As United States citizens, people have certain rights. These rights are protected by the Bill of Rights in the United States Constitution. Rights include freedom of speech, press, and religion and the right to vote. There are also demands that. citizens have placed upon them. Demands include paying taxes, obeying the law, serving on juries, and defending the country.

A person becomes a citizen of the United States by birth. The Fourteenth Amendment to our Constitution declares that all people born in the United States are citizens.

Sometimes people in other countries decide they would like to become citizens of the United States. People who move permanently to the United States but are not yet citizens are called aliens. These people may become naturalized citizens after being in the country for five years. When aliens are naturalized, any children in the family become citizens too.

To prepare for becoming citizens, aliens attend citizenship classes. They learn to read and write English. They also learn about the history of the United States and its government. The adults must pass a literacy test and answer questions about the United States in order to qualify for citizenship.

September 17 is Citizenship Day in the United States. Most naturalization ceremonies occur then. Families assemble in courts throughout the country to be sworn in as United States citizens. They must raise their right hands and take an oath of allegiance. The oath declares loyalty to the United States rather than to the person's country of birth.

Glossary/Gazetteer

abolition The abolishing (complete doing away with) of slavery. (p. 210)

academy A private school. (p. 182)

acid rain Rainfall that carries harmful chemicals. (p. 341)

AIDS Acquired Immune Deficiency Syndrome, a condition that leaves the body with no defense against deadly diseases. (p. 326)

Albany Congress A meeting in 1754 at which Benjamin Franklin presented a plan for union among the colonies. (p. 133)

Albemarle A Confederate ironclad ship that was a threat to Union control of the coastal waters. (p. 232)

Allied Powers The World War I alliance that included Serbia, France, Great Britain, Russia, Japan, and later, Italy. The United States joined the Allies in 1917. (p. 285)

amendment A change in a bill, law, or constitution. (p. 171)

amnesty A pardon. (p. 123)

anarchy The complete absence of government. (p. 117)

annexation The adding of a state, territory, or other unit into another state or nation. (p. 205)

anthropologist A scientist who studies human culture. (p. 23)

Antifederalist An opponent of the new United States Constitution of 1787. (p. 169)

Apollo 11 The spacecraft that took the first humans to the moon. (p. 324)

Appomattox Court House The location in Virginia where Lee surrendered his Confederate forces to Grant. (p. 226)

apprentice A person who learns a trade from a skilled worker. (p. 58)

archaeologist A scientist who studies the remains of early cultures. (p. 14)

arms race The production of vast stores of weapons by the United States and the Soviet Union during the Cold War. (p. 311)

arsenal A weapons depot. (p. 215)

Articles of Confederation The plan, ratified by the states in 1781, that established a national Congress with limited powers. (p. 165)

artifact An object, such as a mask, a clay pot, or a weapon that gives clues to the culture from which it comes. (p. 14)

assembly line A manufacturing process in which workers stationed along a moving belt add parts to a product to complete it. (p. 257)

atomic fallout The tiny radioactive particles carried by global wind currents after an atomic explosion. (p. 310)

backcountry An area of thinly populated settlements that stretched from the fall line to the Appalachians. (p. 106)

Battle of Alamance (1771) The battle—between the militia of colonial North Carolina and the Regulators—which ended the Regulator movement. (p. 125)

Battle of Antietam (1862) The bloodiest day of fighting in the Civil War; neither side won a clear victory. (p. 223)

Battle of Bentonville (1865) The bloodiest Civil War battle in North Carolina; won by the Union. (p. 235)

Battle of Gettysburg (1863) The greatest single battle of the Civil War; won by the Union. (p. 225)

Battle of Manassas (1861) The first major battle of the Civil War; won by the Confederacy. (p. 222)

Berlin Wall A wall erected in 1961 to keep East Germans from fleeing their country. It became a symbol of the Cold War. (p. 328)

bilingual education Education in a student's own language as well as in English. (p.322)

The names of people found in the People, Places, Terms boxes are listed in the Index but not in the Glossary.

Bill of Rights   The first ten amendments to the Constitution, which guarantee the basic rights of (p. 322)citizens. (p. 171)

Black Codes   Laws passed by Southern states after the Civil War that strictly limited the freedom of formerly enslaved people. (p. 240)

blockade   The blocking of a port by ships. (p. 159)

borough town   A town with 60 or more families that had the right to send a delegate to the Assembly in colonial North Carolina. (p. 98)

boycott   The refusal to buy certain items. (p. 141)

Brown v. Board of Education of Topeka   The 1954 Supreme Court decision that declared racial segregation in public schools to be unconstitutional. (p. 321)

busing   The transportation of students from one school district to another as a means of integration. (p. 334)

carpetbagger   An term of insult applied to a Northerner who went South after the Civil War. (p. 244)

Cary's Rebellion   The armed rebellion in 1712, led by former governor Thomas Cary against Governor Edward Hyde, which ended with Cary's humiliating retreat. (p. 95)

cash crop   A crop raised for sale rather than for home use. (p. 111)

casualty   A military person lost through death, injury, or capture or through being missing in action. (p. 235)

census   A count of the population. (p. 338)

Central Powers   The World War I alliance that included Germany, Austria-Hungary, and the Ottoman Empire. (p. 285)

charter   A legal document that gives permission to explore, settle, and govern land. (p. 43)

checks and balances   The system in which each branch of government can limit the powers or actions of the other branches. (p. 173)

civil rights   The rights that are guaranteed to citizens by the Constitution. (p. 294)

clan   A group of related people. (p. 22)

climate   The main kind of weather that a region experiences over an extended period. (p. 6)

Coastal Plain   The broad, flat, region that in North Carolina extends 100 to 150 miles inland from the ocean. (p. 4)

Cold War   The uneasy peace after World War II marked by a rivalry between the United States and the Soviet Union. (p. 310)

colony   A group of settlements far from—but ruled by—the home country. (p. 43)

common   A field in a colonial town or village that everyone shared, usually for grazing their livestock. (p. 69)

commonwealth   A political unit such as a state or a nation; often one that, like Puerto Rico, governs itself but is united with another country. (p. 282)

communism   A system in which in theory the people own all land, factories, and businesses, and power is supposed to rest with the people. (p. 288)

community   A group of people living in a given locale who share some common activities, attitudes, and interests. (p. 345)

compromise   An agreement in which each side gives up something it wants in order to gain something else. (p. 167)

concentration camp   A heavily guarded camp in which political prisoners are held by force. (p. 305)

Confederate States of America   The nation, which lasted from 1861 to 1865, made up of the eleven Southern states that seceded from the Union. (p. 216)

confederation   A joining together, such as the joining together of states. (p. 165)

Congress   The lawmaking branch of government, which was one body under the Articles of Confederation and two bodies—the Senate and the House of Representatives—under the Constitution. (p. 165)

conquistador   A Spanish conqueror. (p. 31)

constitution   A written plan of government. (p. 164)

constitutional reform   The act of changing a constitution. (p. 187)

consumer goods   Products made for use by the average person, rather than for other industries. (p. 295)

containment   A policy aimed at stopping the spread of communism. (p. 311)

Continental Congress   A group of representatives from the colonies who in 1776 voted to declare independence from Britain. (p. 152)

corduroy road   Roads formed by placing logs side by side. (p. 112)

corporation   A business owned by many people. (p. 255)

credit   A way of paying for something in small amounts until it is paid for in full. (p. 296)

Croatoan   An island near Roanoke Island which John White's colonists may have visited. (p. 51)

Culpeper's Rebellion   One of the first popular uprisings in the colonies. An important cause of the rebellion was resentment over the duties imposed by the Navigation Acts. (p. 88)

culture   A people's way of life. It includes the kinds of tools people make, the food they eat, and the language they speak. (p. 15)

culture region   A place where methods of living are similar. (p. 16)

D-Day   The Allied invasion of German-occupied France on June 6, 1944. (p. 309)

Declaration of Independence   The document adopted by the Continental Congress on July 4, 1776, declaring the United States as a nation independent from Great Britain. (p. 152)

depression   A severe and widespread slowdown in the economy that puts many people out of work. (p. 299)

dictator   A ruler who exercises absolute control over his or her country. (p. 304)

direct primary   A special election in which voters who claim membership in one of the political parties choose their party's candidates. (p. 290)

discrimination   Treating some people differently from others because of their race, beliefs, or heritage. (p. 294)

Dissenter   A person who disagreed with the beliefs and rituals of the Anglican church. (p. 93)

draft   A system in which people are required to serve in the military. (p. 219)

Dred Scott v. Sanford   The 1857 Supreme Court case that decided that slaves did not have the rights of citizens and that Congress could not forbid slavery in the territories. (p. 214)

duty   A tax, usually on imported or exported goods. (p. 88)

economy   The way a group of people produces goods and services. (p. 182)

elder   A leader in colonial New England. (p. 69)

elector   A special representative chosen by voters to elect the President and Vice President of the United States. (p. 167)

Emancipation Proclamation   The announcement by President Lincoln freeing all enslaved persons in the Confederate states. (p. 224)

emigrate   To leave one's homeland for another country. (p. 255)

empire   A nation and the lands and people it governs. (p. 33)

environment   All the living and nonliving things that make up a region. (p. 9)

Equal Rights Amendment   A proposed constitutional amendment that would have prohibited discrimination on the basis of sex. (p. 323)

erosion   The slow wearing away of soil by wind or water. (p. 341)

expansionist   A person who favors taking over land outside of his or her own country. (p. 282)

extortion   The obtaining of money or goods by force, threat, or illegal use of power. (p. 123)

fall line   The imaginary line formed by connecting all the points where rivers drop suddenly from highlands to lowlands, forming waterfalls or rapids. (p. 5)

federal system   A government in which power is divided between national and state governments. (p. 171)

Federalist   A person who supported the new United States Constitution of 1787. (p. 169)

Fifteenth Amendment   The 1870 constitutional amendment declaring that the right to vote may not be denied "on account of race, color, or previous condition of servitude." (p. 242)

Fort Fisher   The fort that protected Wilmington and kept its port open longer than any other Confederate port. (p. 229)

Fort Sumter   A fort in the harbor of Charleston, South Carolina, the bombardment of which began the Civil War. (p. 216)

Fourteenth Amendment   The 1868 constitutional amendment declaring that all citizens have the same rights whether they are native-born or naturalized. (p. 242)

free enterprise system   An economic system in which goods are produced in response to the demand of the market, rather than on the orders of government. (p. 329)

Freedmen's Bureau Bill   A bill passed to extend the life of the Freedmen's Bureau, which was a federal agency set up after the Civil War to help formerly enslaved persons. (p. 241)

French and Indian War   A war in which the French and their Native American allies fought British soldiers and American militia from 1753 to 1759; officially ended by treaty, 1763. (p. 132)

fugitive slave law   A law forcing people to return runaway enslaved Africans. (p. 211)

gentry class   People at the top of the social order in colonial North Carolina. Members of this group enjoyed moderate, or even great, wealth. (p. 108)

geographic region   A large area of land with similar features. (p. 3)

Gibbs's Rebellion   A dispute over the governorship of colonial North Carolina between Captain John Gibbs and Philip Ludwell. (p. 91)

glasnost   The policy of openness instituted in the 1980s by Mikhail Gorbachev in the Soviet Union. (p. 327)

graduated income tax   A tax in which the amount paid is increased according to the size of a person's income. (p. 290)

Granville District   The land entitled to John Carteret, Earl Granville, which was one eighth of the land of Carolina. (p. 115)

Harpers Ferry   A location in Virginia where John Brown seized a federal arsenal and tried to start a rebellion against slavery. (p. 215)

Hessian   A German soldier hired by the British soldiers to fight in the Revolutionary War. (p. 153)

High Point   The location of the first factory in North Carolina to produce quantities of furniture. (p. 269)

Highland Scots   People from the mountainous part of Scotland, many of whom joined a large wave of immigrants to the colony of North Carolina in the early 1700s. (p. 104)

holocaust   A huge and terrible destruction of human life, such as the mass destruction of European Jews and other people by Nazi Germany in World War II. (p. 305)

House of Burgesses   The group of elected officials in the Virginia Colony. (p. 58)

Hundred Days   A special session of Congress in which President Roosevelt sent 15 bills to Congress to implement his New Deal. (p. 301)

immigrant   A person who leaves one country to settle in another. (p. 258)

impeach   To charge a public official with wrongdoing. (p. 242)

imperialism   The establishment of political or economic control over other countries. (p. 282)

impressment   The act of seizing people against their will and forcing them into military service. (p. 177)

indentured servant   A person who worked without pay for a specified number of years in return for passage to a colony, clothing, food, and shelter. (p. 58)

individualism   The idea that an individual should be free from interference by the government. (p. 181)

Industrial Revolution   A time of great and rapid changes, when people switched from making goods by hand to manufacturing goods with power-driven machines. (p. 252)

initiative A process by which citizens may propose legislation. (p. 290)

interest A charge for borrowed money. (p. 296)

internal improvement Improvements within a state, such as the construction of canals and turnpikes. (p. 186)

international Relating to more than one nation. (p. 280)

isolationism A policy of staying out of the affairs of other nations. (p. 304)

Joint Committee on Reconstruction A Congressional committee formed to draw up a Reconstruction plan to replace that of President Johnson. (p. 241)

joint-stock company A business owned by many people. (p. 54)

Kirk-Holden War The incident in which Governor Holden called out the militia under George W. Kirk to restrain the activities of the Ku Klux Klan. (p. 248)

Ku Klux Klan A secret society, begun after the Civil War, that used intimidation and violence to return political power to white men in the South. (p. 245)

labor union An organization of workers that tries to help its members receive higher wages and have better working conditions. (p. 259)

latitude A measure of distance north or south of the equator. (p. 30)

League of Nations An organization of nations established at the end of World War I whose purpose was to maintain world stability. (p. 287)

legislature The lawmaking branch of government. (p. 182)

Literary Fund A fund set up by the North Carolina legislature to establish a public school system. (p. 186)

loam A soil made up of a mixture of clay, sand, and decaying plants. (p. 9)

longitude A measure of distance east or west of the prime meridian. (p. 30)

Louisiana Purchase The land west of the Mississippi River that the United States bought from France in 1803. (p. 175)

Loyalist A colonist who sided with Great Britain during the American Revolution. (p. 150)

manhood suffrage The right of white males to vote even if they owned no property. (p. 199

Massachusetts Bay Colony The colony established by the Puritans. (p. 64)

Mayflower Compact The document in which the Pilgrims agreed to set up a government for the colony of Plymouth. (p. 60)

Mecklenburg Resolves A document, created in 1775 by the colonists of Mecklenburg County, which stated that British laws were no longer in effect and which provided for the creation of an independent local government. (p. 151)

mesa A flat-topped, steep-sided plateau. (p. 17)

Middle Colonies The colonies between New England and the Southern Colonies: New York, New Jersey, Pennsylvania, and Delaware. (p. 74)

Middle Passage The journey across the Atlantic endured by captured Africans on their way to slavery in the Americas. (p. 80)

militia Volunteer soldiers. (p. 109)

minuteman An ordinary citizen of the colonies who was armed and trained to fight the British at a minute's notice. (p. 147)

mission A settlement in which people of one religion teach their faith to others. (p. 34)

missionary A person who teaches his or her own religion to people of other faiths. (p. 34)

Missouri Compromise An act of Congress in 1820 whereby Missouri was admitted as a slave state, Maine was admitted as a free state, and slavery was forbidden north of latitude 36° 30' N. (p. 208)

monopoly The complete control of an industry by one person or company. (p. 256)

NASA National Aeronautics and Space Administration. (p. 324)

National Farmer's Alliance An organization whose purpose was to help farmers get higher prices for their products. (p. 274)

natural resources The parts of nature that people use in some way. (p. 9)

naval stores Products from pine trees, such as pitch and tar, used in shipbuilding. (p. 83)

neutral Not taking sides during a conflict. (p. 287)

New Deal Program by Franklin Roosevelt intended to end the Great Depression. (p. 301)

New England Colonies The northern colonies: Massachusetts, Rhode Island, Connecticut, and New Hampshire. (p. 69)

Nisei A second-generation Japanese American. (p. 307)

Nuremberg Trials The post-World War II trials of Nazi leaders for war crimes. (p. 309)

oral history Stories passed down from generation to generation. (p. 20)

Outer Banks The long chain of sandy islands off the coast of North Carolina. (p. 3)

Panama Canal The canal through the Isthmus of Panama that connects the Atlantic and Pacific oceans. (p. 284)

partisan A Patriot follower who was a member of an unofficial military unit. (p. 156)

patent A document that legally protects an inventor from having an invention copied by others. (p. 256)

Patriot A colonist who wanted independence from Great Britain. (p. 150)

Pearl Harbor Hawaiian site of a United States naval base that was attacked by the Japanese in December 1941, bringing the United States into World War II. (p. 306)

Pearsall Plan A plan that allowed schools in North Carolina to close—by majority vote— rather than integrate. (p. 333)

Pennsylvania Dutch The name given by settlers to all German-speaking people who settled in the backcountry of North Carolina in the 1700s. (p. 106)

Persian Gulf A body of water bordered by Saudi Arabia, Kuwait, Iraq, Iran and other Arab countries. (p. 329)

Piedmont The hilly region between the Coastal Plain and the Appalachian Mountains. (p. 4)

Pilgrim A founder of Plymouth Colony. A pilgrim is a person who makes a journey for religious purposes. (p. 60)

plantation A large farm on which crops are grown for sale and on which the people who raise the crops live. (p. 79)

planter A plantation owner. Planters made up the bulk of Southern gentry. (p. 108)

poll tax A tax that charges each person—rich and poor alike—the same amount. (p. 120)

popular party The group in colonial North Carolina that believed that the will of the people through their representatives in the Assembly should determine government actions. (p. 86)

Populist party The party formed to unite working people in factories and on farms; it wanted reforms to help these people. (p. 275)

prerogative party The group in colonial North Carolina that believed in a government as independent of the people as possible. (p. 86)

primary source A firsthand account or an artifact made in the period under study. (p. 4)

privateer A private trading ship armed and commissioned for battle. (p. 155)

Proclamation of 1763 A British act signed that drew an imaginary line along the Appalachian Mountains and closed all lands west of the line to settlement by British colonists. (p. 138)

Proclamation of Amnesty and Reconstruction A plan created by Lincoln whereby all but a few Southerners involved in the Civil War were to be offered a full pardon. (p. 239)

profit The money left over after paying the cost of doing business. (p. 71)

progressives A group of reformers established around 1900 that wanted to solve political, economic, and social problems. (p. 289)

Prohibition A ban on the sale and manufacture of alcoholic beverages. (p. 291)

pueblo The Spanish word for *town*. (p. 17)

Puritan A person who wanted to change and "purify" the Church of England. (p. 63)

Quaker A member of the religious sect known as the Society of Friends. (p. 75)

Quartering Act A law that required colonists to feed and shelter British troops stationed in the colonies. (p. 139)

quitrent A land tax used by the Proprietors to help cover the costs of governing the colony. (p. 86)

quorum The number of members of a group that must be present before the group can function legally. (p. 117)

racism A belief that people of one race are superior to those of another. (p. 110)

Raleigh & Gaston Railroad A railroad that connected the state capitals of North Carolina and Virginia. (p. 195)

ratify To formally approve. (p. 240)

rationing A system in which goods in short supply are distributed fairly. (p. 308)

recession A downturn in the nation's economy. (p. 327)

Reconstruction The process of rebuilding the South after the Civil War. (p. 239)

redistrict To change a congressional district to reflect a change in the population. (p. 338)

referendum A process by which the people vote directly on proposed legislation. (p. 290)

refine To reduce to a pure state. (p. 256)

refugee A person who flees a country out of fear of being persecuted or killed for his or her political beliefs. (p. 319)

Regulator A member of the association formed in North Carolina in the 1760s for regulating public grievances and abuses of power. (p. 123)

rehabilitate To restore. (p. 345)

repeal To withdraw. (p. 141)

republic Any government that is not ruled by a king or queen and in which power rests with the people. (p. 164)

Research Triangle Park A national institute that combines research and industry and benefits the entire state of North Carolina. (p. 340)

revolution A great change. (p. 149)

Richmond The capital of Virginia. It was the Confederate capital in the Civil War. (p. 222)

rural Of the countryside. (p. 258)

satellite A nation ruled by another country. Also a natural or artificial body that circles a planet. (pp. 311, 312)

scalawag A dishonest person; a derogatory name given to any Southerner who aided Reconstruction. (p. 244)

Scots-Irish People of Scots heritage from northern Ireland, many of whom settled in America. (p. 106)

sea dog A veteran sailor. (p. 43)

secede To withdraw from a nation. (p. 211)

sectionalism A strong loyalty to one's own region or section. (p. 114)

segregate To separate. (p. 320)

Separatist A person who wanted to separate from the official Church of England. (p. 59)

settlement house A community center established to help immigrants. (p. 262)

sharecropping A system of farming in which a farmer rented land and provided labor in return for a share of the crop or for part of the income from the crop. (p. 272)

sit-in A means of peaceful protest. (p. 334)

slash-and-burn A method in which trees and brush are burned to provide cleared land for fields and villages. (p. 18)

slave codes Laws in the South that kept enslaved persons from voting, moving freely, or meeting in large groups. (p. 210)

Southern Colonies The southernmost of the 13 colonies: Virginia, Maryland, North Carolina, South Carolina, and Georgia. (p. 77)

Soviet Union A former nation lying in Europe and Asia, which has now split into the nations of Estonia, Latvia, Lithuania and the republics in the Commonwealth of Independent States. (p. 327)

space shuttle A spacecraft that can return to earth under its own power. (p. 324)

Sputnik I An information-gathering satellite created by the Soviets in 1957. (p. 312)

Stamp Act A law that stated that colonists had to pay for the stamping of taxable paper items to prove that the tax had been paid on these items. (p. 139)

stock A share in a company. (p. 299)

stockholder A person who owns stock in a corporation. (p. 255)

Sugar Act A law that raised the duties on luxury items such as wine and silk that Britain sold to the colonies. (p. 139)

Sun Belt A strip of warm-weather states that runs across the southern United States. (p. 6)

surplus An amount over what is needed. (p. 76)

tenant farming A system of farming in which a farmer rented land owned by another, provided the labor, and purchased some of the necessary resources. In return, the farmer received a share of the crop or part of the income from the crop. (p. 272)

tenement An apartment house in which living conditions are poor. (p. 261)

Tidewater The low-lying eastern part of North Carolina's Coastal Plain. (p. 4)

topography The location and elevation of the surface features of an area. (p. 3)

totalitarian Having to do with a government that controls all aspects of life. (p. 311)

transcontinental railroad A railroad that connects the Atlantic and Pacific coasts of the country. (p. 253)

treason The betrayal of one's country. (p. 140)

Treaty of Paris The treaty that in 1763 officially ended the French and Indian War. Also, the treaty signed in 1783 that ended the Revolutionary War. (pp. 137, 161)

triangular trade Triangle-shaped trade routes among the colonies, the West Indies, Africa, and Europe. (p. 72)

tyranny The unjust use of power. (p. 146)

Underground Railroad A series of hiding places forming the route to freedom for African Americans fleeing from slavery. (p. 212)

urban Of the city. (p. 258)

Vestry Act The first church law in North Carolina. It called for laying out parishes, organizing vestries, and building churches, as well as a tax for the support of clergymen. (p. 93)

veto To reject or refuse to sign a bill. (p. 129)

viceroyalty A large colony of the Spanish empire in America. (p. 33)

Wall Street The site of the New York Stock Exchange. (p. 299)

War of 1812 A war between Britain and the United States that ended indecisively. (p. 177)

War on Sugar Creek A riot in 1765 that began when squatters on Mecklenburg County land whipped surveyors who came to map out their land. (p. 123)

Whig party In the United States, a party made up of those who were sympathetic to banks and internal improvements. (p. 189)

Wilmington & Weldon Railroad A railroad built by the citizens of Wilmington, from Wilmington to the Roanoke River at Weldon. (p. 194)

writs of assistance Search warrants. (p. 139)

Yorktown The site of the battle that ended the American Revolution. (p. 159)

Index

The letter *m* stands for map. The letter *g* stands for graph, chart, table, or diagram.

Acknowledgments

Key to Abbreviations: Bettmann Archive—BA; The Granger Collection, New York—GC; North Carolina Collection, University of North Carolina at Chapel Hill—NCC; North Carolina Division of Archives & History, Raleigh—NCDAR

Cover: Martin Paul

Unit 1 • 2:NCC. 4: Bayard Wootten, NCC. 5: William Russ, Travel and Tourism Division, Raleigh. 7: The Charlotte Observer. 8, 9: Travel and Tourism Division, Raleigh. 11:NCC. 14: Courtesy of the Trustees of the British Museum, London. 16: Dennis Hallinan, FPG International. 17: David Muench. 18: Neg. #325898, courtesy Department of Library Services, American Museum of Natural History. 19: #N29452, Hillel Burger, Peabody Museum of Harvard University. 21: North Carolina Division of Archives and History, Raleigh. 22: Courtesy of the Trustees of the British Museum, London.

Unit 2 • 26: *t*, Bibliotheque Nationale, Paris, *b*,GC. 28: National Gallery of Art, Samuel Kress Collection #A–1665. 29: Rare Books and Manuscript Division, The New York Public Library, Astor, Lenox & Tilden Foundation. 30: Historical Pictures. 31:GC. 32: Lee Boltin. 33: From the collection of the Tozzer Library, Harvard University, Alfredo Chavero, Lienzo de Tlaxcala. 34: *t*, Chip and Rosa Maria Peterson; *b*, Laurie Platt Winfrey, Inc. 37:NCDAR. 39:BA. 42–43:BA. 45:NCC. 47: Courtesy, the Trustees of the British Museum, London. 48:NCC. 49:NCC. 51: Walter V. Gresham III, courtesy of The Lost Colony, Roanoke Island Historical Association. 54: Rare Book Division, The New York Public Library, Astor, Lenox & Tilden Foundation. 55: William S. Powell. 57: Virginia State Library & Archives. 58: Culver Pictures. 60:BA. 62: Archives of '76, Bowman Associates. 64: American Antiquarian Society. 65: "The Mason Children," private collection.

Unit 3 • 68: *t*,GC; *b*, North Wind Picture Archives. 70:BA. 73: North Wind Picture Archives. 75: Historical Pictures. 76: *t*,GC; *b*, Historical Society of Pennsylvania. 77:BA. 79: Larry Lefever, Grant Heilman Photography. 80: American Antiquarian Society. 82:NCC. 83: William S. Powell. 84: East Carolina University, Greenville. 85: William S. Powell 87: Reprinted with permission of Charles Scribner's Sons, an imprint of Macmillan Publishing Co., from ATLAS OF AMERICAN HISTORY, 2nd revised edition, Kenneth T. Jackson, Editor, copyright © 1943, 1978, 1984 by Charles Scribner's Sons, renewal copyright © 1971 by Charles Scribner's Sons. 88:NCC. 90:NCDAR. 92:NCC. 94: "Quaker Meeting," (variant of a painting entitled "Gracechurch Street Meeting," Society of Friends, London), bequest of Maxim Karolik, courtesy of Museum of Fine Arts, Boston #64.456. 95:NCDAR. 96, 98, 99:NCC. 100:NCDAR. 102: Courtesy of Old Salem, Inc., Winston-Salem. 105:NCC. 106:BA. 109, 111, 114, 115, 116, 118:NCC. 119: Travel & Tourism Division, Raleigh. 120: Courtesy Tryon Place, New Bern. 121:NCC. 122: Bruce Cotten Collection, NCC. 125:NCDAR.

Unit 4 • 128: North Wind Picture Archives. 130: New York Magazine III 452, August 1792. 132: Washington & Lee University. 133: Library Company of Philadelphia. 134: William S. Powell. 135:NCC. 137: National Archives of Canada, Ottawa #C-2736. 138: National Portrait Gallery, London. 139:BA. 140: New York Historical Society. 142: American Antiquarian Society. 143, 144:NCDAR. 146: Museum of the City of New York, Harry T. Peters Collection, Currier & Ives. 147: Shelburne Museum, Vermont. 149: "The Battle of Lexington," by Doolittle & Barber, Lexington Historical Society. 150: "Battle of Bunker Hill," by Winthrop Chandler acc. #982-281, bequest of Mr. & Mrs. Gardner Richardson, courtesy of the Museum of Fine Arts, Boston. 151:NCDAR. 152:NCC. 154: *t*, Culver Pictures; *b*, "Washington Crossing the Delaware," acc. #97.34 by Emmanuel Leutze, The Metropolitan Museum of Art, gift of John S. Kennedy. 155: U.S. Naval Academy Museum. 156: *t*, Historical Pictures; *b*,NCDAR. 157: *l*,NCDAR; *r*,NCC. 160: Yale University Art Gallery. 164: U.S. State Department. 166: National Portrait Gallery, Smithsonian Institution, Washington, D.C. 167:*t*, GC; "*b*, Washington Leading the Constitutional Debates," commissioned by the Pennsylvania, Delaware, & New Jersey state societies of the Daughters of the American Revolution, © Louis Glanzman. 168:GC. 170: New-York Historical Society. 171: "Salute to George Washington in New York Harbor," by L.M. Cooke, National Gallery of Art, Washington D.C., gift of Edgar William & Bernice Chrysler Garbisch. 172:NCC. 175:NCDAR. 176: "Flora Americae Septentrionalis," 1814, by Frederick Pursh, Print Division, The New York Public Library, Astor, Lenox & Tilden Foundation. 177: *t*,NCDAR; *b*, "Bombs over Fort McHenry," I.N. Phelps Stokes Collection, Miriam & Ira D. Wallach Division in Arts, Prints & Photographs, The New York Public Library, Astor, Lenox & Tilden Foundation.

Unit 5 • 180:NCDAR. 182: *t*, NCC. 183: "Trail of Tears," by Robert Lindneaux, courtesy of Woolaroc Museum, Bartlesville, Oklahoma. 186: Courtesy of Mariner's Museum, Newport News, Va.; 188: "Portrait of Andrew Jackson," by Alonzo Chapell, Chicago Historical Society. 189: NCDAR. 190:NCC. 192, 193:NCDAR. 194:NCC. 197, 199:NCDAR. 200:NCC. 201:NCDAR.

Unit 6 • 204: Library of Congress. 205:NCDAR. 206:GC. 209:NCC. 211: Library of Congress. 212:NCC. 212, 213: Library of Congress. 215: NCDAR. 216:NCC. 218: Anne S.K. Brown Military Collection, Brown University Library. 220: Chicago Historical Society, neg. #IChi07732. 221, 222:GC. 223: "Robert E. Lee," by Theodore Pine, Washington & Lee University. 224, 225: Library of Congress. 226:GC. 227: Archives of '76, Bowman Associates. 228:NCC. 229:NCDAR. 230:NCC. 231: *t*,NCDAR; *b*,NCC. 232:NCC. 233:NCC. 235: Travel & Tourism Division, Raleigh. 236: Jock Lauterer, Chapel Hill. 238, 239: Library of Congress. 240:NCDAR. 241: The New York Public Library. 242: *Harper's Weekly*, March 26, 1868. 243: *t*,NCDAR; *b*,NCC. 244, 245, 246:GC. 247:NCDAR. 249: Library of Congress.

Unit 7 • 252:GC. 254 :BA. 255:GC. 257: Edison Institute, Henry Ford Museum & Greenfield Village. 258: National Portrait Gallery, Washington D.C. 260: *Literary Digest*, 1905. 261: Brown Brothers. 262: *t*, Jane Addams Memorial Collection, University of Illinois Library, Chicago; *b*, Avery Architecture & Fine Arts Library, Columbia University. 263: Culver Pictures. 264: Colorado Historical Society. 266:NCC. 267: Brown Brothers. 268: *t*,NCC; *b*,NCDAR. 269: *t*,NCDAR; *b*,NCC. 270, 272:NCC. 274, 275:NCDAR. 276: Division of Travel & Tourism, Raleigh. 277:NCC.

Unit 8 • 280: Missouri Historical Society. 281: Newspaper Collection, The New York Public Library, Astor, Lenox & Tilden Foundation. 282: Original in Liki'oukalani Trust, Honolulu, photo courtesy of Bishop Museum. 284:GC. 286: *t*,NCDAR; *b*, Herbert Hoover Presidential Library. 288: Trustees of the Imperial British War Museum. 289: Reis Library, Allegheny College. 290:GC. 291:NCC (from an original owned by Una Mae Brown, Catawba, N.C.). 292:NCDAR. 293: Missouri Historical Society. 294:BA. 295:NCDAR. 296: Culver Pictures. 298: Division of Travel & Tourism, Raleigh. 299:NCDAR. 300: Culver Pictures. 302: *t*, Franklin D. Roosevelt Library; *b*,NCDAR. 303:NCDAR. 305: Yivo Institute. 308: Fort Bragg Office of Information. 309: Culver Pictures; *insert*, Wide World Photos. 311, 312: Wide World Photos. 313: Stephen Acai, Jr., Raleigh.

Unit 9 • 316: NASA. 317: Black Star. 318: Van Bucher, Photo Researchers. 320: Wide World Photos. 321: Francis Miller, *Life Magazine* © 1963 Time, Inc.; 322: Leif Skoofors, Woodfin Camp & Associates. 323: Beringer-Dratch, The Picture Cube. 324: Susan Greenwood, Gamma-Liaison. 325: NASA. 326: Yvonne Hemsey, Gamma-Liaison. 327: UPI, Bettmann Newsphotos. 328: Eric Bouvet, Gamma-Liaison. 329: Pierre Perrin, Gamma-Liaison. 332: William S. Powell. 333: Chapel Hill Newspaper, Chapel Hill. 334: Greensboro Daily News, Greensboro. 335:NCDAR. 336: Division of Travel & Tourism, Raleigh. 337:NCDAR. 338: Office of Governor James Martin. 340: Courtesy JoAnn Sieburg-Baker, Photographer, Charlotte. 341: Hugh Morton. 343:NCDAR. 344: Division of Travel & Tourism, Raleigh (Shaftner Buchanan). 345: Chamber of Commerce, Charlotte.